W9-CMC-667

For too long, too many historians have been too much concerned with impersonal forces, underlying structures and long-term developments. Now, 'people' are back. In a post-modern age it is easier to appreciate the decisive role played by individuals, as they ride their luck and seize their opportunity to bend the world to their will. As these essays by twelve eminent historians demonstrate, biography is too important to be left to the amateurs. Among the rich variety of strong characters analysed here are an Austrian emperor, a German kaiser, a Victorian prime minister, an Italian dictator and an American president.

Dedicated to the most accomplished and versatile historian-biographer of his generation, Derek Beales, the range and quality of this collection will stimulate, inform and entertain everyone interested in the history of the modern world and in the biographies of those who have helped to make and to mould it.

HISTORY AND BIOGRAPHY

HISTORY AND BIOGRAPHY

ଈଓଈଓଈଓ

ESSAYS IN HONOUR
OF DEREK BEALES

EDITED BY

T. C. W. BLANNING
University of Cambridge

DAVID CANNADINE
Columbia University, New York

CAMBRIDGE
UNIVERSITY PRESS

Published by the Press Syndicate of the University of Cambridge
The Pitt Building, Trumpington Street, Cambridge CB2 1RP
40 West 20th Street, New York, NY 10011–4211, USA
10 Stamford Road, Oakleigh, Melbourne 3166, Australia

© Cambridge University Press 1996

First published 1996

Printed in Great Britain at the University Press, Cambridge

A catalogue record for this book is available from the British Library

Library of Congress cataloguing in publication data
History and biography: essays in honour of Derek Beales /
edited by T. C. W. Blanning and David Cannadine.
p.   cm.
Includes bibliographical references and index.
ISBN 0 521 47330 6
1. Beales, Derek Edward Dawson. 2. History, Modern.
3. Statesmen – Biography. 4. Kings and rulers – Biography.
I. Beales, Derek Edward Dawson. II. Blanning, T. C. W.
III. Cannadine, David, 1950– .
D223.H57 1996
909.08–dc20 95–36123 CIP

ISBN 0 521 47330 6 hardback

CONTENTS

കയെരയ

CONTRIBUTORS

T. C. W. BLANNING is Professor of Modern European History at the University of Cambridge and a Fellow of Sidney Sussex College.

DAVID CANNADINE is Moore Collegiate Professor of History at Columbia University, New York.

P. G. M. DICKSON is Professor of Early Modern History at the University of Oxford and a Fellow of St Catherine's College.

H. M. SCOTT is Senior Lecturer in History at the University of St Andrews.

JOHN BREWER is Professor of History at the University of California at Los Angeles and at the Istituto Universitario Europeo at Florence.

BOYD HILTON is University Lecturer in History at the University of Cambridge and a Fellow of Trinity College.

R. J. W. EVANS is Professor of European History at the University of Oxford and a Fellow of Brasenose College.

J. P. PARRY is University Lecturer in History at the University of Cambridge and a Fellow of Pembroke College.

DENIS MACK SMITH is Emeritus Fellow of All Souls College, Oxford.

PETER CLARKE is Professor of Modern British History at the University of Cambridge and a Fellow of St John's College.

Until his retirement in 1983 OWEN CHADWICK was Regius Professor of Modern History of the University of Cambridge and Master of Selwyn College.

TONY BADGER is Mellon Professor of American History at the University of Cambridge and a Fellow of Sidney Sussex College.

Introduction

DEREK BEALES AS HISTORIAN

AND BIOGRAPHER

ღოღოღო

T. C. W. BLANNING AND DAVID CANNADINE

THIS collection of essays, by friends, colleagues and former students, is presented to Derek Beales to mark and to celebrate his sixty-fifth birthday. It is at least doubly appropriate that it should be called *History and Biography*. For not only was this the title of his inaugural lecture as Professor of Modern History at Cambridge University, which is reprinted here: it also describes his range and defines his accomplishments as a scholar. Few historians today trouble themselves with large-scale, full-dress biographies. Even fewer biographers write anything that is recognisable as serious history. Derek Beales, by contrast, may justly claim to be both a distinguished historian and a gifted biographer. He has written national history, international history, political history, constitutional history, ecclesiastical history and cultural history. For four years, he taught a Special Subject on Gladstone's First Ministry in Part Two of the Cambridge Historical Tripos. And he is still engaged on his major work: a magisterial biography of the Emperor Joseph II. As all his writing makes plain, Derek Beales is fascinated by the interplay between men and events, individuals and circumstance. He is sceptical of impersonal and structural history, and he has never favoured debunking or mocking biography. And he is as much an historiographer as he is an historian. Not for nothing was the alternative title for his inaugural lecture 'Historians as Great Men, and Great Men as Historians'.

As Derek Beales would be the first to remind us, there are formative influences on historians no less than on statesmen or monarchs. In his own case, he is the distinguished upholder of a great Cambridge tradition of scholars who range across countries and centuries with an ease and an authority which defies the conventional boundaries and vigorously defended specialisms of modern professional academic history. For G. M. Trevelyan, J. H. Clapham, Herbert Butterfield, M. M. Postan, Owen Chadwick and David Thompson (the latter, also of Sidney Sussex College, an especially influential mentor), it was perfectly natural to write about both England and

Continental Europe, and it never seems to have occurred to Derek Beales that he should not follow the same path. He has always been the least parochial of historians: too fascinated by his own country's past to give himself exclusively to Italy and Austria; too much immersed in the languages and culture of the Continent to be completely happy within the insular constraints of British history. All this was made precociously plain in his first book, *England and Italy, 1859–1860*, where the coyness of the chronology was belied by the richness of the research and the significance of the subject. For not only did this book bring alive the close nineteenth-century links between Englishmen and Italians: it also made major contributions to our understanding of mid-Victorian British politics, and to a crucial episode in the Italian Risorgimento.

Ever since this first book, Derek Beales has moved back and forth across the English Channel with an ease and a frequency which long antedates today's subterranean train-travellers. As an historian of Britain, there is one more influence which must be recalled, that of Dr George Kitson Clark of Trinity College, whose research seminar on Victorian England was a mecca for all graduate students working in the field during the 1950s, 1960s and early 1970s. As befitted the life-long admirer of Peel, Kitson Clark's chief interests were political, constitutional and ecclesiastical, and the same may be said of much of Derek Beales's work, although in his case they are devoid of any trace of Kitson's instinctive Toryism. Much of his most influential writing in this area has appeared in pamphlets, scholarly articles or review essays: his accounts of the party system in the eighteenth and the nineteenth centuries; his comparison of Peel and Russell as penal reformers at the Home Office; his meticulous and suggestive dissections of the Gladstone diaries; his robust reassertion of the importance of the Great Reform Act; and most recently, as if bringing this side of his work full circle, his study of Garibaldi's reception in England. Together these pieces constitute a formidable (and often iconoclastic) contribution to our understanding of nineteenth-century Britain, and as such, they both anticipate and develop the broader interpretation advanced in his widely read and long-lasting general survey, *From Castlereagh to Gladstone, 1815–85*.

But this was scarcely one half of Derek Beales's mature output. In the early 1970s, the *embarras de richesses* created by the plethora of historians of nineteenth-century Britain in Cambridge encouraged him to turn back to Continental Europe in a more single-minded and systematic way. It was characteristic of his versatility that he should have moved away from his earlier interest in Risorgimento Italy both chronologically and geographically. He now redirected his focus across the Alps into the Habsburg Monarchy and backwards in time to the eighteenth century. A highly successful Part II Special Subject on Joseph II and Belgium, which attracted many gifted undergraduates, provided the ideal forum for this reorientation.

Its first fruits proved to be one of the most important articles on the history of the Habsburg Monarchy to have been published in recent years. In 'The False Joseph II', which appeared in *The Historical Journal* in 1975, Derek Beales showed that many of the most celebrated – and frequently cited – observations attributed to the Emperor were forgeries. How many times, one wonders, has the resounding proclamation 'I have made philosophy the legislator of my empire' been quoted by historians content to repeat the errors of their predecessors? The worst culprit was also the author of the most widely used biography of Joseph available in the English language, namely Saul Padover, whose study of *The Revolutionary Emperor* had been reprinted as recently as 1967. By showing that no fewer than a quarter of Padover's numerous quotations had been drawn from tainted sources, Derek Beales discredited the whole work.

He himself then filled the vacuum he had created by publishing the first volume of his own biography of Joseph in 1987. As reviewers were quick to recognise, this is the best study in any language, setting new standards of accuracy and objectivity in a field hitherto obstructed by ignorance and prejudice. Rejecting all sources of dubious provenance, he discovered a Joseph who was less 'enlightened', less appealing but very much more credible than earlier distortions. As he also brought to his task two other vital qualities of the biographer – a capacity for getting inside the mind of his subject and an ability to convey his discoveries with clarity, cogency and wit – he also created one of the great biographies of modern historical scholarship. To say that volume two, which will take the story from Joseph's accession as sole ruler in 1780 to his death in 1790, is eagerly awaited by historians of eighteenth-century Europe is very much an understatement.

The interval between the publication of the two volumes has been due to a determination not to hurry a project designed to be durable and an equally laudable refusal to be hurried into premature action by the dismal new world of mindless productivity demanded by our paymasters. It has also been due to Derek Beales's unflagging appetite for new interests. Yet another Part II Special Subject, this time on 'The philosophies and the monarchs', has intensified a long-standing interest in the Enlightenment. His own deep knowledge of and affection for the music of the period has also borne fruit, in the shape of a highly regarded lecture on 'Mozart and the Habsburgs', which has now been published and will cause much fluttering in musicological dovecots. The Birkbeck lectures given to large and appreciative audiences in Cambridge in the autumn of 1993 revealed his continuing ability to ask awkward questions and to find surprising answers, on this occasion about the fall and rise of monasteries in Europe in the late eighteenth and early nineteenth centuries. In short, as release from what has always been a heavy burden of teaching and administration beckons, there is every sign that his retirement will be unusually productive and satisfying, even by the cheering standards of historians. His friends, colleagues and former pupils welcome this opportunity to register their affection, respect and gratitude, together with their best wishes for the future.

1

BARON BARTENSTEIN ON COUNT HAUGWITZ'S 'NEW SYSTEM' OF GOVERNMENT

ↄↄↄↄↄↄ

P. G. M. DICKSON

I N November 1753, at the request of the Empress Maria Theresia, the
aged Baron Johann Christian Bartenstein (he was then 63) wrote two
memorials on the working of Count Friedrich Wilhelm Haugwitz's new
System ('neue Sistemate') of finance and government, introduced in 1748–9.[1]
Bartenstein had recently, and reluctantly, ceded control of the Austrian
Monarchy's foreign policy to Kaunitz, and assumed the largely otiose function
of Austrian and Bohemian Vice-Chancellor, or third man in the hierarchy of
the *Directorium in Publicis et Cameralibus*, created in 1749 to deal with the
main areas of internal finance and administration, and headed by Haugwitz
himself. Bartenstein's sharp-sighted observations on the 'Systemate in internis'
were thus drafted at a time when he was a relative newcomer to domestic
business.[2] In January 1756, again at the empress's request, he compiled a much

---

[1] Vienna, Haus-, Hof-und Staatsarchiv [HHSA], Nachlass Zinzendorf, Hs. 2 b fos. 10–23. For
convenience, Bartenstein's pagination, 1–28, is used here. These memoranda and that
of 1756 (see next) were written by clerks. I am indebted to the Director of the HHSA, DDr
Gottfried Mraz, for sending me a microfilm of this source, and the information about its
handwriting. Bartenstein (23.10.1690–6.8.1767) was a Catholic convert, whose father was
Rector of the Gymnasium at Strassburg. See A. von Arneth, 'Johann Christoph von
Bartenstein und seine Zeit', *Archiv für österreichische Geschichte* [*AÖG*] 46 (1871), 1–214,
which prints Bartenstein's memorandum of 1762 on the Monarchy's foreign relations since
the sixteenth century, and M. Braubach in *Neue Deutsche Biographie* {*NDB*} 1 (1952),
599–600, which corrects Arneth's date of 1689 for Bartenstein's birth. See also J. Hrazky,
'Johann Christopher Bartenstein, der Staatsmann und Erzieher', *Mitteilungen des
österreichischen Staatsarchivs* [*MÖSA*] 11 (1958), 221–51, which adds some further details.
There is a summary of Bartenstein's career in P. G. M. Dickson, *Finance and Government
under Maria Theresia* (2 vols., OUP 1987), i, pp. 343–4, which, however, repeats the
erroneous birth-date 1689. For Haugwitz's 'System' see ibid., i, ch. 1; ii, ch. 1.

[2] As he states in 1756. The idea of a fixed system was not peculiar to Haugwitz. English
diplomatic correspondence at the time is permeated by it, with the Old System of alliance

longer memorial, running to over 100 pages, in response to four specific questions. These were as follows. Could the provinces ('Länder') support the new level of taxation? Should the existing system of collecting taxes be retained? How could the System be made more acceptable to lord and peasant? How could credit, and internal and foreign trade, be encouraged, and the prosperity of the provinces increased? The greater length of Bartenstein's response, though partly due to recapitulation and expansion of his earlier conclusions, reflected his increased experience, and better grip on his subject; and also the mounting difficulties which the System was encountering with each passing year.[3]

I

These three documents, briefly summarised by Prokeš in 1926, but never fully exposed, are liberally peppered with expressions of Bartenstein's humility, insufficiency and deferment to the superior judgement of Emperor and Empress.[4] His protestations were largely window-dressing. The memorials are singularly frank. Bartenstein was, of course, aware that his policy of an alliance with France, and escape from English entanglements, adumbrated as early as 1739, had recently been taken over by his supplanter Kaunitz; and that his own efforts at better mobilisation of Austrian resources had been superseded by Haugwitz's recent 'revolution' in government.[5] From having been, in the 1730s, one who had 'made it rain and made it shine' at court, Bartenstein had become largely marginalised in an honorary role.[6] Some bias on his part is, in

---

between the Maritime Powers and Austria most prominent. Similarly, the Emperor told Robert Keith in July 1749 that the Russian Chancellor Bestuschev 'has no system', PRO SP 80/182, Keith to Newcastle, 30 July 1749.

[3] Nachl. Zinz. Hs. 2 b, p. 29–129. The memorial, like the two others, has brief marginal notes in a different hand; the HHSA identifies it as that of Count Karl Zinzendorf. They are usually in French, sometimes in German or Italian. At p. 65, against Bartenstein's criticism of the superfluity of government commissions, often acting without knowledge of the facts, Zinzendorf comments 'comme en 1790'. He died in 1792.

[4] Jaroslav Prokeš, 'Boj o Haugvicovo "Directorium in publicis et cameralibus" r. 1761', Sitzb. d. böhm. Gesellsch. d. Wiss. (Phil. – Hist. Klasse) 1926, pp. 19–23. The MS source is given by F. A. J. Szabo, Kaunitz and Enlightened Absolutism (CUP 1994), p. 117 n., but the summary in his text is from Prokeš.

[5] PRO SP 80/137, Thos. Robinson to Lord Harrington, 10 October 1739; ibid., 182, Newcastle to Keith, March 1749, 'the supposed System of Mor. Bartenstein, for uniting the House of Austria, more intimately with France and, even, with the King of Prussia'. Count Khevenhüller-Metsch observed of the institutional changes of May 1749, 'People had not expected such a revolution', H. Schlitter (ed.), Aus der Zeit Maria Theresias. Tagebuch des Fürsten . . . Khevenhüller-Metsch . . . 1742–1776 (8 vols., Vienna 1907–72), entry for 2 May 1749.

[6] PRO SP 80/182, Keith to Newcastle, 10 April 1749; Keith quoted that Bartenstein in the 1730s 'faisoit la Pluye et le beau tems'. Between 1739 and 1749 Bartenstein turned from an object of English admiration to one of hate as his dislike of the Old System became evident.

these circumstances, only to be expected. Bartenstein, however, who was not unconscious of his considerable powers, was aware that for a decade he had been Maria Theresa's most trusted adviser, and that she regarded his measures in 1741–2 as having saved the Monarchy.[7] Further, as she again acknowledged, he was himself one of the architects of the 'new System', which he had supported since its inception.[8] In doing so, as he states several times, he had become extremely unpopular, a fact confirmed by the English minister Robert Keith's report in January 1749 that Bartenstein, though in high favour with the Empress, was 'both hated and despised' in political circles.[9] The baron thus spoke with the openness expected of an old and trusted adviser, who had drawn fire in his mistress's service; not as an encrusted defender of former practices. The picture he paints both adds considerably to our limited knowledge of Haugwitz's 'revolution', and qualifies in important respects the view that it was relatively successful and uncontentious.[10]

The first memorial, dated 4 November 1753, summarises the financial changes introduced in 1748, and some of the arguments deployed for and against them. A yearly 14 million fl. Contribution was in future to be paid for support of an army of 108,000 men by 'the entire hereditary kingdoms and lands', except the Austrian Netherlands and Lombardy (*sic*).[11] Bartenstein does not refer to the Decennial Recesses which obliged the Bohemian and Austrian lands, save Tyrol and Further Austria, to provide their part of this total, just over 10 million fl., for a ten-year period. These lands (not the others) were also, Bartenstein continues, to pay 2.25 million fl. p.a. towards debt service, the cameral debts (excluding those charged on the Vienna City Bank) being estimated at 80 million fl., subsequently 70 million fl.[12] However,

---

7 '. . . he alone saved the Monarchy, without him everything would have fallen (. . . zu Grund gegangen)', Maria Theresia's *Testament* of 1750 in F. Walter (ed.), *Maria Theresia. Briefe und Aktenstücke in Auswahl* (Darmstadt 1968), p. 67.

8 Ibid., pp. 81–2. In her *Testament* of 1756 she stated that Bartenstein was second only to Haugwitz in implementing the System, and braving the ensuing hatred, ibid., p. 125.

9 SP 80/182, Keith to Newcastle, 29 January 1749.

10 Charles Ingrao's verdict that 'However dramatic in its results, the First Theresian Reform was hardly revolutionary in the tactics it employed . . . the central government . . . continued to seek the consent and cooperation of the monarchy's estates', *The Habsburg Monarchy 1618–1815* (CUP 1994), p. 169, is not untypical.

11 'Anschuldige, doch bestgemeinte Gedanken des Directorial-Vice-Canzlers Freiherrn von Bartenstein die hiesige innerliche Verfassung betreffend', 4 November 1753, Nachl. Zinz. Hs. 2 b, pp. 1–19. The MS says 100,008 men. Bartenstein does not refer to the Frontier Militia, numbering 47,000 in 1756 according to the Empress (Walter, *Briefe*, p. 128) nor to the planned 50,000 troops in the Austrian Netherlands and Italy. The army in 1754–5 conformed to the pattern Haugwitz proposed, with 108,219 men (excluding Frontier Militia) in the central lands and 25,360 in each of the other two areas, Dickson, *Finance*, II, p. 356.

12 Nachl. Zinz. Hs. 2 b, p. 13. See Dickson, *Finance*, II, pp. 15–16 for the Decennial Recesses and pp. 25–7 for the cameral debts. The Hungarian Lands were excluded from these Recesses and arrangements for debt service.

1.13 million fl. p.a. of this 2.25 millions was to go towards service and reduction of their own debts, which he does not quantify.[13] The upshot, he tells us, was to make them pay one million fl. more than was at first intended. Supplementary taxes ('adminicular funds') were therefore assigned to them from the crown's cameral revenue, put at 7 million fl. in 1748.[14] Meanwhile, 3.2 million fl. was assigned to cover Court expenditure, and 1.3 million fl. for the civil list ('pro aulico civili').[15] Many thought these budgetary ambitions, intended to bring clarity and order into the Monarchy's finances, were unfeasible, Bartenstein tells us: but 'I supported them, and do support them.'[16]

Bartenstein's account of the financial settlement, with its sharply increased taxation, agrees well, if not in all details, with other sources. His description of the arguments used against it adds to our existing information. As Conference Secretary, he had drafted the minutes of the famous session of 29 January 1748 at which Haugwitz's fiscal plans were approved in principle.[17] He was thus in a position to know. They stipulated as a counterpart concession that the Bohemian and Austrian lands should in future not be responsible for providing army recruits, cavalry remounts, cartage, military billets. 'The Länder were to have nothing more to do with the military'.[18] Against this, it was argued (Bartenstein scrupulously refrains from naming persons) that most provinces were short of money, but had a surplus of provisions. Might it not be more rational to continue taxation in kind?[19] As for recruits, if the Länder were no longer to supply them, the government would have to levy them in the Reich, where they would probably be vagrants, prone both to desert and to cause desertion. Would it not be better to lower the hitherto unrealistic domestic recruit quota of 25,000 men (in the Bohemian and Austrian lands) to 8,000 men, which would keep money in the country, and fill the German infantry regiments in three to four years? Bartenstein disclaims an opinion on the merits of these objections, the second of which was his own.[20]

---

13 The figures finally adopted from 1 November 1748 were 2.614 million fl. and 1.184 million fl., ibid., II, p. 376. The expected peacetime Contribution in the Bohemian and Austrian lands increased between 1747 and 1749 from 5,613,779 to 12,738,678 fl., or by 7,124,899 fl., ibid. (War taxes increased the actual amount in 1747.) However, under the new System, all levies for the army ceased, at least in theory, see next. They continued in the Hungarian lands, where tax increased only marginally.

14 Nachl. Zinz. Hs. 2 b, p. 14. For these 'adminicular' taxes, see Dickson, Finance, II, pp. 190–3, 221, 253, 269. They totalled over 2m. fl.

15 Nachl. Zinz. Hs. 2 b, p. 12.   16 Ibid.

17 Dickson, Finance, II, pp. 13–14. Bartenstein refers to this Conference at pp. 40–1 of his text. At p. 5, he calls it 'the famous Conference at Court in February [sic] 1748'.

18 Nachl. Zinz. Hs. 2 b, p. 4.

19 Ibid., p. 7.

20 Ibid., pp. 7–9, 40. A table of wartime recruiting numbers is enclosed in PRO SP 80/176, Robinson to Chesterfield, 7 January 1747: 30,000 were required in the Bohemian and Austrian lands, 8,000 in Hungary, 2,000 in Italy.

As regards (direct) taxation, Bartenstein tells us, it was agreed that it was necessary to have equity ('Peraequatio') both between the *Länder* and within each of them. But Haugwitz's wish to tax income was problematical. Since yields differed greatly, how could income from land in different areas be equally assessed? Further, yields themselves were hard to measure. If sworn declarations ('Fassionen') were used, as eventually occurred, this would not solve the problems of gauging yields, or of protecting the crown from dishonest declarers.[21] These criticisms, directed at the problem of moving from the areas of land declared to estimates of their income, were not necessarily irresponsible, and were only partly overcome by the tax cadastres subsequently introduced. Bartenstein adds the very interesting comment that, had the resources ('die innerliche Kräfte') of each of the *Länder* been known, there would have been no difficulty in imposing a uniform tax system; but they were not.[22] This belief in economic inquiry clearly resembles the approach of the Zinzendorf brothers, whose importance in Kaunitz's circle at this time Professor Klingenstein has recently emphasised.[23] Haugwitz's patronage of the Saxon economist J. H. G. von Justi, who was in Vienna when Bartenstein was writing, and Count Ludwig Zinzendorf's of Johann Mathias Peuchberg, statistician extraordinary and father of the new system of state accounts introduced in 1763, are further examples.[24] Bartenstein himself was responsible later in the decade for collating reports on the various central lands of the Monarchy, drawn up for the benefit of Crown Prince Joseph; who as Joseph II was to make statistics the foundation of government policies.[25]

Such were the main features of the 'new System', Bartenstein tells us. The general verdict on it, he was disturbed to find, was damning. It was thought that it could not last long without exhausting the resources of the provinces: and with its fall would come that of the Monarchy itself.[26] Without wishing to be presumptuous, the baron wrote, I do not share this view. Since the System was introduced, 700,000 fl. has been obtained from Hungary; a fifteen-year *Indultum* [clerical tax] has been conceded by the Papacy; debts have been relieved; income has risen.[27] The main problem, he argued, was expenditure. It threatened to absorb all the extra revenue. The 'very fortunate'

---

21 Nachl. Zinz. Hs. 2 b, pp. 9–10. 'Fassionen' has as its root Latin 'fateor', 'I declare, indicate'.

22 Ibid., p. 11.

23 G. Klingenstein, 'Between Mercantilism and Physiocracy. Stages, Modes, and Functions of Economic Theory in the Habsburg Monarchy, 1748–63', in C. Ingrao (ed.), *State and Society in Early Modern Austria* (Purdue UP 1994), pp. 181–214.

24 Ibid., pp. 188, 195–6, 203–4 (Justi); Dickson, *Finance*, II, pp. 36, 82–5, 135 (Puechberg).

25 Klingenstein, 'Between Mercantilism and Physiocracy', pp. 193–4; P. G. M. Dickson, 'Joseph II's reshaping of the Austrian Church', *Hist. J.* 36 (1993), p. 93.

26 Nachl. Zinz. Hs. 2 b, p. 14.

27 Ibid., pp. 15–17; see Dickson, *Finance*, II, pp. 22, 29 (Hungarian Contribution; debts repaid); 266 (Papal *indultum*); Table 3.1 (income).

increase in royal children had rendered the 3.2 million fl. Court budget obsolete. Salaries had risen to 2 million fl. p.a. Pensions were swollen by the empress's generosity.[28] Even the unplanned increase in the number of army generals had added to costs. And outlay was increasing, not lessening. Meanwhile, the various *Länder* had not grown in wealth, and if need arose might not be able to provide the means to defend themselves. This had serious implications, Bartenstein declared, for the Arch House, given the present situation in Europe.[29]

The baron's first report was thus largely confined to the fiscal content, and consequences, of Haugwitz's System. His next, dated 28 November 1753, is more wide-ranging – and even more alarming.[30] Bartenstein began prudently, on an emollient note. He was a supporter of the new *Sistemate in Internis* – and was hated for being so.[31] It had had three great objectives: a sufficient military establishment; provision for Court expenditure and for the 'civil Lista' in Vienna and the various *Lände*; and the gradual paying off of debts. (Neither here nor elsewhere does Bartenstein refer to the celebrated 'separation of administration and justice' emphasised in 1749.) The army had never been so well provided for; endless (unspecified) public abuses had been curbed; factories founded; the trade of Trieste increased. Mining was flourishing, and if half its products could be hoarded instead of being exported, the Hereditary Lands would in ten years be the richest in Europe. (Bartenstein had evidently not studied the history of Spain.) Defects in religion were being cured, expenditure on education was the greatest 'the Serene Arch House' had ever made. The tender-hearted empress sacrificed everything to the common good.[32]

This may have lifted the spirits of Empress and Emperor. Its sequel, which begins 'nevertheless', cannot have done so. There are complaints (about the new System) everywhere, Bartenstein proceeds. The military, clergy, nobles, burgesses, peasants, are discontented. Why was this? The System, he says, was initiated in such a way as not to arouse any outcry. Subsequently, however, harsh measures had been preferred to mild ones, and not enough

---

[28] Nachl. Zinz. Hs. 2 b, pp. 17–18. These statements are borne out by the figures for expenditure in Dickson, *Finance*, II, p. 385.

[29] Nachl. Zinz. Hs. 2 b, p. 19.

[30] Ibid., pp. 21–8. 'Allerunterthänigste Nota des Directorial-Vice-Canzlers Freiherrn von Bartenstein, die bey der Verfassung des Directorii in Publicis et Cameralibus sich zeigende Gebrechen betr [effend]', dated 28 November 1753.

[31] Ibid., p. 21.

[32] P. 23, 'wird dem allgemeinen Besten alles ausgeopfert'. Cp. Walter, *Briefe*, p. 71, *Testament* of 1750, 'des Staats und gemeinen Besten'. Bartenstein's guarded reference to the discovery of substantial Protestant minorities in Upper and Inner Austria from 1752 understated the seriousness with which it was regarded, see R. Reinhardt, 'Zur Kirchenreform unter Maria Theresia', *Zeitschr. f. Kirchenges.* 77 (1966), 105–19.

attention paid to their presentation. Even in the most unrestricted ('uneingeschränkesten') governments, like that of France, care was taken to sweeten ('versüssen') acceptance of hated edicts. Further, it would have been better to proceed bit by bit rather than all at once. And the constant changes, and flood of orders, have irritated the *Länder* and made a bad impression. Consultation with them before edicts were sent would have been better. At the centre, the *Directorium* had become absorbed in detail, and especially in matters of *Polizei*, instead of concentrating on general issues. If it held joint sessions with other departments, much time and scribbling ('Schreiberey') would be avoided. Its business should be more concentrated, following the Prussian example and its own original model. Ministerial conferences should be held on weighty issues. Lastly, the inequality of the new tax system, both between and within *Länder*, was a source of grievance.[33] All possible means should be considered of lessening this inequality, and reducing the burden of taxes. The present revision ('Rectification') of assessments to the Contribution should be ended, and a full inquiry made whether the present interim assessments ('Interimisticum') fulfilled the intentions expressed in 1748–9. A fully-attended Conference should discuss the results of this inquiry, 'on which the woe and welfare of so many *Länder* depend'.[34]

In these two reports, Bartenstein, though omitting any discussion of institutional change, including the creation of the *Directorium* itself in 1749, shows an insider's knowledge of the need for Haugwitz's new System, and of how it had worked out. The intention, he says, was right, and the new levels of taxation realistic. However, haste, violence and lack of consultation had spoiled the work's initial promise, and generated a level of hatred of it which could have been avoided. Riper deliberation, more expert assessment of the necessity for changes, less writing and more discussion, more attention paid to presentation, would have produced better results. It is interesting to find him signalling the empress's attachment to the general good, and his own both to brevity in business, achieved through verbal discussion, and to economic statistics as a basis for tax assessment, concepts more often attributed to Joseph II. Bartenstein, before Kaunitz, also emphasised the need for greater prosperity, to support higher taxation.[35] Bartenstein shows himself halfway between the unmeasured resistance to Haugwitz's reforms of the Austrian old guard, personified by the Bohemian Chancellor in 1748, Count Friedrich Harrach, and the fire, and will for change, of Count Haugwitz, which corresponded to those of the Empress herself, at least in some of her moods.

Two years passed before the baron's views on the working of the System

[33] Nachl. Zinz. Hs. 2 b, pp. 24–7.

[34] Ibid., pp. 27–8.

[35] Kaunitz's innovative insistence on such policies is a main theme of Szabo's study, see n. 4.

were again solicited. As the questions then asked of him, on 31 December 1755, indicated, royal concern over its defects, and anxiety about the burden of taxation, had increased, not lessened. Moreover, the Empress was aware that Austrian foreign policy, under Kaunitz's guidance, now aimed at an alliance with France and Russia to recover Silesia and decisively humble the upstart Frederick II. The possibility of renewed war, carefully concealed from Bartenstein, thus underlay her renewed approach. In his response, her ancient adviser, now 'of an age [65] where I am indifferent to the world', amply fulfilled his mandate to write 'clearly and openly'.[36] Councillors, he insisted, had in any case a duty to speak out; and their views should not be suppressed.[37] Instead of confining himself to the four questions asked, he embarked on an extended survey of the political history of the Monarchy from 1740, the genesis of Haugwitz's System, the present style, and defects, of government, and, in particular, the weaknesses and injustices of the new Contribution. While repetitious, and unclear in structure, and no doubt maddening to the Empress, and especially to Haugwitz, at whom many of its criticisms were by implication directed, Bartenstein's treatise (it is little less) is a mine of information, greatly extending the scope of his earlier reports.

He was clear that he was writing at a point of crisis in the Monarchy's fortunes. Already in 1753, he states, he had prayed to God to avert the ill consequences which might follow open unrest.[38] Now, two years later, discontent had multiplied. The public ('das Publikum') was confused and fearful. Hope of betterment was shrinking, fear of the future growing. This would cause great problems should war break out. The leading clergy, the nobles, burgesses, peasants, were filled with fear and misgiving.[39] Bartenstein prefaced his analysis of the causes of this alarming state of affairs by a short sketch of 'the revolutions which followed the late Emperor Charles 6's death, and which gave rise to the System'.[40] After Frederick II invaded Silesia 'at the invitation of a few discontented Protestants', Maria Theresia found herself at Pressburg (in 1741) deserted by friends she had most reason to trust, attacked by those she had least reason to suspect. But the measures taken by her, together with her husband Francis Stephen, Count Gundaker Starhemberg, and Bartenstein himself, had pulled Austria back from the brink. Matters quickly improved, friends increased, enemies diminished. The war which had

---

36 Nachl. Zinz. Hs. 2 b, pp. 29–129 (51 is used twice), 'Anmerkungen des Directorial-Vice-Canzlers Freiherrn von Bartenstein, über das im Kahre 1748 eingeführte neue Finanz-Sistem', dated 31 January 1756. The quotation is at p. 30. For the questions Bartenstein was to address, see p. 6 above.

37 Ibid., pp. 94, 102.   38 Ibid., p. 58.

39 Ibid., pp. 53, 58, 64. This discontent is acknowledged in the Empress's *Testament* of 1756, Walter, *Briefe*, p. 126.

40 Nachl. Zinz. Hs. 2 b, marginal note to p. 31.

threatened destruction of the Arch House ended well, and, but for certain mistakes, could have ended even better. Bartenstein closed this unorthodox interpretation of the War of the Austrian Succession by admitting that before it ended the need had been recognised for a 'sufficient Sistema in internis' to meet the danger of weakened territories and increase in the number of enemies.[41] Count Haugwitz's first plan, drawn up before the end of 1747, envisaged an army of 108,000 in the Hereditary hands in place of the former 80,000, costing 14 million fl. a year for 'at least' ten years.[42] The Bohemian Chancellor, Count Friedrich Harrach, the Bank President Count Philipp Kinsky, Field Marshal Count Batthyány, General War Commissary Count Sallaburg (Salburg), 'von der Mark' and Bartenstein himself, studied this plan.[43] Haugwitz, Bartenstein tells us, was accused 'of wanting to put everything on a Prussian footing, given out as tyrannical'.[44] Haugwitz replied that he had no wish to be tyrannical or despotic, but simply to free the Empress from the selfishness and arbitrariness ('Eigennützig- und Eigenmächtigkeiten') of the Estates.[45] Bartenstein advised the empress that the proposed new System was feasible over ten years, provided there was no war, the burden of taxes was equitably shared, and steps were taken to increase provincial prosperity. Astonishingly, he proposed that as much as 13 million fl. of the 14 million fl. military quota should be levied in the Austrian and Bohemian lands.[46] *Länder* abuses must be reformed, but their constitutions (*Verfassungen*) otherwise respected. The extremes of despotism and anarchy must be avoided. Bartenstein continues through the Conference of 29 January 1748; the subsequent dispatch of Haugwitz to talk to the Estates in Moravia; his able management there; the attempts by the (unnamed) enemies of the System to alter it, and frustrate its introduction; his own sufferings in its defence. He needed to sketch this background, he concluded, to make his own proposals intelligible.[47]

---

41 Ibid., pp. 31–4. Bartenstein listed as mistakes the failure to press the French after Dettingen in 1743; going into winter quarters in the Netherlands in the summer of 1744; and the botched Provence expedition of 1747.

42 Ibid., p. 35. A peacetime return of January 1740 shows 30,000 troops in the Bohemian and Austrian lands and 50,000 in Hungary, Dickson, *Finance*, II, p. 356.

43 Nachl. Zinz. Hs. 2 b, p. 37. 'Von der Mark' is not at present identifiable. He may be the Johann von Mark who was a Councillor of the *Directorium* in 1754, *Court Cal.* For the others named, see Dickson, *Finance*, I, ch. 12.

44 Nachl. Zinz. Hs. 2 b, p. 37, 'auf den Preussischen für Tyrannisch ausgegebenen Fuss einrichten zu wollen'.

45 Ibid.

46 Ibid., p. 38. Here, as at p. 12 earlier, he used the phrase 'die in der Proportion stehende Länder' to denote these lands, and those 'outside' the Proportion as the Hungarian Lands, Tyrol and Further Austria.

47 Ibid., pp. 41–6. These developments are discussed in Dickson, *Finance*, I, pp. 223–9; II, pp. 6–24.

A major part of his subsequent report was concerned with the style and defects of internal government. He repeated his contention of 1753 that the *Directorium* had departed from its original, Prussian-style, compactness; and added that there were now so many departments that you needed a good memory even to remember their names.[48] Formerly, commissions ('Commissionen') answering to a department had sufficed.[49] The very helpful practice of a Friday conference each week at Court, attended by the Empress, relevant ministers ('Ministrorum') and their officials, had provided her with the factual knowledge without which even rulers as wise as Solomon made mistakes; but it had been discontinued 'a few years ago' ('seit einigen Jahren').[50] Provincially, administrative and judicial entities, each with their own staffs, had multiplied, an oblique reference to the separation of administration and justice. In consequence of this institutional proliferation, government personnel, and salaries, had sharply increased. Yet many provincial officials knew nothing of the *Länder* in which they were installed.[51] Further, the traditional provincial constitutions ('Verfassungen') had been needlessly trampled on. This increased machinery of state, he argued, had led, not to greater certainty, but to greater confusion. In contentious issues, the councillors of the *Directorium* scarcely knew where to refer applicants.[52] The flood of state edicts on tax and other business, often changed or revoked, baffled their recipients, and gave foreign ministers and their spies the impression of Austrian weakness.[53]

At the centre, Bartenstein insisted, the style of government was hasty, secretive, unconsultative. The advice of two or three was taken, that of more experienced persons neglected. Reports ('Vorträge'), often quickly drafted, were presented to councils as embodying the royal will; and dissenting votes on them omitted from the minutes ('Protocoll'). Business was typically in writing, and this led to bitter paper wars, in which each protagonist defended his position, making royal decision difficult.[54] Bartenstein advised drawing up a formal Instruction for the *Directorium*, and then returning the latter to its initial concentrated form. Official numbers should be frozen, then reduced. More deliberation should precede important decisions, Court conferences be re-introduced, verbal discussion replace the flood of paper. Officials should be encouraged to give their views freely: the proposed Conduct Lists must not

---

48 Nachl. Zinz. Hs. 2 b, pp. 73 (Prussian model), 49 (proliferation of departments).
49 Ibid., p. 79.
50 Ibid., p. 50. This 'Conferenz in Internis' had formalised the *Hofdeputation* created in 1747, see Dickson, *Finance*, I, pp. 223–6.
51 Nachl. Zinz. Hs. 2 b, pp. 78 ('foreign' officials) and 79 (judicial offices).
52 Ibid., p. 49.
53 Ibid., p. 53.
54 Ibid., pp. 63, 66 (neglect); 75 (reports); 84 (paper wars).

allow the chief of a department to ruin their career for doing so.[55] A mixture of royal oversight, verbal discussion, economy, compression, care, would, it appears, replace the current confusion. This prescription resembled in important respects Joseph II's administrative programme at the start of his reign, including the Conduct Lists, finally introduced in 1781, from which Haugwitz evidently drew back.[56]

As an appendix to his remarks on government, Bartenstein, trespassing even further from his brief, threw in an attack on the *Codex Theresianus*, the project to codify civil law in the Bohemian and Austrian lands initiated in 1753. Three drafts had been produced, the second and third trying to correct the faults of their predecessors. Their model was Frederick II's code (of 1749–51), which had not attracted universal praise. The Sardinian monarchy's code ('Codex Victoriano') would have been better. It was too late to change this now, but the separate teams of draftsmen should at least talk to each other. In any case, Bartenstein adds, a much better project would be to compile a digest of the numerous government ordinances, which the empress had herself asked for. Such a *Codex Theresianus*, he says, would bring fame and profit, and amply repay its cost. The very notice of its publication would obliterate the memory of the excessive numbers of edicts. Bartenstein's jaundiced verdict on the official *Codex* was borne out by events. His proposal for a digest of ordinances was only fulfilled by Hempel-Kürsinger's massive project of 1825–33.[57]

Bartenstein's second major concern was the Contribution and its assess-

---

55 Ibid., p. 100 (Instruction for DPC); 73 (concentration of DPC); 116 (reduction of numbers); 102 (discussion); 104 (Court Conferences); 84–5 (verbal discussion); 94 (Conduct Lists). Bartenstein advised limited Court Conferences for particular business, rather than weekly sessions.

56 See P. G. M. Dickson, 'Monarchy and bureaucracy in late eighteenth-century Austria', *English Historical Review* [*EHR*] 110 (April 1995), 323–67.

57 Nachl. Zinz. Hs. 2 b, pp. 70–2, 124. For an account in English of the *Codex Theresianus*, see H. E. Strakosch, *State Absolutism and the Rule of Law* (Sidney UP 1968). For [S. von Cocceji], *Project des Corporis Juris Fridericiani, das ist . . . Landrecht worinn das Römische Recht in eine natürliche Ordnung . . . gebracht wird* (2 vols., Halle 1749, 1751) see H. Weill, *Frederick the Great and Samuel von Cocceji* (Wisconsin UP 1961). A French translation of the code appeared in 1751–5, an English one in 1761. The projected code was only a part of substantive legal reforms which Cocceji enforced, and which related to judicial process and personnel. See *The King of Prussia's Plan for Reforming the Administration of Justice Drawn up by His Majesty himself* (Dublin 1750). Commentary usually blends the projected code with the actual procedural reforms. Both attracted favourable English notice, see M. Schlenke, *England und das friderizianische Preussen 1740–1763* (Munich 1963), pp. 317–22. The 'Codex Victoriano' is *Leggi e costituzioni di Sua Maestà* (2 vols., Turin 1729), published by Vittorio Amadeo II as a re-working of an earlier version in 1723, see G. Symcox in *Storia d'Italia* (ed. G. Galasso, 23 vols., Turin 1979–94), 8/1 (1994), pp. 397–9. Professor Symcox points out that the intended code was really a compilation of existing laws. J. C. Hempel-Kürsinger, *Alphabetisch-chronologische Übersicht der k. k. Gesetze und Verordnungen* (12 vols., Vienna 1825–33) realised Bartenstein's concept of a digest of laws.

ment, which formed the main pillar of Haugwitz's financial edifice. The issues of principle, a major increase in tax total, and the liability of lords, lay and clerical, to pay Contribution on their demesne land in peacetime, had been settled in 1748. What had not been settled was how these decisions were to be implemented. A prolonged process of state-directed inquiry and compulsion, with the uneasy co-operation of the provincial Estates, had ensued. Existing cadastres had been revised in the Bohemian lands, new ones introduced, for example in Lower Austria. In 1756, this process of 'rectification' as it was called, was not complete, and had generated great bitterness.[58]

This was the background to Bartenstein's text. Underlying his exposition was his belief that happiness ('Glückseligkeit') depended on keeping a proportion between the needs of the state and the needs of taxpayers; between defence and opulence. Despite numerous eight-hour meetings on the rectification, he tells us, it had not proved possible to devise uniform rules systematising income taxed, and the division between lords' and peasants' land ('dominical', 'rustical', land). A really accurate survey ('Ausmessung') was not feasible. In its absence, the aim of making 1,000 fl. revenue in Bohemia equal the same amount in Austria was not achieved. Bartenstein argued that the new assessment in Bohemia, where a clear distinction between the land of lord and peasant had been reached, 'could hardly be improved on'. Bohemia, despite its suffering in the recent war, was also flourishing economically. This was largely because its provincial constitution had as far as possible been preserved. Moravia's position was less favourable, and its population was falling in consequence.[59] Bartenstein, however, clearly thought that tax reform had succeeded in the Bohemian Lands, at least in comparison with the Austrian ones. Here, rates of tax for dominical and rustical land varied between provinces. You could write pages, Bartenstein observes, describing the worst abuses.[60] Repeated local investigations of the tax base had produced hasty, and often-changed, results, with over-burdened tax officials wilting under the strain. In Krain, three costly inquiries had simply led to re-staging of disagreements, Count Poztazky (Podstatzky) and Pappa (Papa) repeating the former controversy engaged in by Count Hohenburg and Spiersch.[61] Carinthia was an especially harsh case. The new tax system there (imposed by

---

58 Dickson, *Finance*, ii, chs. i, 6–8.
59 Nachl. Zinz. Hs. 2 b, pp. 76–7 (happiness); 51a (equality); 81 (Bohemia); 112–13 (Moravia). The supposed impossibility of an accurate survey was an obstacle Joseph II later encountered. He surmounted it by employing teams of peasants under state oversight.
60 Ibid., p. 52.
61 Probably Count Aloysius Podstazky, named in the *Court Calendar* as a councillor of the Bohemian *Repraesentation and Cammer* in 1754, in 1779 as President of the Inner Austria *Gubernium*, is intended. J. C. von Papa and B. von Spiersch were prominent tax officials, the latter of Prussian origin, see Dickson, *Finance*, ii, index, snn. I have not traced Count Hohenburg.

royal fiat on the Estates) had, in effect, ruined this 'once prosperous' land. Yet it was Carinthian rules which were now being applied in the rectification of the other Austrian provinces. This, Bartenstein declared, might make their tax burden unsustainable before the ten-year period ended.[62] He reserved particular heat for Lower Austria (where his own lordships lay). The tax levels recently agreed with the Estates there had been suddenly and capriciously changed, without an authorising signature.[63] The new plan was unworkable. A senior adviser ('cavalier') should go through the tax declarations with the Estates, and settle the matter on the basis of the previous assessment. Here, and in the other Austrian lands, application of Carinthian rules should be abandoned, and Bohemian ones substituted.

In contrast to this barrage of description and prescription, Bartenstein's answers to the four questions he had been asked (and which by this stage the Empress may have regretted asking) were restrained. Could the *Länder* support the present levels of taxation? Yes, said Bartenstein, given freedom from plague, famine, floods, foreign invasion. But equal rules must be applied to the rectification, abuses checked, the numerous revising commissions ended.[64] On the second question, how the collection of dominical and rustical tax, and of the 'adminicular' taxes, could be improved, Bartenstein confined himself to the last. He pointed out that there were as many sets of these taxes as there were provinces, and differences of up to one fifth in their burden. The whole should be gone through, local representations heard, and the rules of simplicity and uniformity, which made collection easier, and helped the taxpayer, applied.[65] With this Smithian observation, he turned to the third question, how the tax system could be made more acceptable to lord and peasant. He advised appointing 'an impartial minister of rank and birth' to survey the whole field of taxation, and see how far unnecessary duties could be abolished, and 'the excessive number of riding officers [customs officials] reduced'. It seems, however, that this survey would exclude direct

---

[62] Nachl. Zinz. Hs. 2 b, pp. 85–6, 106. The Contribution was levied by royal fiat in Carinthia, 1750–64, the Estates having refused to agree to the government's demands, see Dickson, *Finance*, II, p. 16. However, the initial (1747) level of tax proposed was subsequently reduced, ibid., p. 221, and the scope of Bartenstein's argument about Carinthian rules requires further investigation.

[63] Nachl. Zinz. Hs. 2 b, pp. 87, 108, 121–3. The absent signature was that of Carl Holler von Doblhof, Bartenstein's brother-in-law. Bartenstein strongly hints that the procedure was illegal. There is much supporting evidence for the government's difficulties with the Lower Austrian Estates, see Dickson, *Finance*, II, ch. 8. The 1754 *Court Calendar* shows that Bartenstein owned the lordships of Ebreichsdorf, Johannesthal and Hennersdorf. Bartenstein repeated in 1761 some of the same points he had made earlier: the defects of the Rectification, the increase in officialdom, the multiple ordinances, etc., see Prokeš, 'Boj', pp. 37–8.

[64] Nachl. Zinz. Hs. 2 b, pp. 88–9.

[65] Ibid., pp. 90–2. See also n. 14 above.

taxes.[66] Lastly, Bartenstein was pessimistic about encouragement of credit, and the prosperity of the provinces, the fourth question. We have only a handful of trading houses of importance (in Vienna), he observed. Merchants are courted when we want loans from them, but otherwise are scorned. Trade has increased in Bohemia, under the skilled hand of Count Rudolf Chotek, and Count Joseph Kinsky's factories there have shown what private enterprise can do. Kinsky, however, had no emulators elsewhere. Bartenstein argued that merchants should be invited from the Austrian Netherlands to settle in the Hereditary Lands, and submitted a plan for this, which is, however, missing from the manuscript.[67]

Bartenstein's text had so far said little about the Hungarian Lands, and their effective exclusion from Haugwitz's System. His last section is of correspondingly greater interest. He argues that the removal of legitimate Hungarian grievances in 1741, and concession to the Serbs ('Raitzen'), whose troops had then astonished Europe by their exploits, had helped save the Monarchy. Continued conciliation of these two nations, he argued, was a necessary condition of the System's survival. But steps must be taken, for the two were now at odds, and Serbs were emigrating, with their property. In view of the latters' services to the state and religion (including Hungarian religion) since 1690, it was vital to confirm their secular and ecclesiastical privileges. Bartenstein thanks the empress for appointing him as president of the *Hofdeputation in Illyricis*, formed to administer this troubled area of the Monarchy, though he does not mention his recent role in helping to settle the mutiny of Serb frontier regiments, whose religious rights he believed had been invaded. It is clear that, though he regarded (Catholic) Hungary as indispensable, his sympathies lay with the equally indispensable (Orthodox) 'Illyrians'.[68]

---

[66] Ibid., pp. 93–4. The word for riding officers which Bartenstein uses is 'Überreuter'. Austrian indirect taxation generated large numbers of officials, see Dickson, 'Monarchy and bureaucracy' for the position later in the century.

[67] Ibid., pp. 95–9. Bartenstein names the trading houses of Bender, 'Dom' [Dohm], Küner, Riesch, 'Smidmer' [Smittmer] all Christian; and Sinzheim (Jewish). For these, see Dickson, *Finance*, I, ch. 7. For literature on Count Joseph Kinsky's enterprises, ibid., p. 113. The Empress refers to the need to enrich the provinces in her 1756 *Testament*, Walter, *Briefe*, p. 129. Prokeš's surmise that Bartenstein's text influenced the *Testament*, 'Boj' p. 19, is plausible.

[68] Ibid., pp. 34, 125–9. The tangled history of the Border Militia ('Grenzer') is discussed by G. E. Rothenberg, *The Military Border in Croatia 1740–1881* (Chicago UP 1966). A fundamental problem appears to have been the mixture of 'Croatian' (Roman Catholic) and 'Serb' (Greek Orthodox) troops. This was a cause of frequent revolts by Serb troops: Rothenberg, *Military Border*, pp. 14, 31, 35–6, lists twelve between 1695 and 1755. In the last, after 12 ringleaders were executed, an amnesty patent was issued on 21 July 1755, on Bartenstein's intercession, ibid., p. 15. The *Hofdeputation in Banaticis, Transylvanicis et Illyricis* was formed in 1745. The literature states that in 1755 it merged with the *Hofkammer*, Dickson, *Finance*, I, p. 293 n., however Bartenstein treats the deputation 'in Illyricis [only]' as still existing.

II

Such was Bartenstein's analysis of the internal affairs of the Monarchy on the eve of the Seven Years War. It would be easy at first sight to dismiss it as motivated by barely concealed resentment at the success of his rival, Haugwitz. Despite the repeated statements in these memoranda of Bartenstein's intention to blame no one, the virtual absence of any mention of Haugwitz by name, and then only favourably, the studied anonymity of the 'experienced councillors' whose advice was being disregarded, the gaps are not difficult to fill. However, there is much evidence to support Bartenstein's statements. The Prussian envoy Podewils described the Empress's unpopularity in January 1747, before the 'System' appeared.[69] 'I am sorry to say that this new Manner of raising the Taxes is by no means palatable to the people in general', Robert Keith in Vienna assured the Duke of Newcastle in April 1749.[70] The Venetian ambassador, Andreas Tron, reported in February 1751 that many said the new tax burdens were so heavy that in a few years noble and peasant alike would be forced to emigrate.[71] In 1756, he wrote that 'all cry out against the new arrangements and the Silesians [*sic*] who made the plan for them'.[72] In 1765, after the war was over, Lord Stormont in Vienna looked back on Haugwitz's administration as 'a very memorable and odious epoch in the Annals of this Country'.[73] The history of the 'rectification' of the Contribution in the Bohemian and Austrian lands in the years 1748–56 provides much evidence for the compulsion, haste and inequality of which Bartenstein complained.[74] Similarly, state expenditure, numbers of departments, numbers of officials and the volume of government decrees all increased, as he stated.[75] Much of the detail of his account, for example of the application of Carinthian rules to the 'rectification', and of his more general statements about the autocratic style of government, is lacking; but the statements themselves are plausible. Whether the more consultative mode of business which he favoured would have procured results, rather than frustrating them, is, of course, open to conjecture. Perusal of these memoranda raises a further, more general, issue. It is usually argued that Haugwitz's System, even if effective in peacetime, was

---

[69] A. von Arneth, *Gesch. Maria Theresia's* (10 vols., Vienna 1863–79), IV, p. 63 n. 59.
[70] PRO SP 80/182, Keith to Newcastle, 10 April 1749.
[71] Arneth, *Gesch. Maria Theresia's*, IV, p. 64, n. 61, 13 February 1751.
[72] Ibid., p. 65.
[73] See Stormont's report on the Monarchy in September 1765, Dickson, *Finance*, I, app. A. The quotation is at p. 391.
[74] Ibid., II, chs. 7–8. ·
[75] Ibid., II, ch. 1 (expenditure) and I, chs. 9 (departments) and 11 (officials, decrees). The issue of increased expenditure in the central offices is discussed by Prokeš, 'Boj', pp. 15–18. Kaunitz in a 1761 memorandum resumed Bartenstein's attack on the number of departments, Dickson, *Finance*, I, pp. 230–1

doomed to failure once the Seven Years War broke out. It is perhaps possible to argue instead that the war, with its confessional overtones, and considerable victories, diverted public attention in the nick of time from the minister's hated innovations; and transformed his unpopular patroness Maria Theresia into a national heroine.

2

THE RISE OF THE FIRST MINISTER

IN EIGHTEENTH-CENTURY EUROPE

∽∾∽∾

H. M. SCOTT

LATER eighteenth-century Europe has recently been viewed through a
royal lens. The publication of a series of major political biographies has
renewed the study of monarchy during the generation before 1789 and
has made clear that, far from being an overture to the French Revolution, these
decades must be considered on their own terms.[1] These terms were overwhelmingly monarchical. It was pre-eminently the age of Frederick the Great,
Joseph II and Catherine the Great, and in retrospect can be seen to have been
the final decades when the institution of monarchy itself was secure and
unchallenged. Kings and queens did not become extinct after 1789, but crowns
were worn less confidently after the upheavals of the French Revolution and
especially the execution of Louis XVI. It had been very different during the
eighteenth century when political authority throughout much of Europe was
exercised by sovereigns of various kinds, most of whom were in practice and
usually in theory hereditary rulers: in Russia, emperors and empresses, elsewhere kings and queens, dukes, and princes of all kinds.[2] These men and

---

[1] The list of major works is headed by Derek Beales, *Joseph II*, I: *In the shadow of Maria Theresa
1741–80* (Cambridge, 1987) and also includes: Adam Wandruszka, *Leopold II.* (2 vols.,
Vienna, 1963–65); Theodor Schieder, *Friedrich der Grosse: ein Königtum der Wiedersprüche*
(Frankfurt-am-Main–Berlin, 1983); Isabel de Madariaga, *Russia in the Age of Catherine the
Great* (London, 1981) and the same author's *Catherine the Great: a short history* (London,
1990); Adam Zamoyski, *The Last King of Poland* (London, 1992) (a biography of Stanislaw
Poniatowski); Michel Antoine, *Louis XV* (Paris, 1989); and John Hardman, *Louis XVI*
(London, 1993). I am very grateful to Professor M. S. Anderson, Dr Melissa Calaresu,
Professor Ole Feldbaek, Mag. Michael Hochedlinger, Dr T. J. Hochstrasser, Dr Christine
Lebeau, Professor Kenneth Maxwell and Dr Julian Swann for generous advice and
encouragement and for sending me specific references and publications.
[2] The office of Holy Roman Emperor is excluded from consideration: nominally elective, it
was in practice held by the Austrian Habsburgs except between 1740 and 1745. Though
the Emperor's powers were considerable, however they were not of the same order as the
sovereignty exercised by a King of France or Spain, or by the Habsburg family itself within
the Hereditary Lands.

women were closely involved in the government of their territories. They participated in the councils which fashioned foreign and domestic policies and even had a limited role in their implementation. One common theme in the recent stream of monarchical biographies has been the personal involvement of these figures in all the dimensions of ruling, even at a period when bureaucratic administrations were supposedly beginning to emerge in some continental states.

I

The rediscovery of monarchy has been both salutary and essential. Yet this emphasis has rather obscured another striking development in eighteenth-century Europe. This is the rise of the dominant first minister, which has received far less attention than it merits. Particularly in the decades after 1750, administrative authority in many states was exercised by a series of pre-eminent and politically long-lived ministers, to whom rulers in practice delegated a considerable amount of their authority and who were responsible for all – or almost all – aspects of external and internal policy. The list of such first ministers is long and impressive. It is headed by Graf (later Fürst) Wenzel Anton von Kaunitz, foreign minister of the Habsburg Monarchy from 1753 and first minister, responsible for its domestic administration as well, from the time of the Seven Years War (1756–63) nominally until his resignation in 1792. In practice his power was severely curtailed after the beginning of Joseph II's personal rule in November 1780. Thereafter his control of foreign policy usually remained unchallenged, but his role in domestic administration was much reduced: as Professor Blanning has recently pointed out, during the 1780s, 'Joseph [II] ruled as a dictator . . . There was no room for a prime minister, only for specialists in certain fields.'[3] Kaunitz would largely escape the downgrading which his fellow ministers experienced, as their functions ceased to be advisory and they became merely executors of the Emperor's policy. But his influence was far less than it had been during the second half of Maria Theresa's reign. At that period Kaunitz had been effectively prime minister and had dominated 'all aspects of the Monarchy's government', as Derek Beales has emphasised, and may even be considered 'the third head of state'.[4]

---

[3] T. C. W. Blanning, *Joseph II* (London, 1994), 60, 61. It is revealing that the references to the *Staatskanzler* in the correspondence printed in Alfred Ritter von Arneth, ed., *Joseph II und Leopold von Toscana: ihr Briefwechsel von 1781 bis 1790* (2 vols., Vienna, 1872) overwhelmingly concern foreign policy.

[4] Beales, *Joseph II*, 92–3; P. G. M. Dickson, *Finance and Government under Maria Theresia 1740–1780* (2 vols., Oxford, 1987), I, 255. There is an impressive detailed study by Franz A. J. Szabo, *Kaunitz and Enlightened Absolutism 1753–1780* (Cambridge, 1994).

In Portugal during this period the marquês de Pombal, who had been a member of the government since 1750, achieved supreme power five years later and for the next two decades effectively ruled the country, until he was over-thrown in 1777.[5] Eighteenth-century France had a whole series of men who enjoyed the authority and sometimes even the title of 'principal minister'. Foremost among these was the veteran churchman Cardinal Fleury, who held power between 1726 and 1743. During the generation before the French Revolution, four men acted as *de facto* first ministers. Only one formally enjoyed the title: the Archbishop of Toulouse, Loménie de Brienne, in 1787–8. The position of the other three was less clear cut, and none enjoyed the pre-eminence of Fleury earlier in the century. The comte de Vergennes was 'virtually a first minister' throughout much of the 1780s. He was most clearly supreme between February and November 1783, but had occupied that position 'in embryo' during the previous two years, and again enjoyed overall authority in 1785–7.[6] His immediate predecessor, the ageing courtier and veteran minister the comte de Maurepas – who had been appointed to his first post as long ago as 1718 – had been the leader of the French government between the fall of Turgot in May 1776 and 1780, when his health began to fail: one recent historian has felicitously described him as an 'informal first minister' throughout these years.[7] This description would apply equally well to the duc de Choiseul, who was in office from 1758 until 1770, though he exercised supreme ministerial authority only from 1761 onwards, when he was able to consolidate his hold over power in the aftermath of the death of the aristocratic maréchal-duc de Belle-Isle.[8] His dominance was less complete than some of the other first ministers of eighteenth-century France. His opponents retained a voice on the council and he did not possess the automatic right to attend meetings between others ministers and the French King which – as will

---

[5] Technically he was only known as Pombal from 1769, when he was created marquês. Originally from a family in the petty nobility, Sebastião José de Carvalho e Melo had been created count of Oeiras in 1759 (Oeiras was a *morgado* (entailed estate) in Lisbon which he inherited from his uncle). In this article he is referred to throughout as Pombal, which is the established usage: Kenneth Maxwell, *Pombal: Paradox of the Enlightenment* (Cambridge, 1995), 2.

[6] Munro Price, *Preserving the Monarchy: the comte de Vergennes, 1774–87* (Cambridge, 1995), 1: the whole book is illuminating on the general problem of the first minister in France at this period; J.-F. Labourdette, 'Vergennes ou la tentation du "ministériat"', *Revue historique* 275 (1986), 73–107; M. Price, 'Vergennes, "Principal Ministre" en 1783', *Revue d'histoire diplomatique* 101 (1987), 323–34.

[7] Price, *Preserving the Monarchy*, 25, 31.

[8] The impressive recent study by Julian Swann, *Politics and the Parlement of Paris under Louis XV, 1754–1774* (Cambridge, 1995) contains (chapters vii–x passim) the most satisfactory available account of French politics during the Choiseul ascendancy; that contained in Antoine, *Louis XV*, chapters xv–xvii, passim is coloured by the author's dislike of first ministers in general and the duc in particular.

be seen – was one crucial source of the power of chief ministers. Yet Choiseul's leadership during the 1760s was undoubted and widely recognised by contemporaries, and he is usually regarded by historians as having been *de facto* first minister.[9]

Lesser states furnish even more examples of the phenomenon. In Denmark, Grev Andreas Peter von Bernstorff exercised his leadership from 1784 until his death in 1797.[10] One of the most politically long-lived first ministers was the marchese Bernardo Tanucci, who served the King of the Two Sicilies, the future Charles III, from 1734 onwards. Tanucci's authority grew, especially during the 1750s. After the fall in 1755 of an earlier first minister, the marchese Giovanni Fogliani, who had been in charge since 1746, Tanucci's influence predominated. He acted as viceroy in Naples from 1759 – when the King was translated to Madrid as Charles III – and remained in power until 1776.[11] In the northern Italian state of Savoy-Piedmont, Carlo Vincenzo Ferrero di Roasio, marchese d'Ormea, rose rapidly in the Savoyard administration during the final two decades of the reign of Victor Amadeus II (1675–1730). Upon the old King's abdication, Ormea became the chief minister for his son and successor, Charles Emanuel III (1730–73) and retained this position until he died in 1745. On a smaller stage, the French exile Guillaume du Tillot served the Duke of Parma and Piacenza, a Bourbon satellite in northern Italy, from 1759–71, spearheading one of the most remarkable programmes of religious reform carried out anywhere in Europe at that time.[12]

The medium-sized and smaller states of eighteenth-century Germany also provide pertinent examples. In Electoral Saxony, which between 1697 and 1763 was linked in a dynastic union with the Polish-Lithuanian Commonwealth, Graf Heinrich von Brühl served as first minister to Augustus III (1733–63) from 1738 until shortly after the King's death in October 1763. In

---

9 E.g. Paul Viollet, *Le roi et ses ministres pendant les trois derniers siècles de la Monarchie* (Paris, 1912), 288–9; Rohan Butler, *Choiseul*, vol. 1: *Father and Son, 1719–1754* (Oxford, 1980), 1; Price, *Preserving the Monarchy*, 23; Labourdette, 'Vergennes ou la tentation du "ministériat"', 73.

10 The best non-Danish introduction is the anniversary publication, *Andreas Peter Bernstorff 28.8.1735–21.6.1797* (Kiel, 1985).

11 The only comprehensive study appears to be Rosa Mincuzzi, *Bernardo Tanucci: ministro di Ferdinando di Borbone 1759–1776* (Bari, 1967). There is currently a notable revival of interest in Tanucci: see, e.g., Giuseppe Galasso, *La filosofia soccorso de' governi: la cultura napoletana del settecento* (Naples, 1989), 337–52, and Marie Grazi Maiorini, *La Reggenza borbonica (1759–1767)* (Naples, 1991). The vintage study by Harold Acton, *The Bourbons of Naples (1734–1825)* (London, 1956) remains a mine of information.

12 Du Tillot is something of a sub-hero of Franco Venturi's *Settecento riformatore*, II: *La chiesa e la repubblica dentro i loro limiti, 1758–1774* (Turin, 1976) because of the importance of his policies for the overall clash between Church and state during the sixties, which is the author's overarching theme; for an account of du Tillot's ministry, see ibid., 215–36.

another German state that came to be part of a dynastic union, the electorate of Hanover, there were to be several examples of dominant ministers. The first was Andreas Gotlieb von Bernstorff – an ancestor of the Bernstorff who headed the Danish administration after 1784 – who was Hanover's *premier ministre* by 1709 and subsequently acted as principal adviser for German affairs to Georg Ludwig when, in 1714, he became Britain's King George I. His most prominent successor was Gerlach Adolf von Münchhausen who was formally first minister only after 1765, but had given a lifetime's service to the Electorate and had long dominated its administration, being chief minister in fact, if not in name. Even the pocket-sized, if politically significant, Rhineland ecclesiastical territory of Mainz provides an outstanding example: Graf Anton Heinrich Friedrich von Stadion, first minister for the Elector during the 1740s and 1750s.[13]

The above list is reasonably comprehensive, though it is far from complete. The phenomenon of the first minister was to be found in states of all sizes during the eighteenth century and especially during the decades after 1750. Until now, however, no attempt seems to have been made to explore this phenomenon. A century ago Lord Acton, in one of his characteristic insights, noted that the second half of the eighteenth century was the great age of the ministers who were 'admired and imitated as Louis XIV had been in a former phase of absolute monarchy'.[14] This verdict came the more easily since one of his own ancestors, Sir John Edward Acton, had served in that capacity in Naples during the late 1780s and 1790s.[15] It identified an important and generalised development which required further investigation. Its defining characteristic was that, within a political system where the ruler exercised full sovereignty, this absolute monarch then delegated at least some of his authority to one figure within the administration.[16] The minister was in turn responsible for a broad area of external and internal policy, amounting in most cases to the majority of issues facing that government. He alone usually discussed and reported upon policy to the ruler, he normally handled the key area of foreign affairs, and he clearly dominated his colleagues within the

[13] See T. C. W. Blanning, *Reform and Revolution in Mainz 1743–1803* (Cambridge, 1974), chapter iii.

[14] Lord Acton, *Lectures on Modern History* ed. J. N. Figgis and R. V. Laurence (London, 1921 edn), 303.

[15] On the early phase of Acton's career in Naples, there is much of interest in the impressive and detailed article by Raffele Ajello, 'I filosofi e la regina: il governo delle due Sicilie da Tanucci a Caracciolo (1776–1786)', *Rivista storica italiana* 103 (1991), 398–454 and 657–738.

[16] This survey therefore excludes those countries – above all Britain, the Dutch Republic, Poland-Lithuania and (from 1718–72) Sweden – where sovereignty was shared with representative assemblies and was therefore incomplete, or where the monarchy remained elective.

administration.[17] Two features were especially noteworthy. The first is the way in which powerful chief ministers emerged in so many states at around the same time. The second is the derogation of sovereignty implied in the willingness of so many eighteenth-century absolute monarchs to delegate effective authority to a group of high officials.

The near-simultaneous appearance of so many first ministers makes this trend a significant development. Yet, though certainly widespread, it was far from ubiquitous. Many states which were at times ruled by or through first ministers also experienced long periods when the sovereign governed either personally or by means of a series of departmental ministers, none of whom achieved supremacy. Bourbon Spain is the best example, among the major states, of authority being exercised – when favourites were not in the ascendant, as under Philip V (1700–46) – through a number of ministers, all of whom had essentially departmental functions and none of whom ever really secured the kind of prolonged ascendancy enjoyed by Kaunitz or Pombal. There is also one striking exception to the phenomenon of the first minister: the Prussia of Frederick the Great (1740–86). Under his father, Frederick William I (1713–40), Heinrich Rüdiger von Ilgen had, for a time during the later 1710s and 1720s, acted as a *de facto* leading minister. Ilgen's effective control of foreign affairs, together with his responsibility for a wide range of domestic matters, made him almost a first minister.[18] His ascendancy, however, was personal in nature and he certainly never eclipsed the King. After Ilgen's death in 1728, Frederick William I was assisted by several officials rather than one man. His son's accession at the end of May 1740 abruptly terminated the influence of ministers and established the most personal system of monarchy to be found anywhere in eighteenth-century Europe, with the exception of the Ottoman Empire and, perhaps, Russia. Throughout his reign Frederick the Great acted as his own first minister: he was foreign secretary and head of the civil service as well as commander-in-chief of the army.[19] His authority, however, came to be exercised not through the established agencies

---

17 Aladár von Boroviczény, *Graf von Brühl: Der Medici, Richelieu und Rothschild seiner Zeit* (Zürich–Leipzig–Vienna, 1930), 76, provides this list of the duties and responsibilities of one first minister. In spite of the preposterous sub-title this is an informative political biography.

18 R. A. Dorwart, *The Administrative Reforms of Frederick William I* (Cambridge, Mass., 1953), 227, n. 28.

19 For the extremely personal style of monarchy after 1740 see Eberhard Naujoks, 'Die Persönlichkeit Friedrichs des Grossen und die Struktur des preussischen Staates', *Historische Mitteilungen* 2 (1989), 17–37; for his role as leading bureaucrat, see Walther Hubatsch, *Frederick the Great: Absolutism and Administration* (London, 1975); for his personal control of foreign policy, see H. M. Scott, 'Prussia's Royal Foreign Minister', in *Royal and Republican Sovereignty in early modern Europe* ed. R. Oresko *et al.* (Cambridge, forthcoming); for his military role, the latest study is Dennis E. Showalter, *The Wars of Frederick the Great* (London, 1995).

of government, above all the *Kabinettsministerium* (Prussia's foreign office) and the General Directory, which was the apex of the vaunted Prussian administration, but directly from his own *Kabinett*. This was quite separate from the *Kabinettsministerium* and comprised a small group of secretaries and clerks who travelled everywhere with the King and lived with him when he withdrew from his capital, Berlin, to reside at Potsdam. At the very beginning of his reign, in early June 1740, Frederick had seized power from the ministers formally responsible for foreign policy, which he conducted personally until almost the end of his life. After the conclusion of the Seven Years War in 1763, this system of direct royal control was also applied to domestic affairs, as the King sought to rule all Prussia from his own *Kabinett*. There were, in practice, important limitations upon this personal royal direction of external and internal policy. Frederick the Great worked tirelessly at the task of ruling, but even he could not cope with the rising tide of official papers and the growing number of issues which he was obliged to resolve, especially as he grew older and, eventually, infirm. The extent of the King's personal control over all aspects of his state's government was nevertheless extremely unusual and probably unique during the generation before the French Revolution.

II

The first ministers who held sway elsewhere, though more prominent and numerous, were a far from new phenomenon. Throughout the early modern period – when the dividing line between royal favourite and government minister was often blurred and could be difficult to draw with any precision[20] – there had been a succession of powerful courtiers and officials who had monopolised all aspects of policy, which they had conducted on behalf of their ruler. In the sixteenth century, Cardinal Thomas Wolsey, chief minister of England's Henry VIII, and two chancellors of France, Antoine Duprat under Francis I and Michel de l'Hôpital in the early phase of the religious wars, were good examples of an all-powerful minister.

From around 1600, the number of such leading ministers had increased sharply, and during the next six decades the trend appeared to establish itself.[21] By mid-century the titles of 'first minister' and even 'prime minister' had

[20] A. Lloyd Moote, 'Richelieu as Chief Minister: a comparative study of the favourite in early seventeenth-century politics', in *Richelieu and his Age* ed. Joseph Bergin and Lawrence Brockliss (Oxford, 1992), 13–43, is a recent and suggestive, if not entirely convincing, survey.

[21] There is a valuable comparative study by Jean Bérenger, 'Pour une enquête européenne: le problème du ministériat au XVIIᵉ siècle', *Annales E.S.C.* 29 (1974), 166–92. Its principal foci are France and the Austrian Habsburg Monarchy. The perspective must be widened to include Spain in particular, for which see especially J. H. Elliott, *The Count-Duke of Olivares: the Statesman in an Age of Decline* (New Haven and London, 1986).

become familiar, reflecting the broader evolution.[22] In France, political authority was exercised by a series of powerful favourites (Concini and Luynes in particular) and then successively by the two great Cardinal-Ministers, Richelieu (1624–42) and Mazarin (1642–61). South of the Pyrenees, Richelieu's celebrated adversary and near contemporary, the Count-Duke of Olivares, guided the destiny of Spain from the early 1620s until his fall in 1643. Olivares was distinguished from his great rival in one crucial respect: unlike Richelieu, who was never the favourite of Louis XIII, the Count-Duke also occupied this position at the court of Philip IV.[23] The same dual role was apparent in the Duke of Buckingham's dominance in England during the 1620s. During the next decade, the Earl of Strafford and Archbishop Laud both served as chief ministers to Charles I during his personal rule.

One of the best examples was to be found in the remote but politically emerging power of Sweden, where the Chancellor Axel Oxenstierna (1583–1654) acted as first minister throughout the reign of Gustav Adolf (1611–32). After the King's death on the battlefield of Lützen in November 1632, Oxenstierna continued to guide the Swedish ship of state during first the difficult regency (1632–44) and then the tumultuous reign (1644–54) of Christina, climaxed as it was by the Queen's unexpected abdication. The seventeenth-century Austrian Habsburg Monarchy also saw the ascendancy of powerful leading ministers. Cardinal Melchior Khlesl had assisted the Archduke Matthias first when he was governor of Lower Austria and later Holy Roman Emperor (1612–18). His successor on the imperial throne, Ferdinand II (1619–37), for a time made Fürst Eggenberg his first minister. Subsequently, Fürst Portia had filled the same role for the young Leopold I (1657–1705) between 1657 and his death eight years later.[24]

The ubiquity of first ministers, especially during the 1620s and 1630s, has convincingly been attributed to the inability of existing administrative structures to bear the new loads imposed upon them.[25] The sixteenth century had seen a significant expansion of government in many states, with a proliferation of councils and the development of more complex adminis-trations. This had been a response to the increasing scale and complexity of the

---

22 J. H. Elliott, *Richelieu and Olivares* (Cambridge, 1984), 50.

23 Richard Bonney, *Political Change in France under Richelieu and Mazarin 1624–1661* (Oxford, 1979), 6; Elliott, *Count-Duke of Olivares*, 169.

24 Khlesl remains an elusive figure, though there are some valuable glimpses in R. J. W. Evans, *The Making of the Habsburg Monarchy 1550–1700* (Oxford, 1979); for Eggenberg, see Robert Bireley, S.J., *Religion and Politics in the Age of the Counter-Reformation* (Chapel Hill, NC, 1981); for Portia's *ministériat* see the brief account in Jean Bérenger, *Finances et absolutisme autrichien dans la seconde moitié du XVII⁰ siècle* (Paris, 1975), 32–7; basic biographical information on all three men can be found in Henry F. Schwarz, *The Imperial Privy Council in the seventeenth century* (Cambridge, Mass., 1943), 256–8, 226–8 and 321–3.

25 Bérenger, 'Pour une enquête européenne', 166–7; Elliott, *Richelieu and Olivares*, 50.

tasks facing rulers during a period of economic expansion and warfare that was both more frequent and also on a new scale. The resulting burdens were more than many monarchs could bear unless, like Philip II, they devoted their whole lives to reading official papers. By 1600, the myriad tasks of monarchy were already beyond the capacity of many rulers to discharge them. The additional burdens imposed by the near-continuous warfare between 1600 and 1660, and the wide-ranging diplomatic activity which accompanied this, forced many European monarchs to delegate some of their political authority to leading ministers, who monopolised foreign and domestic policy-making and quickly became all-powerful.[26]

The novelty of the *ministériat*, however, together with the real power yielded by men such as Buckingham, Richelieu and Olivares, aroused considerable criticism at the time, particularly from the great aristocrats whose domination of the highest level of government these men appeared to be usurping: most of the first ministers originally came from outside the high nobility. Two linked aspects of the system were singled out for attack: that powerful chief officials usurped some of the sovereign's prerogatives, and that they might create their own personal tyrannies.[27] Underlying such criticism was the developing notion that sovereignty was indivisible, a doctrine that the influential French theorist Jean Bodin had revived and notably publicised during the second half of the sixteenth century and which gained ground rapidly after 1600. The French royal councillor and propagandist, Cardin Le Bret, expressed such a belief when he declared during the Thirty Years War that 'The sovereign power of command is so unique that it cannot be transferred to anyone.'[28] The *Princeps in Compendio*, a 'mirror of princes' produced in the very same year on the orders of the Emperor Ferdinand II for the instruction of his son and successor, expressed the same view that sovereigns should rule personally and not through a chief minister; significantly it continued to be used in the Austrian Habsburg family until the age of Maria Theresa.[29]

The experiment of the first minister was not generally sustained after the 1660s, by which point the long decades of generalised warfare appeared to be at an end. Developments in France led the way. Louis XIV (1643–1715)

---

[26] For the position and duties of the chief minister in France after 1624, see Bonney, *Political Change*, 7 *et seq.*

[27] These twin dangers were, for example, highlighted by the abbé Jacques-Joseph Duguet in his *De l'institution d'un prince* (London, 1739; but written in 1699 in France): Bérenger, 'Pour une enquête européenne', 188–91.

[28] Quoted by Roland Mousnier, *The Institutions of France under the Absolute Monarchy 1598–1789* (English trans., 2 vols., Chicago, 1979–84), 1, 666, from *De la Souveraineté* (1632).

[29] Christine Lebeau, 'Le "gouvernement des excellents et des meilleurs": aristocratie et pouvoir dans la monarchie des Habsbourg 1748–1790', *Revue de la Bibliothèque nationale de France* (1993), 22 and 25, n. 56.

inaugurated his personal rule in March 1661 by declaring that he himself would play the central role in government, rather than rule through a chief minister, and he even expressed the hope that not merely the office but the very term itself 'would be forever abolished'.[30] The French King had received his political education during the 1650s from the second of France's Cardinal-Ministers, Mazarin, who had impressed upon his young pupil the disadvantages of the system of the *ministériat*, which he believed had facilitated open opposition to the French monarchy, particularly during the civil wars of the *Frondes* (1648–53). The Cardinal himself and his pre-eminent position in France's government had been vigorously attacked, particularly by *parlementaires* and great nobles who would have hesitated to confront the ruler directly. In an age when opposition to the monarch was still viewed as both treasonable and sinful (since the King of France was viewed as God's anointed), attacking a chief minister was an attractive substitute. For this reason Mazarin, in his celebrated final advice to the young King, had urged that Louis should govern personally and make decisions having received the views of several ministers, rather than one.

Louis XIV was receptive to such guidance, and in any case was himself suspicious that any minister given the position of *de facto* head of France's government might be tempted to abuse his power for his own private ends. Throughout his long reign, the King played the central role in French government and dominated the highest council of state, the *Conseil d'en Haut*, where policy was hammered out in discussions between and with his principal ministers. He was assisted by a series of important advisers: above all Jean-Baptiste Colbert, the celebrated minister of commerce and finance, Louvois, the great war minister, and Colbert de Torcy, responsible for foreign affairs in the final years of the reign. The crucial point, however, is that none of these men ever secured the overarching power earlier enjoyed by Richelieu and then Mazarin. Though several of Louis XIV's ministers, notably Colbert and Louvois, secured an influence which far transcended their formal depart-mental responsibilities, none was to rival the authority wielded by the Cardinal-Ministers. Indeed, Louis XIV deliberately encouraged rivalry among his principal advisers, believing that this would ensure that he received better advice and that a measure of competition was desirable to prevent any one man securing too much power.

Louis XIV's government set the standards for the rest of monarchical Europe. His action in March 1661 was exactly emulated four years later by his great rival, Leopold I. In the early years of his reign the young Austrian Habsburg Emperor had placed his confidence in a chief minister, Fürst

---

30 Andrew Lossky, *Louis XIV and the French Monarchy* (New Brunswick, NJ, 1994), 74–7, 80–6, is the most recent account of this episode and its impact upon French government.

Portia. Upon Portia's death in 1665, Leopold declared that he would not name a successor and would instead rule personally. He restored a system of departmental ministers in Habsburg government which would continue well into the eighteenth century.[31] His system of ruling through the *Geheime Conferenz* (Privy Council) closely paralleled Louis XIV's use of the *Conseil d'en Haut.* The 1660s inaugurated two generations of highly personalised monarchy over much of Europe, as rulers strove to emulate the standards – both political and cultural – set by the Sun King. The following decades saw a series of energetic and powerful kings, who ruled as well as reigned and played the central part in government: men such as Victor Amadeus II in the Savoyard State, Karl XI (1675–97) in Sweden, and Frederick William I in Prussia. First ministers did not become extinct, but they were certainly less common than they had been during the first half of the seventeenth century. Occasionally, a ruler who was weak and, sometimes, incapable would come under the sway of one powerful adviser. A good example was the ascendancy of first the Duke of Medinaceli and then the Count of Oropesa, who were successively grandee chief ministers to the last Habsburg King of Spain, the sickly Carlos II (1665–1700), in the 1680s and early 1690s.

The administrative tide, however, was flowing strongly in the opposite direction: rulers governed personally, with the aid of ministers responsible for specific departments and areas of policy. This was aided by the contemporary trend towards the elaboration of more functional and administratively complex departments of state, which evolved out of, but also in competition with, older conciliar systems of government derived from the ruler's own court.[32] The pre-eminent position occupied by foreign policy at this time ensured that the more elaborate and specialised departments of state to emerge during the later seventeenth and early eighteenth centuries were created initially for the conduct of diplomacy. France led this development and provided the model for other countries to emulate. The second half of Louis XIV's reign witnessed the creation of a much larger and more sophisticated French foreign office.[33] This development was soon copied, as other states created ministers and specialised departments. A new secretariat of state for external affairs was set up in Spain in 1714. Three years later in the Savoyard monarchy the first secretary of state was made formally responsible

[31] Bérenger, *Finances et absolutisme autrichien*, 32–66.

[32] There is still much of interest on this crucial subject in the vintage comparative study by Otto Hintze, first published in *Historische Zeitschrift* 100 (1908) and available in English translation as 'The Origins of the Modern Ministerial System', in *The Historical Essays of Otto Hintze* ed. Felix Gilbert (New York, 1975), 218–66.

[33] For an admirable brief account, see John C. Rule, 'Colbert de Torcy, and Emergent Bureaucracy, and the Formulation of French foreign policy, 1698–1715', in *Louis XIV and Europe* ed. Ragnhild Hatton (London, 1976), 261–88.

for Turin's diplomacy, while in Brandenburg-Prussia a Department of
External Affairs was established in 1728; from 1733 this was known as the
Kabinettsministerium. Side by side with these structures, new administrative
bodies were established to handle internal policy, which was also becoming
more complex during the later seventeenth and eighteenth centuries. States
were exerting greater control over, and demanding more from, their subjects
and this expansion of governmental activity required not simply more
personnel but also greater sophistication from departments of state.[34] The
elaboration of administrative mechanisms for foreign and domestic affairs was
to prove significant in the eighteenth-century rise of the first minister.

III

The appearance of dominant ministers, particularly after 1750, was not due to
any innovative theories concerning government, nor to the development of
new systems of administration. At most, the success of individual first
ministers may have inspired a degree of emulation. Europe's monarchs were
always aware of the actions of their brother rulers, and not slow to copy these
whenever it seemed appropriate. In a similar way these men were not the
forerunners of the constitutional prime ministers of later centuries. They were
rather traditional figures whose careers depended ultimately upon the support
of the absolute monarchs whom they served: this is why 'first minister' is the
most appropriate term to describe these officials, who could be appointed and
dismissed quite arbitrarily and purely on the decision of the ruler. The trend
towards governments headed by dominant ministers was rather the aggregate
of a series of developments, which were in turn the product of the interplay
between individual personalities and particular circumstances. This becomes
immediately apparent when the formal offices which the first ministers
occupied are considered. There is a vagueness and a fluidity about these
official positions. The administrative posts which the ministers held were
remarkably heterogeneous, and their own dominance was essentially personal
rather than institutional. Almost all of these men were primarily responsible
for their state's diplomacy, and many first ministers had initially risen to
prominence in Europe's foreign offices, from where they expanded their
authority: as Kaunitz, Pombal, Choiseul, Vergennes and Bernstorff all
did with notable success. This reflected the primacy of foreign affairs in
eighteenth-century government.[35]

---

34 Though its overall perspectives are not entirely convincing, there is still much of interest in
   the episodic study by Hans Haussherr, *Verwaltungseinheit und Ressorttrennung von Ende des
   17. bis zum Beginn des 19. Jahrhunderts* ([East] Berlin, 1953).
35 Cf. Labourdette, 'Vergennes ou la tentation du "ministériat"', 74.

The formal title was most clearly established in eighteenth-century France, where it was an official designation conferred by letters patent registered in the *parlement* of Paris. Though French contemporaries spoke loosely of a 'premier ministre', this title was never actually granted by the King during the eighteenth century. Instead, certain leading advisers were awarded the designation 'principal ministre', which was bestowed on four men in the decades after Louis XIV's death. Three of these held office during the adolescence of Louis XV: the Cardinal Dubois (1722–3), the former Regent the duc d'Orléans (1723), and the duc de Bourbon (1723–6), while sixty years later the title was awarded to Loménie de Brienne (1787–8).[36] What is immediately striking is that these were among the shortest and least successful French ministries of the period. The most politically long-lived and, probably, most successful first minister of eighteenth-century France, Fleury, never held the title, though he was in power from 1726 until 1743, dying in office when he was in his ninetieth year. The Cardinal, however, did institute a practice which came to be among the crucial attributes of a French chief minister. This was the right to be present at the *travail* (the meetings at which all official business was discussed) of other departmental ministers with the King.[37] Controlling access to the ruler was of immense value in an age of highly personal monarchy, when royal decisions were all-important.[38] All subsequent first ministers in eighteenth-century France, with the single exception of Choiseul, possessed the right to attend their colleagues' *travail*. Indeed, one factor in the duc's weakening hold on power during the later 1760s was the easy access to Louis XV which his ministerial rivals enjoyed. Choiseul was never formally designated as chief minister. During Louis XVI's reign after 1774, neither Maurepas nor Vergennes was styled 'principal ministre', though both were recognised to exercise such leadership. Instead, each came to be officially designated *Chef du conseil royal des finances* during his ascendancy. This underlines the absolute centrality of financial matters during the later 1770s and 1780s. It was an essentially decorative title. The *Conseil royal des finances* had been established by Louis XIV in 1661, but had soon declined in importance. During the eighteenth century, it was little more than an honorific designation which, twice under Louis XVI, was used to distinguish a first minister.

One or two dominant officials were actually styled 'first minister' at this period. The spread of the French language was apparent in the fact that both Brühl (from 1746 onwards) and du Tillot (throughout his period in power)

36 John Hardman, *French Politics, 1774–1789: from the Accession of Louis XVI to the Fall of the Bastille* (London, 1995), 117; Viollet, *Le roi et ses ministres*, 276–8.

37 Antoine, *Louis XV*, 161.

38 Price, *Preserving the Monarchy*, 23.

seem to have been formally designated *premier ministre*.[39] France's political and cultural influence was, of course, strong both in Saxony and in Parma. In eighteenth-century Hanover, the same designation appears to have been established: both A. G. von Bernstorff and G. A. von Münchhausen came to be styled *premier ministre*. Yet such examples of the formal title were the exception rather than the rule. Elsewhere the power of first minister was exercised through a wide variety of formal offices and informal positions, and these could even change during one man's period of predominance. A striking example of this is provided by the situation in Naples. By 1759, Tanucci was formally responsible for the Kingdom's foreign policy and chief minister *de facto*. Upon Charles III's departure for Spain, he became head of the Regency Council and was also tutor to the young King, Ferdinand IV, who was both boorish and incompetent.[40] When the latter came of age in 1767, Tanucci remained head of the Council of State and in the following year he was formally named First Secretary. His power, however, changed far less than the offices which he occupied and the titles he enjoyed: in Naples, as elsewhere, the *ministériat* had essentially personal foundations.

The vagueness over nomenclature possessed a further significance. It facilitated the ambiguity over the important question of the implied derogation from sovereignty represented by the *ministériat*. The reaction against first ministers in the middle decades of the seventeenth century had been due to a belief that sovereignty was impartible and that these men had in any case abused the authority which they exercised.[41] Such attitudes remained alive a hundred years later.[42] Frederick the Great, who had a longer memory than most, was quick to instance the alleged treachery of Graf Adam von Schwarzenberg, who had been chief minister to the Hohenzollern Elector George William (1619–40).[43] Prussia's King articulated the widely held view that sovereignty could not be divided and should ideally be exercised by a hereditary ruler. One of the very few occasions when a monarch formally delegated some of his authority to a chief minister was in France in 1726, when Louis XV declared that Fleury's orders carried the same force as if they came

[39] Robert L. Koehl, 'Heinrich Brühl: a Saxon Politician of the eighteenth century', *Journal of Central European Affairs* 13 (1954), 311–28, at pp. 325–6; Venturi, *Settecento riformatore*, II, 215.

[40] For a recent detailed study of these arrangements, see Maiorini, *La Reggenza borbonica*, 77–116 and 251–325, passim.

[41] Cf. above, p. 29.

[42] See, e.g., *Mémoires et lettres fr François-Joachim de Pierre, Cardinal de Bernis (1715–1758)* ed. Frédéric Masson (2 vols., Paris, 1878), II, 81, for the Cardinal's view that Louis XV's opposition to a first minister was due to his fear of giving up any of his authority to a subject, who might then place the monarchy in chains.

[43] 'Political Testament' of 1768, in *Die politischen Testamente der Hohenzollern* ed. R. Dietrich (Cologne, 1986), 610, 612.

from the King himself.[44] This was exceptional. For the most part eighteenth-century rulers – like the political theorists of the age – seem to have ignored the *ministériat*'s considerable implications for the theory of royal sovereignty, and instead accepted its practical value for the operation of government.

Its fluidity and flexibility were fully apparent in Portugal, where Pombal's predominance came to be directly modelled on the situation in Britain, which he had witnessed at first hand while envoy in London between 1739 and 1748. He joined the government in July 1750 as secretary of state for foreign affairs and war. Having secured his own ascendancy by the mid-1750s, Pombal set up the Portuguese treasury and became its first head, being styled the King's principal minister, in accordance with British practice.[45] This was less important in his long tenure of office, however, than his complete personal dominance both over the King and over his colleagues in the government.

The same was true of Kaunitz. He never possessed the formal title of prime minister, and always remained simply *Staatskanzler*, that is to say head of the *Hofkanzlei* ('Court Chancellery'). This had been established in 1742, controlled the Monarchy's foreign policy and 'confidential [Habsburg] dynastic matters' and was therefore later to be known as the *Haus-, Hof- und Staatskanzlei*, which was soon abbreviated to *Staatskanzlei*.[46] To this post, secured in May 1753, he subsequently added complete control over the government of the duchy of Milan and the Austrian Netherlands. At the beginning of the Seven Years War, the *Hofkanzlei*'s two councils for Italian and Netherlands' affairs were formally annexed to Kaunitz's own fiefdom, the foreign ministry.[47] The governments of Milan and of the Austrian Netherlands were handled by separate departments within the *Staatskanzlei*.[48] Even more important in securing his overall control was the *Staatsrat* ('Council of State'), established in 1760/61 as the central innovation in a series of domestic administrative changes in which he played the leading role. This was the only body in Vienna which supervised internal policy in all of the lands held by the Monarchy within Central Europe: though formally its writ did not extend to the Kingdom of Hungary, notoriously it transacted Hungarian business from its very inception. Kaunitz did not immediately dominate the *Staatsrat*, but slowly he managed to place

[44] Viollet, *Le roi et ses ministres*, 279; Hardman, *French Politics 1774–1789*, 119.
[45] Maxwell, *Pombal*, 51, 18. In May 1756, he was designated 'Secretary of State for the Affairs of the Kingdom': J.-A. França, *Une ville des Lumières: La Lisbonne de Pombal* (Paris, 1965), 61.
[46] For these various changes, see Grete Klingenstein, 'Institutionelle Aspeckte der österreichische Aussenpolitik im 18. Jahrhundert', in *Diplomatie und Aussenpolitik Österreichs: Elf Beiträge zu ihrer Geschichte* ed. Erich Zöllner (Vienna, 1977), 74–93, esp. 82 *et seq*.
[47] Szabo, *Kaunitz*, 50.
[48] For the changes as they affected Italian affairs, see Carlo Capra, 'Il Settecento', in Domenico Sella and Carlo Capra, *Il Ducato di Milano dal 1535 al 1796* (Turin, 1984), 329–38.

his protégés onto this body, and it was an important basis for his power during the period down to 1780.[49]

The political structure and thus the administrative arrangements of the Habsburg Monarchy were peculiarly complex, and this was one source of the multiplicity of official positions which Kaunitz held. Yet it is striking that he consistently opposed the creation of the specific post of first minister. In 1758, at a time when his control of foreign policy was secure and his role in internal affairs was expanding, he explicitly opposed the establishment of such an office, ostensibly on the grounds that the Empress Maria Theresa filled this role herself.[50] Though her involvement in government during the Seven Years War was undoubted, this argument had more tact than credence. Two years later, during a period of administrative reorganisation, Kaunitz argued that the Monarchy's system of government actually precluded a first minister. 'Un premier ministre', he wrote to the Empress, 'ne me parait pas pouvoir convenir à la forme du gouvernement', especially when (he was careful to add) Maria Theresa herself played an active role in government. The *Staatskanzler* went on to point out how difficult it would be to find someone with the abilities necessary for the post of chief minister.[51] He would subsequently argue that his own creation, the *Staatsrat*, was in any case 'a form of corporate prime minister'.[52]

Kaunitz was aware that he was suspected of aspiring to the position of premier, and this may have been one reason why he was opposed to the creation of the formal office.[53] Since the seventeenth century the *ministériat* had been viewed with suspicion within the Habsburg family, and this may have contributed to the *Staatskanzler*'s reluctance.[54] More importantly, he also understood that administrative power remained personal rather than institutional and, at least until 1780, his overwhelming influence was usually sufficient. The principal challenge to it was the bid for personal power made by Graf Karl Friedrich Hatzfeld zu Gleichen in 1771.[55] He was defeated, but only after several months during which it seemed as if he might secure the dominant position in domestic affairs at least. Kaunitz's protégé and long-time second-in-command, Freiherr Friedrich Binder von Kriegelstein, in the course

---

[49] Szabo, *Kaunitz*, 83, 103, 105, 118–19.

[50] Szabo, *Kaunitz*, 56.

[51] 9 Dec. 1760, printed in Friedrich Walter, ed., *Vom Sturz des Directoriums in Publicis et Cameralibus (1760/61) bis zum Ausgang der Regierung Maria Theresias: Aktenstücke (II. Abteilung*, vol. III, in the series *Die österreichische Zentralverwaltung* (Vienna, 1934)), 3–10, at 5.

[52] Dickson, *Finance and Government*, I, 234, n. 48.

[53] This is suggested by Dickson, *Finance and Government*, I, 233–4.

[54] Lebeau, 'Le "gouvernement des excellents et des meilleurs"', 22.

[55] For which see Beales, *Joseph II*, chapter vii, and Dickson, *Finance and Government*, I, 248 *et seq.*

of a diatribe against Hatzfeld, made the significant charge that he was seeking to 'acquire the power of an uncontrolled prime minister'.[56] Part of the reason for Kaunitz's political longevity may be that, although he was avid for power, he was careful to avoid the appearance of being a first minister, while in practice acting as this for over two decades.

Kaunitz's overall power was thus more than the sum of the range of offices which he filled, and was in essence personal. In Denmark, the same situation existed when A. P. von Bernstorff enjoyed a dominance after 1784 which rested upon his political leadership of the *Staatsrad* (Danish Council of State). Eighteenth-century Denmark remained a composite monarchy. Though certain specialised bodies, such as those for finance and commercial affairs, along with the *Staatsrad*, dealt with the entire kingdom, its central government was divided on a regional basis into two separate agencies. The German Chancellery governed the duchy of Holstein (which was also part of the Holy Roman Empire) and that of Slesvig, together with the ancestral territories of Delmenhorst and Oldenburg. Its head was also responsible for Denmark's foreign policy, which was handled by a separate department within the Chancellery. The Danish Chancellery was responsible for the government of the remaining territories: Denmark itself, Norway, Greenland, Iceland and the Faroe Islands. Though he was – briefly – to be head of the Danish Chancellery in 1788–9,[57] Bernstorff throughout most of his second period in office (1784–97)[58] directed only foreign policy and the German Chancellery. This was exactly the same duties and posts that his famous uncle and predecessor, J. H. E. von Bernstorff, had occupied between 1751 and 1770.[59] The elder Bernstorff was in some measure dependent upon the royal favourite, Count A. G. von Moltke.[60] Though a powerful figure in Danish government, he never secured the overall direction of affairs achieved by his nephew. The younger Bernstorff dominated Danish government after 1784 and was master of the *Staatsrad*, through which the remarkable reform measures passed which were the main feature of his ministry.[61]

The importance of individual events and particular circumstances in securing the dominance of one minister was most apparent in the case of Pombal. He had entered office in 1750, shortly after the accession of a new King, Dom José I (1750–77). Though at this stage Pombal was simply one of

[56] Quoted by Dickson, *Finance and Government*, I, 249.
[57] H. A. Barton, *Scandinavia in the Revolutionary Era 1760–1815* (Minneapolis, 1986), 213.
[58] He had earlier been in office 1773–80 but was not pre-eminent at that time.
[59] Lawrence J. Baack, 'State Service in the eighteenth century: the Bernstorffs in Hanover and Denmark', *International History Review* I (1979), 323–48, at 331–2.
[60] This is apparent from the letters between the two men printed in Aage Friis, ed., *Bernstorffsche Papiere* (3 vols., Copenhagen, 1904–13), II, 343–90 *passim*.
[61] Barton, *Scandinavia*, 213; Baack, 'State Service', 344.

Portugal's three secretaries of state and formally responsible only for foreign policy and the army, his energy and ability – together with the decrepitude of his veteran ministerial colleagues – soon secured for him a measure of dominance.[62] What propelled him to complete power, however, was the Lisbon earthquake of 1755 and its aftermath.[63] On All Saints' Day (1 November) Portugal's capital was devastated by an earthquake which killed some 15,000 of its inhabitants and left only 3,000 houses out of 20,000 habitable. Bodies were everywhere, the threat of epidemic disease was very real, and law and order were breaking down. The official response to this was paralysis. The King, who with other members of the royal family had escaped injury by virtue of being at the palace at Belém just outside the city, was bewildered and terrified in equal measure. One Secretary of State (de Mota) took to his bed and another (Mendonça) actually fled,[64] which left only Pombal, who faced the emergency with fortitude and energy. Fires were extinguished, looters unceremoniously hanged, food and shelter provided for the living, and the dead were quickly buried at sea.[65] Pombal's success in dealing with the earthquake's aftermath earned him the abiding gratitude of his King, and for the remaining twenty-two years of Dom José I's reign his power was total.

A rather different kind of emergency propelled Kaunitz to a dominant position.[66] The continental Seven Years War, which began in late August 1756, led to the evolution of an *ad hoc* advisory body of ministers and army commanders. It was formed to organise and direct the military effort and particularly Austria's attempts to recover Silesia, lost to Prussia in the 1740s. In practice, this amounted to a War Cabinet, which was dominated by the *Staatskanzler*. According to his most recent historian, this ensured that

---

[62] The reform of 1736 had reorganised the secretaryships, creating one for the interior, one for the navy and colonies and one for the army and foreign affairs. In 1750, the Secretary of State for the interior, Pedro de Mota, was elderly and frequently ill, while the Naval and Colonial Secretary, the Abbé Diogo de Mendonça, was ineffective: A. H. de Oliveira Marques, *History of Portugal* (2nd edn, 2 vols., New York, 1976), I, 394; David Francis, *Portugal 1715–1808* (London, 1985), 102, 103.

[63] See França, *Une ville des Lumières*, 51–66; the whole book provides an admirable account of the rebuilding of the city and of Pombal's central role in it.

[64] Francis, *Portugal 1715–1808*, 122.

[65] Maxwell, *Pombal*, 24.

[66] The standard authority was for long the writings of the Austrian administrative historian, Friedrich Walter, and especially his substantial article, 'Kaunitz' Eintritt in die innere Politik: ein Beitrag zur Geschichte des österreichischen Innenpolitik im den Jahren 1760/61', *Mitteilungen des Instituts für österreichische Geschichtsforschung* 46 (1932), 37–79. These arguments were subsequently to be repeated almost word for word in his standard survey, *Die Geschichte der Österreichischen Zentralverwaltung in der Zeit Maria Theresias (1740–1780)* (*II. Abteilung*, vol. I:i of 'Die Österreichische Zentralverwaltung' (Vienna, 1938)), 261–81. In recent years, however, Walter's conclusions have been significantly modified by the researches of P. G. M. Dickson (*Finance and Government*) and Franz Szabo (*Kaunitz*).

Kaunitz became prime minister in fact though not in name at the beginning of the Seven Years War.[67] The administrative practices and problems of the war years inexorably drew him more deeply into domestic affairs and thereby strengthened his own overall control of policy. By the time the struggle with Prussia ended unsuccessfully early in 1763, he was established as the Monarchy's first minister.

Bernstorff's emergence was the result of the changing personalities and politics of the Danish Court. In the 1770s, he had been part of the administration which had ruled after the downfall of Struensee early in 1772. This régime, headed by the King's step-mother, Juliana Maria, and Ove Høegh-Guldberg, was strongly Danish in tone and was a form of cabinet absolutism, ruling for the schizophrenic Christian VII. Bernstorff, in fact, resigned from this ministry in November 1780, when his foreign policy was severely criticised; he was already something of a rallying point for aristocratic opposition to Høegh-Guldberg. He spent the next four years in the political wilderness, returning to office as a consequence of a further political upheaval. Though the King, by now completely mentally disabled, would live until 1807, authority was exercised by the Crown Prince, Frederik, who carried out a *coup* when he came of age in 1784. Frederik's unwillingness and, perhaps, inability to direct Danish government led him to place his full confidence in Bernstorff.

Developments in Copenhagen highlighted the personal foundations of the *ministériat*. Indeed, one noted observer, Frederick the Great, sardonically commented in 1768 that the spread of first ministers was due entirely to the failings of Europe's sovereigns, who if capable should rule personally: as he himself was doing.[68] His assumption that monarchs should provide decisive leadership coloured his observation, but Prussia's King certainly had a point. In a number of states, the appearance of first ministers was clearly linked to the inexperience and, sometimes, incapacity of particular sovereigns. When a monarch ruled personally, as Frederick the Great and, after 1780, Joseph II did, there was no need and, indeed, no room for a first minister. Elsewhere, however, the ruler's age and personality were decisive.

Portugal provides an excellent illustration. Pombal's ministry exactly coincided with the reign of Dom José I, a well-intentioned but lazy and pleasure-seeking king who preferred the hunt and the opera to the business of government.[69] Tanucci's dominant role after 1759 was due to the extreme

---

[67] Szabo, *Kaunitz*, 51; Dickson, *Finance and Government*, I, 349, notes the *Staatskanzler's* growing involvement in internal policy from this point onwards, but does not go as far as Professor Szabo.

[68] 'Political Testament' of 1768, *Die politischen Testamente* ed. Dietrich, 610.

[69] Maxwell, *Pombal*, 4 and *passim*.

youth and weakness of Ferdinand IV, who became Naples's ruler in that year. It had been engineered by Charles III, now King of Spain, who intended Tanucci to act as a viceroy, and the formal end of the Regency in 1767 made no real difference to the minister's authority. In a similar way, Münchhausen acted as a viceroy for the absent British King George II, who paid periodic visits to his German Electorate, and then for George III, who never did. Du Tillot was first minister to another youthful and weak Bourbon prince, Duke Philip, who was as little interested in ruling as his brother King Ferdinand in Naples.

Royal weakness was also a factor in France. Both Louis XV and Louis XVI paid lip service to the intensely personal monarchy of their great predecessor. Each emulated the Sun King in declaring that he would rule personally and not through a first minister. Louis XV announced at the beginning of Fleury's premiership and again after the Cardinal's death that he would extinguish the title and functions of 'principal ministre' and would govern himself, while Bernis subsequently commented that the King had a 'répugnance invincible' against appointing another first minister.[70] His successor was also influenced by Louis XIV's actions in 1661, which he tried to emulate by announcing that he would also be his own first minister.[71] Neither King, however, could live up to the standards he had set himself. Though always stubborn and capable of isolated initiatives, Louis XV's enthusiasm for the hard work of government quickly waned, while Louis XVI recognised his own youth and inexperience and in addition found a way out of his chronic indecision through reliance upon a first minister.[72]

Personal factors and particular circumstances were everywhere significant and, in certain countries, quite decisive. At the same time, however, the appearance of first ministers was also linked to a structural shift within European government, which evolved from its traditional judicial function into a more modern administrative mode. This transformation was apparent in the emergence of new terms: the word 'administration', together with the use of 'gouvernement' in an absolute sense, both became established in France during the early part of Louis XV's reign.[73] It had two linked dimensions. In the longer perspective, the expansion of administrative activity which had stimulated the seventeenth-century rise of the *ministériat* continued and even accelerated after 1700. The functions and institutions of government were growing rapidly, in terms of both activities and institutions, and in the

---

[70] Viollet, *Le roi et ses ministres*, 278; *Mémoires . . . de Bernis*, ed. Masson, II, 81.

[71] Price, 'Vergennes, "Principal Ministre"', 324.

[72] Viollet, *Le roi et ses ministres*, 278; Price, *Preserving the Monarchy*, 112.

[73] K. M. Baker, 'Introduction', and Michel Antoine, 'La monarchie absolue', both in K. M. Baker, ed., *The Political Culture of the Old Regime* (vol. 1 of 'The French Revolution and the Creation of Modern Political Culture'; Oxford, 1987), xv, 1–24.

broadest sense this contributed to the widespread emergence of first ministers. More important, however, was the particular nature of administrative expansion by the eighteenth century.

Generalisations concerning this topic are difficult to frame, since state administrations in individual countries were at distinct stages of development: there was a world of difference between the relatively modern state apparatus to be found in Prussia and the situation in neighbouring Saxony, where during Brühl's ministry government remained an extension of the Elector's household administration.[74] The general trend, however, is clear. The eighteenth century saw the transition to functional ministries in many continental states. They were headed by an executive director dealing with a particular branch of government and not, as hitherto, a distinct geographical area. The change was far from complete. Even at the end of the eighteenth century, the older territorial principles of government had not finally been abandoned. But the trend in most states towards modern-style ministerial departments was clearly evident and probably irreversible.[75] The resulting gain in executive energy was considerable. By concentrating upon their own specialist function, these ministries were able to govern more extensively and efficiently than the older, territorially based agencies. Yet this could be at the expense of the strategic overview which the older conciliar style of government had provided, and which the expansion of administrative activity made even more desirable.

The problem was that the new kind of departments acquired a life of their own, at times pursuing their individual aims with scant regard for the broader objectives of state policy. In December 1760, during the discussions which preceded the establishment of the *Staatsrat*, Kaunitz had emphasised the power of the separate departments and their heads, and the lack of unified central direction, something which was especially serious during the war against Prussia.[76] There was an element of special pleading in all this: his solution of course, was the establishment of the *Staatsrat* which he hoped to dominate and which would provide the necessary co-ordination. Five years after the *Staatsrat*'s establishment, its founder noted complacently that it had 'saved the situation'.[77] Though its role was originally declared to be consultative, it quickly expanded its remit. It was, quite crucially, the first body to consider each and every part of the scattered lands of the Habsburg Monarchy.[78]

---

[74] Koehl, 'Heinrich Brühl', 313–14.
[75] Hintze, 'Origins of the Modern Ministerial System', 250 and *passim*.
[76] To Maria Theresa, 9 Dec. 1760, printed in Walter, ed., *Vom Sturz des Directoriums*, 6–7.
[77] Dickson, *Finance and Government*, I, 234, n. 48.
[78] Szabo, *Kaunitz*, 37.

Developments in France during the second half of the eighteenth century were broadly similar. The fiscal and financial problems of the French state, exacerbated by the unsuccessful war of 1756–63 and a marginally more successful conflict in 1778–83, highlighted the lack of central control over the various departments, especially where financial questions were concerned. There was no successor to Fleury as principal minister after 1743. During the 1740s and 1750s, the problem of departmental independence was exacerbated by the weakness of the King and then highlighted by military defeat, in particular that suffered at Rossbach in November 1757. This led well-placed contemporaries to urge unsuccessfully the necessity of a first minister. He would provide the co-ordination and direction which Louis XV could not exert and, specifically, secure some control over expenditure.[79] Indeed, the Cardinal de Bernis's proposal that, in addition to the appointment of a 'premier ministre', the Conseil du roi should be a corporate first minister and co-ordinate the actions of the separate branches of government is strongly reminiscent of Kaunitz's view of the function of the Staatsrat.[80]

A quarter-century later, the enormous financial problems which accompanied French intervention in the War of American Independence were one reason for the revival of the ministériat.[81] Maurepas had strongly advised Louis XVI to appoint a first minister in order to co-ordinate the work of the various departments. This was to be his intended role in 1776–80 and that of Vergennes during the 1780s. The degree of independence which individual departmental ministers enjoyed could be considerable. The actions of the naval minister, the duc de Castries, who arranged his departmental budget in meetings with the King rather than with the contrôleur-général was an especial problem: this was why the right of a first minister to sit in on his colleagues' travail with the King was so vital. The need to regulate the various departmental budgets lay behind Vergennes's desire to become first minister and the determined but unsuccessful attempt in 1783 to establish the comité des finances, with himself at its head.[82]

A generation earlier, Frederick the Great had stigmatised the confusion and strife of the departmental ministries in France as something to be avoided at all costs, declaring that French government had degenerated. This verdict

---

79 This had been advocated by the marquis d'Argenson at the end of 1753: Journal et mémoires du marquis d'Argenson ed. E. J. B. Rathery (9 vols., Paris, 1859–67), VIII, 197–9. It was consistently urged by the Cardinal de Bernis during the early stages of the Seven Years War: Mémoires . . . de Bernis, ed. Masson, II, 81–7, 141 (written shortly after news arrived of the disaster at Rossbach), 172–3, 185, 239.

80 Mémoires . . . de Bernis, ed. Masson, II, 82–3.

81 Labourdette, 'Vergennes ou la tentation du "ministériat"', 99 et seq.

82 Hardman, French Politics 1774–1789, 118; Price, Preserving the Monarchy, 69, 237 and chapters iii–iv passim; Price, 'Vergennes, "premier ministere"', 328–9.

exemplified his broader view, that ministers would always squabble and intrigue, to the detriment of effective government, and that authority should be exercised by one individual.[83] His own extremely personalised style of monarchy – which was emulated by Joseph II after 1780 – was thus intended to provide exactly the same direction and co-ordination which in many states was exercised by a first minister. Bernstorff's ministry was linked in a similar way to the emergence of a more complex administrative machine in later eighteenth-century Denmark. He provided necessary unity and direction to a governmental system that was not yet fully integrated.[84] This was why first ministers often established their power by accumulating a series of different offices. By personally becoming head of several separate departments, they imparted a degree of unity and direction to the government of their state, as well as securing their own supremacy. The rise of Brühl during the later 1720s and 1730s was a classic example of a dominant position being secured through the aggregation of a series of influential posts.[85] The role of individual human agency in this was all-important. While the expansion of government was significant, these administrative structures did not determine developments. It was rather the reaction of individual personalities to the problems they confronted which underlay the emergence of the *ministériat* in many countries after 1750.

IV

Eighteenth-century central government was everywhere a hybrid. It retained in different degrees features of older conciliar and territorial administrations while simultaneously acquiring some of the features of the modern bureau-cratic forms later to be idealised by Max Weber. The *ministériat* itself reflected this Janus-like nature, exhibiting both significant continuities and some important breaks with the past. Principal among these was the nature of the men who exercised power. The first ministers of the age of the Enlightenment were distinguished from their predecessors in two significant respects: with one notable exception and several minor ones, they were not churchmen; and they did not hold great legal offices. In earlier times there had been a significant number of clerical statesmen: Wolsey, Richelieu, Mazarin, Khlesl, to name only the most prominent. In the eighteenth century, however, there was to be only a handful of such figures and only one after 1750. Three of these men held sway in France: first the Cardinal Dubois who was briefly principal

[83] His views are in the 'Political Testament' of 1752: *Die politischen Testamente*, ed. Dietrich, 324–8 *passim*, 336; see also Hintze, 'Origins of the Modern Ministerial System', 245.
[84] See Ole Feldbaek in *Andreas Peter Bernstorff*, 9–19.
[85] Koehl, 'Heinrich Brühl', 316–20, passim.

minister during the Regency for Louis XV, then the veteran Cardinal Fleury, and finally Loménie de Brienne, in 1787–8. In Portugal the Cardinal de Mota was chief minister under Dom João V (1707–50) during the years after 1736. Elsewhere, however, clerical statesmen were a vanishing species by the eighteenth century. In a similar way, the chief advisers of earlier periods had often occupied a great legal office: for example in the sixteenth century, Duprat and l'Hôpital had both been chancellors of France as well as chief ministers. This reflected the vital role of legal issues and legal offices in an earlier period. By the eighteenth century, if not actually before, these were being eclipsed: in Denmark, for example, the last *Grosskanzler* served in the 1720s. Law remained an important element in the education of some first ministers and one – Tanucci – had been a professor of jurisprudence at the University of Pisa, before he accompanied Don Carlos to Naples. But none resembled the legal or clerical statesmen of earlier generations. In both respects the *ministériat* corresponded to the broader evolution, as central government became more secular in nature and less purely a matter of enforcing the kingdom's laws, as interventionist domestic programmes came to be pursued.

A less clear-cut break with the past was apparent where social origins were concerned. By the eighteenth century, aristocratic families were providing fewer and fewer ministers in central government, while continuing to dominate the higher levels of command in the army and the major diplomatic posts. The first ministers all correspond to this broader evolution. Their social origins were actually surprisingly similar. They were, in the first place, drawn almost exclusively from the nobility, which still provided the overwhelming majority of officials. All the first ministers came from noble families, or in a small minority of cases were quickly admitted into the Second Estate. Even more striking is the fact that some, though far from all, came from noble Houses with an established tradition of service to ruler and dynasty. This was particularly true of Pombal, Kaunitz and Bernstorff. The Portuguese first minister was descended from a family of lesser nobility who had served over many generations in Portugal's army and administration, at court and in the Church, both in Europe and occasionally in the extensive empire overseas. Though Pombal's own first marriage to a member of the Arcos family made him a relative of Portugal's high nobility, his early career owed more to family traditions of service and especially to his uncle's influential support. Indeed, throughout his ministry he was to be fiercely opposed by the aristocratic élite, who resented his rise and pre-eminence, abhorred his policies and never ceased to regard him as an upstart who had married above himself.[86] The attempted assassination of the Portuguese King in 1758 was at one level an attempt by the old aristocracy to bring down Pombal, whose power was

---

[86] Maxwell, *Pombal*, 2–4, 78.

believed to depend upon the support of Dom José. In the event, it backfired dramatically, since it was used by the minister to strengthen his own position still further.

A. P. von Bernstorff came from a family with a tradition of service, first in Hanover and then in Denmark, which stretched from 1671 until 1797,[87] and in the nineteenth century would be continued in the government of Prussia. The Bernstorffs were originally members of the petty nobility of North Germany, who found careers and fame in the region's larger and more powerful states. Their ascent was striking, but it was eclipsed by that of the Kaunitz family in the Habsburg Monarchy. The rise of the House of Kaunitz constitutes a classic case of successful service to a dynasty extending over almost two centuries and bringing a noble lineage from near-obscurity to pre-eminence.[88] The Kaunitz were originally a Bohemian family, but at an early stage they had acquired property in neighbouring Moravia, with which they were always to be associated. Their fortunes had begun to rise during the upheavals of the Thirty Years War when they secured more lands through links with the powerful Dietrichstein family, who dominated the region. Lev Vilém von Kaunitz (1614–55), who made the crucial breakthrough, had been the ward of the celebrated Cardinal Franz Dietrichstein as a child and subsequently fashioned a career in the service of the Holy Roman Emperor. His son, Dominik Andreas (1654–1705) was an imperial diplomat and ultimately *Reichsvizekanzler*. The family's upward trajectory was consolidated by Max Ulrich (1679–1746) – the father of the *Staatskanzler* – who undertook a few short-lived diplomatic missions and, more importantly, served as governor of Moravia from 1720 until 1746. His son, Wenzel Anton, was thus born into a family with a long tradition of service and (after the death of his elder brother), received an education carefully designed to prepare him for a ministerial career.

Two of France's first ministers, Choiseul and Vergennes, also came from noble families with strong traditions of state service, though in rather different capacities. The Stainville/Choiseul were originally from eastern France and had long served its Kings, principally as soldiers.[89] In the 1720s, however, the father of the future duc de Choiseul had entered the service of neighbouring Lorraine, where the family also owned property. The Duchy's growing links with France, which reached their climax in 1766 with its formal annexation, together with earlier family traditions, obliged the young

---

[87] Baack, 'State Service in the Eighteenth Century', 323–4.

[88] There is an illuminating study by Grete Klingenstein, *Der Aufstieg des Hauses Kaunitz: Studien zur Herkunft und Bildung des Staatskanzlers Wenzel Anton* (Göttingen, 1975), on which the following account largely depends.

[89] Butler, *Choiseul*, part I, provides a detailed account of this family background.

Choiseul to make his career at the French Court, which he did with spectacular success. The family background of Charles Gravier, comte de Vergennes was rather different: as befitted members of the minor *robe* nobility of Burgundy, his own grandfather and father had served in the *parlement* and sovereign courts of Dijon. He himself was a third-generation nobleman and the first in his family to be considered a true member of the traditional *noblesse*: his father and grandfather owed their privileged status to the venal offices which they occupied. He himself moved into the world of diplomacy and state service when his uncle, Chavigny, took him as secretary on diplomatic missions to Portugal and Germany.[90] Two important embassies of his own were stepping-stones for Vergennes to the foreign ministry and, eventually, supreme power. Not all first ministers came from noble families with traditions of service: both du Tillot and Tanucci were outsiders who rose in their own lifetime and through their own abilities and efforts, while Brühl's path to power was at court through the favour of two successive Elector-Kings.[91] Yet even here there was a family background of service to one of the minor Wettin lines, that of Saxe-Weissenfels.

Though none of the first ministers was initially a member of the aristocratic elite, most entered it at some point in their careers as a reward for their contributions. By the eighteenth century, the nobilities of almost all continental countries had become clearly stratified. At the apex of the Second Estate there was a distinct group of high nobility – now coming to be known as an 'aristocracy' – who were distinguished by their wealth and power, and also by their monopoly of the higher titles of nobility: above all baron, count, marquis and prince. His family's earlier importance endowed Wenzel Anton von Kaunitz with the rank of 'Graf' upon his father's death in 1746, and his own success was rewarded by the title of 'Fürst' in 1764, while Choiseul was originally 'comte' and became 'duc' only when he first entered office. The Chevalier de Vergennes was created 'comte' in May 1771, on the eve of his departure for Stockholm, where he was to be ambassador until 1774.[92] The social origins of the other first ministers were rather more modest. Indeed, Pombal's father – painfully aware of his roots in the lesser nobility – had actually falsified his family's genealogy, in an attempt to enhance his social standing, and as a result suffered a period of disgrace.[93] Portugal's first minister rose through the nobility as a direct consequence of state service, securing the title of 'count' in 1759 and that of 'marquês' a decade later. A

---

[90] Jean-François Labourdette, *Vergennes: Ministre principal de Louis XVI* (Paris, 1990), chapter i.

[91] A convenient account of his rise is Otto Eduard Schmidt, ed., *Minister Graf Brühl und Karl Heinrich von Heinecken: Briefe und Akten* (Leipzig–Berlin, 1921), 223–9.

[92] Labourdette, *Vergennes*, 14.

[93] Maxwell, *Pombal*, 4.

similar elevation of status was secured by all the important first ministers: Brühl became 'Graf' in 1737; du Tillot was awarded the title of 'marchese' in 1764, along with the landed estates of Felino and San Michele di Tiorre, and an income to match, while Tanucci also secured the rank of 'marchese'.[94]

Promotion within the noble hierarchy was everywhere the expected reward for loyalty and diligence. Such advancement was, however, far from the only reward which first ministers secured. Often lacking a substantial fortune of their own, many acquired a considerable income from state service to support the lifestyle and expenditure expected of a high official. The absence of any reliable studies of the finances of a first minister make generalisations especially difficult. But it can be suggested that many left office significantly richer than they had entered it. Pombal, for example, came from a relatively modest family, but amassed immense wealth initially by marriage and inheritance, and then during his ministry. He actually ended up as one of the three wealthiest noblemen in Portugal, which provided one additional source for the disdain and hostility felt towards him by the traditional aristocracy. His wealth was partly secured through gifts, principally of estates, from a grateful ruler. But it was also created by Pombal's skilful exploitation of the commercial opportunities open to a resourceful and unscrupulous state servant. The dividing line between public duty and private opportunity was difficult to draw in the later eighteenth century.

One chief minister who undoubtedly crossed over it and unscrupulously exploited his official position for naked private gain was Brühl, who at the time enjoyed an unenviable reputation for financial corruption both in Saxony and in Poland-Lithuania.[95] Brühl's private affairs and public career overlapped to an extent that was judged to be extraordinary and unacceptable even in the more relaxed circumstances of the eighteenth century and he clearly exploited his official position to advance himself financially. Aided first by Graf Johann Christian von Hennicke (1692–1752) and after the latter's death by Karl Heinrich von Heinecken (1706–91), Augustus III's first minister gathered a considerable private fortune, mostly in the form of landed property, built several palaces and was a noted collector of books and *objets d'art*. Hennicke seems to have been an adventurer who began life as a valet and entered the service of the Saxon Elector, enjoying a reputation equally as unsavoury as that of his patron. He came to Brühl's attention by assisting the minister in a series of shady property deals during the 1730s and 1740s and rose to control the Saxon *Kammer* (Treasury). During his six-year tenure of this

---

[94] Koehl, 'Heinrich Brühl', 320; Henri Bédarida, *Parme et la France de 1748 à 1789* (Paris, 1928), 81.
[95] J. T. Lukowski, *Liberty's Folly: the Polish-Lithuanian Commonwealth in the eighteenth century, 1697–1796* (London, 1991), 161.

post (1746–52), ended only by his own death, it seems probable that he diverted state funds to aid Brühl's private financial operations.[96] After his death, Heinecken became the minister's private intendant and handled his numerous and complex financial and artistic transactions.[97]

Brühl's corruption was unusual and probably unique. Most first ministers were content to enjoy the perquisites and income traditionally conferred by high office. None could in any case afford to be indifferent to the rewards of state service. Though Kaunitz's financial disinterestedness seems clear, he was happy to accept gifts from his grateful sovereign and himself spent lavishly: on his private establishment, on entertainment, and on his celebrated collection of paintings and his renowned love of horsemanship. Like his fellow ministers, Kaunitz also expected to spend some of his private income in support of his public duties: in the eighteenth century the two worlds intersected at several points. This is one further reason why judgements concerning finance are especially problematical.

V

The essentially traditional nature of government and politics during the second half of the eighteenth century and the important continuities from earlier epochs were apparent in certain characteristics of the *ministériat*. The first was the central place still occupied by the royal and princely courts. There has been an understandable tendency to emphasise the more modern aspects of eighteenth-century government, at the expense of its traditional elements. In an age of personal monarchy, however, courts still stood at the very heart of government and continued to play a significant and occasionally decisive role in the political process.[98] The fact that first ministers were everywhere appointed, maintained in office and dismissed by their sovereigns made the monarchs' immediate entourage the crucial location of power. This was exemplified by the remarkable career of du Tillot, who was a courtier before he became a minister. Though born in France, his early life had been spent south of the Pyrenees. His father was one of the group of French *émigrés* who served the early Bourbon monarchy in Madrid, and he himself began his career at the Spanish court. He accompanied Don Philip to Italy in 1749 and rose in his service, becoming cabinet secretary and then intendant of the

---

96 Boroviczény, *Graf von Brühl*, 82 *et seq.*; Koehl, 'Heinrich von Brühl', 320–1.

97 The letters between the two men illuminate these operations and have been printed: Schmidt, ed., *Minister Graf Brühl und Karl Heinrich von Heinecken*, 20–222; for Heinecken see *ibid.*, 239–48 and Boroviczény, *Graf von Brühl*, 96ff. He was a noted apostle of Cameralist teachings which he had studied at Lübeck and Leipzig.

98 A recognition of this is one of the special strengths of Derek Beales's *Joseph II*; cf. Dickson, *Finance and Government*, I, 212.

maison. In 1756 he was given the economic portfolio and, three years later, became first minister.[99]

Courts were especially important in those countries where administration remained very elementary, such as Naples and Saxony. The turbulent court life of the Kingdom of the Two Sicilies during the second half of the eighteenth century would provide an excellent libretto for an opera. Yet it was quite crucial to that country's ministerial politics, as Tanucci found to his cost. He had been inclined to discount the rise of the Habsburg Queen, Maria Carolina, but he was summarily removed from office in 1776 when her party became predominant at court and his pro-Bourbon policies were rejected. Not even the continuing support of Charles III in distant Madrid could save the veteran minister from his fate. The fall of du Tillot in late 1771 was also the consequence of court intrigue. In Electoral Saxony, Heinrich von Brühl owed his predominance to his skills as a courtier rather than to his undoubted administrative abilities. He had risen to power within the Wettin Court, and increasingly he was forced to buttress his position by pandering to the whims of Augustus III. One particular source of his power was his own marriage: his mother-in-law, Countess Kolowrat, was close to Augustus III's wife, Maria Josepha.[100]

Few of the first ministers were also royal favourites, as Brühl was: the dividing line was now more clearly drawn than during the first half of the seventeenth century. But none could neglect the arts and graces of the courtier within a political system where their continuation in office and in power depended ultimately upon the support of their sovereign. This was also true of those states with more developed administrative structures. All across Europe, the world of the first minister embraced the court, which had not been displaced from the centre of political life, as well as the bureaux of the government. A striking demonstration of this was provided by Choiseul's dominance, which was created by his own successful rise within Louis XV's court and especially by the support of the King's official mistress, Madame de Pompadour.[101] Though the duc was eventually to be brought down by divisions within the French ministry and by the actions of Louis XV, his position had long been undermined by his enemies at court. This was a serious source of weakness throughout his premiership and it proved to be fatal, with the rise of a new royal mistress, Madame du Barry, during the later 1760s.[102] The political career of Maurepas had its roots in the French court. Though he had endured a quarter-century's exile after his first extended period in office ended with dismissal in 1749, he remained the quintessential courtier

---

[99] Bédarida, *Parme et la France*, 75–87.
[100] Koehl, 'Heinrich von Brühl', 319.   [101] Butler, *Choiseul*, especially part IV.
[102] Swann, *Politics and the Parlement of Paris*, 319 and chapters vii–x *passim.*

during his Indian summer under Louis XVI.[103] The case of his successor, Vergennes, is even more instructive. Though Vergennes enjoyed the reputation, at the time and subsequently, of being the antithesis of a courtier, he himself always acknowledged the crucial importance of Louis XVI's court and its rivalries for his own political power and survival. As a secretary of state, be actually resided at Versailles and was a member of the *maison*; he participated in the complex rivalries and in-fighting of the courtiers; and the court provided the essential context to his premiership during the 1780s.[104] His Habsburg counterpart Kaunitz was no less skilful where court politics were concerned.[105] Indeed, all first ministers necessarily had to become courtiers as well, though after 1750 many and perhaps a majority initially came to prominence through their administrative abilities.

The second traditional aspect of the *ministériat* was the continuing and significant role played by clientage within government. Most of the first ministers staffed key posts with their own clients, friends and even close relatives. In 1761, after he himself consolidated his own ascendancy following Belle-Isle's death, Choiseul catapulted his cousin the duc de Praslin from the obscurity of a routine military and diplomatic career into the foreign ministry. Pombal's two most important collaborators were even closer relatives: his brothers Paulo de Carvalho e Mendonça and Francisco Xavier de Mendonça Furtado, while many other relatives of the marquês secured posts in the Portuguese administration.[106] In one sense this was a necessary consequence of the policies pursued and the opposition they encountered from vested interests in Church and State. Implementing radical initiatives involved advancing committed people to champion these measures.

There was a structural, as well as a practical, reason for using one's clients. Eighteenth-century state administrations were far less formalised than governments subsequently became. In particular, recruitment of personnel was still surprisingly haphazard. Kaunitz was always searching for talented subordinates, whose careers he carefully advanced even if he did not always agree with their views and policies.[107] The *Staatsrat* came to be staffed by a whole series of protégés, who were also strategically located throughout the Habsburg administration and the Monarchy's diplomatic service. The *Staatskanzler*'s dependence on the ever-reliable Binder as his own deputy and on specialists such as the step-brothers Ludwig and Karl von Zinzendorf in the field of public finance and commerce is well known. A surprising number of

---

[103] Price, *Preserving the Monarchy*, chapters i–ii.
[104] See especially J.-F. Labourdette, 'Vergennes et la Cour', *Revue d'histoire diplomatique* 101 (1987), 289–321.
[105] Beales, *Joseph II*, 143. [106] Maxwell, *Pombal*, especially pp. 3, 106–8.
[107] Szabo, *Kaunitz*, 118–19, 150, 162, 316 and *passim*.

these men had been members of the 'Kaunitz circle', as it has been styled. This emerged at an early stage in his career. Binder, Ludwig von Zinzendorf and the comte de Mercy-Argenteau (who would subsequently occupy the key Paris embassy for a quarter of a century) had all been part of his private brains trust when he was ambassador to France in the early 1750s. A surprising number of his circle were also related to Kaunitz through marriage, which was another important adhesive within his entourage.[108] In a similar way, Pombal's policies were carried through by a team of collaborators, some of whom were also his relatives; many, though not all of his followers were removed from office in the aftermath of his fall.[109] Brühl depended heavily upon his loyal subordinates and particularly on Hennicke and Heinecken, especially during the second half of his ministry.[110] Though Choiseul's predominance was never completely secure, he was still able to insert Praslin first into the foreign office and then in 1766 into the naval ministry. Two years later, one of Choiseul's protégés, Maupeou, was made Chancellor and another, Maynon d'Invault, *contrôleur-général*.[111] Vergennes's use of his clients in administrative posts was ever more extensive.[112]

This exemplified the way in which personal contacts and interchange remained the key to government in this period: in the later eighteenth century, state administrations were still primarily a reservoir of people and ideas, rather than a collection of formalised administrative structures. Personal initiatives and private connections oiled the wheels of the state machine, which were not yet driven by the bureaucratic routines of a later age. Kaunitz, for example, expected his friends and protégés to draw up policy initiatives and then to carry them through. This essay has sought to clarify the personal and administrative dimensions of the *ministériat* in the age of the Enlightenment. The policies pursued, individually and collectively, by these men were scarcely less significant. The first ministers were in the forefront of the notable reforming initiatives of this period. In recent years, Enlightened Absolutism has been seen to be less a purely monarchical phenomenon and more a matter of ministerial initiative. Statesmen such as Bernstorff, Kaunitz and Pombal presided over and, to a considerable extent, inspired the reformist policies pursued in their countries.

---

[108] The study of this dimension of the *Staatskanzler's* career has been renewed by Christine Lebeau in her thesis on the Zinzendorf brothers: this is summarised in 'Le "gouvernement des excellents et des meilleurs"', *Revue de la Bibliothèque nationale de France* (1994), 17–25. The notion of the 'Kaunitz Circle' is explored in her article, 'Verwandschaft, Patronage und Freundschaft: die Rolle des Buches in der Kaunitzschen Verflechtung', in *Wenzel Anton von Kaunitz-Rietberg, 1711–1794* ed. G. Klingenstein and F. A. J. Szabo (Graz, forthcoming).

[109] Maxwell, *Pombal*, 106–8, 152–3 and *passim*.   [110] Koehl, 'Heinrich von Brühl', 321–2.

[111] Swann, *Politics and the Parlement of Paris*, 317.

[112] Labourdette, 'Vergennes ou la tentation du "ministériat"', 93, 97.

This highlights the crucial importance of their own education and of the intellectual influences upon them. Derek Beales has rightly emphasised that 'Intellectual formation is far more powerful than social or geographical origin or physical location.'[113] The formative background of several first ministers is elusive: the essential research remains to be done, if indeed it can be undertaken, given the gaps in the sources. The importance of reformist and even Enlightened ideas for the outlook and the actual policies of Pombal and Kaunitz has been clearly established.[114] In a broad sense Bernstorff, Choiseul, du Tillot and Tanucci were all influenced by the ideas of the Enlightenment. Yet there does not seem to be a modern and comprehensive scholarly biography of any of these four crucial figures, or of some of their counterparts. The significance of the revival of the *ministériat* during the eighteenth century is clear and certain of its key features have been identified. But detailed research is needed on many dimensions and, above all, on the actual individuals who rose to prominence. When we have a series of major biographies of all of these men, of the kind urged by Derek Beales[115] and exemplified by his own study of Joseph II, we shall be able to speak with more confidence on the eighteenth-century rise of the first minister.

---

113 *History and Biography: an Inaugural Lecture* (Cambridge, 1981), 12; cf. below, p. 273.
114 Thanks to the pioneering recent studies of Kenneth Maxwell, *Pombal;* Grete Klingenstein, *Der Aufstieg des Hauses Kaunitz,* 112–253 *passim* (on the *Staatskanzler's* formation and early career); and Franz A. J. Szabo, *Kaunitz,* on the period when he was clearly first minister.
115 *History and Biography,* 22, 24 and *passim;* cf. below, p. 281–2.

3

AN OLD BUT NEW BIOGRAPHY

OF LEOPOLD II

eoeoeo

T. C. W. BLANNING

U NTIL the publication of the first volume of Derek Beales's biography
of Joseph II in 1976,[1] what scholars 'universally regarded as the best
account of the emperor's work' (in Beales's own words)[2] was the two-
volume study by the Russian Paul von Mitrofanov, published in German
translation by C. W. Stern of Vienna and Leipzig in 1910.[3] The original
Russian edition had appeared three years earlier in a single volume.[4] Although
the translation was given a different title – 'Joseph II, his political and cultural
activity', as opposed to 'The political activity of Joseph II, his supporters
and his enemies (1780–1790)' – a comparison of the two texts shows that the
translator was entirely loyal to the original version. The historiographical
domination established by this remarkable work for most of this century
is a tribute both to its quality and to the intractability of the problems
posed by its subject. In the introduction to his own book, Beales ruefully
conceded:

> I know that this is a foolhardy undertaking on many counts. First, Mitrofanov's
> book, though nearly eighty years old, is by no means easy to rival. He says that
> it took him eight years to write, and it is remarkable that he accomplished the
> task so quickly. He was not one of Chekhov's feckless, unproductive Russian
> professors. The two volumes are vigorous, intelligent, wide-ranging, and based
> for the most part on unimpeachable sources.[5]

---

[1] Derek Beales, *Joseph II*, vol. 1: *In the shadow of Maria Theresa 1741–1780* (Cambridge, 1987).

[2] Derek Beales, 'The false Joseph II', *The Historical Journal*, 18, 3 (1975), 472.

[3] Paul von Mitrofanov, *Joseph II, seine politische und kulturelle Tätigkeit*, 2 vols. (Vienna and Leipzig, 1910).

[4] P. Mitrofanov, *Politicheskaia deiatel'nost' Iosifa II, eia storonniki I eia vragi (1780–1790)* (St Petersburg, 1907). It was published as volume 83 of the series *Zapiski istoriko-filologicheskago fakul'teta imperatorskago S.-Petersburgskago Universiteta.*

[5] Beales, *Joseph II*, p. 12.

Everyone who has ever written seriously about the history of the Habsburg Monarchy in the period has always begun with Mitrofanov. Although the debt is not always acknowledged with appropriate candour or gratitude, it is always apparent. Moreover, his reputation is all the more remarkable in that it is based exclusively on this one work. Nothing else, not even an article or a review by him is ever cited. It is one of the best-kept secrets of Habsburg historiography that he was also the author of a major study of Joseph's brother and successor Leopold. The first part of the first volume was published in Petrograd in 1916.[6] If that sounds like a fragment, it should be added at once that it runs to 460 pages. In the preface, Mitrofanov wrote that the work was designed to appear in two volumes, the first dealing with foreign policy and the second with domestic. At the time of writing, he added, he had all of the former ready for the press and an incomplete draft of the second. All that was needed to bring the latter to completion was another year's work in the Viennese archives, alas now rendered impossible by the war. As there was not enough paper available for the printing of volume one in its entirety, and as he was in failing health, he had decided to publish the first part at once. If providence spared him, the second part of volume one, dealing with Leopold's relations with the French Revolution, would appear at the first opportunity.

Providence was turning a blind eye to most people in Petrograd at this time and Mitrofanov seems to have been no exception. For after this the scent goes cold. Neither the second part of volume one, nor volume two was ever published. Indeed, nothing more was heard of Mitrofanov either, and it can be assumed that he died of the illness he refers to in the preface.[7] In a brief entry, the *Great Soviet Encyclopedia* recorded his dates as 1873–1917, adding disapprovingly: 'As a historian of a bourgeois-liberal tendency, Mitrofanov devoted special attention to reforms stemming from above – from monarchs. As an idealist, he saw the state as belonging to a category standing above classes.'[8] Even that part of his manuscript which was published failed to reach the scholars for whom it was intended. No copy seems to have reached the

---

6 P. Mitrofanov, *Leopold II avstriiskii: vneshniaia politika*, vol. i, pt i (Petrograd, 1916). I am indebted to Dr John Barber of King's College, Cambridge, for obtaining a microfilm from what was then called the Lenin Library in Moscow, and to Derek Beales for its loan.

7 A plan to investigate the last days of Mitrofanov and the fate of his manuscript in St Petersburg was frustrated by the difficult situation currently prevailing in that troubled city. It is to be hoped that one day the remainder of his book will resurface. I am grateful to Dr Simon Dixon of the University of Glasgow for undertaking what proved to be a fruitless search for further evidence.

8 B. A. Vvedenskii (ed.), *Bol'shaia sovetskaia entsiklopediia*, vol. xxvii, 2nd edn (Moscow, 1954), p. 601. There was no mention at all of him in the third edition of 1974. In a preface to an open letter written by Mitrofanov in April 1914 on the reasons for Russo-German hostility, Hans Delbrück recorded that Mitrofanov had received part of his education at the University of Berlin – Paul von Mitrofanoff [*sic*], 'Offener Brief über das Verhältnis von Russland und Deutschland', *Preußische Jahrbücher*, 165 (April–June 1914), 385.

West, for it is not recorded in the catalogues of any of the major collections. No historian outside Russia, so far as I have been able to establish, has ever cited it.[9] The author of the only major complete biography of Leopold II ever written – Adam Wandruszka – appears to have been unaware of its existence. Not only did he not refer to it, he stated categorically in his preface that until then (1965) there had been no scholarly study of Leopold.[10] Mitrofanov was equally neglected inside the Russian Empire, or rather the USSR as it became six years after the publication of *Leopold II*. None of the many Soviet studies of the period has ever referred to it.[11]

I

In view of the veneration paid to his biography of Joseph II, the resurrection of Mitrofanov's study of Leopold requires no justification. Moreover, the thirty years which have elapsed since the publication of Wandruszka's major biography have yielded little of value on the history of the Habsburg Monarchy at the time of the French Revolution.[12] In particular, Mitrofanov provides an important supplement to Wandruszka by dealing in great detail with the resolution of the Eastern Question in 1790–1 and the reconquest of Belgium in 1790. Wandruszka's great service was to provide a very full account of Leopold's career as Grand Duke of Tuscany before succeeding Joseph as ruler of the Habsburg Monarchy, indeed more than three-quarters of his book was devoted to the period before 1790. This was not unreasonable in a biography, given that Leopold was then forty-two and had only two years of his life left. From a more general perspective, however, it has to be said that Tuscany was a middling Italian principality of minor importance. When Leopold travelled north in March 1790 he moved from a *comprimario* role to centre-stage at a truly world-historical moment in European history.[13]

Mitrofanov was exceedingly well equipped to do justice to the drama which then unfolded. This he reveals in a thirty-page introduction in which he

---

[9] I myself did refer to it when writing *The French Revolutionary Wars* (London, 1986).

[10] Adam Wandruszka, *Leopold II*, 2 vols, (Vienna and Munich, 1964–5), I, p. 7.

[11] See for example the numerous historiographical essays to be found in A. L. Narochnitskii (ed.), *Velikaia frantsuzkaia revoliutsiia i Rossiia* (Moscow, 1989).

[12] The only notable exceptions are Peter F. Sugar's important article: 'The influence of the Enlightenment and French Revolution in 18th century Hungary', *Journal of Central European Affairs*, 17, 4 (1968) and Leslie Bodi, *Tauwetter in Wien. Zur Prosa der österreichischen Aufklärung 1781–1795* (Frankfurt am Main, 1977), although the latter is flawed by a simplistic conceptual framework into which the fascinating material is crammed. The best account remains Denis Silagi, *Jakobiner in der Habsburger Monarchie. Ein Beitrag zur Geschichte des aufgeklärten Absolutismus in Österreich* (Vienna and Munich, 1962).

[13] I have argued elsewhere that 'it was between 1787 and 1792 that a decisive and permanent shift in the configuration of power in Europe took place' – 'The French Revolution and Europe', in Colin Lucas (ed.), *Rewriting the French Revolution* (Oxford, 1991), p. 187.

describes and analyses the sources he has used. At the top of his list he placed the diplomatic archives in Vienna, which he had combed with a fine tooth-comb and a critical eye. Among other things, all scholars will share his exasperation at the grouping in separate fascicles of instructions sent to the envoys at foreign courts and their reports. His excellent account of the fate of the Belgian archives following the revolt of 1780 both explains why the holdings in both Brussels and Vienna are so patchy and reveals how meticulous his researches had been. As might be expected, his account of the Russian archives is particularly helpful and reminds historians of the period what riches remain to be explored.

It was with the authority of a man who had worked through all the major and many of the lesser archives that Mitrofanov wrote a critical review of the numerous printed sources available. Although unable to repress a sneer at Arneth as the 'indefatigable archivist',[14] for the most part he was objective and judicious, later paying generous tribute to the high level of Arneth's scholar-ship and also praising the collections of Beer and Schlitter. But he could also be severe and was no respecter of reputations, especially when dealing with the much-vaunted collection of documents edited by Vivenot, who is charged – among other things – with confusion, error, misdating, selective quotation, a wilful failure to date certain crucial documents, a clumsy arrangement and an inadequate index.[15] Even that pales by comparison with his strictures on another key source – Adam Wolf's edition of Leopold's correspondence with his sister, the Archduchess Marie Christine.[16] It was surely not asking much, Mitrofanov suggested scornfully, to publish two hundred letters in chrono-logical order, only diligence and a knowledge of the events of the times being required. Yet Wolf contrived to make a mess of it, misdating documents by up to a year and demonstrating repeatedly his general ignorance.[17]

It is this rigorous, meticulous attention to the official documents which distinguished Mitrofanov's methodology. He had a low opinion of memoirs, finding only the odd nugget of information hidden in a great heap of special pleading. Newspapers and the like he dismissed outright, using the occasion to make some trenchant observations about public opinion in general. The historian does not need to take it into account, he stated, for the good reason that the governments did not: the eighteenth century was the great age of

---

14 Mitrofanov, *Leopold II*, p. 2.
15 Alfred Ritter von Vivenot (ed.), *Quellen zur Geschichte der deutschen Kaiserpolitik Österreichs während der französischen Revolutionskriege, 1790–1801*, vol. I: *Die Politik des österr. Staats-kanzlers Fürsten Kaunitz-Rietberg bis zur französischen Kriegserklärung, Jänner 1790–April 1792* (Vienna, 1873).
16 Adam Wolf (ed.), *Leopold II. und Marie Christine. Ihr Briefwechsel (1781–1792)* (Vienna, 1867).
17 Mitrofanov, *Leopold II*, pp. 23–4.

the authoritarian state and the public counted for nothing. Pamphlets may be important for a study of the domestic scene, he added, but they are meaningless as a guide to foreign policy, for their authors could have had no knowledge of what was really happening.[18] Foreign affairs, he concluded, are the business of foreign offices and for their historian there is no salvation to be found outside the archives.[19]

The same sharp pen is also employed when the historiography is reviewed. It is important to remember that the events of Leopold's brief reign had an intense topical relevance to Mitrofanov and his contemporaries, lending their scholarship both the vitality inspired by commitment and the distortion engendered by prejudice. The ejection of Austria from Germany in 1866, the defeat of France and the creation of a *kleindeutsch* German Empire, the continuing partition of Poland and the equally enduring intractability of the Eastern Question culminating in the First World War, all had obvious parallels and indeed origins in the events of 1790–2. So, for example, Ernst Herrmann's Hegelian belief in Prussia as the chosen vehicle of the *Weltgeist* and corresponding aversion to the multi-national Habsburg Empire strongly coloured his hostile attitude to Leopold II, whom he depicted as a black reactionary. As Mitrofanov shows, the picture he painted was drawn from a palette so selective as to be positively fraudulent.[20] On the other hand, Mitrofanov draws a line under the long-running and very bitter dispute between Herrmann and Heinrich von Sybel about Poland, showing that Sybel was quite wrong in his assertion that the 'revolution' of 3 May 1791 was orchestrated by Leopold.[21]

Mitrofanov was particularly severe on historians displaying national prejudice. Albert Sorel, for example, was taken to task for his excessive dislike of *Preussentum*, which led him – *inter alia* – to present a spitefully inaccurate picture of Frederick William II and to exaggerate Prussian incompetence. Nor did Mitrofanov spare his fellow-countrymen, even criticising the great Solov'ev for allowing his Russian patriotism to take him 'over the frontier of objectivity'.[22] He himself succumbed to what might be deemed excessive admiration of Catherine the Great, usually referring to her simply as 'the great woman' (*velikaia zhena*), but he did not try to conceal the rapacity of her

---

[18] Ibid., pp. 31–3.
[19] Ibid., p. 32. These are the closing words of the preface.
[20] Ibid., pp. 8–9.
[21] Ibid., p. 9. Mitrofanov was wrong, however, in criticising Sybel for not having used the Austrian archives. This error arose from using only the third edition of Sybel's five-volume *magnum opus*, *Geschichte der Revolutionszeit von 1789 bis 1800*. He seems to have been unaware that a fourth edition (Stuttgart, 1882) was published, *after* Sybel had worked in the Austrian archives.
[22] Ibid., p. 10.

policy, especially towards Poland. If he suggested that the Poles were living in cloud-cuckoo land in the period leading up to the second partition, expecting Prussian assistance but not prepared to pay the necessary price, he was only anticipating the verdict of the most authoritative modern Polish analysis.[23]

One further striking merit of this remarkable book is Mitrofanov's concern to write about people as well as events. This is no dry-as-dust register of what one diplomat said to another but a drama in which vividly drawn characters interact. The intellectual and literary quality is evident on the very first page of chapter one, as the *dramatis personae* are presented: Kaunitz, old but clever, swollen with pride, and arrogance, insatiably avid for flattery; Hertzberg, obstinate; Louis XVI, spineless; Marie Antoinette, masterful; Frederick William II, impetuous, short-tempered, devoted to the occult, bloated, 'an enormous meat machine' (*eine ungeheuere Fleischmaschine*), as Spielmann described him; William Pitt, the chief salesman of the Great British Stores; Catherine the Great, steadfast (and great, of course); Leopold, slippery, elusive, but perhaps the most important of them all.

Later in the book, a substantial section of some twenty pages long is devoted to contemporary views of Leopold's character. As Mitrofanov demonstrates by deft use of quotation, drawing on his matchless command of the sources, the collective picture presented was deeply hostile. Leopold was depicted by foreign diplomats as a dyed-in-the-wool Florentine conspirator, never to be trusted or believed, whose cunning stemmed not from cleverness but from weakness, cowardice, indecision and lack of character.[24] This tells us more about the distorting perspective of the observers than about their subject, Mitrofanov reasonably concludes. His own verdict is much more nuanced – and convincing. Naturally sympathetic to a man who constantly suffered from ill-health, he acquits him of all charges stemming from the 'greasy Florentine' stereotype, identifying his only significant vice as 'son penchant immodéré pour le sexe', as contemporaries called it.[25] Among other things, it made Leopold the target for an imaginative ruse by the French *émigrés*, who sent the beautiful Madame de Cassis to exploit his notorious priapism, although her willingness to make the supreme sacrifice proved to be of no avail.

When it comes to Leopold's political achievements, Mitrofanov is generous but judicious. By a combination of skill, cunning, patience and determination, the new emperor took the Habsburg Monarchy back to safety from the brink of ruin to which his brother's folly had brought it. Moreover, this tactical dexterity was underpinned by a strategic vision of a stable Europe

23 Ibid., p. 171; Jerzy Łojek, 'The international crisis of 1791: Poland between the Triple Alliance and Russia', *East Central Europe*, 2, 1 (1975), 13, 17.
24 Mitrofanov, *Leopold II*, pp. 35–8.
25 Ibid., p. 43.

which had turned its back on the restless greed which had brought so much warfare in the past. This was developed most clearly in the course of Leopold's interview with the secret Prussian envoy Bischoffwerder on 25 February 1791, which Mitrofanov recounts in detail. Not only did Leopold make the predictable noises about his desire for peace, he also stated that the current ferment was the outcome of forty years of error. Everyone in Europe had been so anxious to grab everyone else's property that general ruin had been the inevitable result. It was therefore essential for Austria and Prussia to turn their backs on past practice and set an example of cooperative restraint which would put an end to the ruinous international anarchy.[26] This provides powerful support for Paul Schroeder's admiration of Leopold, delivered by means of a comparison with Metternich:

> Leopold resembled Metternich in some ways, especially in his flexibility and tactical skill, but excelled him in other, more important respects, and lacked only the longevity and luck to which Metternich would owe his fame. Metternich was a skilful diplomat; Leopold was a great statesman . . . Leopold anticipated [Metternich] in breaking with eighteenth century politics and trying to create a new international system. Only thus, and not just as expedients to get Austria out of trouble or to manage an increasingly chaotic situation, must Leopold's actions in the summer of 1791 and later be understood.[27]

Schroeder concedes that Leopold could not have prevented war with revolutionary France or saved Poland, but suggests that at least he would not have thrown good money after bad in fighting a string of disastrous wars, 'nor, after his policy suffered shipwreck, would he have jumped overboard clinging to the anchor', as his undistinguished son and successor Francis II did.[28] Unless and until the remaining parts of Mitrofanov's book are found, we shall have no way of knowing whether he fully anticipated Schroeder's enthusiasm. There is an occasional hint, however, that his overall verdict was a good deal less favourable. Although he rejected the 'scheming Florentine' image, he did explicitly endorse Marie Antoinette's view that her brother was 'a petty Tuscan Grand Duke on the Austrian throne', adding by way of qualification that he died too soon, before he had had the chance to grow into his new role.[29] In particular, Mitrofanov liked to stress what he believed to be Leopold's timidity, as for example in his comment on the approach made to Catherine the Great in late 1790 urging a quick peace with the Turks on

---

[26] Ibid., p. 288.
[27] Paul W. Schroeder, *The transformation of European politics 1763–1848* (Oxford, 1994), p. 88.
[28] Ibid., p. 98.
[29] Mitrofanov, *Leopold II*, p. 53.

moderate terms: 'the entire project bore the seal of that timidity and anxiety which were so dear to the heart of Leopold II'.[30]

As this verdict suggests, Mitrofanov was fond of making confident judgements about historical figures. Indeed, he was much too fond. His intensive study of the archives had yielded a mountain of material about personalities, especially about the diplomats whose reports he relied on so heavily, and he was very loath to leave any of it out. The result was a series of pen-portraits of all the main and many of the minor actors – five pages on Count Mercy, four pages on Prince Reuss, and two pages on Joseph Ewart, for example.[31] These contain many acute characterisations (no one who has ever trudged through Sir Robert Murray Keith's ponderous correspondence will fail to share Mitrofanov's exasperation with this 'amiable but dull-witted' diplomat) but they slow the pace of the narrative to an irritating amble and sometimes bring it to a complete standstill.

Mitrofanov's most serious failing as a historian was his lack of selectivity, not so much his inability to see the wood for the trees as his determination to treat the smallest sapling with the same attention as the mightiest sequoia. Nowhere is this more apparent than in his enervating account of the Congress of Sistova, surely the most tedious diplomatic episode of the century. From December 1790 until August 1791, a group of wretched diplomats were obliged to kick their heels in a small town on the lower Danube while one great power after another intervened to prevent the negotiations reaching a conclusion. One is almost (but not quite) inclined to feel sorry even for Keith, who told his sister that he was leading 'such a life as would *tire an oyster*'.[32] Yet Mitrofanov remorselessly charts every arid twist and turn in their deliberations.[33] It is at moments such as these that his maxim '*nulla salus extra tabularium*' makes one feel that hell should be risked.[34]

II

The substantive range of the surviving torso of Mitrofanov's book is revealed best by his table of contents:

---

[30] 'Ves' proekt nosil na sebe pechat' toi robosti i boiazlivosti, kotoraia tak mila byla serditsu Leopolda II' – ibid., p. 369. See also his comment that his response to news of the Polish revolution of 3 May 1791 was typical of the mentality of 'the little Tuscan duke' – ibid., p. 444.

[31] Ibid., pp. 73–7, 115–18, 127–9.

[32] Sir Robert Murray Keith, *Memoirs and correspondence (official and familiar)*, ed. Mrs A. Gillespie Smyth, 2 vols. (London, 1849), II, p. 381.

[33] Mitrofanov, *Leopold II*, pp. 426–40.

[34] I am grateful to Professor James Diggle of Queen's College, Cambridge, for his assistance in translating Mitrofanov's Russian maxim into Latin.

Preface

Introduction

1. Leopold II and his ministers
2. Austria and Europe at the end of Joseph II's reign
3. Reichenbach
4. The Belgian Republic of 1790
5. First attempts at a rapprochement between Austria and Prussia
6. The European crisis of the spring of 1791
   i.   The victory of Russia in the Eastern Question
   ii. The Congress of Sistova
   iii. The Revolution of 3 May 1791

Despite the existence of excellent accounts of this period both old (by R. H. Lord) and new (by Paul Schroeder),[35] no historian of the period could fail to find something of interest in Mitrofanov's account, if only because he knew the archives so well and quoted from them so liberally. His major service to the historiography of the revolutionary period was his demonstration of the minor role played by the French Revolution in international affairs in 1789–91. Explicitly following Ranke and criticising the opposite view advanced by Häusser, Mitrofanov stressed that the French Revolution should be seen as part of international politics, not the other way round.[36] During this crucial period it was only in Belgium that events in France made a direct impact. Elsewhere in Europe it was the ramifications of the reopening of the Eastern Question by the Turkish declaration of war on Russia on 17 August 1787 which determined the course of events. In what follows, I propose to examine Mitrofanov's account of the crucial opening months of Leopold's reign, to demonstrate the nature, scope and limitations of his achievement.

At the beginning of chapter two, Mitrofanov provides an eloquent account of the problems facing Leopold II when he succeeded his brother. The Belgians had seceded, the Magyar gentry of Hungary were preparing for revolt and even the normally docile Hereditary Lands were restive. Still more menacing was the threat from abroad, as the war against the Turks continued and invasion by Prussia allied to Great Britain, the United Provinces, Poland, Sweden and Turkey threatened. Of Austria's own allies, revolutionary France

---

[35] Robert Howard Lord, *The second partition of Poland. A study in diplomatic history*, Harvard Historical Studies, vol. 23 (Cambridge, Mass., 1915), *passim*; Schroeder, *The transformation of European politics*, ch. 2. Despite the almost exact coincidence of the publication of Lord's and Mitrofanov's books, their authors do not appear to have known of each other's existence, although it would have been most surprising if their paths had not crossed in the archives at some point.

[36] Mitrofanov, *Leopold II*, pp. 5–6, 9–10. I have advanced my own version of this argument in 'The French Revolution and Europe' and at greater length in *The French Revolutionary wars 1787–1802* (London, 1996).

was both impotent and deeply hostile, while Russia was fighting Sweden in the north, was on the defensive in the Caucasus and was operating sluggishly on the Danube. Mitrofanov concludes that the last hour of the house of Habsburg seemed to have struck.[37]

But he also asks – did not the situation look worse than it really was? – and then advances a number of cogent reasons for Leopold's escape. With the advantage of hindsight, he suggests, we can see that the critical moment had passed. The Monarchy had been at its weakest in the summer of 1789, with Belgium erupting in revolt and the hitherto unsuccessful war against the Turks not yet turned round. It was then that the Prussians had their best chance of making significant territorial gains at Austrian expense. For some time, Count Hertzberg had been advocating a diplomatic *démarche* which would settle the Balkan conflict by means of a multiple exchange of territory: the major losers were to be the Turks, who were to cede the 'Danubian Principalities' of Moldavia and Wallachia to the Habsburg Monarchy, receiving in return an international guarantee of their remaining territories. For their part, the Austrians were to restore Galicia to Poland, which in turn would reward Prussia with Danzig and Thorn and surrounding districts.

Mitrofanov did not have a high opinion of Hertzberg, damning him with faint praise as 'a first-rate chancellor with unrivalled knowledge of the archives'. As a diplomat he was handicapped by his conceit, pedantry, egocentricity, loquacity, indiscretion and boorishness.[38] No wonder that Kaunitz regarded him as a 'scoundrel' (*Schurke*) and an 'homme abominable et très dangereux',[39] although that might well be seen as a classic case of the pot calling the kettle black. Kept on a tight rein by Frederick the Great, who was well aware of his deficiencies, Hertzberg came into his own under Frederick William II, whose favour he had curried for many years. Reaping his reward with the title of Count, the Order of the Black Eagle and the presidency of the Berlin Academy, he achieved an early and dazzling success with the resolution of the Dutch crisis in the autumn of 1787. This put Prussia in the driving seat on the European continent and placed Hertzberg behind the wheel.

Yet all his efforts came to nothing. Paradoxically, the chief reason for failure in 1788 was the unexpected vigour displayed by the Turks in their campaign of that year, which together with the habitual lethargy of their Russian and Austrian opponents, brought unaccustomed military success. They were correspondingly reluctant to make any territorial concessions. By the summer of 1789 it was becoming clear that the Hertzberg plan could not be achieved by peaceful diplomacy, especially as the new Turkish Sultan Selim III had announced his intention of prosecuting the war in the Balkans

[37] Mitrofanov, *Leopold II*, p. 69.   [38] Ibid., p. 103.   [39] Ibid., p. 54.

à outrance. Losing patience, Hertzberg advised Frederick William II to take advantage of the pressure created by the Prussian summer manoeuvres in Silesia to issue an ultimatum to Russia and Austria demanding their consent to the annexation of Danzig and Thorn. If they refused, the Prussians should simply occupy Great Poland; and if they resisted, then so much the worse for them, for, in alliance with Sweden, Turkey and Poland, possession would prove to be ten tenths of the law.[40] As Hertzberg told the Prussian agent in Warsaw, the supremely devious Marchese di Lucchesini, if Frederick William II waited until the following year to 'frapper le grand coup', he would miss the 'heure du berger', a singularly appropriate metaphor for his notoriously amorous sovereign.[41]

When it came to politics, however, Frederick William was nothing if not irresolute.[42] His natural inclination to procrastinate was then reinforced by a diplomatic counter-offensive launched by Catherine the Great. Her new envoy to Berlin, Maksim Maksimovich Alopeus, quickly established good relations with the rising star at the Prussian court, the royal *aide-du-camp* Colonel Johann Rudolf von Bischoffwerder.[43] The latter, Mitrofanov justly remarks, was just as mysterious as his name, which was spelt by contemporaries in several different ways.[44] Although he had no official position in the Prussian foreign office, he was rapidly emerging as the prime influence on the king, their relationship strengthened by their common membership of the Rosicrucian Order.[45] Despite his military background, Bischoffwerder was a complete pacifist, if not by conviction, then certainly by self-interest, for he knew that what Frederick William wanted most was to be left in peace to pursue his hedonistic way of life. For that reason alone he was utterly opposed to Hertzberg's restless schemes and used his influence in the summer of 1789 to prevent a decisive initiative over Danzig and Thorn.[46]

Alopeus and Bischoffwerder were lent powerful support by the British envoy in Berlin, Joseph Ewart. As Mitrofanov rightly stresses, the alliance

---

[40] Ibid., pp. 109–10.

[41] Bronislas Dembinski, *Documents relatifs à l'histoire du deuxième et troisième partage de la Pologne*, vol. I: *Politique de la Russie et de la Prusse à l'égard de la Pologne depuis l'ouverture de la Diète de Quatre Ans jusqu'à la promulgation de la Constitution du 3 Mai, 1788–1791* (Léopol, 1902), p. 403.

[42] It was said unkindly of the confirmed bachelor William Pitt that he was 'stiff in everything but congress with women'. In the case of Frederick William II, this *mot* should be reversed.

[43] Alopeus was given his first audience on 4 July 1789 – Otto Friedrich Winter (ed.), *Repertorium der diplomatischen Vertreter aller Länder*, vol. III: *1764–1815* (Graz and Cologne, 1965), p. 362.

[44] Mitrofanov, *Leopold II*, p. 99.

[45] Mitrofanov corrects the view expressed by Adam Wolf (*Österreich unter Maria Theresia, Joseph III und Leopold II* (Berlin, 1883), p. 376) and others that Bischoffwerder did not become influential until 1790.

[46] Mitrofanov, *Leopold II*, p. 111.

between Prussia and Great Britain, concluded in 1788 in the wake of their joint triumph in the Dutch Republic, was fatally flawed from the start. The Prussians wished to use it to redraw the map of central and eastern Europe in their favour, while the British regarded it as a bulwark of the status quo. Throughout the summer of 1789, Count Alvensleben reported from London that Pitt and his colleagues were sticking firmly to the letter of their defensive alliance and would do nothing to help Prussian territorial expansion.[47] As a result, Ewart changed from being Hertzberg's friend and confidant into his declared opponent. In a private letter, conveyed by Bischoffwerder, Ewart implored Frederick William II not to proceed with his foreign minister's plan.[48]

British disapproval might have been disregarded, but the refusal to send a naval task-force to assist Prussian land operations along the Baltic coast was a different matter. Moreover, by mid-summer the generals, led by Möllendorff and the Duke of Brunswick, were beginning to argue that the season was too far advanced for a campaign to be started.[49] Postponing action until the following spring, they pointed out, would allow proper mobilisation. Anyway, by that time, it was confidently expected, the Habsburg Monarchy would be imploding: a revolt was already underway in Belgium and plans were well advanced for fomenting similar insurrections in Hungary and Galicia. Perhaps more important than all these considerations was Frederick William II's natural hesitancy when faced with a potentially momentous decision. Whatever the reason, at some point late in August 1789 he rejected finally Hertzberg's pleading for immediate action, although expressing his determination to go to war the following year.[50]

Mitrofanov agreed with Hertzberg: Prussia had missed a golden opportunity. As Lucchesini wrote on 27 August: 'The events of ten centuries could not bring about a situation more favourable to Prussia for putting the last touches on her aggrandizement.'[51] No sooner had Frederick William II allowed the sword to slide back into its scabbard than the fortunes of war began to turn. At long last, the Austrian and Russian armies began to go on the offensive, winning decisive battles against the Turks at Focşani in Moldavia on 31 July, at Martinesci on the river Rymnik on 21 September and

---

47 Friedrich Carl Wittichen, *Preußen und die Revolutionen in Belgien und Lüttich* (Göttingen, 1905), pp. 19–21.
48 Mitrofanov, *Leopold II*, p. 110. A fuller account can be found in Friedrich Luckwaldt, 'Zur Vorgeschichte der Konvention von Reichenbach: englischer Einfluß am Hofe Friedrich Wilhelms II.', *Delbrück-Festschrift. Gesammelte Aufsätze, Professor Hans Delbrück zu seinem 60ten Geburtstage dargebracht von Freunden und Schülern* (Berlin, 1908), pp. 252–5.
49 Mitrofanov, *Leopold II*, p. 110.
50 Lord, *The second partition of Poland*, pp. 118–19.
51 Quoted in ibid., p. 118.

at Porceni on 8 October. Most important of all was the storming of the great Turkish fortress of Belgrade by an Austrian army commanded by Laudon, also on 8 October. The campaign was brought to a triumphant conclusion with the capture of Bucharest by another Austrian army under Prince Coburg on 10 November.[52]

With the advantage of hindsight, we can see that this was the crucial moment for the Habsburg Monarchy. Many more anxious moments would have to be endured, but it turned out that the great victories of the autumn of 1789 had ensured survival. It is a tribute to Mitrofanov's breadth of vision that, unlike most historians of the period, he is able to give credit where it is due – to Joseph II. It was Joseph who had built the army and it was Joseph who took full advantage of its success. Although gripped by a terminal illness (tuberculosis), he showed impressive energy and determination during the last few months of life, organising the defence of the northern frontier against the impending attack by Prussia and launching a diplomatic offensive to split the Anglo-Prussian alliance.[53]

One last success of Joseph's reign was the securing of Saxon neutrality in the event of war. This was less easy than it sounds, for the Prussians had launched a major initiative of their own, sending Lucchesini down from Warsaw with all manner of blandishments. In return for military assistance, Frederick Augustus of Saxony was promised support in acquiring the throne of Poland, free passage for Saxon shipping on the Elbe and even a piece of Brandenburg territory. His advisers were simply bribed. For their part, the Austrians fell back on a device as old-fashioned as it was effective, using the Elector's confessor to play the card of religious solidarity. The deeply pious Frederick August succumbed. On 10 February – just ten days before Joseph's death – the Austrian envoy, Hartig, was given the necessary assurance that Saxony would not support Prussia militarily. Great was the rejoicing in Vienna when news of this diplomatic coup arrived. As Mitrofanov acidly observed, even Kaunitz cheered up.[54]

So when Leopold arrived in Vienna on 12 March 1790 (he had refused to set out until his brother actually died), the situation was much less gloomy than it might have been. It was well known that Prussian preparations for war were not going smoothly, a fact recently dramatised by the suicide of the officer in charge of assembling supplies. To make matters worse, the previous year's harvest in Silesia had been particularly poor, a prolonged drought had lowered the level of the Oder, making the transport of supplies difficult, the cavalry was short of horses, desertion was rife, ammunition was short and morale was low. As a result, the original schedule, which had called for the army to be in place

---

[52] I have examined this campaign in my *Joseph II* (London, 1994), pp. 176–82.
[53] Mitrofanov, *Leopold II*, p. 113.   [54] Ibid., pp. 113–14.

by the beginning of May, had to be put back again and again.[55] News of Prussian problems prompted Kaunitz to encourage his new master to take a tough stand. He told Leopold with his habitual imperiousness that he should maintain close links with Russia, continue negotiations with Great Britain, spin out negotiations with the Turks and resist resolutely any offensive in the north – if it came. In fact, Kaunitz doubted very much whether there would be any attack: the Polish 'army' was worthless, he argued, and Frederick William II would back off if the Austrians stood up to him.[56]

Leopold did not agree. Having always disapproved of the alliance with Russia in general and of Austrian participation in the Turkish war in particular, he was determined to achieve a quick peace.[57] So he and his chancellor were at loggerheads from the start. Not even Leopold's best Florentine flattery could win Kaunitz round. As Mitrofanov commented, the latter had received so much during his long career that he was now immune – even when it was lavished on him by his sovereign.[58] Yet although disagreeing about the correct strategy, they were agreed about tactics. At the suggestion of Kaunitz, on 15 March Leopold wrote a personal letter to Frederick William II, announcing his accession to the throne and making friendly noises about his desire for a peaceful resolution of their differences. By this démarche, Kaunitz hoped to win time for further military success in the Balkans, while Leopold hoped it would initiate a permanent peace process.[59]

It has been generally assumed that it was Leopold who decided on this personal appeal to Frederick William II[60] – and not unreasonably, given his well-known desire for peace. Yet Mitrofanov could show that it was the Prussophobe hawk Kaunitz who had advised this course of action. He had found in the Viennese archives a document entitled 'Draft of a memorandum (which however was changed in different ways two or three times before assuming its final form), which Prince Kaunitz composed for Emperor Leopold on his accession to the throne, in order to demonstrate, by reference to the mistakes committed by Emperor Joseph II, how he should conduct himself towards foreign states.' Among other pieces of advice, there was the following unequivocal recommendation:

---

[55] Ibid., p. 139. This was Count von Schulenburg-Blumberg, who had sold his stocks in 1789 in the hope of being able to buy them back more cheaply the following year. Alas, prices had gone up.

[56] Ibid., p. 137.

[57] Wandruszka, Leopold II., II, p. 188.

[58] Mitrofanov, Leopold II, p. 138.

[59] Ibid., pp. 170–3.

[60] See, for example, Lord, The second partition of Poland, pp. 128–9 and Wandruszka, Leopold II., II, p. 265.

There is just one step which can still be taken, and this would be for Your Majesty to send an autograph letter to the King of Prussia on the occasion of the formal notification of your accession to the throne, so that there can be no doubt as to your views on all the big issues of the present day, and indeed in the future.[61]

Moreover, it was Kaunitz and Kaunitz alone who drafted the better-known and much fuller communication to Frederick William II which was despatched on 26 March, even though it went out under Leopold's name. As Kaunitz told the signatory:

> In the case of letters of so great importance as that which Your Majesty is now sending to the King of Prussia, there is not a thought, not a turn of phrase or even an expression which does not need to be weighed and considered, if one does not wish to run the risk of failing to achieve the desired end. For that reason I took the view that I could allow myself time to think about it.[62]

Ranke stated that this draft of Kaunitz was altered by Leopold to make it more conciliatory but Mitrofanov could find no document in the archives to suggest that this had been done.[63]

There is neither need nor space to follow Mitrofanov's detailed account of how this peace initiative of March 1790 led to a resolution of the Austro-Prussian dispute by the Convention of Reichenbach, signed on 27 July. Although shorter and less securely based on archival sources, the account to be found in R. H. Lord's *The Second Partition of Poland* provides an adequate substitute. What does deserve to be highlighted is Mitrofanov's demonstration of just how pivotal was the role of the British. It was their adamant refusal to assist Prussian expansion which forced Frederick William II to take off his armour and play the role of peace-maker. This was no foregone conclusion. There were times during June and July 1790 when his bellicose eruptions made war seem certain.[64] Only a categorical statement from London delivered by Ewart on 6 July that, if war resulted from an attempt to impose the Hertzberg plan, the British would not participate, brought a change. Now Frederick

---

[61] Mitrofanov, *Leopold II*, p. 173: 'Ein einziger Schritt dürfte jedoch noch zu machen seyn, und dieser wäre, ein eigenhändiges Schreiben E. M. bey Gelegenheit der feyerlichen Notification Ihrer Thronbesteigung an den König von Preußen zu erlassen, um ihm Ihrer Gesinnungen wegen über aller dermalen vorliegende große Gegenstände und sogar auf die Zukunft nicht in Zweifel zu lassen.' This document is to be found in the Haus-, Hof- und Staatsarchiv, Staatskanzlei, Vorträge, 220.

[62] Mitrofanov, *Leopold II*, p. 173. It should be noted that Mitrofanov's transcriptions from languages other than Russian were often defective. It is possible, of course, that he died before he could correct the proofs.

[63] Ibid. Ranke's statement is to be found in Leopold von Ranke, *Die deutschen Mächte und der Fürstenbund*, 2 vols. (Leipzig, 1871–2), II, pp. 174–5.

[64] Mitrofanov, *Leopold II*, p. 194.

William II insisted that the Austrians must agree to make peace with the Turks on the basis of the strict *status quo ante bellum*.[65]

This news caused consternation in both camps. On the Prussian side, the deepest disappointment was felt by Hertzberg, who saw what he believed to have been a uniquely favourable position abandoned for no reason and for no profit. It also involved abandoning Prussia's allies in Poland, Turkey, Belgium, Galicia and Hungary. On 1 August he wrote to Schlieffen: 'I cannot contain myself for grief and shame.'[66] His counterpart in Vienna, Prince Kaunitz, was no less appalled by Leopold's sacrifice of all the great gains made the previous year. In particular, the need to hand back Belgrade, the symbol of Balkan control, stuck in his (and many other Austrians') craw. In a memorandum on the Congress and Convention of Reichenbach, he described the outcome simply as a 'humiliation'.[67] That these two old cold-warriors should be equally disapproving might prompt the comfortable conclusion that they were both wrong. That was not Mitrofanov's view. He believed that Reichenbach was indeed a defeat for both the German powers. Hertzberg was right: Prussia had indeed missed the boat, squandering sixteen million talers into the bargain.[68] On the other hand, those historians led by Sybel who believed that Leopold had achieved just what he wanted had been confused by the imprecise language employed. When the Austrian negotiators had spoken at Reichenbach of being prepared to return to the 'status quo', they did not mean the term to be taken literally. While prepared to hand back some of their conquests to the Turks, they intended to keep those within the 'Passarowitz line', i.e. the territory won at the Peace of Passarowitz in 1718, including Belgrade. When they learned that the status quo was to be interpreted quite literally, they were horrified.[69]

---

65 Ibid., p. 207. Mitrofanov believed that in effect this amounted to a declaration of war, for in his opinion Frederick William II did not believe that Leopold II would accept the strict status quo 'in secret he hoped that Vienna would not yield to his ultimatum and would decide for war' (Vtaine on nadeialsia, chto v Vene ne primut ego ul'timatuma i reshat'sia na voinu). However, the only evidence he cites is a remark made by Frederick William to his envoy in Vienna, Jacobi: 'Je ne puis que concevoir des doutes sur la bonne foi de la Cour de Vienne.' Lord was quite emphatic that Frederick William did *not* think he was provoking war by insisting on the strict status quo – *The Second Partition of Poland*, p. 147.

66 Ibid., p. 150.   67 Mitrofanov, *Leopold II*, p. 216.

68 Ibid. This was a verdict which has been echoed recently by Paul Schroeder: 'For Prussia . . . Reichenbach was really a defeat. By mobilizing at great expense and then failing to act, it had let down the Turks, betrayed the Poles, irritated the Russians, worried its English and Dutch allies, and finally let its opponent off the hook, all for an ephemeral gain in prestige' – *The transformation of European politics*, p. 66.

69 Mitrofanov, *Leopold II*, p. 217. The latest historian to have fallen into this trap is Jeremy Black, who has written 'the terms were essentially those outlined by Leopold II in his correspondence with Frederick William II', a comment which suggests that he has not mastered the German literature – *British foreign policy in an age of revolutions 1783–1793* (Cambridge, 1994), p. 262.

As Mitrofanov stresses, the real victors were the British, who duly crowed with delight. Their foreign minister, the Duke of Leeds, told Keith that the news had been received in London 'with great satisfaction'.[70] But as Mitrofanov also points out, this orgy of self-congratulation on a diplomatic triumph – all the more intense for being so rare – was fated to end in tears. Prussia emerged from the crisis deeply resentful at an ally who had behaved like a mediator. As Reichenbach also marked the final eclipse of Hertzberg's influence, the Anglo-Prussian alliance was now tottering. The Ochakov fiasco the following spring proved to be the *coup de grâce*. Nor were the Austrians any less embittered, blaming the British for robbing them of the fruits of their victories. Kaunitz told his envoy in London, Count Rewiczky, that British tactics at Reichenbach had been 'outrageous'. Rewiczky reciprocated with the comment that it was simply unbelievable that perfidious Albion should first break faith – and then expect to be thanked for its treason.[71] The chief victim, however, was Poland. As Paul Schroeder has written:

> An inconclusive draw for Prussia, Austria and the Ottoman Empire, it [Reichenbach] was for Poland a disaster. It ended Polish hopes of forming a great league with the Triple Alliance and the Ottoman Empire for purposes of war on Austria, and the recovery of its independence and territory, and it left Poland dependent on support from a greedy, unsatisfied, unreliable Prussia against the inevitable future challenge from Russia.[72]

But was it a triumph for Leopold II? No unequivocal answer is possible, for so much depends on how one assesses both his intentions and the dangers he faced. If one believes that he had intended all along to settle the war on the basis of the strict status quo and that in doing so he saved the Habsburg Monarchy from certain ruin, then a triumph it certainly was. That is not Mitrofanov's view, however. He did not believe that the threat of domestic insurrection was at all serious. He conceded that much discontent had been aroused by the reforms of Joseph II and that it was equally true that Prussian agitators were everywhere at work, fomenting unrest.[73] He did not believe, however, that either the Germans or the Slavs of the Monarchy would

---

[70] British Library, London, Add. Mss. 35,543, fo. 30, 30 July 1790. For Keith's own rejoicing, see his letter to Ewart of 24 July – *Memoirs and correspondence*, II, pp. 294–5.

[71] Vivenot (ed.), *Quellen zur Geschichte der deutschen Kaiserpolitik Österreichs*, I, p. 8, Kaunitz to Rewiczky, 24 July 1790; Vienna, Haus-, Hof- und Staatsarchiv, Staatskanzlei, England, Berichte, Kart. 127, no. 341, Rewiczky to Kaunitz, 20 August 1790.

[72] Schroeder, *The transformation of European politics*, p. 76.

[73] Mitrofanov has a great deal to say about Baron Jacobi's conspiracy with dissident Magyars in Hungary, quoting long extracts from his reports to Frederick William II. These would be immensely helpful, were it not for the fact that the ground was covered in much greater detail by Robert Gragger in his *Preußen, Weimar und die ungarische Königskrone* (Berlin and Leipzig, 1923).

cut off their noses to spite their faces, especially when they considered Leopold's record as a constitutionalist in Tuscany, the concessions he made as soon as he arrived in Vienna and the awful warning posted to the privileged orders everywhere in Europe by the French Revolution.[74] Even the threat from Hungary was 'not so very terrifying' once Joseph had revoked on his death-bed the most unpopular of his reforms. Once that victory had been gained, the great majority of the Magyar gentry would not have followed foreign adventurers like Hompesch, for in doing so they would have risked becoming the victims of a peasant jacquerie unleashed by Vienna. The Prussian diplomat Count Podewils, who did not share his colleague Jacobi's enthusiasm for fishing in Hungarian waters, told Frederick William II bluntly on 5 March 1790:

> In general, it seems that this planned insurrection can never be accomplished. It would be very difficult at a time when there are so many German troops in this country and the Turks are on the frontiers. Hungary cannot exist alone; it has to defend its position against either the Turks or the House of Austria and the domination of the latter will always be preferable.[75]

This was also the view in Vienna. On 4 July, General Mack told Spielmann that he doubted whether the insurgents could mobilise even 30,000 men – they would all run away at the first shot anyway.[76]

III

So, Mitrofanov concluded, whether one was referring to the Hereditary Lands, Galicia or Hungary, the danger from within was not worth taking into account. It should certainly not have prompted Leopold to abandon the great gains made by his late brother in the campaign of 1789. All of his incorrigible timidity was required to prompt him to give way at Reichenbach, as he deluded himself about the severity of the problems he faced.[77] This assessment runs directly counter to modern analyses, most notably those of Paul Schroeder and Adam Wandruszka. The latter concluded that with the Convention of Reichenbach, Leopold achieved the first and most important point of the programme he had expounded in letters sent to his sister, the Archduchess Marie Christine, before he left Florence. He had avoided the imminent war with Prussia, he had laid the basis for a peace with the Turks, he had paved the way for his election as Holy Roman Emperor, he had established better relations with Great Britain and the Dutch Republic, he had kept his alliance with Russia intact, he had deprived the Belgian rebels

---

[74] Mitrofanov, *Leopold II*, p. 145.   [75] Ibid., p. 151 n. 3.
[76] Ibid., p. 151.   [77] Ibid., p. 152.

and the Hungarian dissidents of foreign support and had thus begun the pacification of the Habsburg Monarchy.[78] This verdict has been given recent and authoritative support by Schroeder, who sees Reichenbach as Olmütz in reverse: 'apparently a shameful retreat, actually a lucky escape'.[79]

It is difficult not to argue with this more generous view of Leopold's achievement, not because the Habsburg Monarchy was facing internal dissolution – Mitrofanov was right about that – but because *any* alteration of the status quo, however apparently beneficial, would have been to its detriment. This is where the advantages of hindsight come into play. When Mitrofanov wrote his *Leopold II* in the years before the First World War, it was still possible to believe that the pursuit of territorial advantage in the Balkans could be conducted with impunity. Indeed, his own state was currently engaged in just such an exercise. He did not live to experience its terrible consequences. Although he can hardly be blamed for that, his knowledge of the revolutionary-Napoleonic wars should have taught him the dangers of acquisitive balance-of-power politics. What Mitrofanov castigates as Leopold's 'cowardice' and 'timidity' are better seen with Schroeder as intelligence and breadth of vision.

[78] Wandruszka, *Leopold II*, ii, pp. 271–2.
[79] *The transformation of European politics*, p. 66.

4

JOHN MARSH'S *HISTORY OF MY PRIVATE LIFE 1752–1828*

✿✿✿✿

JOHN BREWER

The political history of great men is useful and necessary to many; but the domestic history of all men is useful and necessary to all.

Memoirs of a Printer's Devil interspersed with local descriptions
(Gainsborough, 1793)

I

In the spring of 1796 John Marsh, a forty-four year old gentleman composer and pillar of genteel society ensconced in a fashionable Chichester townhouse, began to write a memoir of his family and ancestors. Marsh was leader of the Chichester orchestra, an enthusiastic reader of histories, scientific treatises and modern novels, a contributor to literary and musical journals and a regular performer on the organ and piano. He was eventually to compose at least twenty-eight overtures and symphonies and twelve concerti grossi, numerous services, chants, anthems and voluntaries as well as catches, glees and songs, making him one of the most prolific English composers of the eighteenth century.

But in March 1796 he was at a loose end. He had just finished composing his concerto in D, and had also completed writing his 'Musical Definitions and Thoughts on the Different Styles of Music', a primer for young musicians, as well as a treatise on the intermediate state of the soul, *The Excursions of a Spirit*. Determined to have 'a job always at hand to employ my leisure' (17.87),[1] he began an account of his ancestors and the Kentish estate to which he owed his wealth. By April, and despite spending much of his spare time reading William Godwin's 'eccentric performance' (17.107) *Caleb Williams*, he had written a first draft. Nine months later, after antiquarian researches had

---

[1] All references to Marsh's private *History* are to the Huntington Library version, Mss. 54457. The first figure refers to the volume number, the second to the page.

taken him back to the family vault in Kent, the task was complete, transcribed into two quarto copybooks.

There was, of course, nothing unusual about John Marsh's action. Doubtless many inheritors of a patrimony that brought in a little more than a thousand a year were prone to rummage in deeds and scrutinise pedigrees for their ancestors. Some of them may even have been industrious enough to record their findings systematically. But Marsh found himself embarked on a larger task. He had planned to conclude his account of his family with a short 'History of my private life' (17.134) but, deciding that his family would be more interested in 'the *principal* circumstances of the Family' than in 'the minute particulars' of his own existence, he had begun a separate personal history 'wrote more for the sake of the amusement the thus tracing over my life again afforded me at the time, and the amusement afterwards than for anything else' (17.134). Marsh had kept detailed diaries since he had been thirteen years old. He had a fund of memories which he began to record methodically and with such exceptional detail that his new task threatened to consume all his time. As he wrote:

> the present History I thought might take up 6 or 8 of these Books, & employ me at my leisure for 2 or 3 years, instead of wch I found so many circumstances to relate that I am now arriv'd at the middle of the 17th book, the writing and composing which, & the previous draft, or rough Copy, has taken me up above four years and a half in bringing it down to the present time [31 Dec. 1800] in addition to which, I have now to continue the relation to the present time, having however hitherto work'd pretty hard at it having generally when at home written from 3 to 5 pages per day, besides the rough copy, I shall in future not devote to much time to it, that I may have more leisure for my Musical Studies and other things. (17.134-5)

Marsh did not stick to his resolution. In 1802, on the occasion of his fiftieth birthday, he had brought his *Life* up to date. In the six years since 1796 he had produced twenty-two of the eventual thirty-seven volumes covering his life. His attitude towards the task had also changed. He no longer viewed his *Life* as merely a source of amusement. On his fiftieth birthday he wrote of his plan to re-read his earlier volumes before going on with his journals:

> the natural Reflection from which will, I hope, tend towards inspiring me with Gratitude to my Creator, & with the Determination to spend the remainder of my life in such a manner as shall be most likely to insure a continuance of the earthly blessings I have hitherto enjoyed, & to induce me at the close of it (whenever that awful period may arrive) to have a lively hope of being admitted, through the Merits & Mediation of my Saviour, into a future state of Bliss and Glory! (22.127-8)

Unflaggingly Marsh continued his record. In 1811 he gave his son, Edward Garrard, a fellow of Oriel College Oxford and evangelical cleric who became editor of the *British Review*, the twenty-eight volumes he had completed up to that date. He continued his labours until shortly before his death in 1828. Though the last pages are in another hand, several of them contain what is clearly a transcription of his own draft entries before they go on to record his death.

There are two surviving versions of Marsh's *History of my Private Life*: a complete text in Marsh's own hand now in the Huntington Library in California (Ms 54457), and an incomplete version in sixteen volumes in the Cambridge University Library (Ms Add. 7757). The latter is written in the same hand as the final few pages of the full text. Though I have yet to verify this, I believe the incomplete version and the final few pages of the California text to have been written by Marsh's son, Edward. Certainly the final sentiments recorded in the *History* about Marsh are those of his evangelical son:

> He had long known where to rest his hope, and whilst he sought more and more in the use of his time and property to promote the cause of his redeemer and the spiritual and temporal interests of his fellow-creatures, he saw more clearly as he advanced in life, the necessity of casting himself for acceptance entirely in the free mercy of God, made sure to believers through the everlasting covenant of Jesus Christ. (37.183)

The full text contains many pencilled annotations apparently intended to prepare an abbreviated version of Marsh's *History*, some though not all of which correspond to the omissions made in the Cambridge text. It is probable that Edward, the most scholarly of Marsh's children as well as the editor of a journal, tried to prepare the manuscript for publication. And it is even more likely that the work was never published because its editor was defeated by its sheer bulk, though there were reasons why Edward, a far more strait-laced evangelical than his father, might have had reservations not only about its contents but also about its general tenor.

Marsh's *History* is unquestionably one of the most illuminating surviving sources for the study of late eighteenth- and early nineteenth-century provincial life. The abbreviated Cambridge version concentrates on Marsh's musical activities. It records his participation in the orchestras, festivals, catch and glee clubs in the three cathedral cities – Salisbury, Canterbury and Chichester – where he lived and the performance of his sacred music – psalm tunes, chants, anthems and voluntaries – in such abbeys, churches and cathedrals as St Paul's, St Martin's in the Field, St Margaret's Westminster and Westminster Abbey. And it captures Marsh's enthusiasm on his annual spring visits to London for metropolitan concert life, including the performances staged by Wilhelm Cramer, Muzio Clementi and Johann Peter Salomon at Hanover Square, and the concerts of the Philharmonic Society and the Concert of Ancient Music. The manuscript is filled with musical private parties, services, concerts, operas and festivals, its pages crossed by the likes of Haydn as well as by a number of fashionable English composers, singers and instrumental performers.

The incomplete Cambridge text appeared to be chiefly a musical memoir and it was used by a number of musicologists and music historians both to secure Marsh a place in musical history (he appears in both the 5th edition of *Grove* and the *New Grove*) and to illuminate concert life in eighteenth-century England.[2] But the Cambridge manuscript was rarely used by historians, and the full riches of Marsh's *History* only became apparent with the Christie's sale of the full text of thirty-seven volumes to the Huntington Library in November 1991.

What was sometimes sketched in the Cambridge manuscript but often left undrawn was delineated with astonishing clarity in the full text. Marsh wrote not just about music-making and concert life but drew a series of exceptionally detailed pictures of the social dynamics of genteel provincial society in three English cathedral towns: their obsessive punctilio and scrupulous regard for social niceties; their quarrels and misunderstandings about politics, religion, etiquette and personality; their rich and varied forms of sociability, including visiting, assemblies, reading clubs and concerts; the relations between the church and society, and between rich and poor. And there is no better source for the activities of a lay evangelical who supported the numerous religious societies and charities that were the backbone of the evangelical movement.

Marsh's vision is at once highly local – drawing a detailed picture of the small number of individuals and families who comprised the elite of a small town – and much broader, for his account shows how the local gentleman's life connected with larger national and international developments in politics, religion and the life of the mind. Like many provincial gentry, Marsh made regular visits to the capital, usually spending part of the spring in London visiting not just concerts and musical-instrument makers, but art exhibits, the

---

[2] *Grove's Dictionary of Music and Musicians*, 5th edition, ed. E. Blom (London, 1954), vol. v, pp. 588–9; *The New Grove Dictionary of Music and Musicians*, ed. Stanley Sadie (London, 1980), vol. xi, pp. 706–7; Stanley Sadie, 'Concert Life in Eighteenth-Century England', *Proceedings of the Royal Musical Association*, 78 (1958–9), esp. p. 17; Brian Robins, 'John Marsh: A Georgian Gentleman Composer', *Southern Early Music Forum*, 3 (1984), pp. 10–14; Ian Graham-Jones, 'An Introduction to the Symphonies of John Marsh', *Southern Early Music Forum*, 3 (1984), pp. 15–18; Simon McVeigh, *Concert Life in London from Mozart to Haydn* (Cambridge, 1993). McVeigh has also used the Huntington Mss; Peter Underdown, 'The Symphonies of John Marsh', Cambridge University, unpublished PhD thesis.

theatre, scientific lectures, libraries and bookshops. And his literary and scientific interests were as cosmopolitan as his enthusiasm for the operas of Mozart and the works of Beethoven.

But what I propose to do in the following pages is not so much use the content of John Marsh's *History* to discuss the features of genteel provincial (musical) life,[3] but rather to raise the question of what Marsh was *doing* in writing his life in the way that he did. In order to do this we have to place his work in two contexts: the history of journal keeping and autobiography and their relation to other forms of eighteenth-century 'life writing', and the relationship between Marsh's *History* and other works which he read and wrote while working on his *magnum opus*.

II

Marsh's diary and *History* were in keeping with a Protestant tradition in which the recording of one's life was seen both as a means of self-examination and self-understanding and as an example to others of the Christian life. Such journals and personal histories set down the details of everyday life, which were usually cast as a Christian narrative either of Pauline conversion from wickedness and sin to Christian faith, or as the story of an Augustinian struggle to achieve a godly life in the face of worldly temptation.[4]

There are, as we shall see, some important connections between such narratives and Marsh's *History*, but there is also a significant difference. Most Protestant accounts, especially those of the seventeenth century, looked on the material and social world, the world of taste and the senses, as subordinate to questions of faith, conversion and salvation. A moral struggle between the forces of darkness and light, between the depraved body and the religious spirit, overshadowed all else. What mattered was Christian divinity and the eternal life, not the quiddities of ordinary existence, which were only important as signs of a transcendent truth. Indeed in many accounts the material and social world is suspected of being nothing more than a snare and delusion which distracted Christians from the higher truth of Christ and the afterlife. Though in the entry for his fiftieth birthday, Marsh displays a Christian humility and takes stock of his life, in the *Life* as a whole he exhibits no such anxiety about the visible, social world. Rather he revels in an unevangelical way in its oddities, seeing life less as an arduous journey than as

---

3 Something I have attempted elsewhere in a forthcoming book on British culture to be published by Harper-Collins in 1996.
4 John O. Lyons, *The Invention of the Self. The Hinge of Consciousness in the Eighteenth Century* (Carbondale, Ill., 1978), pp. 19, 61.

theatre, a modern comedy of manners.[5] Society is not treated as a delusive shadow but is detailed in substance.

Marsh was a man of social refinement and good taste as well as a man of God. He believed strongly in the importance of manners and politeness and his *History* displays that concern for genteel self-fashioning the roots of which lay in the courtly literature of the Italian renaissance and which had been so effectively popularised in Britain by the *Spectator* and a plethora of self-help manuals. The *Spectator* and its epigones urged their readers to keep diaries not to record temptation, conversion and salvation but as a means to cultivate the arts of politeness and good conversation. Society, individual forms of conduct and the world of appearances featured centrally in such journals. Taste and virtue, sociability and the good life were married. The literature of politeness looked on the diary less as a godly aid (though it could certainly be that) than as a form of self-representation. The novelist Frances Burney called her journal, 'My Life and Opinions Addressed to Myself'; one of her female contemporaries recorded in her diary, 'I love this conversation with myself.'[6]

The self existed only in relation to others, even if that other was oneself; it was labile not fixed, shaped by and in society. Personal conduct and the conduct of others were therefore judged not just according to their conformity to a universal moral law but on the basis of how they affected others. The sort of impression made on other people, how you appeared to them, acquired greater importance. Morality became embedded in the world of appearances. At the same time such a view, elaborated by seventeenth-century psychology, supposed an interior or inner self, as well as one of outward appearance. Matching the inner and outer selves, reconciling individual feeling and public obligation became a key moral question, a process which was recorded and understood by means of a diary or journal. Keeping a written record was the way in which polite persons could be constituted and could represent themselves to others.

In such circumstances, the status of a journal or diary was highly ambiguous. On the one hand it was a private record; on the other, it presupposed a reader other than the author (or The Author), the possibility of bringing a private life into public view. More often than not, diaries and journals disavowed an audience beyond the author and his or her immediate family. Yet such rhetorical gestures should be treated sceptically, for they were necessary in order to establish the credibility of the work as a private journal. When, for example, Job Orton published *Memoirs of the Life, Character and Writings of the Late Reverend Philip Doddridge*, he claimed that his use of 'such

---

[5] For the novelty of this idea, see Donald A. Stauffer, *The Art of Biography in Eighteenth-Century England* (Princeton, 1941), p. 28.

[6] Anna Larpent Diary, Huntington Library Ms. 31201, vol. 17, no pagination, 1781.

Extracts from his [Doddridge's] Diary and other Papers, written solely for his own Use, and his Letters to his intimate Friends in which he laid open his whole Heart' made his account truer and more illuminating, though he also conceded that some felt that 'what was principally written for a Person's own Use, ought not to be made public'.[7]

The public value of a journal or diary depended on its privateness, whose authentication came either from the author and text or from the editor who acted as a midwife bringing the private journal into the world.[8] Yet private journals frequently contained traces of their authors' consciousness of a larger readership – the care with which manuscripts such as Marsh's were copied and edited,[9] or the occasional lapse in the texts themselves where they explicitly address a greater audience. Even if such documents did not find their way into print, diaries and journals, like familiar letters, were sometimes read aloud or circulated among friends. In addition to his *History*, Marsh kept at least two other journals of particular parts of his life, which he wrote for the express purpose of the amusement and edification of his friends (35.28; 36.98).

Given the extraordinary proliferation of private writing which found its way into print, often without the consent or after the death of its author, it is hard to imagine an eighteenth-century diarist or autobiographer, or for that matter a writer of familiar letters, who was not aware of a potentially unfamiliar reader looking over their shoulder. There were always plenty of friends or relatives who felt it their duty to save the public and rescue family honour by tossing a private life into the fire, as John Murray did with Byron's autobiography. (This must be one of the few occasions on which a publisher deliberately destroyed what would unquestionably have been a bestseller.) But there were even more who valued the private thoughts of their friends and ancestors, believing that much could be learnt from accounts of the private lives of ordinary men or women or that, at the very least, their publication could be turned to a profit. Memoirs, biographies of criminals, actors and freaks, as well as monarchs, clerics and statesmen, collections of private letters, and compendia of lives poured from the eighteenth-century press. Donald Stauffer's list of collected biographies captures the wealth of such publications:[10]

---

[7] Job Orton, *Memoirs of the Life, Character and Writings of the Late Reverend Philip Doddridge* (London, 1766), p. vi.

[8] Robert Iliffe, 'The role of the editor', in Ann Bermingham and John Brewer (eds.), *Culture and Consumption: Word, Image and Object in the Seventeenth and Eighteenth Centuries* (London, forthcoming).

[9] For an interesting account of authorial doctoring and editing see James L. Clifford, *From Puzzles to Portraits. Problems of the Literary Biographer* (London, 1970), esp. chapter 1.

[10] Stauffer, *The Art of Biography*, p. 236.

there exist collected lives of botanists, of ancient philosophers and of those who died in the year 1711, of professors at Gresham College; royal and noble authors, English regicides, and learned women; of Roman empresses and pious foreigners; of Etonians and converted American Indians; of Parliamentary leaders, or London aldermen, and of those individuals whose portraits happened to hang in Knole House; there are collections of women because they are women and of Scotsmen because they are Scotsmen.

There were two related but distinct views that conferred value on the publication of private life. One argued that even the most trivial and personal matter about persons (usually men) of genius, rank and talent was revealing and instructive. The second, more radically, maintained that the lives of ordinary men and women also taught valuable lessons. The former attitude had its roots in classical antiquity. Dryden, drawing a distinction between biography, on the one hand, and history and annals on the other, invoked Plutarch in pointing to the value of intimate detail:[11]

> There are proper places in it [biography] for the plainness and nakedness of narration, which is ascrib'd to Annals; there is also room reserv'd for the loftiness and gravity of general History, when the actions related shall require that manner of expression. But there is withal a descent into minute circumstances, and trivial passages of life, which are natural to this way of writing, and which the dignity of the other two will not admit. There you are conducted only into the rooms of state; here you are led into the private Lodgings of the Heroe: you see him in his undress, and are made familiar with his most private actions and conversations. You may behold a *Scipio* and a *Laelius* gathering cockleshells on the shore, *Augustus* playing at bounding stones with boys, and *Agesilaus* riding on a hobby horse among his children. The pageantry of life is taken away: you see the poor reasonable animal as naked as ever nature made him; are made acquainted with his passions and his follies, and find the *demi-god* a man. *Plutarch* has more than once defended this kind of relating little passages: for, in the Life of *Alexander*, he says thus: '*in writing the lives of illustrious Men, I am not tyed to the Laws of history; Nor does it follow, that, because an action is great, it therefore manifests the greatness and vertue of him who did it; but on the other side sometimes a word, or a casual jest, betrays a Man more to our knowledge of him, than a Battel fought wherein ten thousand Men were slain, or sacking of Cities, or a course of Victories.*'

This passage from Plutarch was a favourite amongst eighteenth-century biographers of literary figures and humble people – Boswell invoked it to justify his *Life of Johnson* – though, as Glen Bowersock has shown, citing such an authority involved a wilful misreading of Plutarch who, as he points out,

---

[11] 'The Life of Plutarch', *The Works of John Dryden*, vol. XVII, *Prose 1668–1691*, ed. Samuel Holt Monk (Berkeley and Los Angeles, 1971), pp. 275–6.

'had no interest in human character on its own, but only as a basis for moral instruction. He had no interest in socially insignificant people, but only in the great. He cared little for the lives of literary figures.'[12] For all that, the invocation of classical authority to bolster a literary innovation (a character-istic eighteenth-century move), helped to establish the convention that private life and personal detail were of public import.

This sort of justification, as readers of the modern gutter press know well, was something that could easily be abused. Early in George I's reign a periodical complained of 'a race of men lately sprung up . . . Grub Street biographers, who watch for the death of a great man like so many under-takers'.[13] Edmund Curll, the scourge of Alexander Pope, was only one of a number of publishers who specialised in sensational biography,[14] and in exposing the private lives of the famous without their knowledge or consent. Prurience was legitimised. By the end of the century, it had become a cliché that curiosity fuelled the interest in biography. As the anonymous author of a life of the notorious Duchess of Kingston put it – and he should have known[15] –

> This is an age when the prying eye of curiosity penetrates the privacy of every
> distinguished person; neither the living nor the dead escape. The most trivial
> pursuits of the one, and the former table-talk of the other, are exposed, and
> narrated, with all the pomp of importance, by some officious hand, engaged to
> furnish anecdote for the world.

We should, however, hesitate before being too censorious about this often prurient pursuit of private detail. For the complexity of character as well as sense of time and place which are so vividly conveyed in the best life-writing of the period, whether by Marsh or Boswell, depended on the telling anecdote or revealing detail.

The view that the private doings of famous public figures exposed the true person was often elided with the claim, more Protestant than classical, that accounts of ordinary lives were the most effective means of providing moral instruction to their readers. Both private life (even of the great) and humble life were deemed more intelligible to the ordinary reader and therefore more effective as means of instruction. As the biographer Roger North explained:[16]

---

12 Glen Bowersock, 'Suetonius in the eighteenth century', *Biography in the Eighteenth Century*, ed. John D. Browning (London, 1980), p. 29.
13 *The Freeholder*, 20 April 1716.
14 See, for instance, *The Case of John Atherton, Bishop of Waterford in Ireland. Who was convicted of the sin of uncleanness with a cow, and other creatures, for which he was hanged in Dublin, Decem. 5, 1640* (London, 1710).
15 *Life and Memoirs of Elizabeth Chudleigh, Duchess of Kingston* (London, 1789), p. 2.
16 Quoted in James L. Clifford (ed.), *Biography as an Art. Selected Criticism 1560–1960* (Oxford, 1962), p. 27.

> The history of private lives adapted to the perusal of common men, is more
> beneficial (generally) than the most solemn registers of ages, and nations, or the
> acts and monuments of famed governors, statesmen, prelates, or generals of
> armies. The gross reason is, because the latter contain little if any thing,
> comparate or applicable to instruct a private economy, or tending to make a
> man either wiser or more cautelous [*sic*], in his own proper concerns.

Such an emphasis on the ordinary, private, domestic and intimate was sometimes elevated into the claim that true history was not a saga of grand events
but a question of understanding the nature of the human condition which 'can
only be illustrated by the actions of the individual'.[17] This was Goldsmith's
position in the famous preface to his life of Beau Nash, the master of
ceremonies at Bath:[18]

> no one can properly be said to write history but he who understands the human
> heart, and its whole train of affections and follies. These affections and follies
> are properly the materials he has to work upon. The relations of great events
> may surprise, indeed; they may be calculated to instruct those very few who
> govern the million beneath; but the generality of mankind find the most real
> improvement from relations which are levelled to the general surface of life,
> which tell – not how they gained the shout of the admiring crowd, but how they
> acquired the esteem of their friends and acquaintance . . . There are few who do
> not prefer a page of Montaigne or Colley Cibber, who candidly tell us what
> they thought of the world and the world thought of them, to the more stately
> memoirs and transactions of Europe, where we see kings pretending to
> immortality, that are now almost forgotten, and statesmen planning frivolous
> negotiations, that scarcely outlive the signing.

Goldsmith's account is, of course, overdrawn and certainly does not reflect the
direction in which British historical writing went in the next generation, but
it embodies a belief in the value of private histories which was well established
in the second half of the eighteenth century and which lay behind Marsh's
mammoth endeavour.

III

Marsh was familiar with a large body of historical and biographical writing.
He was an avid reader, helping to found a book society in Chichester in 1789,
which he was still attending a few weeks before his death in 1828, and a library
society set up in 1794 (112.148; 16.88; 37.179–80). He and his wife read for
several hours a day, 'taking each always a Book at Breakfast & at Tea Time,

---

[17] Miss Ambrose, *Life and Memoirs of the late Miss Ann Catley* (London, 1789), p. 5.
[18] [Oliver Goldsmith], *The Life of Richard Nash, of Bath, Esq., Extracted from his original papers*
(London and Bath, 1762).

. . . and also for sometime after Dinner & Supper, by wch means we each read about 2 hours or more every day, in common' (15.92). The Library Society provided Marsh with his non-fictional reading – history, biography and travel literature. When travelling, sick or on holiday he also read a great many current novels, often at the recommendation of his friend, the fashionable poet William Hayley, who lived just outside Chichester. Marsh also acquired books from James Lackington's London emporium, where he exchanged books he had bought at a cut price from the Book Society or made purchases outright.

From his earliest youth Marsh enjoyed history. As his first school prize he chose *La vie privée des Romains* as well as two volumes of Telemachus (1.94). As a boy he read Rapin's *History of England* and by his twenties he had read Goldsmith's *History of England in a series of letters from a nobleman to his son* twice (2.36; 6.65). In his maturity he read the whole of what he called 'Clarendon's History of the Civil wars' (20.116; 21.32), as well as a large number of historical accounts of other nations which had been acquired by the Book Society (e.g. 12.134, 137, 148; 19.168; 21.24; 22.28, 56, 78). But he preferred biography, reading Johnson's *Lives of the Poets*, Horace Walpole's *Anecdotes of the Lives of the Painters*, Murphy's *Life of Garrick* as well as Hayley's biographies of Cowper and Romney. Over the years he enjoyed lives of the classicist Mrs Carter, the poet Geoffrey Chaucer, the silver- and goldsmith Benvenuto Cellini, as well as collected works on clerics, Scottish chiefs, popes and painters. He was, in short, fully conversant with the conventions of eighteenth-century history and life-writing (15.77; 17.70; 18.4; 22.78; 23.62, 83–4; 24.26; 26.93, 136).

At the same time he was an avid reader of fiction. During the 1790s he read a great many novels, usually selecting the most fashionable and topical from the reviews. But Marsh's abiding attachment was to the picaresque novel. As early as his fifteenth year he was translating Lesage's *Le Diable boiteux* (2.36). His enthusiasm for Lesage remained unabated. At fifty he was delighted to find both French and German versions of *Gil Blas* in the library at Worthing (23.22). His favourite English novels were by Fielding (especially the Quixotic *Tom Jones* which Marsh read on many occasions) and Smollett, the translator of Cervantes. When he married in 1774, Marsh bought 'a small assortment of books' to read aloud to his bride, beginning with Fielding's works and with Don Quixote (5.13). As late as 1795 Marsh was able to while away the time when caught in a shower of rain by reading *The Adventures of Ferdinand Count Fathom* which he 'had in his pocket' (16.181). This sort of comic fictional writing, with its emphasis on action rather than character and on the incongruity between human aspirations and their realisation, was to have every bit as much influence on the form of Marsh's *History* as the biographies and histories he had read.

John Marsh did not refer to his thirty-seven volumes as a 'memoir' but as 'A History' of his private life. He might have chosen to call it an autobiography – the term had first been used in 1797 by William Taylor of Norwich when reviewing Isaac D'Israeli's Miscellanies in the *Monthly Magazine* and had quickly come into general usage[19] – but instead he opted for an oxymoronic title. This decision was, as I have shown, in line with eighteenth-century developments in life-writing which made it possible to view a private life as a history. But Marsh does not present himself – as we might well expect for the late eighteenth century – as a man of sentiment or explore his interior feelings. Despite his persistent presence in the *History* we are more conscious of Marsh as an author than as actor, struck by his ability to describe a world he inhabits rather than his feelings about what it was like to be in it. This sense of historical distance from its subject is reinforced by the form of the text. It is clearly not a diary or personal journal, as is demonstrated by the frequency with which Marsh interpolates retrospective commentary reminding us of his rewriting of his sources. Like a history (and unlike a novel or memoir) the reader is provided with marginalia to guide his reading and regulate the tempo of the narrative. Marsh exercises extraordinary care in recording the facts of his life. No detail seems too picayune to be omitted. The death of a family dog, the birth of a litter of kittens, the silent inebriation of a neighbour, a nose-bleed, visits to the dentist, a shave from a female barber, an overturned chamber pot full of urine, the discoloured fingernails of a school friend are all recorded with the same exactitude that he brought to his precise descriptions of concert programmes or the events of a local election.

When he wrote up the fair copy from his rough notes, Marsh listed what he considered to be the most important events in his life, breaking up the narrative. Though musical performance and composition predominate, he includes occurrences that range from the outbreak of war and the death of kings to teaching his grandson to play the piano and observing a solar eclipse. It is a history, but it is *his* history, not only because it is an account of his life but because it reconstructs the world from his own perspective, one where local detail often looms as large as the most important national event.

Marsh's attention to detail does not seem designed, like many biographies and memoirs, to explain his own character or that of others around him. The telling detail is corporeal rather than psychological, as when we learn of his father's girth by being told that he always booked two places when travelling by stagecoach, or of his valetudinarian wife's obesity by his mention of the

---

[19] For a general discussion see Jerome Hamilton Buckley, *The Turning Key. Autobiography and the Subjective Impulse since 1800* (Cambridge, Mass., 1984), p. 18. Marsh read the *Monthly Magazine* regularly.

small stool she carried so that she could rest if she had to walk any distance (1.147). Marsh sticks to his narrative and rarely pauses to offer moral commentary or any sort of criticism. His position is that of the seemingly dispassionate observer, recording events of which he was a part, but also distancing himself from them. He never pauses to offer a homily or sermon on a moral or political issue, and on the rare occasions when he does intrude – as when he offers up prayers when he survives being knocked down by a horse in 1822 – the voice seems jarring (34.54). What then was Marsh up to? Why did he devote so much time to this prodigious work which, as he sometimes complained, took up so much of his time?

Marsh hints at the answer to these questions in his private history, but there is more evidence of his intentions in his other writings, notably his essays on musical performance, and two remarkable works, the first a mock travel book, *A Tour Through some of the Southern Counties of England. By Peregrin Project and Timothy Type*, published in 1804, the second a study of the intermediate state of the soul, begun in 1800, but not published until 1821.[20] Almost all of these published writings draw on materials from his manuscript private history; in the case of the *Tour*, large chunks are quoted verbatim. These works therefore transcribed parts of his history into another genre. But they were published anonymously; the only means by which we learn of their author is through the history itself. (Though we should add that most of Marsh's circle of acquaintances knew him to be the author of these works. Several of them read drafts of the different manuscripts (21.18, 26; 22.72; 25.78; 26.42; 28.167; 33.99).)

One of the first impressions derived from the private history is of a world of accidents, absurdities and thwarted intentions. Concerts are spoiled by players who cannot keep time; Marsh's wife is excluded from Salisbury's polite society because of an incomprehensible piece of etiquette; 'A fellow of a most consummate impudence' who mounts 'the orchestra to perform an imitation of daft birds' spoils the earlier pleasure of listening to the divine Miss Linley; the last night's performance in the old theatre in Salisbury attended by the flower of local society degenerates into a riot, and a drunk cleric makes a fool of himself on stage (4.172–3; 5.88, 118). The lord of misrule is often present in Marsh's account of polite society.

Marsh's *History* is full of the comedy that he admired in Fielding and Smollett. He reminds us of the high price paid for the pursuit of social and aesthetic cultivation: how easily harmony turns into discord, how difficult it is to observe the proprieties of social life. Marsh's frequent invocation of the banal and the carnal, his repeated demonstration of the imperfectibility

---

[20] *The Excursions of a Spirit; with a Survey of the Planetary World: A Vision, with four illustrative plates* (London, printed for F. C. & J. Rivington, 1821).

of man, subverts his own attempt at cultivation but, by emphasising its unattainability, renders its pursuit heroic, if not tragic. The culture of the provinces, Marsh implies, can only be understood as a mock-heroic story in the manner of one of Marsh's favourite books, *Don Quixote*.

In his *Tour* Marsh adopts the persona of Peregrin Project, a bookseller deluded by reading travel literature into believing that he can make a fortune by publishing his own travel account. Accompanied by his Sancho Panza, the printer Timothy Type, Project visits the cathedral towns that Marsh knew so well, gathering materials for his narrative. But, instead of offering his readers lists of old masters and memorials to the great, Project records the prints in tavern parlours, the subject-matter of Delft tiles around the tavern fireplace, and the epitaphs of drunken soldiers and women shellfish sellers.[21] In both fiction and history Marsh presents himself as a mock-heroic character in pursuit of an unattainable end.

Marsh's self-deprecation seems at odds with the seriousness and enthusiasm with which he pursued his musical passion and the piety that dominated his later life, but it is of a piece with his desire to escape censure as a social oddity who saw music as more important than any other aspect of his life. By treating himself humorously, he manages to retain his distance, to imply that he is not as totally absorbed by his musical passions as might appear at first sight.

Throughout his life Marsh looked askance at all forms of conflict. When two organists in Salisbury began a quarrel that was to tear the local musical community apart and ruin concert life for nearly a decade, Marsh refused to take sides and signed a paper asserting his neutrality. Similarly, in the electoral conflict in Chichester in 1790 he refused to join the Duke of Richmond's party, though he felt obliged to vote in the Duke's interest (13.82–3).[22] He found both high church and radical dissenting views inimical, though, quite typically, he enjoyed close friendships with people whose views he did not share. He was ecumenical and tolerant of people, though he regarded opinions outside the broad consensus of moderate, mainstream Anglicanism as perverse. His first instinct in almost every conflict was to seek reconciliation, to secure an agreement acceptable to all parties. This served him well in local government and explains why he was so often chosen as a leader of convivial and musical societies, of charities and local commissions. But it also brought home to him the difficulty of ensuring unanimity, of obtaining what he called 'perfect harmony'.

In an essay on the impossibility of attaining 'perfect harmony' in the

---

[21] *A Tour*, pp. 142–3, 163.

[22] In later years he resisted the Duke's pressure to be a more ardent supporter and, in consequence, incurred the Duke's resentment.

Quarterly Musical Magazine for 1826,[23] Marsh made clear his wistful longing for an unattainable perfection: 'whatever approaches we may make towards perfection in this or any other science, whilst in this sublunary state, they are yet *but approaches*, or attempts to attain what we shall ever find to be beyond our reach'.[24] All we can do, he says, is obtain a foretaste 'of that heavenly harmony with which we may hope to be hereafter gratified in the realms of bliss'.[25] As these comments reveal, Marsh regarded his private history as not only a mock-heroic story but a Christian tale that revealed the imperfectibility and incompleteness of the human state. The private history was didactic as well as droll, a work that he could present to his evangelical son as a study in the vanity of human wishes and as a saga of one man's pursuit of musical and Christian harmony. The foibles and intimate details of provincial life were important because of what they revealed about the nature of man and his earthly existence; they were also invaluable in revealing one man's inevitably flawed struggle to lead a virtuous Christian life and to achieve musical perfection. Throughout his life, Marsh had written didactic works: books on astronomy, bookkeeping, musical notation and composition. The private history was another such work; it offered instruction and illumination.

Towards the end of his life Marsh published a treatise on the intermediate state of the soul. In *The Excursions of a Spirit* he revealed the world to which he aspired but which he never achieved in the genteel communities and musical societies of the provinces. In outlining the fate of the virtuous Christian soul between death and the day of final judgement, Marsh constructs a heavenly world devoid of conflict and filled with musical harmony. Instead of squabbling religious factions, 'all controversy is at an end, and every thing that is revealed by the holy Scriptures, is fully and compleatly understood by every individual, and, . . . *all*, however different may have been their religious creeds and opinions upon earth, here join in one and the same kind of worship of their Creator and Redeemer'.[26] Instead of musical quarrels between inept amateurs and temperamental professionals, heaven offers 'no distinction of professor and amateur: and . . . not the smallest idea, or notion of competition; as every spirit wishing to become proficient . . . will soon arrive at the *ne plus ultra* of perfection, and, of course, will find himself upon a level with all other practitioners therein', avoiding 'the prevalence of the malignant passions of envy, jealousy, hatred, &c so as to poison most of the enjoyments of life'.[27]

Marsh's heaven offers infinite variety of music and the opportunity to play

---

23 'To the Editor. SENEX', *Quarterly Musical Magazine*, vol. VIII, no. 30 (1826), pp. 186–90.
24 *Quarterly Musical Magazine*, 1826, p. 186.   25 Ibid., 1826, p. 190.
26 *The Excursions of the Spirit*, pp. 128–9.   27 Ibid., p. 145.

the finest organs ever perfected. Its epiphany is the sacred oratorio performed by thousands united in their celebration of perfect harmony:

> What therefore would you think of an orchestra of a thousand (or ten thousand if you please) vocal and instrumental performers, the abilities and powers of every one of which are so nearly equal, so as to be scarcely distinguished from each other by the nicest ear, each of which is likewise infinitely superior to any one that was ever heard on earth?[28]

The sensations he describes at hearing such a perfect concert are redolent of the words he uses in his private history to describe his feelings when he first heard Handel's Messiah and on the occasion of the Handel Commemoration of 1784. It was, he says,

> the most sublime and interesting sight I had ever yet witnessed; that of many thousands of spirits, actuated as it were by one soul, uttering their united praises and thanksgivings, and afterwards joining together in one grand and universal chorus of simple and expressive melody and perfect harmony, the force and effect of which filled me with the most exquisite sensations I have ever yet experienced.[29]

Moral completeness, social harmony and musical perfection were all united in a single ecstatic moment. But, as Marsh realised, such a climax could not be achieved in the mundane, querulous and sharply divided society which he had worked so hard to transform into a realm of social and musical harmony.

Marsh's *History* brings together a number of different ways of life-writing. It represents Marsh's life both as a series of theatrical tableaux and as a spiritual journey; it is both comic and pious; and the success of its execution – I know of no one who has not been moved, amused and enlightened by it – shows that Marsh was right: sometimes a private life makes some of the best history.

---

[28] Ibid., p. 139.   [29] Ibid., p. 69.

5

THE GALLOWS AND

MR PEEL

GOGOGO

BOYD HILTON[1]

D EREK Beales has always delighted in the ballistic statistic, such as the fact that *in Scotland nobody at all voted in the general election of 1826*.[2] Probably no statistics have detonated more destructively in the face of a prevailing historiography than those contained in his review article, 'Peel, Russell and reform'.[3] By 1974 the scholarly laudation of Sir Robert Peel and corresponding denigration of Lord John Russell were at their height. For half a century historians such as Elie Halévy, G. M. Young, George Kitson Clark, Robert Blake, Asa Briggs and Norman Gash had presented Peel as a uniquely skilful administrator and far-sighted statesman, a leader whose ability to straddle the gap between reform and reaction had ensured Britain's peaceful progression through the 'age of revolutions' and 'the great transformation' of society. Gash summed up this tradition in 1972 when he claimed that by the mid-nineteenth century 'the larger problems of his time had been met and solved. The age of revolt was giving way to the age of stability; and of that age Peel had been the chief architect.'[4] Just two years later, in 1974, Beales planted his incendiary device, and Peel's reputation has never looked quite the same since, though Russell's has yet to benefit significantly.[5]

---

[1] I have benefited immensely from conversations with Vic Gatrell, my disagreement with whom on the subject of Peel in no way diminishes my admiration for his magnificent work on the ideological, cultural and emotional meanings of capital punishment. The point at issue is a small one from his angle but not from mine, since his interpretation of Peel's penal policies runs directly counter to my view of Peel's political philosophy.

[2] Derek Beales, 'The electorate before and after 1832: the right to vote, and the opportunity', *Parliamentary History*, 11 (1992), 139–50 (original emphasis).

[3] Derek Beales, 'Peel, Russell, and reform', *Historical Journal*, 17 (1974), 873–82. On the respective merits of Peel and Russell, see also Derek Beales, *From Castlereagh to Gladstone 1815–1885* (London, 1969), p. 150.

[4] Norman Gash, *Sir Robert Peel: the Life of Sir Robert Peel after 1830* (London, 1972), p. 714.

[5] However, Russell might be said to be, at least implicitly, the heroic embodiment of 'main-stream Liberalism', 'liberal Anglicanism', and 'Foxite Whiggism' as defined (respectively) by Drs Parry, Brent, and Mandler. Jonathan Parry, *The Rise and Fall of Liberal Government in*

The most devastating blasts were to Peel's reputation as a great penal reformer. Here Beales acknowledged his debt to Sir Leon Radzinowicz's pioneering *History of English Criminal Law* – a study which, in waspish rather than bombing mood, he described as so voluminous that 'few historians have mastered its contents'. However, it was some stark statistics, culled from G. R. Porter's *Progress of the Nation* (1851), and recording the number of capital sentences and executions in England and Wales in each year from 1817 to 1840, which did the real damage. Beales's verdict was unequivocal:

> This table [of statistics] makes it absolutely clear that the decline in the number of death sentences passed began only after Peel had left the Home Office in 1830. The mitigations of the law's severity with which he is so generally credited can have amounted only to repealing statutes and sections of statutes which were totally disused, and to a more generous commutation policy . . . Noticeable change in the effective criminal law arrived only under the Whig governments of the thirties, first as a result of private members' pressure, then impelled from above by Lord John Russell as Home Secretary from 1835 to 1839. Some of these reforms were opposed by Peel, and he was active in none of them . . . So, on the criminal law, Peel tinkered, while Russell made drastic reforms.[6]

This denigration of Peel was significant because penal reform was the only area of policy which had offered any real ammunition to those many historians who had wished to emphasise his 'progressive' credentials. His conversion to Catholic emancipation came too late and was too heavily qualified for him to be given much credit as an ecclesiastical reformer. He opposed parliamentary reform strenuously as well as the extension of the civil rights of dissenters. His hostility to trades unions, and his commitment to what would now be called monetarism, freer trade, and non-interventionist social market policies, aligned him with the employers and capitalists against the labouring classes, and only took a populist turn at the very end of his career when he carried the repeal of the corn laws. Given this record, it is not surprising that Peel's twentieth-century admirers should have made so much of his famous if absurd boast in 1827 that 'there is not a single law connected with my name, which has not had for its object some mitigation of the severity of the criminal law'.[7]

Victorian Britain (New Haven and London, 1993); Richard Brent, *Liberal Anglican Politics: Whiggery, Religion, and Reform 1830–1841* (Oxford, 1987); Peter Mandler, *Aristocratic Government in the Age of Reform: Whigs and Liberals, 1830–1852* (Oxford, 1990). Recent evaluations of Peel have been mainly unenthusiastic, with the notable exception of Donald Read, *Peel and the Victorians* (Oxford, 1987).

6 Beales, 'Peel, Russell and reform', 880.

7 HC [House of Commons], 1 May 1827, 2PD [*Hansard's Parliamentary Debates*, second series], XVII, p. 411.

There is much debate and uncertainty with respect to criminal law reform, but three points are not in dispute. First, that between 1688 and 1820 the number of capital offences, that is the number of crimes for which one might be hanged, increased hugely from about fifty to more than two hundred. Secondly, that owing to the use of the 'royal pardon' the number of persons hanged did not rise commensurately with the number of capital offences or with the rise in population. About one-half of those who were condemned to death in the eighteenth century had their sentences reduced to transportation or imprisonment, either on the recommendation of the presiding judge after the trial or else by the King in Council. This resort to mercy increased further in consequence of a near-doubling of capital convictions during the distressed years after 1815, so that between 1821 and 1825 some 93 per cent of persons sentenced to be hanged were subsequently pardoned. Thirdly, it is not in dispute that during the home secretaryships of Peel (1822–7, 1828–30), Melbourne (1830–4) and Russell (1835–9) the number of capital offences, the number of convicts sentenced to death, and the number of executions all declined (Table 5.1). Under Russell the number of capital offences was reduced from 37 to 16, and in practice to 2 – murder and attempted murder. Furthermore, it is hardly in dispute that the changes made under Melbourne were largely due to back-bench pressure, whereas those under Russell resulted from his own initiative, building on and going further than the report of the Royal Commission on the Criminal Law (1836).[8] What *is* in dispute is still the nature of Peel's contribution to the process whereby the penal régime of the 'long eighteenth century' was brought to an end. After all, it is not inherently surprising that Peel, who preceded Russell, should have achieved less. Perhaps this is a case where (to borrow Bagehot's phrase) Peel rather than Russell actually 'bore the burden and heat of the day', and so should be given a substantial share of the credit.

In fact, since Derek Beales's intervention the myth of Peel as a great penal reformer has been in rapid retreat.[9] So much so that it is hardly an exaggeration to describe Peel as the villain of V. A. C. Gatrell's *The Hanging Tree*, the most passionately magisterial book to have appeared on modern English social history since E. P. Thompson's *The Making of the English Working Class*. Having worked in the archives of the Home Office, and seen Peel's dismissive formula, 'The law to take its course', scribbled on the verso of numerous pleas for mercy lodged by the friends and relatives of condemned felons, Gatrell

---

[8] Parry, *Rise and Fall of Liberal Government*, p. 122; W. R. Cornish and G. de N. Clark, *Law and Society in England 1750–1950* (London, 1989), pp. 574–8.

[9] Though it survives in J. M. Beattie, *Crime and the Courts in England 1660–1800* (Oxford, 1986), pp. 13, 632, 635.

Table 5.1. *Number of convicts sentenced to death
and number of executions, 1822–39*

	Number of convicts sentenced to death	Number of executions
1822	1016	97
1829	1385	74
1831	1601	52
1834	480	34
1835	523	34
1839	56	11

even qualifies Beales's suggestion that Peel adopted 'a more generous commutation policy' than his predecessors. Gatrell shows conclusively that, whatever else might be said about his role as a penal reformer, Peel was distinguished among home secretaries by his reluctance to reprieve those whom the judges had condemned to hang. Of course, many convicts were reprieved by the King in Council while Peel was home secretary, but in marginal cases Peel was almost always to be found on the side of severity. Confronted by a monarch who inclined to leniency, Peel 'more than any preceding home secretary ensured that the prerogative came *de facto* to lie in his, the executive, hands rather than the king's'. Moreover, this was unfortunate for the condemned felons, since 'petitioners found little mercy in Peel, . . . and certainly no matching sense of that commonsensical fairness which seems increasingly to have moved lay opinion'. 'However high-mindedly, Peel still let more people hang in the 1820s than any predecessor in office, and he meant to go on killing them.'[10]

Despite his obvious abhorrence of Peel, Gatrell seeks to 'get into the mind of a great hangman'. He acknowledges a religious perspective – the 'ethical pessimism', the providential fatalism, and the fact that – for someone of Peel's evangelical disposition – the termination of mortal existence, even on the scaffold, would not have seemed the worst of fates. Essentially, however, Dr Gatrell's understanding reflects a conventional spectrum which places old-fashioned and 'bloody' Toryism at one end, with a reformist and humanitarian Whig-Liberalism at the other. According to this interpretation, 'Peel, hailed as a great penal reformer, was the most committed protagonist of the old order. He tried to conserve as much of it as he could.' His adjustments

---

[10] V. A. C. Gatrell, *The Hanging Tree: Execution and the English People 1770–1868* (Oxford, 1994), pp. 553, 567, 585.

to the penal code eliminated only those capital statutes which were widely thought to be absurd and were never used. It was a 'holding operation' – a means of outflanking more wholehearted reformers like Sir James Mackintosh – and was not intended to lead on to the further relaxations of the following decade. Peel's aim, as Gatrell sees it, was not to reform the bloody code but to make it more credible, 'more efficient, even more punitive – more of a terror, not less'. This explains why an unreformed and Tory-dominated Parliament readily acquiesced in his policy – it knew that the ancien régime was safe with Peel. In order to maximise terror, moreover, Peel deemed it necessary, not only to leave the death penalty on many different types of offence, but also to retain 'huge areas of judicial and executive discretion in sentencing'. 'What is [not] often recognized is his passionate defence of the central principles of the old régime: the royal prerogative of mercy and the discretionary element in judicial and executive power.'[11]

In terms of the polarity which Dr Gatrell is mainly concerned with, between an older régime of judicial terror and a newer and more merciful humanity, this placing of Peel is undoubtedly correct. He *was* a hanger. It is just that the polarity itself seems too one-dimensional, too whiggish. Nor does it bring out the ambivalence of a politician whose instincts were simply to get on with the executive job in hand, but who found himself caught in various ideological crossfires. Indeed, any attempt to schematise early nineteenth-century attitudes to penal reform should start by recognising that there were at least two separate polarities.

In the first place, there was a polarity between the retributionists and the humanitarians; between those who believed that a ferocious penal code was both practically necessary and morally right, and those who wished to spill as little blood as was compatible with the preservation of law and order. Those whom Gatrell calls ethical pessimists tended to regard exemplary and retributive punishment as an integral part of the providential dispensation, necessary both for the well-being of society and for the spiritual correction – or, in a favourite phrase of Peel's, the 'moral discipline' – of individuals. Some 'extreme' or pre-millenarian evangelicals such as R. B. Seeley thought that human (i.e. ruling-class) punishments reflected the floods, famines and pestilences liberally meted out by the Old Testament God whom they worshipped, but most moderate evangelicals and High Churchmen, more sympathetic to the general mores of society, simply emphasised the 'salutary' effects of punishment and the need for expiation and atonement. Thus Peel in private expressed a strong doubt as to whether, without sincere repentance, mere death-bed remorse could purchase remission of sins, or prevent the

---

11 Ibid., pp. 566, 568–70, 583, 585.

infliction of 'severe punishment' for eternity.[12] At the other end of this spectrum stood ethical optimists like Bentham, who wished to limit the quantum of punishment to the minimum that was necessary for the discipline of society. 'All punishment is mischief: all punishment in itself is evil.'[13] Therefore the amount of punishment should be no greater than whatever level was requisite to deter the offender (and others) from repeating his guilty conduct. In practice, of course, the gap between exemplary and deterrent punishment might be a narrow one, but even so there is no reason to doubt the sincerity of Bentham's desire to limit the quantum of judicial pain.

A second and quite separate polarity divided those who believed in a paternalistic or discretionary administration of justice from whose who wished to make justice as self-acting and systematic, as mechanical and non-discretionary, as possible. The first of these, which might be called the Hay-model after the brilliant exposition by Douglas Hay in 1975,[14] represented the status quo in early nineteenth-century England and was forcibly upheld by lawyer-politicians such as Lords Eldon and Ellenborough. Certain aspects of Hay's thesis have come under heavy fire – notably its emphasis on ruling-class exploitation – but for present purposes the key to the Hay-model was, not class exploitation, nor even the theatricality and 'majesty' of the judicial system, but rather the extensive discretion which was given to judges to recommend mercy, and to the King in Council to commute the death penalty. Judicial discretion meant that sentencing policy was conducted with an eye to the needs of society more than to the rights of the individual, and was part and parcel of eighteenth-century paternalism. On this basis it was right for sentences to vary. 'The grounds for mercy were ostensibly that the offence was minor, or that the convict was of good character, or that the crime he had committed was not common enough in that county to require an exemplary hanging.'[15] The alternative model, deriving from the ideas of Beccaria and Bentham, is widely held to have influenced Whig reformers such as Sir Samuel Romilly and Sir James Mackintosh.[16] Bentham advocated more scientific sentencing with only a minimum of discretion devolved on judges. In Hay's

---

[12] Peel to Charles Lloyd, 11 February 1826, Peel Papers, British Library, Add. MSS 40342 ff. 320–1, *Sir Robert Peel from His Private Correspondence*, ed. C. S. Parker (London, 1891–9), I, pp. 385–6.

[13] Jeremy Bentham, *An Introduction to the Principles of Morals and Legislation*, ed. J. H. Burns and H. L. A. Hart (London, 1789, new edition 1823) Chapter 13, ¶. 2; *The Collected Works of Jeremy Bentham*, ed. J. H. Burns (London, 1970), p. 158.

[14] Douglas Hay, 'Property, authority and the criminal law', in Douglas Hay, Peter Linebaugh, John G. Rule, E. P. Thompson and Cal Winslow, *Albion's Fatal Tree: Crime and Society in Eighteenth-Century England* (London, 1975), pp. 17–63.

[15] Ibid., p. 43.

[16] Randall McGowen, 'The image of justice and reform of the criminal law in early nineteenth-century England', *Buffalo Law Review*, 32 (1983), 95.

words, 'gross and capricious terror should be replaced by a fixed and graduated scale of more lenient but more certain punishments'.[17] By taking into account all the various circumstances of an offence – consequences, intentionality, consciousness and disposition – together with all the various qualities of a punishment – variability, equability, commensurability, characteristicalness and other such typically Benthamite neologisms – judges would be able to arrive with some precision at a correct 'proportion between punishments and offences'.[18] Once such punishments had been codified, moreover, potential offenders would be able to calculate in advance the likely consequence to themselves of their own unlawful actions, and society as a whole would benefit through their prudent use of that knowledge.

Where then did Peel stand in all of this? With regard to the first polarity, Dr Gatrell is clearly correct to place him at the bloodthirsty end of the spectrum, that is at the opposite end from Bentham. He was indeed an ethical pessimist, who believed in original sin and saw 'the great scheme of human redemption' as providing a providentialist rationale for the system of judicial murder. He was more appalled than most by 'pious perjury', the practice whereby jurymen, unwilling to risk a defendant being hanged for a relatively trivial offence, underestimated the value of items stolen, or even on occasion found 'not guilty', in order to pre-empt that possibility. And in rendering the capital code a little more 'merciful', he undoubtedly hoped that there would be a greater resort to punishments such as transportation, imprisonment, whipping and the treadmill. However, with regard to the second polarity – between discretionary and non-discretionary systems of justice – it is surely wrong to place Peel at the opposite end of the spectrum from Bentham. Historians tend to assume that discretionary justice necessarily implied harsh justice, as though the ruling class always behaved like an outraged Jehovah, but this was by no means axiomatic. In fact the opposite was true, since in practice to exercise discretion was to exercise mercy. Eldon, for example, strongly advocated the 'salutary' effects of 'vesting a very large share of discretion in the judges'. In his view, it was 'not from the circumstances of the severity of the law being put into execution to the fullest extent, so much as the imaginary terrors of it on the mind, that produces the abhorrence of crime'. He 'favoured the retention of severe laws that were rarely, if ever, enforced' in preference to a regime of softer but more certain punishments.[19] Yet although he was such a firm believer in judicial

---

17 Hay, *Albion's Fatal Tree*, p. 23.

18 Bentham, *Principles*, Chapters 14, 15; *Collected Works*, pp. 165–86.

19 Rose Anne Melikan, 'A lawyer's political apprenticeship: the early career of John Scott, Lord Eldon, 1751–1799', University of Cambridge PhD thesis, 1992, p. 169; HC, 30 May 1810, 1PD [*Hansard's Parliamentary Debates*, first series], XIX, Appendix p. cxii; 24 May 1811, 1PD, XX, p. 301.

discretion, Eldon came low down on the scale of bloodthirstiness, and might even be described as 'squeamish' about capital punishment.[20] By the same token, then, there is no theoretical reason why Peel should not have opposed too much discretion and yet have been retributive in his attitude to punishment.

Central to any understanding of Peel is the fact that he disapproved of material (as distinct from moral) paternalism. Men must stand on their own feet, free from the operations of caring or coercion by government or other ruling-class agency. All such manipulation disrupted the workings of the great machine of society, and thwarted God's 'system of social retribution', that 'just reward of merit, and just penalty of folly and vice'.[21] In this respect Peel was a mechanistic 'liberal individualist' like Bentham. The difference was that Bentham was an ethical optimist who believed that individual choice would lead to a harmonisation of social relationships, whereas Peel was an ethical pessimist whose vision of a healthy society was one that tamed 'the unruly passions and corrupt natures of human beings'.[22] Yet despite this enormous difference in tone and underlying philosophy, the two men concurred in many areas of practical policy, and with regard to penal reform both men valued visibility and predictability.[23] Thus Peel was uneasy about the excessive deployment of spies and informers, and utterly hostile to the use of *agents provocateurs*. 'God forbid that he should mean to countenance a system of espionage; but a vigorous preventive police, consistent with the free principles of our free constitution, was an object which he did not despair of seeing accomplished.'[24] He set up the Metropolitan Police in 1829 to represent a small but visible state, insisting that the new 'Bobbies' or 'Peelers' should wear uniform.[25] He also wanted to see a visible relationship between the seriousness of a crime and the degree of punishment it met with. Otherwise individual citizens could not be expected to make rational prudential calculations as to the disutility of criminal behaviour. In both its optimistic mode (Bentham's 'greatest happiness principle') and its pessimistic mode (Peel's 'moral

---

[20] Dr Melikan's word (private information); see Gatrell, *The Hanging Tree*, p. 546.

[21] Phrases from *A Correct Report of the Speeches Delivered by Sir Robert Peel at Glasgow* (London, 7th edn 1837), pp. 42–3, 59–60.

[22] For the way in which this duality operated in economic and social policy, notably the poor law, see Boyd Hilton, *The Age of Atonement: the Influence of Evangelicalism on Social and Economic Thought, 1785–1865* (Oxford, 1988), pp. 64–70, 237–48.

[23] The best discussion of the relations between Peel and Bentham is in Renée B. Lettow, 'Codification and consolidation of English law in the age of Peel and Brougham', University of Oxford M.Litt. dissertation (1992), pp. 75–9.

[24] HC, 4 June 1822, 2PD, VII, pp. 803–4.

[25] Leon Radzinowicz and Roger Hood, *A History of English Criminal Law and its Administration since 1750* (London, 1948–86), IV, p. 162. However, for Peel's subsequent admission that spies could not be altogether dispensed with, see ibid., IV, p. 242.

discipline'), this approach was essentially preventative – based on what Malthus might have called the jurisprudential check to crime.

Of course, Peel with his retributive attitudes faced a difficulty which Bentham did not face in advocating a system of graduated or proportionate punishments. Whereas Bentham could reserve the death penalty for the most heinous crimes only, and measure all other punishments downwards, Peel's scale was necessarily skewed by his belief that a large number of the more serious crimes should continue to attract the same penalty. However, though this distorted the fearful symmetry of the criminal code, it did not impair the basic principle (shared with Bentham) that an intending criminal should have a pretty accurate notion of what would happen to him if he were to be charged and convicted. Peel stated this view clearly in his speech on criminal law consolidation in 1826:

> I presume that I shall not have to combat at the outset any objections to the principle of an attempt to consolidate and simplify the criminal law. It appears so conformable to the dictates of common sense, that the law, of which all men are supposed to have cognizance – and which all are bound under heavy penalties to obey, should be as precise and intelligible as it can be made – that it is almost needless to fortify by reasoning or authority, the first impressions of the understanding.[26]

Peel, it must be remembered, was unconsciously steeped in a system of belief which located God's moral government of the universe in a nexus of natural rewards and punishments, especially the latter. The judgements handed out by temporal authorities should therefore seek to emulate such providential dispensations. This point had been made explicitly by the influential evangelical moralist Hannah More in 1813:

> We govern our country by laws emulative of those by which he governs his creatures: – we train our children by probationary discipline, as he trains his servants. Penal laws in states, like those of the Divine Legislator, indicate no hatred to those to whom they are proclaimed, for every man is at liberty not to break them; they are enacted in the first instance for admonition rather than chastisement, and serve as much for prevention as punishment.[27]

It followed from God's natural laws that excessive haste would lead to a broken leg, as alcohol led to the gout, lust or laziness to the workhouse, and avarice to the debtor's prison. Such lessons of life were learned by experience – what Peel called 'the first impressions of the understanding' – rather than by precept or ratiocination, and the criminal code should, so far as possible, reinforce such sense impressions.

---

26 HC, 9 March 1826, 2PD, xiv, pp. 1214–15.
27 Hannah More, *Christian Morals* (London, 1813), i, pp. 69–70.

In seeking to make law less arbitrary and more predictable, Peel did not of course seek to eliminate all elements of discretion or uncertainty from the criminal code. But he did take some significant steps in that direction. He reduced the number of capital offences, albeit cautiously. He was invariably reluctant to recommend the royal prerogative of mercy in marginal cases. By an Act of 1823 he allowed the courts, in cases not involving murder, to 'record' the death penalty – thereby letting the prisoner know at once that he would be reprieved – rather than keeping him on tenterhooks by 'pronouncing' the death penalty and merely 'recommending' a reprieve. By Acts of 1823, 1825 and 1827 he consolidated many venerable statutes in a manner which, according to one recent commentator, and 'allowing for the differences between the French and British systems, was not unlike Napoleon's methodical procedure prior to the enactment of the *Code Civil*'.[28] Indeed, his clearly stated desire to remove existing 'exceptions to the general principle' prompted the Whig lawyer Denman to accuse him of 'placing too precise and exact limits to the conduct of magistrates' and of 'too technical a laying down of their duties'.[29] In all these ways Peel cut down on the amount of flexibility in practice and to that extent he rendered the law more certain.

And yet so formidable an authority as Dr Gatrell believes that Peel enthusiastically upheld the discretionary elements of the old régime. He can moreover cite twice from Peel's speeches in support of his contention. The first occasion was in 1822, after Burdett had called on the House of Commons to address the King on behalf of Henry Hunt, who had been sentenced to two-and-a-half years' imprisonment for his part in the Peterloo incident. Burdett hoped to secure a remission of the remaining part of the sentence, but Peel protested that the prerogative of mercy was 'exclusive' to the executive, and should never be interfered with by 'the democratic part of [the] constitution'. Gatrell cites this comment as expressing Peel's 'passionate defence of the central principles of the old regime: the royal prerogative of mercy and the discretionary element in judicial and executive power'.[30] But in fact all Peel was saying was that the power to remit a sentence (not, of course, the death sentence in Hunt's case) lay with the executive (the King in Council) rather than with the legislature. His comments had nothing to do with the extent of discretion per se.

Gatrell's other citation, from Peel's response to Mackintosh's proposals for criminal law reform in 1823, is much more interesting and superficially much

---

[28] Desmond H. Brown, 'Abortive attempts to codify English criminal law', *Parliamentary History*, 11 (1992), 17.
[29] HC, 17 April 1826, 2PD, xv, pp. 286, 290.
[30] HC, 24 April 1822, 2PD, vii, p. 34; Gatrell, *The Hanging Tree*, pp. 583–4.

more compelling. First Peel defended the Council's power to grant pardons on
the grounds that

> It would . . . be impossible to establish any code of laws which would prevent
> the necessity of a discretionary power on the part of the executive . . . Would it
> be fair, then, to take away the discretion by which those punishments had been
> thus apportioned; or could they hope to make a law so precise in all its
> provisions as to substitute it with effect?[31]

Peel also defended the power of judges to vary sentences (by recommending a
royal pardon or not) according to local or temporal circumstances. If, for
example, there had been a prevalence of horse stealing in a particular locality,
then a degree of exemplary toughness might be called for in dealing with such
an offence: 'It might be hard to say to a man, that his life should be valued at
a particular rate, depending upon local or temporary expediency. But this was
the very reasoning upon which law was founded.'[32] These remarks may seem
to align Peel firmly alongside Eldon as a believer in the discretionary model of
justice, for if sentences were to be varied according to local contingency, the
penal law would become that much less visible or predictable.

However, it is important to remember that the criminal law, unlike the
common law or equity, was mainly governed by statute. This being so, no one
could sensibly have taken an extreme position on the question of judicial
discretion. That is to say, no one suggested that judges should have complete
discretion to punish however they liked, or to be able to sentence a person to
death for crimes which did not carry a statutory death penalty. Conversely, few
suggested that there should be virtually no discretion at all along the lines of
the French Code Pénal of 1791, or that execution should be mandatory for
all capital crimes, with the only point of a trial being to determine guilt
or innocence. So to talk of Peel (or for that matter Bentham) standing at
the mechanistic or non-discretionary end of the spectrum is not to suggest
that they opposed *all* discretion whatever. There was never any question of
Peel opposing discretion totally or of attempting to fabricate a completely
scientific criminal code which would be able to anticipate all felonious
situations.[33]

Moreover, a close look at what he said in the parliamentary debate of 1823
suggests that his attitude to penal discretion was fairly complex. It seems very
likely from their speeches that both Mackintosh and Peel were conscious of
the arguments contained in Bentham's *Principles of Morals and Legislation*
(1789), the second edition of which had appeared shortly before the debate

---

[31] HC, 21 May 1823, 2PD, IX, p. 422.

[32] Ibid., p. 424, quoted in Gatrell, *The Hanging Tree*, p. 584.

[33] After all, moderate evangelicals believed that even God interfered with his own machinery –
his 'moral system of government by rewards and punishments' – from time to time.

took place.[34] Bentham had argued that 'the value of the punishment must not be less in any case than what is sufficient to outweigh that of the profit of the offence', meaning not just pecuniary gain but the quantum of pleasure derived from its commission. It followed that 'the greater the mischief of the offence, the greater is the expense, which it may be worth while to be at, in the way of punishment'.[35] Mackintosh countered that the mischief of an action could not be the sole regulator of the amount of punishment, since punishment must also be exemplary, but he too called for 'proportionate punishments' instead of the extensive 'arbitrio judicis' which then obtained. Of all countries England was the one in which the law was least literally executed, and in which issues of life and death most depended on the feelings of individual judges. In Mackintosh's view, judges ought not to pronounce a sentence of death when they had no expectation that it would be carried out – Hay's theatricality model – since if only one out of 66 men condemned to death for a certain offence was actually executed, then his death could not possibly act as a deterrent and would be 'a wanton and criminal waste of human existence'. Likewise the fate of a convict ought not to depend on whether the particular district in which he happened to live was thought to require an exemplary punishment. 'That the life of man should depend on temporary or local policy, on the necessities of a particular district, or the interests of particular classes, was a principle utterly inconsistent with justice and humanity, and tending to confound all our notions of right and wrong.'[36]

In advocating the abolition of capital punishment for forgery and for various categories of larceny (such as the theft of horses, sheep and cattle), Mackintosh explicitly favoured a more merciful penal code along French lines.[37] Since abolition of the death penalty would have meant the abolition of discretionary mercy in such cases, Mackintosh came across as a Benthamite in so far as he wished to minimise the amount of discretion in sentencing. It is therefore significant to find Peel beginning his reply by saying that the difference between himself and Mackintosh was 'only as to degree,' and that, since he too had been about to suggest amendments to the law, 'there could be no necessity for him and [Mackintosh] to debate that point'. Indeed, Peel's main objection was that Mackintosh's mode of proceeding 'was the most inconvenient which could be taken'. In other words, Peel broadly accepted the principles which Mackintosh had laid, quibbled about procedural matters, and displayed some pique at having had his priority stolen.[38]

---

[34] At least it *appears* from internal evidence that the second edition was published in the early months of 1823. (The responsibility for this statement is mine, but I am extremely grateful to Professor J. H. Burns for his skilful detective work.)

[35] Bentham, *Principles*, Chapter 14, §§. 8, 10; *Collected Works*, pp. 166, 168.

[36] HC, 21 May 1823, 2PD, IX, pp. 403–11.

[37] Ibid., p. 406.   [38] Ibid., pp. 420–1.

Then, pretending that Mackintosh had advocated 'a more fixed proportion' between convictions and executions for all categories of capital offence, Peel objected that such a 'fixed proportion' would 'be impossible to establish', and there would remain 'the necessity of a discretionary power on the part of the executive'. This comment leads Dr Gatrell to say that Peel passionately approved of 'the discretionary element', but it is not so simple. It is not even clear what Peel meant by the 'executive' in this context. In London and Middlesex discretion was clearly vested in the executive – the King in Council – rather than in the judges, though the latters' trial notes were available to the Council. With respect to the provincial circuits it was the judges who decided whether or not to recommend a reprieve, so that executive discretion was delegated to them. In cases where mercy was not recommended, the Home Office frequently had to consider petitions appealing against the death penalty, and to that extent there was a second and higher level of discretion in operation, but what is not clear is whether either Peel or any other Home Secretary used this power to moderate judicial decisions. Available evidence suggests that Peel nearly always deferred to the opinions of the judges in such appeal cases,[39] though he might sometimes push a judge gently in a particular direction. In view of all this, it is clear that Peel's allusion to 'the necessity of a discretionary power on the part of the executive' hardly carries the weight which has been put on it. Either he was simply saying that a system of mandatory death penalties required that there should be some provision for mercy, which no one – least of all Mackintosh[40] or Bentham – would have contested; or else he was advocating a need for executive discretion over and above that of the judiciary. If the latter, then in exercising such discretion either the executive always submitted to the views of the judges, in which case its effect on the system as a whole was neutral; or else it imposed a degree of central interference, presumably in an attempt to harmonise judicial decisions and secure some small degree of uniformity across circuits and assizes. There is no known evidence of a sustained attempt at such a corrective use of executive power, but the important point is that whichever way Peel's words are interpreted, they do not amount to a plea for large amounts of discretion.

Peel clearly thought it right to value a man's life 'at a particular rate, depending upon local or temporary expediency'. It had also been right to allow the judges discretion in sentencing the Gordon rioters, for example,

---

[39] I am especially grateful to Dr Gatrell for advice on this point.

[40] In a blatant piece of polemical table-turning, Peel even managed to imply that he was more 'humane' than Mackintosh in defending the practice of executive reprieve for crimes such as arson, attempted murder and burglary, which would have remained capital offences even if Mackintosh's resolutions had been passed.

since no law could have been framed which would have taken into account all the circumstances of the case. However, this does not mean that he was siding with Eldon, Paley, and other exponents of the Hay-model of justice. After all even Bentham, who deprecated judicial discretion, thought that judges should have the power to measure a punishment according to the circumstances of a case, by which he meant motive, intentionality, consciousness, age, and so forth, in other words exactly those circumstances which Peel said should be taken into account. All that Bentham wanted was that judges should take these factors into account scientifically – in such a way as potential criminals might anticipate – rather than arbitrarily, out of personal feeling, or for the sake of theatre, and exactly the same is true of Peel. For it is clear that, in defending such discretion 'against' Mackintosh in 1823, Peel was tilting at a windmill. What Mackintosh had thought abominable was that a man might be sentenced to death simply because of 'the particular temper and opinions of the judge [or] the peculiar necessity which might exist for making a signal example in some particular district'.[41] In other words, he objected to arbitrary harshness and to the use of exemplary punishments in regions where the guilt was collective. But he would probably not have disagreed with the more precise way in which Peel defined discretion in his reply. This was to say that a horse stealer might rightly be hanged in a part of the country where there was justified 'alarm on account of offences of this sort', whereas it would be equally right for judges to remit the death penalty in regions where there was 'no such common dread to actuate them'. If punishments had to be set at (or above) the minimum level necessary to act as a deterrent, then in deciding what that minimum level was in practice it was entirely proper for judges to take local circumstances into account. Where sheep stealing was a serious nuisance, it required a high degree of deterrence. Potential horse stealers could also be expected to take this factor into account when they made their rational and prudential calculations as to whether they should steal a horse or not.

In other words, Peel's formulation of the case for discretion was entirely in line with utilitarian philosophy. Bentham never supposed that punishments had to be the same everywhere and for everybody, and he would have agreed with Peel that it was a 'principle of sound law' for locally prevailing degrees and kinds of lawlessness to be taken into account. What judges were *not* to do was impose the death penalty simply in order to impress the populace with the power of the governing class, or because it was thought in a general and unspecified way that a particular locality needed to be taught a lesson. That was the sort of arbitrary discretion which had no rational basis and which could not therefore act in a tutelary way on potential criminals.

Indeed, not only are Peel's comments in 1823 compatible with Benthamism,

[41] HC, 21 May 1823, 2PD, IX, p. 411.

they are far more compatible than Mackintosh's. Mackintosh was clearly at one with Bentham in wishing to minimise bloodshed and to minimise judicial discretion, and so historians of penal reform have tended to think in terms of Beccaria → Bentham → Romilly → Mackintosh. Yet this flies directly in the face of those intellectual historians who have rightly emphasised that Bentham and Mackintosh were opposites. For example, William Thomas writes of Mackintosh's attack on Bentham's *Plan of Parliamentary Reform* in the *Edinburgh Review* in 1818: 'Mackintosh's approach was the very antithesis of Bentham's and [James] Mill's. Where they saw society as a mechanism, he saw it as an organism. They appealed to reason; he appealed to history.'[42] Donald Winch cites Mackintosh and Bentham as the central protagonists in his chapter on the very bitter if occasionally 'playful' battle between 'Philosophic Whigs' and 'Philosophic Radicals'.[43] And Seamus Deane points out that, though it would have hurt the author of *Vindiciae Gallicae* (1791) to admit it, Mackintosh was really a Burkean who complained in the *Dissertation on Ethical Philosophy* (1830) that Bentham had confused ethics and jurisprudence and had excluded the operation of 'feeling' from his calculations. Mackintosh constantly denounced the Utilitarians' 'selfish system of morals', and in reply the Utilitarian James Mill rubbished Mackintosh's 'sentimental system', which he said was potentially despotic (i.e. discretionary).[44] In the light of these judgements, it is not difficult to see that in some important respects it was Peel and not Mackintosh who played the Benthamite in the Commons debate on the criminal code in 1823.

For example, Mackintosh 'objected strongly . . . to the principle of making the amount of property stolen any criterion for the punishment inflicted upon an offender', since 'there was no greater moral depravity in stealing a large sum than a small one'.[45] Now Bentham would have objected strongly to the first of these propositions, while accepting the second one wholeheartedly. Indeed, he went further than Mackintosh in respect of the second proposition, arguing that there was often a *greater* 'depravity of disposition' in offenders who had yielded to a slight temptation than in those who had yielded to a large one.[46] However, the question of a felon's disposition or 'degree of depravity' was a sentimental consideration which should not be allowed to affect the quantum of punishment.

[42] William Thomas, *The Philosophic Radicals: Nine Studies in Theory and Practice 1817–1841* (Oxford, 1979), p. 125.

[43] Stefan Collini, Donald Winch and John Burrow, *That Noble Science of Politics: a Study in Nineteenth-Century Intellectual History* (Cambridge, 1983), pp. 91–126.

[44] Seamus Deane, *The French Revolution and Enlightenment in England 1789–1832* (Cambridge, Mass., 1988), p. 55.

[45] HC, 21 May 1823, 2PD, IX, p. 408.

[46] Bentham, *Principles*, Chapter 11, ¶. 42; *Collected Works*, pp. 140–2.

The strength of the temptation, *cæteris paribus*, is as the profit of the offence: the quantum of the punishment must rise with the profit of the offence: *cæteris paribus*, it must therefore rise with the strength of the temptation. This there is no disputing. True it is, that the stronger the temptation, the less conclusive is the indication which the act of delinquency affords of the depravity of the offender's disposition. So far then as the absence of any aggravation, arising from extraordinary depravity of disposition, may operate . . . the strength of the temptation may operate in abatement of the demand for punishment. But it can never operate so far as to indicate the propriety of making the punishment ineffectual, which it is sure to be when brought below the level of the apparent profit of the offence.[47]

Bentham was adamant that judges should base sentences primarily on the consequences of a criminal's actions rather than on their (inevitably imperfect) estimation of his motives. This central element in Bentham's system – that punishment should be calculated according to the sin and not the sinner – is a clue to the subterranean links between his thought and that of moderate evangelical Christians like Hannah More, links which help to explain why utilitarians and evangelicals so often found themselves on the same side of policy issues, despite being poles apart psychologically.

On the other hand, nothing could be less Benthamite than Mackintosh's remark that 'the criminal law could never be effectually administered, but when it was in perfect unison with the moral feelings and sympathies of the people'.[48] As Randall McGowen puts it in a sophisticated re-appraisal, this reflected his belief that the law was strongest 'when it was an extension of the spontaneous feelings of the community'.[49] Mackintosh was anticipating the mid nineteenth-century's Whig-Liberal conception of law as an evolving set of rules which accommodated to the developing mores of particular societies. It was wholly different from the utilitarian/evangelical view of societies as static-mechanical and of the law as a transcendent set of universal rules, the purpose of which was to curb the 'unruly passions' and anti-social behaviour of men.

Peel was not given to philosophising, yet his riposte to Mackintosh contains at least one clear enough statement of utilitarian and evangelical juris-prudence.

It might be hard to say to a man, that his life should be valued at a particular rate, depending upon local or temporary expediency. But this was the very

---

[47] Bentham, *Principles*, Chapter 14, ¶. 9; *Collected Works*, p. 167.
[48] HC, 21 May 1823, 2PD, IX, p. 413.
[49] Randall McGowen, 'A powerful sympathy: terror, the prison, and humanitarian reform in early nineteenth-century Britain', *Journal of British Studies*, 25 (1986), 312–34.

reasoning upon which law was founded. On what other ground could they pretend to inflict capital punishments? It was not that they, in the deficiencies of human nature, were able to determine that which could only be effected by a tribunal above – the exact degree of moral turpitude attached to each particular offence. But while mankind were constituted as they were, having to struggle with all the imperfections of their senses, this was the last [i.e. least] mode which legislation could devise for the preservation of civil order.[50]

Dr Gatrell describes this pronouncement as a paraphrase of one of Paley's most celebrated passages. It buttresses his belief that Peel was a Paley-ite in penal matters, and therefore a die-hard exponent of the ancien régime's discretionary philosophy. In 1785 Paley had written that

> The proper end of human punishment is, not the satisfaction of justice, but the prevention of crimes. By the satisfaction of justice, I mean the retribution of so much pain for so much guilt; which is the dispensation we expect at the hand of God . . . From the justice of God we are taught to look for a gradation of punishment, exactly proportioned to the guilt of the offender; when therefore, in assigning the degrees of human punishment, we introduce considerations distinct from that guilt, and a proportion so varied by external circumstances, that equal crimes frequently undergo unequal punishments, or the less crime the greater; it is natural to demand the reason why a different measure of punishment should be expected from God, and observed by man.[51]

The reason which Paley gives is that God can penetrate the innermost secrets in the hearts of his creatures, whereas with human justice there is always an element of doubt as to motive, so that judges can never know how bad an offender really is. And while there can be no escape from God's judgements, in terrestrial affairs crooks often go undetected and so 'the uncertainty of punishment must be compensated by the severity'.[52]

There are indeed resemblances between Paley's views and those of Peel, but there was also one very important difference. Both men believed in God's moral government of his creatures by means of rewards and punishments. However, in Paley's moral cosmology, such dispensations were not envisaged in a terrestrial sense. When he referred to 'a gradation of punishment exactly proportioned to the guilt of the offender', he meant that the final quantum of punishment which was inflicted in the afterlife would exactly reflect the quantum of human guilt incurred during a person's lifetime.[53] This sense of a gradation was possible because he did not see heaven and hell as absolute

---

50 HC, 21 May 1823, 2PD, IX, p. 424, quoted in Gatrell, *The Hanging Tree*, p. 584.
51 William Paley, *The Principles of Moral and Political Philosophy* (London, 1785), pp. 526, 530 [Book VI, Ch. 9]; Gatrell, *The Hanging Tree*, pp. 517–19, 584.
52 Paley, *Principles*, p. 531.
53 The phrase 'gradation of punishment' here implies not 'graduation' (as in 'graduated scale') but the final climactic step in accumulation of punishment.

opposites. To those who objected that, in terms of their just deserts, there might be little to choose between the worst soul in heaven and the best soul in hell, Paley retorted that neither might there be much difference in their respective conditions. As for God's administration of the earth, Paley was adamant that there were no punishments. On the contrary, the world was contrived for man's pleasure:

> Evil no doubt exists; but is never, that we can perceive, the object of contrivance. Teeth are contrived to eat, not to ache; their aching now and then is incidental to the contrivance, perhaps inseparable from it; or even, if you will, let it be called a defect in the contrivance; but it is not the object of it.[54]

There was nothing calculated to produce 'pain and misery' in the works of nature. The most Paley would admit was that the order of nature proceeded according to general laws which, 'however well set and constituted' in themselves, 'often thwart and cross one another' with inconvenient results for mankind.

> Of all views under which human life has ever been considered, the most reasonable in my judgment is that, which regards it as a state of *probation* . . . It is not a state of unmixed happiness, or of happiness simply; it is not a state of designed misery, or of misery simply; it is not a state of retribution; it is not a state of punishment. It suits with none of these suppositions. It accords much better with the idea of its being a condition calculated for the production, exercise, and improvement, of moral qualities, with a view to a future state, in which, these qualities . . . receive their reward, or become their own.[55]

All this was utterly different from the evangelical cosmology, as propagated by Hannah More and William Wilberforce and unconsciously imbibed by Peel. For a start, evangelicals were disinclined to recognise a gradation of spiritual guilt, since all sin was a rebellion against God and as such equally heinous. Similarly there could be no gradation of punishment after death. Heaven and hell were diametrical opposites, meaning that all saved souls were gloriously happy and all the damned were excruciatingly tormented. It made no sense therefore to say that there was little difference between the lot of the most favoured in hell and the least favoured in heaven. The great – indeed only – object was to scourge as many souls into heaven as possible, and in order to advance this object God had instituted a system of *earthly* rewards and punishments. They were therefore distressed by Paley's refusal to countenance such a system. As Wilberforce complained, 'the goodness of God is the only moral attribute which is apprehended by Dr Paley to be manifest, from the

54 William Paley, *Natural Theology: or, Evidences of the Existence and Attributes of the Deity, Collected from the Appearances of Nature* (London, 1802), p. 501.

55 Ibid., pp. 561–3, 527.

appearances of the natural world. No observation occurs . . . concerning the holiness or justice of the deity, nothing of those tendencies of virtue to produce happiness, and of vice to produce misery'.[56] The crucial point here is that these rewards and punishments were dealt during man's lifetime, not after death and judgement as with Paley. Again, evangelicals objected to Paley's lack of emphasis on vice and to his belief that characters were '*formed* by circumstances',[57] a type of environmentalism.

Peel's reference to a 'natural system of social retribution', with its 'just reward of merit, and just penalty of folly and vice', reflected his view of the proper relationship between human and divine law. For Paley divine law (as registered in the next world) was certain and precise, whereas human law was bound to be arbitrary. For Peel, human law should be as precise and intelligible as it can be made – that it is almost needless to fortify, by reasoning or authority, the first impressions of the understanding – in other words, that the law should silently reinforce men's understanding of what Peel was wont to call (in the argot of the day) 'the dispensations of providence', without having to justify those dispensations by resort to the arbitrary and special pleading of legal experts. That law could be so regulated as to do this was the view of some contemporary legal writers such as Anthony Hammond, whose combination of Benthamite consequentialism and Malthusian ethical pessimism provides much more insight into Peel's ideas than Paley does.

Hammond was the main author of the report of the 1824 Criminal Law Commission, and although the precise degree of his influence is uncertain, he corresponded in some detail with Peel, who evidently valued his assistance in drafting the consolidating legislation of 1826–7.[58] His several essays on 'the science of natural jurisprudence' are interesting because they reveal how an explicitly Benthamite approach to the proper principles of punishment could be combined with an un-Benthamite severity in wishing to retain the death penalty for as many crimes as possible. Hammond argued from the premise that punishment was only justified by 'utility'. Although crimes originated solely in a 'malevolent disposition of mind', they only became punishable when they issued in actual malefaction. 'Effects and consequences alone support and oppose the ends of our creation; every thing, therefore, is good or

56 William Wilberforce in *Christian Observer*, 2 (1803), 373.

57 'When we speak of a state of trial, it must be remembered, that characters are not only tried, or proved, or detected, but that they are generated also, and *formed*, by circumstances.' Paley, *Natural Theology*, p. 564.

58 Radzinowicz, *History of English Criminal Law*, 1, p. 576, n. 31; Hammond to Peel, 15 November, 22 December 1825, Peel Papers, British Library, Add. MSS 40383 ff. 18–19, 40384 ff. 102–4. I am grateful to Dr Peter Gray for his help with the Hammond correspondence.

evil, the object of our desire or aversion, our gratitude or resentment, as it actually and in fact produces benefit or injury.' The only justification for punishing a criminal was to deter others from committing the same crime 'by setting before them the dreadful consequences of such proceedings'. The 'dissuading or reformation of the criminal himself' was very much less important than ensuring that the rest of the community did not imitate his actions; indeed, if reformation of the criminal were the criterion of punishment, then no first offender would ever be executed.

It followed that punishments must neither exceed nor fall short of the level needed to deter others from committing the same crime. This meant that the death penalty should be retained for a large number of offences. Like Malthus, Hammond believed that, 'as pain is a sensation more pungent than the opposite and corresponding sensation, so the passion of fear, which is founded on pain, must always predominate over that of hope, which is founded on pleasure'. It followed that 'the dread of death' was 'the most important principle in human nature',[59] and death was the only punishment which could influence the minds of those who had little sense of shame. Admittedly, the *certainty* of death was slight in a system which allowed so many reprieves; still the awfulness of not being reprieved was such as to deter most potential offenders from taking the risk.

The problem for society, as Hammond saw it, was the natural tendency for men to connive in mitigation of punishment. Their sensibilities – 'humanity, kindness, natural affection ' – disposed them to welcome sentences which fell short of the mark, while judges often experienced 'not only agreeable, but delicious' sensations in exercising an unwarranted mercy. It was therefore important that the 'wise legislator' should 'sometimes do the utmost violence to his benevolent affections' by punishing certain anti-social offences with death, while being less severe on persons whose crimes he found more abhorrent. 'He will pass over the guardian who has defrauded his ward of her property, and then seduced and turned her out upon the world as a beggar and a prostitute. And will put to death the father, who reduced to want by inevitable misfortunes, robs, to satisfy the hunger of his helpless children.' To those reformers who complained that public executions had the effect of degrading the multitude of sightseers, Hammond argued that executions should continue to be both public and frequent in order to desensitise the public to capital punishment – 'to lose, by frequent calls upon its fellow feeling, that sensibility to the sufferings of others, at the first appearance of

---

[59] However, he connected the death of villains – not with the prospect of Hell-fire or Peel's 'severe punishment' – but with deprivation: i.e. exclusion from the 'light of the sun' and from 'life and conversation', and obliteration from 'the affections and . . . memory of their dearest friends and relations'. Hammond, *Scheme*, p. xlii.

which it is so keenly excited'. Repeated exposure to the sight of death on the gallows was the only way to train a community to accept punishments as harsh as the needs of society demanded, the only way to ensure that the 'dictates of understanding' overrode those of 'compassion'.[60]

In some ways, Peel's brief responses to penal developments as leader of the Opposition in the 1830s reveal more about his beliefs than his laboured and self-regarding set pieces as Home Secretary. Gatrell is correct to say that he regarded the Whig Governments as travelling too fast down the road which he himself had opened up, and was inclined at every point to counsel caution, but he was by no means wholly negative or reactionary.

In the first place, he was closer to Russell than to many of his own back benchers. As on almost every other Whig reform of the 1830s, the Conservative opposition split into a Peelite and an Ultra camp, and as on other reforms the Ultra line was pressed most vigorously by Inglis. Robert Harry Inglis was an evangelical with a fierce loathing of the 'liberal' march of mind. He had been an enemy ever since Peel's apostasy over Catholic emancipation in 1829, and had beaten Peel in a bitter by-election for the Oxford University seat. His motto in penal matters was, 'Whoso sheddeth man's blood, by man shall his blood be shed' (Genesis 9: 6), and he frequently reminded the House of the number of crimes under 'the old Scripture dispensation in which the punishment of death was enjoined'. He upheld the need for vengeance, and called for MPs to consider what their feelings would be if their own relatives had been victims of crime. Invariably Peel showed his distaste for such expressions of Ultra philosophy. Indignation should play no part in legislation, and 'the main consideration was what course should be taken which, upon the whole, was most calculated to prevent offences'.[61]

Peel's views on the French legal system are also revealing. He disliked the fact that judges examined prisoners and witnesses and took an active part in trials, since this impaired their impartiality and was redolent of investigative paternalism, but in other respects he expressed much admiration for the French criminal code. For example, in 1836 the Radical MP William Ewart attempted to prevent juries from being given evidence of previous convictions, while conceding that such information 'should be urged after conviction in aggravation of punishment'. This is of course the situation current in English law today, but Peel took a contrary view. 'He had rather that the Jury should

---

[60] Anthony Hammond, *Scheme for a Digest of the Laws of England, with Introductory Essays on the Science of Natural Jurisprudence* (London, 1820), pp. xxv–lv. Like Hammond and also Bentham, Peel believed that executions should take place in public.

[61] HC, 19 May 1837, 3PD [*Hansard's Parliamentary Debates*, third series], XXXVIII, pp. 920–1; 3 May 1831, 3PD, LVII, pp. 1416–17, 1419.

know the fact of a man's previous conviction than the Judge', just as Poor Law Guardians were told whether alleged rogues and vagabonds had proved 'incorrigible' in the past. The disagreement is significant. Whereas Ewart objected that such knowledge 'could not possibly assist' juries in arriving at a correct decision as to guilt, Peel thought that this was nonsense since his view of human nature led him to suppose: 'once a thief always a thief'. Information as to previous convictions should be given to juries because it would help to determine guilt or innocence; it should *not* be used for sentencing because sentences needed to relate to offences rather than to individuals if they were to act as a deterrent to others.[62]

However – and again the qualification is significant – it *would* in Peel's view have been expedient to disclose evidence of previous offences for the purpose of sentencing *so long as* the consequences of re-offending were built into the legislation for all to see. So long, that is, as a potential offender could know how much more severely he would be punished for a second or subsequent offence. Historians have tended to disregard the fact that during the 1820s Peel had 'extensively readjusted the scale of punishments for lesser offences against property', even while retaining the death penalty for more serious crimes. For example, 7 Geo. 4, c. 69 (1826) replaced legislation prescribing transportation for anyone stealing any vegetable matter from any orchard or garden. The new legislation distinguished between types of property – between stealing, destroying and damaging – between different values of property stolen – and between a first and subsequent offence. Peel's belief was that, having refined and defined culpability in this way, it should be possible to specify a range of secondary punishments such as transportation, solitary confinement, the treadmill, whipping (public or private – once, twice or thrice).[63] Dr Gatrell sees Peel's relish for corporal punishment as reinforcing the charge of cruelty arising from his commitment to hanging, but on the contrary it could be regarded as a necessary prelude to any significant reductions in the number of executions. For as Peel reasonably pointed out to Radical and Whig MPs who wished to cut down on all types of punishment, 'it was peculiarly incumbent upon those who advocated the necessity of mitigating the severity of the penal code, in respect to capital punishments, to beware of rendering such an experiment impracticable by narrowing too much the scale of minor punishment'.[64]

In view of this it is unsurprising that Peel's main response to the removal of capital statutes in the 1830s was, not to repine, but to argue the case for a graduated scale of secondary punishments. Take, for example, his comments

---

[62] HC, 9 March 1826, 2PD, XIV, p. 1234; HC, 7 June 1836, 3PD, XXXIV, pp. 167–9.
[63] Radzinowicz, *History of English Criminal Law*, I, pp. 585–7.
[64] Ibid., pp. 570–1; HC, 30 April 1823, 2PD, VIII, pp. 1440–1.

on a Bill for Abolishing the Punishment of Death in the Burning or Destroying of Buildings and Ships:

> If it were intended to rely on transportation and imprisonment as the principal means for repressing crime, it would be satisfactory to have some precise information as to the effects produced on the conduct and habits of criminals by the duration of those punishments . . . It was not his object to have the Bill postponed, but as it was proposed to vest much discretion in the Judges, it would be well to afford the House an opportunity of ascertaining in what manner the system of secondary punishments would be likely to work, and by that means to enable them to exercise their discretionary power in the best manner possible.

Then, after another MP had pointed out that the Bill did not give the judges more discretion than they had already,

> Sir Robert Peel, in explanation, did not mean to say that a wider discretion was vested in the Judges. His object was, to enable the Judges to exercise any discretion with which they might be vested in the best manner possible; and to do this, it would be well that they had every information as to how the system of secondary punishment worked – as, for instance, what was the difference in the result of five years imprisonment, as contrasted with transportation; the various manner in which the different modes of punishment operated, in reclaiming males and females, and which were the results of those separate modes of punishment as applied to the younger and the older offenders.[65]

These comments reflected a belief, fashionable in the 1830s, that statistics were a useful tool of social science, and as such they were entirely consistent with Bentham's project of government. They might not reveal much sympathy with the humanitarian impulse of the early nineteenth century, but they certainly did not betoken a commitment to 'the old order' or to 'the central principles of the old regime'.

Peel's philosophy of punishment is worth bothering about if only because it helps to explain something rather surprising about the direction which penal policy took in the first half of the nineteenth century. Because historians tend to assume that what happened was always likely to happen, their narratives are often inadequate in conveying the unexpectedness of most outcomes. It therefore needs to be emphasised how surprising it was that – without any political revolution or noticeable transfer of power – one of the bloodiest codes in Europe was transformed so quickly into one of the mildest. It is no less surprising that the same highly mercantilist and patronage state should have been transformed into a relative meritocracy and beacon of free trade. The

---

[65] HC, 19 May 1837, 3PD, XXXVIII, pp. 924–6.

political debates which raged on both these developments revealed a sharp polarisation of views – as Mackintosh famously put it in 1830, when debating law reform, he felt as though he 'lived in two different countries, and conversed with people who spoke two different languages'.[66] In saying this he felt himself to be ranged against the full force of establishment privilege and influence, and he had no inkling that in a very short period of time his own language would in turn become normative.

It is well beyond the scope of this essay to explain how the somersault was turned, either on penal or fiscal policy. Whig and Whig-Liberal politicians clearly played an important role, and in Dr Gatrell's view they played the all-important role so far as penal reform was concerned. However, it is contended here that two such surprising transformations could not have occurred so quickly or so painlessly without the agency of what might be called 'liberal Tory' or 'Peelite' politicians. In saying this, it is important to emphasise that 'liberal Toryism' should not be conceived spatially, as though – to cite a recent formulation – 'the Conservative party really does have edges, that the left-hand one abuts or overlaps the right-hand edge of the Liberal party and that if a dissident progressive Tory falls off the end of the Conservative world it is the Liberal one that prevents him from tumbling into nothingness'.[67] For liberal Toryism was emphatically *not* 'simply a mild variant of Tory politics',[68] or a 'half-way house' which 'straddled the gap between liberal reform and tory reaction'. On the contrary, 'liberal Toryism' was a dialectical construct whose practitioners had a foot in both camps. This did not betoken ambiguity or ambivalence, and it only seems to do so if one supposes that there was a single spectrum of opinion on issues such as fiscal and penal policy.

What made liberal Tories so effective as free traders, when they finally came round to asserting that doctrine in full, was that they were free traders who did not subscribe to the pro-manufacturing philosophy which made that doctrine so repulsive to a Parliament of landowners. Likewise, liberal Tories such as Peel were able to promote Benthamite views of jurisprudence so successfully, mainly because it was well known that they did not want to emasculate the judges or dismantle the death penalty. They were liberals in one sense – that of the free market and individual responsibility – without being remotely liberal in the sense of feeling tender to underdogs. Thus Peel espoused a liberal-individualist jurisprudence in order to maintain a high degree of retribution at a time when the old paternalist régime seemed to be going soft under the influence of squeamish judges and over-benevolent Poor Law

---

[66] HC, 24 May 1830, 2PD, xxiv, p. 1033.
[67] Michael Bentley, 'Liberal Toryism in the twentieth century', *Transactions of the Royal Historical Society*, 6th series, 4 (1994), 180.
[68] Ibid., p. 186.

Guardians and magistrates. In doing so he was able to make inroads on the old régime, and to weaken its defences. It is unlikely that humanitarian reformers, acting merely on behalf of the underdog, could have brought about so swift and complete a revision of the bloody code, had it not been for the instrumentality of a liberal Tory.

6

SZÉCHENYI AND AUSTRIA[1]

ᴄᴐᴇᴐᴄᴐ

R. J. W. EVANS

I N all that central-European terrain which Derek Beales has made so much his own during the past two decades, we find no more classic example of a dominant personality than Count István (Stephen) Széchenyi. By words and actions, Széchenyi transmuted Hungary and introduced an Age of Reform there which issued in the Revolution of 1848. Or at least – and that is no less important for the biographical concerns of the present volume – he was *perceived* to have done so. No doubt rapid change would have come anyway; but he catalysed it, and gave it its distinctive configuration. Besides, for Széchenyi himself that perception was crucial: the conviction of his own historic, individual transformatory role drove him to eminence – and to ruin. He was the 'greatest Hungarian' as his equally great adversary Kossuth put it; that was so because, as Kossuth added, he had 'put his finger on the artery of the age and had felt its pulse . . . [He] became the tongue of his age. This is the secret of his influence.'[2]

Not only is Szechenyi's prominent public career most copiously documented in the contemporary record; we have well-nigh unique access to his private life too. For nearly the whole of that career, 35 years in all, he kept

---

[1] This essay, concentrated on the person of Széchenyi, relates to the broader discussion of Austro-Hungarian relations in this period in my articles on 'The Habsburgs and the Hungarian Problem, 1790–1848', *Transactions of the Royal Historical Society*, 5th ser., 39 (1989), 41–62, and 'Hungary and the Habsburg Monarchy, 1840–67: A Study in Perceptions', *Etudes Danubiennes*, 2 (1986), 18–39. In what follows, secondary references have been held to a minimum. The best introductions to Széchenyi for present purposes are George Barany, *Stephen Széchenyi and the Awakening of Hungarian Nationalism, 1791–1841* (Princeton, 1968), excellent on the first part of his career; and Denis Silagi, *Der größte Ungar: Graf Stephan Széchenyi* (Vienna–Munich, 1967), a suggestive sketch. Cf. also the thoughtful assessment in C. A. Macartney, *The Habsburg Empire, 1790–1918* (London, 1968), pp. 243ff.

[2] Quoted in Barany, *Széchenyi*, p. 399. For a similar contemporary judgement, but from an enemy of Kossuth, see Zsigmond Kemény, 'Még egy szó a forradalom után' (1851), reprinted in *Változatok a történelemre*, ed. Gyula Tóth (B[uda]p[est], 1982), pp. 379ff.

113

Diaries. In them he reveals, day by day by day, both the spring for his activities, and many of his most intimate thoughts and emotions: Széchenyi as he saw himself; and as he saw others; and as he saw others seeing him, for he registers the praise and especially the criticism.[3] The Diaries were published over half a century ago; yet they are not altogether easy to use – alongside much allusiveness and obscurity, their extreme bulk, over 4,000 pages of printed text, is itself forbidding. To non-Hungarians they remain largely a closed book; but even from Hungarian historians they continue to withhold many secrets, despite the compelling nature of their contents. Whereas the Diaries have been fruitfully drawn upon as a store of political information, and called to witness to Széchenyi's psychological state, much can still be discovered in them about his intellectual ambience, while their immense value as a source for his social milieu has still hardly been exploited.

I

My purpose here is to examine one of the chief issues in that intellectual and social world of Széchenyi's. What can we learn from the unvarnished evidence of the Diaries, alongside that – at times scarcely less personal – of his other writings, about Széchenyi's relation to Austria, where he was born and died, and where he spent half his life? Wherein lay the significance for him of its culture, with which he was so closely acquainted, and of its German language, which he mostly used in the Diaries till the end? The conventional view identifies this dichotomy, but stresses a dramatic shift in Széchenyi's career from one pole of attraction to the other. There was, we are told, a fundamental tension, exposed in one of his most famous diary entries: 'The fault of the Austrian Monarchy and Hungary is that God in his wrath joined them together.' And is it not indeed indicative that this remark, though it dates from the early 1820s, should already be recorded in Magyar?[4]

Széchenyi, it is said, began as an 'Austrian'. He grew up in the highly conservative, even reactionary environment of his father Ferenc, who, when

---

3 The main sequence of Diaries covers the years 1814–48, and is printed as far as 18 March 1848 in *Gróf Széchenyi István naplói*, ed. Gy Viszota (6 vols., Bp., 1925–39) [hereafter *N*.]. For the sections covering the revolutionary months (19 March–5 September 1848) and the last months of Széchenyi's life (November 1859–March 1860), see below, nn. 98, 115. The circumstances of the Diaries' production are discussed by Viszota in his introduction to *N*., I, and by Barany, *Széchenyi*, pp. 58ff. On the express command of Széchenyi (who had initially wished them all to be burned after his death), some passages of an intimate, especially sexual, character were excised or obliterated by his secretary, Antal Tasner. These erasures – always indicated in *N*. – do not, I think, affect the present argument.

4 'Az az Austriai Monarchiának és Magyar Országnak hibája, hogy az Isten a haragjába kaptsolta öszve': *N*., II, 214. All those (shorter or striking) diary entries which have been left in German in the text of this essay are translated in the notes.

middle-aged and terrified of revolution, retired to live mostly in Vienna – only a day's ride from the family estates on Hungary's Austrian border. In 1809, the eighteen-year-old István joined the Habsburg army, and that military career alienated him further from any native element in his early experience.[5] During a misspent youth, which he later freely admitted, he enjoyed the salon life of Vienna in the age of the Congress, and a series of liaisons – all with Austrian, or rather Austrianised, women: he was a restless traveller.[6] From the 1820s, however, Széchenyi's priorities changed radically, and he became 'Hungarian'. Influenced by the political situation, as the country defended its traditional constitutional liberties against assault from Vienna, by new friends like Miklós Wesselényi, and by his own intellectual and emotional impulses, he quit the army and moved to what has been well described as an 'active but abstract patriotism'.[7]

Prodigal henceforth in pursuit of his ideals – 'mon tems, mes talents, ma fortune sont à ma patrie'[8] – Széchenyi developed a twofold programme. He championed Hungarian culture, with the famous offer of a year's revenue 'for flowering of the national spirit', which soon yielded an academy to refine and propagate the Magyar language, and much else besides, as well as a Hungarian theatre. As he demonstrated increasing verbal and written mastery of that tongue, so the German diary entries perhaps came to represent no more than a quaint survival.[9] At the same time Széchenyi created new social and economic institutions. He threw himself into organising horse-races (with attendances of 15,000 within three years), then broadened into agrarian improvement as a whole, from bloodstock to silkworms. He established 'casinos' as meeting-places and forums for debate. He promoted steamships, and better navigation on the Danube, Tisza and Lake Balaton. Above all he laboured for a bridge to span the river between Buda and Pest and reduce divides of class (by charging an equal toll) as of geography. In a series of treatises, the first major title of which was *Hitel* (1830), he exposed the rationale for his crusade.

5 Cf. András Gergely, *Széchenyi eszmerendszerének kialakulása* (Bp., 1972), pp. 13ff.
6 Cf. István Széchenyi, *Világ vagy is felvilágosító töredékek némi hiba 's előitélet eligazitására* (Pest, 1831), pp. 47ff., on the sins of his youth, and much agonised comment in *N*. Széchenyi was emotionally involved, at very least, with Caroline Meade, daughter of the (Irish) Earl of Clanwilliam and wife of his brother Paul; then with another married woman, Gabriella Saurau (a Hungarian Hunyady by birth); then with Selina Meade, younger sister of Caroline, who subsequently married a Clam-Martinitz.
7 Barany, *Széchenyi*, pp. 88ff.   8 *N*., III, 100f.
9 'A nemzeti szellem felvirágzására': *N*., II, pp. cxxxvii ff., 739–50, on the 1825 démarche. Cf., in general, *A Magyar Tudományos Akadémia másfél évszázada, 1825–1975*, ed. Zsigmond Pál Pach (Bp., 1975). Széchenyi came to employ Hungarian more frequently in the Diaries over the years, but usually in recording his own or others' direct speech. Passages in other languages – Italian, English, and especially French – sometimes appear for the same reason, but often seem to occur to Széchenyi spontaneously.

Whether basically liberal or conservative, whether spreading the vernacular language or creating an urban focus for the material advancement of the kingdom, Széchenyi's concerns were recognised by his countrymen as squarely national.[10] By 1840 he was quite simply a totem figure – though even this supreme accolade as 'größte[r] Ungar', like his first 'academic' initiative fifteen years before, is recorded in his Diary with characteristic misgivings. Furthermore, his activities were manifestly un-Austrian: bridge technology formed only the clearest evidence of English influence upon so many of his doings and ideas.[11] In one respect alone did Széchenyi hold back from full prosecution of the Hungarian cause: he scrupulously avoided any move towards political independence of the country, any confrontation with the essentially Austrian régime. In the mid-1840s he accepted a quasi-ministerial post with responsibility for waterways, especially for the formidable task of regulating the wayward River Tisza.

Széchenyi's association with Viennese government has usually been seen as tactical and contingent, an exercise in conflict limitation. As he put it already in 1826, apparently distancing himself from the central source of power even as he acknowledged it: 'The more I reflect on everything which concerns *our* relationship with Austria, the more convinced I am that any violence *from our side* is harmful.'[12] All Széchenyi's activities were viewed with much suspicion by the régime, and he often felt rebuffed and resentful. Yet he stayed in line, more or less, even in the authoritarian 1830s; then entered into closer alliance with Vienna, as part – arguably – of an aristocratic reaction against the Kossuthist opposition movement in the immediate *Vormärz* years.[13] As early as the cholera disturbances of 1831 – 'c'est le commencement de la fin' – Széchenyi undoubtedly nursed a powerful fear of revolution. Later this was heightened by the deterioration in Hungarian public order as the home-rule debate took root, and as his worries grew about the campaign for Magyarisation, the forced assimilation of minorities, afoot in the country. Hungarian historians are apt to indict Széchenyi of exaggeration in the latter regard, and of a degree of faint-heartedness in respect of the former.[14]

---

[10] The classic liberal portrayal is by Mihály Horváth, *Huszonöt év Magyarország történelméből, 1823-tól 1848-ig* (2 vols., Geneva, 1864), I, 151–3, 177–9, (esp) 194ff., 264ff., 463–7. Gyula Szekfű, *Három nemzedék. Egy hanyatló kor története* (2nd edn, Bp., 1922), pp. 51ff., is no less nationally bound in his famous conservative argumentation.

[11] *N.*, II, 642; III, 251; V, 422, etc.

[12] *N.*, III, 54 (my italics). For the general argument, see, e.g., Silagi, *Der größte Ungar*, pp. 37f., 56ff.

[13] On Széchenyi's relations with the secret police, see *N.*, iii, Introduction. János Varga, *Helyét kereső Magyarország. Politikai eszmék és koncepciók az 1840-es évek elején* (Bp., 1982), pp. 141–85, esp. 178, 183, stresses his class interest.

[14] *N.*, IV, 193; ibid., 168 ('In die Zunkunft sehe ich [in December 1830], oder dass das Land blühen wird, oder wir von den Bauern und dem kleinen Adel erschlagen'); V, 46, VI, 556f.,

The revolutionary months of 1848 seem to have rekindled all Széchenyi's national fervour. He gave strong support to the reform agenda, and held a portfolio in Lajos Batthyány's government, till an acute sense of personal responsibility for the deepening crisis, coupled – if the most expert analysis is to be believed – by his desolation when belatedly made aware of Austrian perfidy, unhinged his mind.[15] Having achieved partial recovery as a voluntary inmate of an asylum outside Vienna, Széchenyi revealed his true sentiments in bitter anti-Austrian recrimination during the 1850s. First he composed an astonishing satirical *tour de force* in Hungarian; then, omitting most of the venomous passages about the Emperor himself and rendering it into Széchenyi's equally labyrinthine German, he published it in early 1859 to exacerbate the problems of the Austrian authorities and cause them maximum international embarrassment.[16] This affair, though it proved the indirect cause of Széchenyi's suicide the following spring, confirmed his place in the national pantheon, and contributed mightily to Hungary's upsurge in the 1860s.

We thus find four phases in the received view of Széchenyi's relationship to Austria: youthful acceptance; maturer disavowal; limited collaboration; and eventual repudiation. Yet the problems of this relationship remain crudely formulated and little attended to. It is worth asking again how his perception of Austria contributed to the patriotic identity which Széchenyi created for himself; and how exclusive, consistent and coherent that identity was. Moreover, since ethnic allegiance is inseparable from other forms of inter-personal bond, we need to consider what kind of social space he occupied, what sort of community he actually belonged to. Did Hungary alone give him the necessary base for his life of action?[17] What of the attitudes of those who, on the evidence of the Diaries, were his close associates? Széchenyi's aristocratic values, loyalties and preoccupations, freely commented on in other contexts, are rarely adduced in this one. I shall refer particularly, as a marker, to his immediate relations and friends, notably those in the Zichy family.

588, 630 (reading Thiers, and later Lamartine on the French 1790s); cf., in general, ibid., pp. xxxvii ff. On all this: Horváth, *Huszonöt év*, II, 59ff., 122–6, 154f., 283–7, 377–9, 394ff., 467ff.; Varga, *Helyét kereső Magyarország*; Iván Z. Dénes, 'The Value Systems of Liberals and Conservatives in Hungary, 1830–48', *Historical Journal*, 36 (1993), 825–50, esp. 840, 849f.

[15] György Spira, *1848 Széchenyije és Széchenyi 1848-a* (Bp., 1964); also in English with more prosaic title as *A Hungarian Count in the Revolution of 1848* (Bp., 1974). Cf. below, pp. 135–7, and esp. n. 104.

[16] Domokos Kosáry, *Széchenyi Döblingben* (Bp., 1981); and cf. below, pp. 138–40, and esp. n. 110.

[17] As argued by Gergely, *Széchenyi eszmerendszere*, pp. 17ff.

II

From the first, Széchenyi wanted a fatherland. As he notes in 1815, it is the most perfect human attribute – alongside a happy marriage (for which he would have to wait), and even above love for women.[18] But what kind of *patria?* The young Széchenyi imbibed a vague sense of Austrianness just in those years, around 1809, when the Monarchy sought and attracted emotional recognition for her stance against Napoleon. His father's circle, which included immigrants from Germany and elsewhere, was a prominent vehicle for such conservative and Catholic patriotism. By the same token, the enthusiasm would ebb away, even suffer official discouragement, when the fighting was over. At the same time, Széchenyi already showed himself markedly critical of Austrian institutions and personnel: the country mocks serious thinkers; its representatives abroad are 'ludicrous'; its administrative is expensive and *untauglich*; its high politics are misconceived.[19] One strikingly unguarded comment about the essential fragility of the Habsburg state may have cost him his army promotion.[20]

Such outspokenness already foreshadowed the Széchenyi of the 1850s: perhaps, as I shall suggest later, one needed to be some sort of a patriot to feel so strongly. But it incorporated a Hungarian component too, not least in the grumbles about the army, where Széchenyi – a brave but hardly dedicated soldier – suspected ethnic discrimination and felt a tension with other kinds of loyalty.[21] Anyway he was always aware of Hungary as a territory and people. István could hardly be unmindful that his father had recently donated the family's collections to form a National Museum in Pest and continued to work hard to consolidate it; nor that his uncle, György Festetics, was doing the same for the material development of the country by founding an agrarian academy.[22] From boyhood, István was a genuine native speaker of Magyar,

---

18 *N.*, 1, 209f., 634.
19 *N.*, 1, 167, 235 (thinkers), 300 (representatives), 373; 11, 639 (administration), 130, 136, 146 (high politics). Commentary ibid., 1, pp. cxxxvii ff.; cf. Barany, *Széchenyi*, pp. 69, 76, 112. For Ferenc Széchényi (the family name was historically spelled thus: István – but not his brothers – dispensed with one of the accents), see László Bártfai Szabó, *A sárvár-felsővidéki gróf Széchényi család története* (3 vols., Bp., 1911–26), 11, 269–505; his milieu in later life, cf. Katalin Gillemot, *Gróf Széchényi Ferenc és bécsi köre* (Bp., 1933). See also, on the brief episode of 'Austrian' patriotism: Hellmut Rössler, *Österreichs Kampf um Deutschlands Befreiung. Die Politik der nationalen Führer Österreichs, 1805–15* (2 vols., Hamburg, 1940).
20 A. Fournier, *Die Geheimpolizei auf dem Wiener Kongreß* (Vienna–Leipzig, 1913), pp. 310–11.
21 *N.*, 11, 159f., 325 (discrimination); ibid., 11, 169, 442f. (loyalty).
22 Barany's calculation (*Széchenyi*, pp. 46, 83) that Széchenyi first felt Hungarian in 1809, and decisively so by 1818, is rather mechanical. On the Museum (mainly a library at first): J. Berlász, *Az Országos Széchényi Könyvtár története, 1802–67* (Bp., 1981), esp. pp. 9ff., 41ff., 63ff., 114ff. On Festetics: Dezső Szabó, *A herceg Festetics-család története* (Bp., 1928), pp. 119–313.

and his Hungarian education, directed by his tutor Liebenberg, prepared him for life by no means as badly as he later inclined to imply.[23] By the early 1820s he began to discover the country better, though still mainly as a place of garrisons and stud-farms. The experience was not a comforting one, eliciting a crescendo of invective in the Diaries about this 'armes gesunkenes Land'; the comment on 'God's wrath', cited above, dates from his first visit to Transylvania.[24]

Did this state of mind of Széchenyi as a young man amount to 'Austro-Hungarian' identity? Certainly he appears to have felt himself fairly indifferent about belonging to either polity or to both of them. One reference to the 'land in which I was born' surely connotes Austria; another seems wholly unclear; a third, with mention of the constitution, may have Hungary more in view.[25] A sudden pang when leaving England in 1815 for his 'armes unglückliches Vaterland' suggests Hungary; but abroad again, ten years on, he still feels for 'das arme alte Österreich'; and later mention of 'mein zurückgebliebenes Land' may likewise signify Austria. At times Széchenyi can act the ardent local patriot too, though never the adulatory one: 'armes kleines Vaterland' – he seems to be thinking of the rolling country of Transdanubia – 'bist ja doch garstig'.[26] But there is always an irreducible cosmopolitanism, reflected in the linguistic and cultural range of the Diaries, and a contempt for anything smacking of pettiness or xenophobia, above all in the high society of his dual homeland.[27]

More reflective and articulate, more ethical and idealist than most of his fellows, Széchenyi did not at this stage differ much in his loyalties from those around him. The immediate family was small: just parents, and his two brothers and two sisters, all senior to István. Most prominent was the eldest, Louis, who after endless bureaucratic delay in finding him a suitable position in the Hungarian administration, became major-domo to the Archduchess

---

[23] Language: cf. *N.*, I, 25, 175, 529; cf. Gergely, *Széchenyi eszmerendszere*, pp. 10f. It certainly grew somewhat rusty. Education: *N.*, I, 593, 702–4 (protesting his 'gänzliche Unwissenheit' as a young man); cf. Barany, *Széchenyi*, pp. 39ff.

[24] *N.*, II, 42, 53 ('poor sunken land'), 67f., 92f., 101ff., 107f., 166 ('Ungarn hat ausgelebt'), etc. Cf. above, n. 4.

[25] *N.*, I, 235, 457 ('mein Vaterland') with 459 ('unser österreichischer Handel'), 629f., 636f. ('mein Land . . . nie mehr zu sehen . . . Ich verliess Wien'). Such comments were regularly critical, as when the 'Miserie der Östreichischen Staaten' was only forgotten in a sense of the 'Dienst den jeder Mann seinem Vaterlande schuldig ist' (ibid., 686). Cf., in general, ibid., pp. cxlvii–cliv.

[26] *N.*, I, 165 ('poor unfortunate fatherland'); II, 568ff. ('poor old Austria'); IV, 49 ('my retarded land'); I, 461 ('poor little fatherland . . . how horrid you are').

[27] As in Széchenyi's disdain for the xenophobia of the young Count Ráday: *N.*, II, 72; cf. ibid., 89ff.

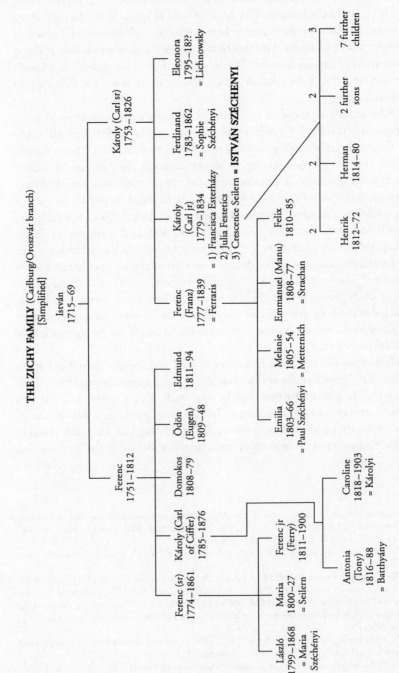

THE ZICHY FAMILY (Carlburg/Oroszvár branch)
[Simplified]

István
1715–69

Ferenc
1751–1812

Károly (Carl sr)
1753–1826

Ferenc (sr)
1774–1861

Károly (Carl of Ciffer)
1785–1876

Domokos
1808–79

Ödön (Eugen)
1809–48

Edmund
1811–94

Ferenc (Franz)
1777–1839
= Ferraris

Károly (Carl jr)
1779–1834
1) Francisca Esterházy
2) Julia Festetics
3) Crescence Seilern = **ISTVÁN SZÉCHENYI**

Ferdinand
1783–1862
= Sophie Széchényi

Eleonora
1795–18??
= Lichnowsky

László
1799–1868
= Maria Széchényi

Maria
1800–27
= Seilern

Ferenc jr (Ferry)
1811–1900

Antonia (Tony)
1816–88
= Batthyány

Caroline
1818–1903
= Károlyi

Emilia
1803–66
= Paul Széchényi

Melanie
1805–54
= Metternich

Emmanuel (Manu)
1808–77
= Strachan

Felix
1810–85

Henrik
1812–72

Herman
1814–80

2 further sons

7 further children

Fig. 6.1 The Zichy family (Carlburg/Oroszvár branch) (simplified)

Sophie in 1824.[28] The Széchényis were intimate with the dynasty and semi-Viennese, but not professional Austrians. That was left to the much larger clan of Zichys, their immediate kinsfolk (see Fig. 6.1) and owners of nearby estates, who came closest of any in the Hungarian political élite to storming the heights of Habsburg government. Carl Zichy senior, after rapid rise to the senior Hungarian dignities under Joseph II, became President of the Chamber, minister of war, and a member of the highest state council. But he also attracted censure, especially in Hungary, and even ridicule. Széchenyi often visited him in his dotage, and was not very impressed.[29] Carl had three sons, all István's older contemporaries. Franz married Molly Ferraris, one of the fashionable hostesses of Congress Vienna; their children would feature largely in Széchenyi's social circle, and not only Emilia, who married his brother Paul.[30] Carl junior followed in his father's footsteps as Habsburg administrator; his third wife, Crescence, was to play a crucial role in Széchenyi's life. The youngest son, Ferdinand, a soldier like Franz, became comrade-in-arms as well as brother-in-law to Széchenyi: Ferdinand was the first to predict great things for István – but in imperial service.[31]

By 1825 there seemed no immediate prospect of that. Frustrated in the army, and passed over for Louis's court appointment, Széchenyi now faced a political dilemma, as the rebellious Hungarian nobility forced a reluctant government to resummon the diet. The country needed a firm 'regimen'; but should this be enforced by gendarmes? It needed liberty; but just the liberty for lords to beat their peasants? Where, in this situation, did treachery lie?[32] Still slow to respond, to break with the rhythms of a metropolitan existence in Vienna and thought prompted by leisured reading of Voltaire or Madame de Staël, Széchenyi remained resolved that 'we should seek our interest in the general well-being of the Austrian Monarchy'.[33] Now, however, he sensed powerfully that the wider service of humanity to which he aspired had to

---

[28] *N.*, II, 384, 516. I have for the most part left the spelling of Christian names within the Szécheny/Széchényi (cf. above, n. 19) circle in the German or French or mixed forms used in *N.* On Louis (Lajos), cf. Bártfai Szabó, *Széchényi család*, III, 5–62.

[29] Zichy's political career remains unwritten. There are relevant documents in O[rszágos] L[evéltár] [= Hungarian National Archives], Budapest, P 707 and especially 708. Jokes about him: *N.*, I, 15; *Aus Metternichs nachgelassenen Papieren*, ed. Richard Metternich-Winneburg (8 vols., Vienna, 1880–4), III, 38f. Széchenyi's view: *N.*, III, 62, 70f.; he says Zichy was hated throughout Hungary at the time of his death: ibid., 93.

[30] Cf. *N.*, I, 132–4; Molly's association with Tsar Alexander I is documented in OL, P 708, rsz. 12, kútfő xxi. Cf. the latter's congratulations on Paul's marriage: ibid., fos. 15–19.

[31] *N.*, II, 426, 429, 444.

[32] Cf. *N.*, II, 339, 349, 352f., 361–4.

[33] *N.*, II, 449ff., esp. 490ff.: he remained in the capital during the whole period November 1823–May 1825; ibid., II, 617 (quoted).

proceed through a single *patria*,[34] and that it was Hungary which offered scope for his endeavours. It was Buda and Pest which needed a connecting bridge – even if Széchenyi first felt the need to make sacrifices for one, 'as a significant service to the fatherland', when hurrying back to Vienna in 1821. Hungary was here and now: 'hic Rhodus, hic saltus', as Hegel put it in that very same year.[35]

III

Széchenyi's comments on his pioneering zeal for the material improvement of Hungary often make it sound like the White Man's Burden. Virtue and satisfaction lie in the task itself, since conditions are so primitive, even repellent, and he expects no thanks. From the first he knows that 'these ingrates will hate me as long as I live'; and as late as 1846 things seem little better: 'C'est dans l'avenir que la Hongrie sera peut être aimable! – Ich liebe Ungarn aus muss . . . '[36] Whereas in his programmatic publications of the 1830s Széchenyi stressed how the country's very backwardness furnished the opportunity for reform initiatives led by ruler and aristocracy,[37] in private his disenchantment with apathy, barbarity and ugliness remained a constant theme. Religious metaphors spring regularly to his mind: 'There's a curse on everything; Hungary must have sinned very deeply.' So do unflattering comparisons with the outside world: 'Hungary appears to me as a great zero', he noted on a visit to Oxford in 1832.[38]

What really fired this high Gladstonian moral purpose for Széchenyi's homeland was a cultural programme, inextricably associated with it, for Széchenyi's nation: the ethnic, indeed racial – as the word was then understood – propagation of Magyardom. His Romantic vision was an organic one. Hence all the morbid imagery of Hungary as lifeless, as a corpse even, which stretches through his Diaries to the very eve of revolution: 'tout me dit que la Hongrie est morte; Ungarn ist nahe an seine Agonie'. Regeneration could only come through the Magyar nation, led by its nobility.[39] Already in 1814 Széchenyi showed himself conscious of coming 'aus der aller ächtesten race der

---

[34] *N.*, I, 224, in 1818: 'um ein Heil und Seegen bringendes Wesen dem Vaterlande und der Menschheit sein zu können'; repeated ibid., III, 101–3, in 1826: 'Mein Leben sey meinem Vaterlande, sey der Menschheit geweiht'; cf. ibid., 137.

[35] *N.*, II, 108. *Hegel's Philosophy of Right*, trans. T. M. Knox (Oxford, 1942), p. 11.

[36] *N.*, I, 609f. and VI, 416 quoted ('I love Hungary because I must'); cf. I, 688, 707ff., IV, 159.

[37] *Hitel* (Pest, 1830), p. xiv etc.; *Világ*, pp. 78, 103, etc.

[38] *N.*, IV, 559 and 310 quoted; cf. IV, 3, 12, 24ff., 34, 38, 40, 53ff. *passim*, 120ff., 250, 262f., 281, etc., from the early 1830s alone.

[39] E.g. *N.*, III, 183 and V, 729, 742f. ('Hungary is near to her agony'); cf. III, 187f., 225, 236, 248ff., 263f., 266, 271; IV, 484; V, 17, 735, 748; VI, 461, 484, 488, 511, 524, 532, 534, 576, 632. Cf. also Gergely, *Széchenyi eszmerendszere*, pp. 75ff., on the role of the nation in Széchenyi's thought. Examples of the language of regeneration: *N.*, III, 13f., 65.

huhnen', and as a young man he sometimes revelled in its pristine condition. But by 1821 he was worried about the fate of 'der alte ungarische Stamm' and agonising – like many another intellectual of the day – about how to handle 'das rohe Volk', whose crudeness stemmed from betrayal by their social betters.[40] Fascinated with Magyar origins, with the Hungarians as a 'people of the East' (the title of one of his most important writings), Széchenyi dabbled in the genteel orientalism of the period for the rest of his life: his identification with the central-Asian traveller, Körösi Csoma, led him to have a special miniature made of the explorer's tomb in Darjeeling, with his own senti-mental inscription.[41] He continually weighed up the racial pros and cons of the Magyars; worried about the prophecies of their national doom, first hinted at by Herder; lamented foreign ignorance of Hungary; agitated for the virtues of true ethnic community.[42] He sought to encourage Magyarisation of the other 'Stämme' in the country, though this theme, so conspicuous in his printed work, occupies much less space in the Diaries.[43]

Central to Széchenyi's commitment and his plans was linguistic nationalism. The démarche of 1825, when he broke with tradition by speaking Magyar in the Upper House of the diet, was indeed partly impelled by his real inadequacy in Latin: a few years later he actually set himself to learn the latter properly, 'to send my detractors to sleep'.[44] But the main fruit of his diet interventions was the establishment of a learned society 'for national spirit and the flourishing of the language', as the authorities – to whom that was no recommendation – put it. Although a broader educational and literary programme flourished around it, the main purpose for Széchenyi was promotion of the native tongue; he ardently supported the legislation which led to full official status for Magyar by 1844 and contemned fellow aristocrats who did not (yet) speak the language.[45] These concerns found their fullest

---

[40] *N.*, I, 45 ('from the most authentic Hunnish ["huhnen" = "Hunnen"] stock'); I, 168, 460 (pristineness); II, 156 ('the old Hungarian tribe'), 101 ('people in the raw'), 237 (betrayal).

[41] This small oil painting, in the Department of Manuscripts of the Hungarian Academy of Sciences, is described by Kornél Divald, *A Magyar Tudományos Akadémia palotája és gyűjteményei* (Bp., 1917), pp. 82–3. The 'people of the East': *A' Kelet népe* (Pozsony, 1841).

[42] *Világ*, 241ff. (race); *N.*, III, 320 (doom), 326 (foreigners); *Világ*, 63ff. (community). This last passage, with its stress on *nemzetiség* and *közértelmesség*, is important for the interpretation of Széchenyi in Szekfű, *Három nemzedék.*

[43] Examples of it there are the offence he feels at the absence of a Magyar element at Fiume, Hungary's only port (*N.*, III, 226ff.), and at Austrian praise of other nationalities in the country (IV, 266). The word 'Stamm' (cf. Hungarian 'törzs'), so popular at that time, conveyed overlapping senses of 'tribe' and of 'nationality'.

[44] *N.*, III, 19n., 774; IV, 34, 65, 87, 95, 131 (quoted), 167. For a while Széchenyi devoted himself to this task with his customary energy, despite his scepticism about the possibility of translating Adam Smith into Latin (IV, 160).

[45] *N.*, III, pp. lvii ff., esp. lxi–ii (quoted); cf. above, n. 9. *N.*, III, 110f., with scorn at one of the Nádasdys.

expression during the mid-1830s in a tract entitled 'Hunnia', which Széchenyi decided, for the time being, to leave unpublished – we shall encounter it again.[46]

How far did Széchenyi's activities for Hungary involve dilution of his 'Austrianness'? The question has a political and a cultural aspect. In political terms, Austria was a ruling dynasty, and a state coterminous with the authority of that dynasty. Széchenyi had no difficulty at all with loyalty to the imperial institution: it is revealing that he frequently refers to the monarch as 'Kaiser', even in strictly Hungarian contexts. Nor did Austrian statehood necessarily give him pause. Austrian government in this period singularly failed to evoke real ethnic affinity – after 1815 it hardly tried to – but by the same token it was, as a series of neutral instances, not necessarily challenged by national rivalries. 'Nation, Nation, was ist das?' asked Metternich of Széchenyi in 1839, then asserted: 'Staat ist alles.'[47] That sentiment, if problematical for the Habsburgs' Hungarian subjects, was no less so for their Germanic ones.

Széchenyi displayed continual impatience with the government's overall feebleness and incompetence, its misrule and arrogance in Hungary; the terms of his disapproval of a speech by the reactionary Chancellor Pálffy are that he 'spoke worse than an Austrian minister'.[48] Yet Széchenyi had hardly more time for the traditions of Hungarian separatism. A visit to the place of Rákóczi's Turkish emigration aroused no patriotic sentiments in him; and when the Rákóczi March became popular in the later 1830s he condemned it as roundly as the Marseillaise. 'Quelle horreur', he observed of the 'Jacobin' conspiracy of 1795.[49] He could well understand the Austrian view of his fellow nobles as tax-dodgers, who 'chatter about liberality and flay their own peasants'.[50] There are, it is true, certain contrary hints in the Diaries. Why couldn't Hungary be as independent as Mecklenburg, he asks while on a German tour – and curses the ancestors who neglected that fundamental requirement. At another point he speaks up for 'monarchie representatif [sic]' à l'anglaise. He may, however, have meant little more here than existing Hungarian constitutionalism – which he at other times thought they had too much of.[51]

That kind of comment was anyway rare; not in print and in public alone

---

46 Töredékek gróf Széchenyi István fennmaradt kézirataiból, vol. i: Hunnia, ed. János Török (Pest, 1858). Cf. below, pp. 125, 136, 138. At one point Széchenyi thought 'Hunnia' such an explosive text 'dass ich nicht recht sicher in Österreich [sic] werde bleiben können': N., IV, 502.

47 Examples of 'imperial' terminology: N., IV, 358ff., 528–30. Metternich quoted: V, 274 ('Nation, nation, what is that? State is all').

48 E.g. III, 189f., 351; IV, 281, 625 (quoted).

49 N., I, 343 (Rákóczi); V, 39, 402; cf. V, 413ff. (Marseillaise), and 243, 266, with disgust at the behaviour of the Hungarian public in general when fed with 'rev[olutionärer] Gährungsstoff'. On the 'Majestätsprocess': III, 371; IV, 29.

50 N., III, 96f.; IV, 190.

51 N., III, 331, 346 (Mecklenburg); V, 515 (constitution); cf. VI, 208.

did Széchenyi tend to stress loyal purpose and co-operation, what in *Hitel* he describes as 'concentration', especially to bridge the divide between Habsburg officialdom and the country at large.[52] While scrupulously avoiding claims for the Hungarian state in particular, he appears largely to eschew the vocabulary of 'state' in general. His obsession with 'good rule' for the 'common weal', to be achieved through rational processes,[53] with scant regard for local autonomous bodies, or for the privileges of the Catholic Church, may remind us – especially in the setting of the present Festschrift – of Joseph II. Széchenyi had mixed feelings about that controversial emperor, discussion of whom had provoked his earlier outburst about God's wrath. He comments favourably on Joseph's 'edles Wollen', despite 'weakness' and 'superficiality', and proclaims the need for a second Habsburg in that vein: hence his apparent willingness to embrace an 'intelligent tyrant' in 1847.[54] István must have recalled the strongly 'Josephinist' phase of his father's life in the 1780s – albeit Carl Zichy constituted a less distinguished link between that age and his own. At all events, many of those earlier reformist plans re-emerged in modified form in Széchenyi's 1830s proposals.[55]

Where Széchenyi differed radically from Joseph was in his perception of the whole Habsburg operation *sub specie Hungaritatis*. 'I seek my salvation in close association with Austria', he told Buda's commanding general in 1830; but added that there must be no 'Österreichisirung'. Over breakfast in London in 1834 he agrees with his ambassador friend Esterházy on two points: '(1) to bind ourselves tightly to our dynasty'; but (2) not to give up *unser Hungarthum*'. In a sort of 'profession de foi' – his own words – to the Upper House in 1839, he describes the link with the Habsburgs as the 'National-Schlußstein', but represents himself as an 'Ungar im strengsten Sinne'.[56] Undoubtedly some subjects of the Habsburgs were more equal than others in his eyes. 'In the Austrian Monarchy', as he put it in 'Hunnia', 'the Magyar is the chief nation'.[57]

Here we reach the cultural aspect of Széchenyi's thinking about Austrianness in the 1820s and 1830s. It was the supposed threat from German language and culture – indelibly associated in the Hungarian mind, of course, with Joseph II's strategy of rule – which prompted much of Széchenyi's rescue

[52] *Hitel*, pp. 171ff.; cf., e.g., *Világ*, pp. 106ff., 273ff.

[53] *Hitel*, pp. 76ff., 102 ('nem a munka, hanem a *jól elrendelt munka*, szóval az ész a nemzeti gazdaság talpköve'), 153; *Kelet népe*, pp. 131ff., and *passim*.

[54] *N.*, III, 306 (quoted: 'noble volition'); cf. above, n. 4; VI, 525 (tyrant).

[55] Cf. Gergely, *Széchenyi eszmerendszere*, pp. 139ff.

[56] *N.*, IV, 51 (1830: no 'Austrianisation'); IV, 450 (1834: sustain 'our Hungarianness'); V, 295 and n. (1839: 'national keystone', but 'Hungarian in the strictest sense').

[57] 'Az Austriai birodalomban a Magyar a fő nemzet', cited by Gy. Bárány, 'Széchenyi István nacionalizmusa', in *Európa vonzásában. Emlékkönyv Kosáry Domokos 80. születésnapjára*, ed. Ferenc Glatz (Bp., 1993), pp. 139–54, at 149.

package for the country, especially the academy foundation. As he said in 1840: 'We always had to fear the link with a powerful German intelligentsia menacing our nationality . . . A nation can attain everything, even a free constitution, but it cannot regain its nationality and idiom any more, once it has lost them.' By that stage, much had already been achieved; yet it had been touch and go, a mission to halt assimilation at, as Széchenyi believed, the eleventh hour.[58] Small wonder that he identified and approved an anti-German edge to his projects, a stance the more natural to him since, for all his Romantic sensibility, Széchenyi had been so little touched by the movement's great German expositors.[59]

The problem was first and foremost a domestic one. Can Hungary's liberty be assured without Magyardom, on a Slav or German base? The idea strikes Széchenyi as preposterous.[60] He nursed an at times deep mistrust of 'Swabians', the local German-speaking population, whom he suspected of demanding preponderance (hence also, though it is peripheral to the present argument, of Hungarian Jews, who were 'zu deutsch gesinnt'). To forestall the reverse process, the Magyar nation, the only true Hungarians, must absorb their German neighbours – Széchenyi's old tutor Liebenberg showed the way, changing his name to Lunkányi in the process. Széchenyi was enthusiastic about efforts to propagate Hungarian values in the German world, as by the Magyarised Swabian Kertbeny (*né* Benkert).[61] He saw his estate at Cenk, over against the Austrian frontier, as 'the first Hungarian community in the west and thus, so to speak, a Defence Post of our Hungarian Fatherland'. When one of his typical projects, a county mulberry society, ran into trouble, his first impulse was to blame 'das deutsche Element'.[62]

Széchenyi knew, however, that things were never so simple. In fact, he soon realised that only the 'teutsche[s] u. bürgerliche[s] Element' could rescue local silk cultivation, just as he appreciated the solid virtues of a prosperous Swabian *Bauer* whom he met along the lower Danube – the man could not and should

---

58 Barany, *Széchenyi*, pp. 358f., 366 (quoted) idem, 'Széchenyi István nacionalizmusa', 150. Cf. *Széchenyi István írói és hírlapi vitája Kossuth Lajossal*, ed. Gy. Viszota (2 vols., Bp., 1927–30), II, pp. cdxliv–v.

59 *N.*, IV, 46: 'Alle meine Anstalten griefen um sich – aber drehen sich gegen das Teutsche' (1830). Cf. the earlier sentiments at II, 100, and the evidence of Széchenyi's library catalogue: László Bártfai Szabó, *Gróf Széchenyi István könyvtára* (Bp., 1923).

60 *N.*, VI, 268.

61 *N.*, VI, 391: 'Aus Ungarn kann noch etwas werden, und zwar in ungrischer (mint ránk fogják: magyarischer, mi felette nevetséges, mert a Német, Görög, Olláh vagy Tóth csak nem "Ungar") und constitutioneller Entwickelung.' Notice especially the parenthesis. Liebenberg's influence on Széchenyi is stressed by Silagi, *Der größte Ungar*, pp. 72–3. On the Jews ('too German-minded'): v, 271f., n. K. M. Kertbeny, *Erinnerungen an Graf Stephan Szécsenyi* (Geneva–Basle, 1860), pp. 13ff.

62 Barany, *Széchenyi*, pp. 224f. (Cenk, in German Zinkendorf); *N.*, VI, 190 (mulberries and 'the German element').

not be 'hungarisirt'. Széchenyi stood close to prominent Hungarian Germans, like the devious but capable Wirkner, who had at least one foot in the Austrian camp.[63] Indeed, contemplation of the situation across the border only unsettled him: in Vienna, and especially in Bohemia, there was much to admire. In 1829 frustration with his compatriots' *Schlendrian* inclined him to 'forswear all my nationality and even become an Austrian'; and the unfavourable comparisons persisted. People in Bohemia are 'big and strong', even 'nobler' than those at home, and they are making faster progress.[64] Between governmental insolence, on the one hand, and aggressive Teutonism, on the other, Széchenyi still nursed some kind of affiliation with a better Austria.

IV

The personal dimension remained crucial in that search for affiliation. And the first person of *Vormärz* Austria was Prince Clemens Metternich. The young Széchenyi knew the State Chancellor (as Metternich became in 1824) only slightly, mainly via the Zichys. Metternich was on intimate terms with Carl Zichy and his family by 1815, using them as his source of information about Hungary; moreover, he nursed an unrequited passion for Carl junior's second wife (who, as a Festetics, was also related to István through his mother).[65] Then, in 1825, Széchenyi made a direct, private appeal to the Chancellor for support in his endeavours, pleading for 'mutual understanding'; but earned only a rebuff as a 'Decembrist', a 'hothead', full of 'vanity and *Ruhmsucht*', a 'lost soul' who misled others, though one quite responsive – thought Metternich – to his sagacious oratory.[66] It was the beginning of over two decades of interaction, a long series of one-sided dialogues, which continually frustrated Széchenyi, but which – equally relevant to our purposes – he always sought to keep alive.

The starting-point of *Hitel* only played into Metternich's hands: he promptly lectured Széchenyi on Hungarian backwardness. Then the

---

[63] Ibid. ('German and burgher element'). *N.*, IV, 60 (Swabian peasant from Futak). On Wirkner, besides the regular references in *N.*, see Ludwig von Wirkner, *Meine Erlebnisse* (Pressburg, 1879), esp. 188n., on the fate of Széchenyi's many letters to him.

[64] *N.*, III, 324f. ('Schlendrian'; i.e. carelessness, unconcern); VI, 515ff., 564, 567ff., 599, 612 (Bohemians); VI, 244ff. (Bohemia's progress). Cf. the much earlier thoughts, II, 170, 217; and István Gál 'Széchenyi and the Czechs', *Studia Slavica Hungarica*, 18 (1972), 129–45.

[65] *N.*, I, 262, 286. OL, P 708, rsz. 12, kútfő xxi, fos. 90–100, letters from Metternich to Zichy, 1813–15: 'Du weißt wie sehr ich in allen Gelegenheiten deine Ansichten theile, ich werde also in Allen Gelegenheiten beitragen sie geltend zu machen . . . Ich habe von hungarischen Gütern gar keinen begriff. Ich werde darnach deine Freundschaft in Anspruch nehmen und dich um Rath und beystand bitten . . .'

[66] *N.*, II, 644ff.; *Nachgelassene Papiere*, IV, 235ff. Cf. Erzsébet Andics, *Metternich und die Frage Ungarns* (Bp., 1973), pp. 45ff.; Barany, *Széchenyi*, pp. 123–34.

Chancellor quite misunderstood the reform plans laid out especially in *Stadium* – even if his Hungarian connections eventually persuaded Metternich to buy shares in Széchenyi's steamship company. In the mid-1830s there were further exchanges: Széchenyi aspired to convert Hungarian nobles from being 'drones in the Austrian beehive'; but Metternich still condemned his attempt to find a political middle way. Harangues from the Chancellor's side again took the place of ideas: on one occasion, according to the Diaries, Metternich spoke for one and a half hours, Széchenyi for two minutes – a fine fate for a compulsive talker with whom others could not get a word in edgeways. No wonder Széchenyi was scathing! Yet his visits to the palace on the Rennweg (the boundary-stone of civilisation, in Metternich's supercilious vocabulary) did not grow any less frequent.[67]

Metternich's links with Hungary in general and Széchenyi in particular were strengthened by Melanie Zichy-Ferraris, who became Clemens's third wife in 1831, having earlier been seen as a possible bride for István. Revealed in her own diaries as direct and homely, but uxorious and *borniert*, she was a Pooterish presence in Austro-Hungarian high society.[68] Instead of Melanie, with whom his relationship remained suitably mundane, or one of his earlier flames, Széchenyi eventually married Crescence Seilern, scion of a typical Austrian aristocratic family of mediocre accomplishments. His platonic infatuation for Crescence in the later 1820s and earlier 1830s, while she was the wife of another, furnished, by his own admission, a good part of the inspiration for all his initiatives: 'that demented love . . . from which all my actions spring'. It was also a major factor in his move to live in Buda-Pest, where her husband ran the Hungarian Chamber. In his fixation about Crescence's role, Széchenyi came close to identifying her with his motherland *tout court*: 'lebte C. nicht . . . wäre Hungarn nicht'.[69] The incongruity of this from a perspective of linguistic nationalism is apparent. In that constituency of well-born ladies whom Széchenyi was so concerned to address – with the

---

67 *N.*, IV, 24, 39 (*Hitel*); IV, 435 (shares); IV, 696–703 (quoted); V, 31, 384f., 770ff. (loquaciousness), and cf. the caustic comment at V, 79; V, 274 (Rennweg). See also, in general, Andics, *Metternich*, ch. 4, *passim*; Barany, *Széchenyi*, pp. 302ff., 319ff., 375ff.

68 *N.*, II, 640, 648, 663; III, *passim*. Melanie's diaries are printed as the first section of vols. V–VIII in *Nachgelassene Papiere*. Her comment on the revolutionary events of 13 March 1848 speaks for itself: 'Ich habe nie viel von den Menschen gehalten, aber ich gestehe, daß ich sie mir nicht so niedrig vorgestellt hatte.' Cf. also Heinrich von Srbik, *Metternich: der Staatsmann und der Mensch* (3 vols., Munich, 1925–54), I, 244ff. Grillparzer, *Sämtliche Werke* (Munich edn (below, n. 74)), I, 433f., 479, 1249, 1263, takes a dim view of Melanie.

69 *N.*, III, 236 ('wahnsinnige Liebe . . . '), 290, and cf. II, p. cxlvi; II, 532 n., and III, 144, 167, 197 (Buda-Pest)); IV, 597 ('Without C. . . . there would be no Hungary'). The Seilern family descended from an early eighteenth-century Austrian Chancellor, but had done little since. Crescence's brother, who likewise married into the Zichys, played his own modest part in the Age of Steam: he was General Commissioner of the First Austrian Steam Laundry and Bleaching Institute.

motto of *Hitel,* for example – and on whose obligation to know their native tongue he so insisted, the cynosure was an unredeemed German-speaker: his wife's proficiency in Hungarian never seems to have exceeded the level of a party piece.[70]

If, however, the ideal Crescence operated as a kind of Magyar demiurge, the flesh and blood one was a typical Austro-Hungarian and also a paid-up Zichy, widow of Carl junior. Through her, István gained an instant Zichy family (cf. Fig. 6.1): besides Crescence's own seven children, there were four adult (step)-stepsons, to whom Széchenyi became closely attached. Altogether his life was full of Zichys – over fifty of them appear in his Diaries for the years around 1840. Some gravitated towards magnate opposition (Lajos Batthyány and György Károlyi, two of Széchenyi's associates in the moderate reform interest, married Zichy sisters). Others filled executive positions in Hungary. Others again moved into 'Austrian' employment, most prominently Ferdinand, who rose to be a field marshal and military commander of Venice.[71] The Zichys, then, were true amphibians, and this may be the *mot juste* for Széchenyi too (if the pun be excused, with reference to a man so preoccupied with water, whether to swim in, sail on, travel over, or regulate). It proved fatal to his mission that there was no Austrian equivalent to such amphibiousness; hence the failure of that 'mutual understanding', which Széchenyi had advocated to Metternich. Contact with the rest of the Monarchy remained a social reality for Széchenyi; it did not become a meeting of minds. We shall shortly see the consequences of that for him in 1848 and beyond, but a brief comment is needed here on some Austrian views of the 'Greatest Hungarian'.

The state was notoriously suspicious of Széchenyi, and kept him under surveillance by police informants, albeit some of them reported on him reasonably favourably, recognising his work as a loyal mediator.[72] No less serious were broader unofficial attitudes towards the 'Hottentotten Land', as Széchenyi's banker friend, Baron Sina, described Hungary. At times Széchenyi felt totally unloved and humiliated as a Magyar in Vienna.[73] Austrian

---

[70] *N.,* II, 39: 'reizende Frauen' should speak their mother language; III, 146, 260, and IV, 266: but hardly any Hungarian ladies do. One closely connected exception seems to have been Emilia Zichy-Ferraris, to judge by the exchange recorded at IV, 544. For Crescence's own efforts with Hungarian: *N.,* III, 261, 271, 304, 366; V, 18, 25, 108, 160, 223, 268; VI, 302ff.

[71] Ferdinand Zichy's career can be pieced together from the documents in OL, P 708, rsz. 100, kútfő xlviii–il.

[72] *N.,* IV, 9–12, 66off., 684–92, with the censor's views on *Hitel* and *Világ.* At one point Metternich invited Széchenyi to comment on informants' reports: IV, 545ff.

[73] *N.,* VI, 279 ('land of the Hottentots'). Viennese attitudes: e.g. VI, 232: 'Ej be nem szeretik a magyart. Welche klägliche Figur spielen wir!' Cf., in general, the brief comments in R. J. W. Evans, 'Austrian Identity in Hungarian Perspective: The Nineteenth Century', in *The Habsburg Legacy. National Identity in Historical Perspective,* ed. Ritchie Robertson and Edward Timms (Austrian Studies, V, Edinburgh, 1994), pp. 27–36 at pp. 33f.

intellectuals discovered Hungary roughly when Metternich – and Széchenyi himself – did, but largely as antiquarians or Romantic enthusiasts for the *puszta*. Grillparzer, who had once been tutor to Crescence's brother, seemingly displayed no interest in Széchenyi (albeit the latter makes a ghost appearance in Grillparzer editions).[74] Bauernfeld merely noted Széchenyi's extreme Magyar feeling – and Széchenyi paid him back in the same coin, finding 'Dissolution und Subversion' in his play *Großjährig*.[75] The famous hostess Caroline Pichler seems to have been friends with Ferenc, not his sons; and although his brother Louis's literary salon continued something of the father's tradition, István had little to do with it. There was no contact, apparently, with Anastasias Grün (his poems are 'miserable', notes Széchenyi).[76] Nor did Széchenyi have recorded dealings with the émigré Nikolaus Lenau: predictably, perhaps, given his tendency to view Swabians as a fifth column, though he did develop harmonious relations with Franz Liszt. Széchenyi, even at the height of his career and powers, was still a *quantité négligeable* in Austrian eyes.[77]

V

In the 1840s Széchenyi's practical activities attained their fullest extent. Though based on Buda-Pest, his commercial undertakings were by no means narrowly Hungarian in their scope. The steamship company, the Erste Donau-Dampfschiffahrtsgesellschaft, like horse-racing from an earlier stage and the railways later, was a joint venture with Austrian enterprise and capital. Regulation of the Danube ought to lie in the interests of the whole empire, as Széchenyi insisted all along; and over railway-building he may

---

[74] Grillparzer, *en route* to Constantinople on 4 September 1843, between Mohács and Belgrade, met 'ein[en] Graf Seczen mit seiner liebenswürdigen Gemahlin. Beide sprechen recht gut': *Sämtliche Werke*, ed. A. Sauer, Abt. II, vol. XI (Vienna, 1924), p. 29, with gloss p. 285; cf. *Sämtliche Werke*, ed. P. Frank and K. Pörnbacher (4 vols., Munich, 1965), IV, 654. István and Crescence were in Pressburg at the time, besides being native speakers of German in a way which belies this reference. Perhaps Grillparzer did know how to write Hungarian names, more or less, and met a pair of Szécsens. Still, the complete absence of mentions of Széchenyi in his extensive diaries does tell a story. On Crescence, see also *Sämtliche Werke*, ed. Sauer, Abt. I, vol. XVI, p. 113.

[75] *N.*, IV, 531n., VI, 517.

[76] Caroline Pichler, *Denkwürdigkeiten aus meinem Leben*, ed. Emil Karl Blümml (Munich, 1914), II, 13–15. For Louis, see *Nachgelassene Papiere*, V, 91, 546; VI, 632; VII, 531; *N.*, VI, 338, 340, 346. Grün (Count Auersperg): IV, 229. Széchenyi did, however, meet the semi-official poet, Joseph Zedlitz: V, 73, 294, 375f.

[77] Dealings with Liszt: VI, 337ff. *passim*. Széchenyi even had little contact with the Austro-Hungarian prelate and poet Pyrker: cf. VI, 427. It took the inimitable Constant von Wurzbach to redeem this situation later, by giving Széchenyi a 38-page entry in his *Biographisches Lexikon des Kaiserthums Öesterreich* (60 vols., Vienna, 1856–91), XLI, 251–89.

actually have liaised with Metternich.[78] Already in 1833 he felt frustrated over a fruitless evening at the Metternichs', precisely because the economic 'future for the Austrian Monarchy' was at stake; he had stressed the same point in *Hitel*, and written its sequel, *Világ*, partly to deflect Hungarians' attention from their tariff grievances – while asserting that the Habsburgs needed to meet them half-way.[79] Széchenyi's industrial enterprises relied on Austrian and German finance and expertise (like the Buda rolling mill built by Swiss workmen, with a Viennese engine). Hence his robust opposition to the Védegylet, the Kossuth-inspired protection society: Széchenyi anticipated with some malice that Hungarians would soon be as sick of native products as Jews in the wilderness were of quails.[80] He insists – returning to an earlier metaphor – that his countrymen must find their greatness and satisfaction in an Austrian beehive; and repeats that they must not flourish at the expense of the Erblande which are – in another favourite expression – 'intermarried with us'. His 'basic purpose' continued to be that of persuading government that the development of Hungary was a key (maybe *the* key) imperial interest.[81]

At the same time Széchenyi withdrew from the cutting-edge of the Hungarian reform movement. Already in the mid-thirties he had disowned his old liberal colleague Wesselényi, even while defending him against persecution by the regime. Then came the crucial public step of his polemic with Kossuth and coolness towards Batthyány, Deák, and others when they failed to toe the Széchenyi line. Once his language goals had been achieved, thanks to almost the only productive diet legislation of these years, Széchenyi was more readily persuaded of the government's bona fides. Indeed, he now feared rather the excesses of Magyarisation, and this aggravated nationality problem at home only enhanced the significance of good relations with Austria. By 1845 Széchenyi moved to firm support for official initiatives to control ever more unruly opposition in the counties.[82] Did that now make him a conservative,

---

[78] In general: Vince Mészáros, *Széchenyi és a magyar vízügyek* (Bp., 1979). *N.*, IV, 65–7 and *passim* (Danube). Railways: Andics, *Metternich*, pp. 170ff.

[79] *N.*, IV, 433: 'Ich bearbeite die Aera einer Zukunft für die Österreichische Monarchie – man lässt mich antichambrieren, sollicitiren, etc. etc. etc. J'en suis indigné, mais je le souffre.' *Hitel*, p. xii, condemning those who 'szomszédink – kikkel közös Urunk van – kárán akarják alapítni a magyar szerencsét'; *Világ*, pp. 434f.

[80] *N.*, VI, 117ff.

[81] Varga, *Helyét kereső Magyarország*, pp. 141, 148 ('velünk egybeházasított'), 165. Cf., in general, Barany, *Széchenyi*, pp. 244ff.

[82] Much on all this in *N.*, *passim*; Széchenyi had been moving to such a position since at least 1842: cf., e.g., V, 559. For the background, see Hanns Schlitter, 'Die Wiener Regierung und die ungarische Opposition im Jahre 1845', in *Beiträge zur neueren Geschichte Österreichs*, vol. IV (Vienna, 1908), 241–95; idem., *Aus Österreichs Vormärz* (4 vols., Zurich etc., 1920), III, 4ff.; Varga, *Helyét kereső Magyarország*, pp. 185ff. Earlier, on the Wesselényi case: *N.*, IV, 526ff., 546, 617, 650, 653, etc.; on the breach with Kossuth: János Varga, *Kereszttűzben a* Pesti Hirlap. *Az ellenzéki és a középutas liberalizmus elválása 1841–42-ben* (Bp., 1983).

alongside his aristocratic friends like Apponyi and Dessewffy? Increasingly he was reputed so, despite his protests of being 'a man of progress', and his continual laments about Hungarian magnates' selfishness and superficiality.[83] Yet in fact Széchenyi's political goals stayed remarkably consistent from 1825 on, with similar mediatory manoeuvrings throughout, between the equal and opposite threats of 'separation' and 'amalgamation', as he put it in 1835, at the height of a trivial but intemperate dispute over whether the new ruler should be described in Hungary as Ferdinand I or V. As he nicely remarked on another occasion: where the likes of Wesselényi found devil's horns in the Vienna administration, he could only detect donkey's ears.[84]

This stance seriously compromised Széchenyi's patriotic reputation. Having 'honourable intentions for both Hungary and Austria', he felt himself between two stools: 'Here badly thought of, in Vienna no influence; j'ai perdu mon jeu.' He moped that nothing had gone right for him since he declared for the government, and that neither side would accept him: 'sie werden mich in Wien für zu Ungrisch – hier zu Österreichisch halten'. Particularly painful was the accusation that he was bringing Hungary 'auf einem österreichischen teutschen Fuss'.[85] On the other hand, Széchenyi found encouragement in his improving relations with the aged Palatine, Archduke Joseph, the first Habsburg to show any understanding of Széchenyi's purposes. (When he laid out a public park – shades of Joseph II again – the Palatine wrily suggested Széchenyi plant it with sunflowers and maize.) He was also in friendly touch with Bombelles, tutor to the young Archduke Franz: the future Emperor Francis Joseph must have been well informed about Széchenyi, passages from whose books were actually set for his Hungarian reading practice.[86] Even Metternich blundered towards a Széchenyi-esque view, and at last promised deeds rather than words, though there were still plenty of the latter, as when, ignoring most of Széchenyi's argument, the Chancellor 'spricht mir 3 Stunden a peu pres unverständliches Zeug', or lectures him on the lessons of peasant insurgency in Galicia without even offering him a seat. Metternich's 'Aphoristical Observations' on the Hungarian situation at the end of 1844 took side-swipes at Széchenyi's activities, but actually endorsed his priorities; by 1845 the two men seem more or less in agreement on the prospects of

---

[83] N., VI, 470 (quoted); e.g. III, 12, 227; VI, 599f. (complaints).

[84] N., IV, 559 (Ferdinand I/V); Barany, Széchenyi, p. 234 (donkey's ears).

[85] N., VI, 9 ('ich meine es ehrlich'); V, 760 ('I've lost the game'); VI, 154 ('Es gehet mir nichts vom Fleck . . . seit dem ich mich für die Regierung aussprach'), 203, 254 ('they'll find me too Hungarian in Vienna, too Austrian here'), 322 ('Austro-German footing').

[86] For relations with the Palatine: N., III, 158, 257, 264, 360, 377; IV, 48, 148, 155, 195, 237, 266, 275, 415, 425, 434, 459f., 484, 514ff., 554; VI, 173f. (sunflowers and maize), 240, 253. For Bombelles: V, 642f., 696, 711, 762, 772f.; VI, 8f., 19, 214, 231f., 288, 333, 354, 505, 741; cf. Dávid Angyal, 'Ferenc József ifjúsága', Századok, 68 (1934), 391–409, at 407.

revolution in the country.[87] And another telling semantic detail: whereas Széchenyi habitually refers to the Hungarian diet as merely a 'Landtag', it is actually Metternich who dignifies the assembly by designating it 'Reichstag'.

Széchenyi's personal links with Austria remained correspondingly important for him. Although his material ambitions centred on Pest, and he pressed for those to be crowned by removal of the diet thither, he long felt so rootless in the town and disgusted by its atmosphere that he contemplated moving away: in 1842 he still found the place 'dreckig und düster'.[88] Vienna had its irritations too, notably when old aristocratic acquaintances there referred to him patronisingly as 'Steve' (Stefferl); but it was a 'pays de Cocagne', whose social and cultural round he could enjoy, admire – 'was alles in Wien geschieht!' – and sometimes envy, and where he could imagine resettling for good. Moreover, it now became the focus for his political strategy, as he undertook negotiations at a high level with Kolowrat, Kübeck and other ministers.[89] Széchenyi's own quasi-ministerial office, the Tisza portfolio, notably enhanced his standing in Austria, and he seemed pleased to become *Geheimer Rat* and *Excellenz* – even while grumbling about inadequate financial help and taking offence that Crescence was not a *dame du palais*. At the same time this great civilian activist, despite his mixed experience in the Habsburg colours decades before, maintained cordial relations with senior army officers, including some who would be prominent in 1848: Lederer, Lamberg, even Windischgrätz.[90]

Most of all, the mature Széchenyi continued to find his confidants in the 'Austro-Hungarian' aristocratic milieu. They included the likes of Lamberg, born and bred in Transdanubia and author of a mildly reformist pamphlet

---

87 *N.*, v, 695f. *passim*, 764f.; vi, 154 (deeds), 7ff. and *passim* ('delivers me three hours of pretty unintelligible rubbish'), 337 (Galicia). The 'Aphoristische Bemerkungen' are in *Nachgelassene Papiere*, vii, 51–63. *N.*, vi, 287f. (revolution). In the 1850s Széchenyi and Metternich, in their very different kinds of retirement, seem to have felt a mutual esteem: Aurél Kecskeméthy, *Gróf Széchenyi István utolsó évei és halála, 1849–60* (repr., Bp./Bratislava, 1987), pp. 75f.; *DIH* (below, n. 98), i, 140f., 489.

88 Critical comments: e.g. *N.*, v, 158, 177, 243 ('Der Séjour von Pesth degoutirt mich bereits ganz ungemein'), 270f. ('Ich denke von hier ganz wegzuziehen'), 327, 414, 446, 600f. ('filthy and dismal'), 705. But by 1844 he is housebuilding (vi, 98, cf. 274f., 292ff.) and already in 1843 he calls for the diet to move there (v, 739). It should be borne in mind that the powerful Swabian and Jewish element in Buda-Pest was a running sore for Magyar patriots.

89 *N.*, iv, 213, vi, 350 (the 'Stefferl' tag, commented on as late as 1846); v, 4 (Cocagne), 382 ('It's all going on in Vienna ... Der grösste Neid erfasst mich'), 584 ('wie froh und zufrieden dort alle Leute'), 275, 506 (thoughts of resettling in Vienna, or at least living there jointly with Pest, though contrast v, 683, vi, 172, 175). For the negotiations: e.g. vi, 190ff.; cf. the odd thesis of Gyula Miskolczy, *A kamarilla a reformkorszakban* (Bp., [1938]), but with its grain of truth, that these men frustrated a Széchenyi–Metternich reform programme.

90 *N.*, vi, 209ff. *passim* (appointment), 349 (lady-in-waiting). Many references to Lederer, iv, v, vi *passim*. Lamberg: see next note. Széchenyi had known Alfred Windischgrätz since his youth, though he was no friend, and perhaps sometimes an enemy.

on *Ungarns politische Zunkunft*.[91] They also still included a lot of Zichys. Besides spending much time with his step-stepsons, Henrik and Herman, and attending to the needs of Crescence's own Zichy offspring at Viennese schools, Széchenyi in the 1840s moved close to an elder branch (see Fig. 6.1), the children of Minister Carl's first-born brother, several of whom were active in Hungarian public life. Ferenc Zichy senior (not to be confused with Ferenc Zichy-Ferraris), twenty years older than Széchenyi, was a conservative, like his son Ferenc junior ('Ferry'), already an important loyalist lawyer and administrative officer: the latter fought a duel over his antagonism towards the Védegylet. Carl ('from Ciffer', as he was known, to avoid confusion) did not win the favour of Széchenyi, who described him as a patriot only till he had to open his purse; but Széchenyi endured him for the sake of his spirited daughters Caroline (Károlyi) and Antonio or Tony (Batthyány).[92] Then there were the much younger siblings: at Domokos, a reactionary bishop, Széchenyi again drew the line, whereas Eugen and Edmund, both whole-hearted government supporters, were his regular companions in social, sporting and political circles.[93]

Széchenyi stood equally close to the younger generation of Zichy-Ferrarises, who were – it may be recalled – Metternich's in-laws as well as his. Felix mediated between Széchenyi and the régime, and acted as an energetic administrator of Vas county; whereas his elder brother Emmanuel ('Manu') moved towards mild opposition. Széchenyi's intimate relationship with Emmanuel and his wife, the 'charmante . . . sehr aimable' Englishwoman Charlotte, *née* Strachan, must be reserved for analysis on some other occasion.[94] But it was typical of the ambience in which he moved in the 1840s, from the summer days spent in country houses on the Austrian border, through the encounters at race-meetings or commercial functions, to the constant attendance at the theatres of Pest, German as well as Hungarian,

---

91 *N.*, IV, 487, 646; V, 498, 600, 631, 635, 722, 731, 735, 740, 780; VI, 29, 32, 34f., 41f., 113, 131f., 207, 253, 279, 289, 333, 509, 533, 556.

92 *N.*, VI, 117ff. (Ferenc Zichy jr's duel), 241, 259 (cifferi Károly Zichy).

93 Domokos seems to have been the brains behind the notorious (and perhaps government-backed) drive against Ferenc Deák's candidature as delegate to the diet from Zala county: András Molnár, 'Deák Ferenc és a zalai liberális ellenzék megbuktatása az 1843-as követválasztáson', *Levéltári Szemle*, 37 (1987), 2, 47–59. Széchenyi's contacts with Eugen (known in Hungarian as Ödön) and Edmund are far too numerous to be recorded here, and extended to Danube trips (*N.*, V, 478ff.), athletics (V, 432, 460), swimming and Hungarian theatre (e.g., VI, 185, 227), even plans for joint house-building (VI, 596ff.).

94 On Felix, e.g. *N.*, VI, 190; cf. OL, P 708, rsz. 98–9, kútfö xlviii, with records of the county congregations etc. Széchenyi first met Emmanuel and Charlotte in the summer of 1840 (*N.*, I, 407), then again in 1841 (V, 495), and increasingly often thereafter. From 1844 he was seeing more of them than of almost anyone else, both in Pest and at Carlburg (Oroszvár). The relation with Charlotte was evidently close, and important to Széchenyi, but frank and not without friction.

punctuated by István's scathing comments on most of the productions in both languages. This world-view remained cosmopolitan and grand-seigneurial; typical of it was the excessive (and quite unworthy) gratification which Széchenyi derived, in his feud with Kossuth, at introducing the latter to a visiting Frenchman in full knowledge that Kossuth would be unable to sustain a conversation with him.[95]

VI

On the eve of the revolutionary events of 1848 Széchenyi was subject to bouts of desperation. He worried about the future of the nation: 'Mein Volk, mein Stamm – der Magyar ist in Agonie.' Even more, he worried about radicals and 'enthusiasts'. He worked openly to frustrate the designs not only of Batthyány in the Upper House of the diet, but also of the 'charlatan' Kossuth in the Lower: 'I offer myself as a holocaust', he said, on seeking election there, while also endorsing the suggestion that Kossuth would be a more suitable victim.[96] Then came the March days, and the last meeting with a Metternich suddenly very attentive to his views, and with the incurably silly Melanie ('Bonjour citoyen', she said to István, 'merci délicieuse sansculotte', he replied). As the régime collapsed, Széchenyi's first impulse was to summon a conference amid his fears for 'our homeland and especially our nationality . . . our race'.[97] Yet his second was to rally dramatically to the national political cause in a mood of apparent euphoria. Suppressing his premonition of 'complete dissolution', Széchenyi acknowledged that the gamble of Kossuth and Batthyány had worked. That is clear enough on the pages of his Diary; still clearer in his correspondence: 'I am full of the most beautiful hopes . . . It seems to me as if heaven has at last opened up for us Magyars.' He even took the lead in stretching the scope of the Pragmatic Sanction to heighten the constitutional role of Hungary's Palatine.[98]

---

[95] For this episode, see *N.*, v, 625. Széchenyi clearly did give the Hungarian theatre a rather higher priority than the German one (cf. vi, 595), but he experienced frustration with it too (e.g. v, pp. xliv–lxiii). His opinions about Magyar literature appear to have been mixed: though he wishes that Crescence could read Berzsenyi (iii, 227f., 298), he describes a work by Károly Kisfaludy as a 'bêtise' (ii, 439f.), and takes a thoroughly 'Austrian' view of Katona's *Bánk bán*: 'Unbegreiflich, dass es die Regierung erlaubt solchen Unsinn zu spielen – Schlechte, gefährliche Tendenz' (*N.*, v, 259f.).

[96] *N.*, vi, 181 (quoted: for 'Stamm' and 'Agonie', cf. above, nn. 39, 43), 636, 657 (nation); 685f., 719, 724 (outbursts against Batthyány and Kossuth); 650 (holocaust).

[97] *N.*, vi, 740 (Metternich); pp. xlv–vi, 743f. (conference).

[98] *N.*, vi, 746ff. ('Heute sehe ich Ungarn gehet seiner vollkommenen Auflösung entgegen'); Spira, *1848 Széchenyije*, pp. 28–32 (quoted), 11ff. (role of the Palatine), 128–30 and *passim*. Széchenyi's diary entries for the period 19 March to 4 October 1848, long separated from all the preceding ones by the accident that they were part of his property confiscated from Döbling in 1860, are printed in *Gróf Széchenyi István döblingi irodalmi hagyatéka*, ed. Árpád

Was this a cautious calculation that Széchenyi's ultimate goals could now be achieved directly, and that those goals essentially involved personal union alone? 'Henceforth Hungary will no longer be a misunderstood and always undervalued colony of Austria', as he told the diet, 'but a self-sufficient country which turns on her own axis.' He even approved separate Hungarian administration of finances and the army.[99] If we bear in mind, however, that Hungary's changed role within and beyond the Monarchy came as a surprise to all, should we not see Széchenyi's response rather as heady enthusiasm, associated with a temporary belief, not only that nothing so far was illegal or damaging to the Habsburgs, but, on the contrary, that it served his vision – as in 'Hunnia' – of strengthening the Magyars so that their constitutional traditions could benefit the rest of the Monarchy?[100] The previous year he had already registered the need for national self-assertion: 'Ungern muss eine eigene Achse bekommen, oder mit Österreich ganz verschmelzen.' But the context seems strictly that of economic tutelage. Now he continued to regard Hungary as 'an *integral* part of the whole Empire' (*közbirodalom*), and to envisage fiscal and military affairs regulated 'in engem Zusammenhang mit der Monarchie'. Whereas he joined his new colleagues in resisting the assumption of any Austrian debt, that was linked to the expectation that the Habsburgs would soon move their seat of government to Buda.[101]

Széchenyi threw himself into activities as Minister of Public Works, with Ferenc Zichy junior as his deputy and a staff of Austrophiles. There was no money – but anyway routine quickly became overshadowed by the constantly deteriorating situation. First, domestic strife revived all Széchenyi's terrors: 'The Slavs will annihilate us, since they loath us, and with justice . . . The Magyar race will be extinguished.' He agonised ever more as a Croat invasion loomed. But concern for the relation between Hungary and Austria came to subsume all these fears, aggravated by a terrible sense of personal responsibility: 'I've ruined the whole country *and the whole*

Károlyi (2 vols., Budapest, 1921–2 [hereafter *DIH*], 1, 275–390). On 11 April, the day of the April Laws, he writes: 'Herrlicher Moment! Fühle mich ergriffen! Obschon das Grab sich vor mir aufmacht!' (ibid., 294).

99 See Spira, *1848 Széchenyije*, p. 85 (quoted), 128–30, and *passim*. On the 'joint affairs', see the draft printed in *Széchenyi István írói és hírlapi vitája*, II, pp. cccl–li; cf. Spira, pp. 88ff.

100 Ibid., p. 200; cf. Barany, *Széchenyi*, pp. 296ff. My impression is, *pace* much Hungarian historiography (e.g. recently Varga, *Helyét kereső Magyarország*, pp. 115ff.; Dénes, 'Value Systems', 833f.), that Hungary's oppositional politicians took the constitutional relationship with Austria almost as much for granted as Széchenyi did before 1848. The one conspicuous exception, Miklós Wesselényi's *Szózat a magyar és szláv nemzetiség ügyében* (Leipzig, 1843), was dismissed by Széchenyi at *N.*, v, 714.

101 *N.*, VI, 581 ('Hungary must acquire an axis of her own – or merge with Austria totally'); Spira, *1848 Széchenyije*, p. 85 ('integrans része a közbirodalomnak'); *Széchenyi István írói és hírlapi vitája*, II, pp. cccl–li ('in close connection with the Monarchy'); Spira, pp. 105f., 218ff. (debt and move).

Monarchy.'[102] The last straw was the Austrian note of 31 August to Batthyány's government, claiming that all Hungarian legislation since March had been unconstitutional, including the role of the Palatine. Bidding a pathetic farewell on 5 September to his city and his bridge – which he would never quite see completed – the demented Széchenyi entered on a desperate journey, punctuated by suicide attempts, which ended at Dr Görgen's sanatorium on the edge of the Vienna Woods.

Historians agree: Széchenyi's 'madness' was not merely physical or psychological, although he did suffer in both those ways, from internal ailments, particularly of liver and kidneys (exacerbated by continual overeating!), and from remorse and penitence. It derived from real factors in his personal life and in the Hungarian situation at mid-century.[103] Széchenyi was driven into insanity partly by his sense of guilt over Hungary's fate – that refrain, now endlessly repeated, had its roots much earlier, as with his unease when passages from *Hitel* were allegedly read aloud to rebellious peasants in 1831; but also by the breakdown of the whole symbiosis apparently achieved in the March days, by the destruction of an ideal greater Austro-Hungary. No less, surely, can be signified by his anguished reference to 'this frightful world-historical catastrophe, of which we stand on the threshold'. This it was – rather than outrage at Vienna's perfidy, still less some kind of recreancy – which unseated Széchenyi's reason in the aftermath of the Austrian ultimatum.[104]

Széchenyi's breakdown in September 1848 coincided with the flight, at his prompting, of his assistant Ferenc Zichy. Worse soon followed for the Széchenyi circle. Eugen Zichy, apprehended in contact with the Austrian authorities, was executed by the local Hungarian army commander. Lamberg, sent by the Austrian side as a mediator, was murdered by the Buda-Pest mob. Felix Lichnowsky, another relation on the Zichy side, underwent the same fate in Germany.[105] Loyalties were deeply divided: whereas Edmund sought to

---

[102] *DIH*, I, 295, 306, 311, 316f., 354 ('whole Monarchy' [my italics]), 359, 368, etc.; cf. Spira, *1848 Széchenyije*, pp. 110, 201ff., 268, 276ff.

[103] There is a good discussion by Viszota in *N.*, IV, pp. xxv ff.

[104] *N.*, IV, 222, 226, 241 (1831). Spira, *1848 Széchenyije*, pp. 304ff. (quoted). Spira argues, against conservative commentators, especially Viszota (in *Széchenyi István írói és hírlapi vitája*, II, pp. cdxiii–liv), that Széchenyi's collapse followed from recognition that Batthyány and Kossuth had been right all along, but his evidence – e.g. the last draft of a letter before madness set in – is not very persuasive. At the same time it must be allowed that the testimony of Görgen, who reported that Széchenyi accused himself of betraying the dynasty as well, is not always reliable either.

[105] *Széchenyi István írói és hírlapi vitája*, II, pp. cdxxiv–v, on Ferenc Zichy; contrast Spira, *1848 Széchenyije*, p. 333. On Eugen Zichy and Lamberg, whose mission, condemned by most Hungarian historians, is better represented as 'the last attempt to save the Monarchy in its old decentralized form': István Deák, *The Lawful Revolution. Louis Kossuth and the Hungarians, 1848–9* (New York, 1979), 175f., 171–3. Lichnowsky was the son of István's Zichy sister-in-law.

mobilise Habsburg troops, and the decamping Domokos temporarily forfeited his property to the new state, their sisters became bitter enemies of the dynasty. Crescence's children also split between supporters and opponents of a separatist Hungary; so did the brothers Felix and Emmanuel, the latter's marriage to Charlotte failing to survive the conflict.[106] Meanwhile Ferdinand Zichy, that might-have-been Austrian Széchenyi, had spent the mad March days surrendering Venice to the Italian insurgents. This dereliction of duty, though by no means all Ferdinand's fault – its antecedents are recorded in his unpublished correspondence with Radetzky and others – earned him a sentence of ten years in prison. After eighteen months, this was commuted to house arrest at Pressburg and on one of the family estates.[107]

Széchenyi too endured some eighteen months of quasi-durance vile, followed by house arrest, which was, in his case, more or less voluntary. While his delirium persisted, he eschewed most personal contact and fell prey to bouts of frenzied self-castigation. During these paroxysms, Széchenyi, scarred but uplifted by the experience of 1848, imagined Hungary as a potential paradise, giving the lead to the rest of Habsburg central Europe, even gradually assimilating it. That was – it will be recalled – the theme of 'Hunnia'; and when some mental stability returned, Széchenyi indeed looked to publication of that treatise.[108] He also gradually reverted to some social intercourse, receiving a trickle of visitors from among his pre-revolutionary friends, most of them now pillars of that political grouping which came to be known as 'old-conservative'.

From the mid-fifties, Széchenyi took up his pen again, writing violent satirical diatribes against 'Osztrákia', the regime of Francis Joseph and Alexander Bach, that despicable exercise in centralisation and *Gleichschaltung*. These hundreds of pages in manuscript Hungarian are full of deeply felt, highly intemperate and personalised abuse, but their larger significance lies elsewhere. They are obsessed with the threat, at home and especially from abroad, to the survival of the Monarchy, its great-power status endangered

---

106 Edmund – revealingly – even earned an entry in the *Allgemeine Deutsche Biographie*. On Domokos: Erzsébet Fábián-Kiss, 'A honárulók vagyonának lefoglalása és kezelése: az 1848–49-es pénzügyi adminisztráció egyik speciális feladata', *Századok*, 128 (1994), 46–89, at 87f. Caroline Károlyi's hatred of the Habsburgs, particularly in the aftermath of the execution of her brother-in-law Batthyány, was experienced by her grandson: Mihály Károlyi, *Egy egész világ ellen* (Munich, 1923), pp. 19f. I hope to treat the fortunes of the Zichy-Ferrarises in and around 1848 on another occasion; there may have been some collusion between Felix and Emmanuel in their attitude to the revolution.

107 Documents in OL, P 708, rsz. 99, kútfő xlviii, fos. 495–500, 'Meine Verteidigung'; rsz. 100, kútfő xlviii–il, fos. 91ff., including letters from Radetzky, 594ff., 522, 624, 630. The brothers-in-law had not had much contact since their dealings over the military career of one of István's stepsons (*N.*, vi, 174).

108 Some of the moving letters from his madness are printed in *DIH*, i, 427–46; cf. Kosáry, *Széchenyi Döblingben*, pp. 7f. (visions), 167ff. ('Hunnia').

by the catastrophic politics of neo-absolutism. Moreover, the critique is a conservative one, which even laments the alienation of Russia.[109] The essentially domestic theme of breakdown in pristine Austrian harmonies was, however, soon to take over again, in the last and most extraordinary of Széchenyi's published works.

VII

The *Blick auf den anonymen Rückblick* was provoked by a peculiarly vapid, condescending and tasteless government propaganda pamphlet about the beneficial transformation of Hungary under direct rule from Austria since 1849.[110] Not least of the *Blick*'s peculiarities – beside the enigmatic title and the circumstances of its own anonymous publication – is the format: it affects to comprise fragments passed to the putative editor 'F.K.' by a dying Hungarian émigré. 'F.K.', however, is German, and he decides to publish the work, in order to give 'us Germans' food for thought, to show how unpopular his nation has made itself in the world. The international situation certainly still mattered to Széchenyi; but more central now was surely the parallel thread of a reckoning with Vienna's cultural claims, with a decade of unrestrained German nationalism, destructive not just of Magyar nationhood, but of Austrian traditions and Austrian compromises, in the name of a factitious neo-Austrian state. Should we not see 'F.K.' as a part of Széchenyi's persona too? Hence the constant in-jokes about the Vienna milieu, and the withering home-truths which are that much nearer the knuckle for being delivered in the Austrianised German patois to which Széchenyi still committed his innermost thoughts. The dearest wish of Hungarians, according to the *Blick*, is to join with the rest of the Monarchy, on the right terms for all; but the currency of Austrian patriotism has been debauched, by those who should have guarded it most fiercely.[111]

The *Blick* openly espoused the Old Conservatives' cause, announcing that

---

[109] Good discussion ibid., pp. 91ff. Cf. Széchenyi's earlier comment, from 1843, on how the Russian ambassador 'kennt unsere [i.e. the Monarchy's, not Hungary's] Schwäche vortrefflich' (*N.*, v, 704).

[110] The full title indicates this: *Blick auf den anonymen 'Rückblick' welcher für einen vertrauten Kreis in verhältnismässig wenigen Exemplaren im Monate October 1857 in Wien erschien.* It appeared in London in early 1859: cf. *DIH*, I, 52ff., 175ff.; Kecskeméthy, *Széchenyi*, pp. 92ff.; Kosáry, *Széchenyi Döblingben*, pp. 123ff. For the circumstances of this *Rückblick*, see R. J. W. Evans, 'From Confederation to Compromise: The Austrian Experiment, 1849–67', *Proceedings of the British Academy*, 87 (1995), 135–67.

[111] *Blick*, pp. 355ff., for this assumption. It is true, as Kosáry, *Széchenyi Döblingben*, 175f., points out, that Széchenyi filtered criticism of Emperor Francis Joseph out of the *Blick*; yet home-truths remained for the dynasty too – Archduke Albrecht is a prime target – to be pondered in its own best interests. Kosáry seems to exaggerate the role of foreign policy considerations in the *Blick*.

their recent petition to the ruler was backed by the whole of Hungary;[112] it echoed a chorus of dissent from Austrian nobles too about their exclusion from authority. Altogether, Széchenyi's political vision, now that he finally came to broach the subject in print, proved distinctly traditional and aristocratic, like his mode of utterance, still more arcane, bewildering and self-indulgent than before, though brilliantly effective for the initiated. It gave final literary expression to the concerns of his Austro-Hungarian relations and friends – but now became rather 'Hungaro-Austrians' by a mixture of alienation and neglect. Zichys remained to the fore: besides the immediate family, the aesthete Edmund was one of Széchenyi's most regular companions; Henrik composed an *Offenes Promemoria*, a short, fierce, anonymous pamphlet in the spirit of the *Blick*. Even the ultra-loyal Felix expressed his dissatisfaction in the 1850s.[113] All contributed, innocently, to István's nemesis. The authorities, in their unwisdom, had long feared some internal conspiracy hatched by conservatives as much as any Kossuthist insurgence abroad. Publication of the *Blick* could hardly fail to confirm them in their suspicion and direct them to reprisals against Széchenyi, so patently its author. His personal tragedy was symbolised by his asseveration to the police chief who came to carry out a house search at Döbling: 'My fatherland was never just Hungary, but the united Austrian state.'[114] If my interpretation stands, that was perfectly true.

On 7 April 1860 István Széchenyi, seated in his armchair, blew out his brains with a shotgun. It was Easter eve: the terminal symbolism of regeneration is numbing. Readers of his Diaries will recognise that theme, as well as others: 'I have no luck and Hungary is dead – and so I must die' (1831).[115] His Austrian legacy proved fateful for Széchenyi: both assimilation and separation were deadly to him, yet he was no man for the status quo. In his deepest derangement, around the first anniversary of the March days, he accused himself of provoking 'the ferment which has destroyed old Austria'. A trivial but emblematic illustration of the same predicament had been his impasse

---

112 *Blick*, pp. 112ff.; cf. Kosáry, *Széchenyi Döblingben*, pp. 213ff.; Miksa Falk, *Gróf Széchenyi István utolsó évei és halála* (1866, repr. Bp., 1984), pp. 54ff.

113 On Edmund: Kosáry, *Széchenyi Döblingben*, pp. 250, 258; Kecskeméthy, *Széchenyi*, pp. 99–104. The anonymous *Promemoria*, so close to the spirit of the *Blick* that it was still attributed to Széchenyi in *DIH*, II, 214f. and n., is assigned to Henrik by Gyula Viszota, 'Ki az Offenes Promemoria szerzője?', ed. Vilma H. Boros, *Századok*, 105 (1971), 1205–16. On Felix: OL, P 708, rsz. 99, kútfő xlviii, fos. 481ff.; cf. *DIH*, I, 79.

114 *DIH*, I, 461: 'sein ganzes sehr actives Leben dem Wohl der herrschenden Dynastie und seines Vaterlandes – das er nie ausschlisslich in Ungarn, sondern im vereinigten österreichischen Staate fand – treu und ehrlich widmete'.

115 *N.*, IV, 210f. On 2 October 1859 Széchenyi had resumed writing his Diary, and he continued it, beginning in another book when one was confiscated at the beginning of March, until 1 April 1860. These entries (printed in *DIH*, I, 393–423) are on the whole briefer and less revelatory than those which ended in 1848, but similar in manner.

when the foundation stone to one of the bridge piers was laid in 1845: Széchenyi declined to make a speech, since he thought German would be inappropriate for it, but Hungarian would be farcical. His bitterness about the ruin of German–Hungarian relations became an *idée fixe*.[116] Its concomitant was the demise of international Austrianness. Thirty years before, in a remarkable passage in *Hitel*, Széchenyi had condemned the cosmopolitan as a wandering, characterless and ridiculous creature, a 'chained dancing bear', who would end in self-destruction.[117] As so often in the *oeuvre* which we have been examining, his words were both personal and prophetic.

[116] *DIH*, I, 428 (ferment); *N.*, VI, 242 (bridge); Kertbeny, *Erinnerungen*, pp. 23ff. (bitterness).
[117] *Hitel*, p. 162.

7

PAST AND FUTURE IN THE LATER
CAREER OF LORD JOHN RUSSELL

തോന്ത

J. P. PARRY

IN 1856, the Stroud Mutual Improvement Society heard its most distinguished member talk about history and biography.[1] That speaker was experienced in both literary forms. He had published the life of a famous ancestor, and had edited three other biographical works; he had written a history of eighteenth-century Europe and various historical essays. But he was also Stroud's former MP, and the country's former prime minister: Lord John Russell, the subject of this essay. Russell is perhaps a particularly appropriate subject for treatment here. This is partly because of the importance of historical study and example for his own political career. It is also because one of Derek Beales's many interests as a teacher and writer has been to restore Russell from long neglect to his proper place in the nineteenth-century Liberal pantheon.[2] In 1930, Tilby commented that 'fame has treated few men more scurvily';[3] fifty years later, the position had hardly changed. Russell's only postwar biographer, John Prest, produced important unpublished material but paid little attention to his views or to many of his policy initiatives.[4] Twenty years ago Derek Beales almost took up the challenge; but in the event Joseph II's gain has been Russell's loss. Recent work, which he has largely inspired, has helped to rectify the situation.[5] But the major reassessment is still awaited.

---

[1] Following Tacitus, he argued that the historian required 'the calmness of a judge' and the biographer 'the zeal and passion of the orator': *Times*, 16 May 1856, p. 7.

[2] See, for example, his 'Peel, Russell and Reform', *Historical Journal* 17 (1974), 873–82, esp. 880–2.

[3] A. W. Tilby, *Lord John Russell* (London, 1930), p. vii.

[4] John Prest, *Lord John Russell* (London, 1972).

[5] Principally Richard Brent, *Liberal anglican politics: whiggery, religion and reform 1830–1841* (Oxford, 1987), whose account of Russell's intellectual influence on whiggism in the 1820s and 1830s is illuminating and important. I have tried to emphasise Russell's significance in my *The rise and fall of Liberal government in Victorian Britain* (New Haven, 1993) and in an essay in *The Routledge Dictionary of British Prime Ministers*, ed. R. Eccleshall and G. Walker

This essay does not attempt anything so bold. It aims to shed light on Russell's political philosophy, and to examine the part of his career which has done most damage to his reputation, and which Prest treated most lightly: the 1850s. Until that decade, Russell's contribution to British history had been incontestable. He led the Liberal party in the House of Commons from 1834 to 1855 and in government for over fourteen of those years – a longer period of governing power than any other politician has enjoyed since 1832. He should take much of the credit for the Reform Act of 1832, the Municipal Corporations Act of 1835, the repeal of the Test and Corporation Acts in 1828, the new Irish policy from 1834, the abandonment of the death penalty other than for murder or treason, the vigorous programme of church and education reform in the 1830s, the attack on the corn tariff in the 1840s, and the beginnings of public health reform. In the 1850s, his career was overwhelmed by disaster. He must bear some of the blame for his fate: the Durham letter of 1850, the sacking of Palmerston in 1851, the resignation from Aberdeen's cabinet in January 1855 and the disastrous Vienna affair that spring must count among the 'gross blunders' to which, at the end of his life, he admitted.[6] But these were not the main reasons for his eclipse, which was caused, as we will see, by the deranged party system of the 1850s.

Russell's decline in the 1850s was assisted by one other factor which has damaged his subsequent reputation: the hostile propaganda about him circulated by some radicals and by his Peelite and Palmerstonian rivals for the Liberal leadership. The latter were competing with him to rally MPs behind a stable non-Conservative government. His title to support was legislative reform, which they disliked. They retaliated by presenting him as a relic of the politics of aristocratic faction, out of touch with the needs of a commercial society. They had a set of weapons ready at hand for this job. Russell believed that it was the duty of the whig aristocracy to take a high-profile leadership role. So in 1846 he had included eight peers (including his father-in-law), an Irish peer and an heir to an earldom in his cabinet of sixteen. This policy made it easy for disappointed place-hunters, angry radicals, or socially insecure Oxbridge meritocrats like Lowe and Harcourt, to mock his following as a 'mere family party'.[7] Russell compounded this reputation for social exclusiveness because of his shyness and taciturnity. Always delicate, he had not endured the socialising experience of a public school education, and

---

(forthcoming). Another stimulating recent book to take Russell seriously, though not from the Beales stable, is Peter Mandler, *Aristocratic government in the age of reform: whigs and liberals, 1830–1852* (Oxford, 1990).

[6] Russell, *Recollections and suggestions 1813–1873* (London, 1875), p. 221.
[7] See e.g. Roebuck, *Hansard['s Parliamentary Debates*, third series], CXIX, 128, 3 February 1852; Duchess of Argyll, *George Douglas eighth duke of Argyll: autobiography and memoirs* (2 vols., London, 1906), I, 362.

preferred quiet literary talk to hot, noisy, superficial London society. His preferences were strengthened by his protective, unworldly, cloyingly religious second wife; after 1847 they would retreat to Pembroke Lodge in Richmond Park, granted to them by Queen Victoria, for half the week even in the parliamentary session.[8] Russell's shyness could easily make strangers think him abrupt, proud and self-centred, and increased his reputation for hauteur. He seemed to take no advice from outside his uncritical family circle. In crises, this advice was frequently to take, or to cling to, office. Russell saw this as public-spirited behaviour; to his critics it was 'self-seeking, place-loving ambition' on his part, and sheer greed on the part of assorted Russells and Elliots (his second wife's family) who stood to benefit from government patronage as a result.[9] Russell seemed oblivious to these charges. He led the opposition to the introduction of competitive examinations for the civil service, on the grounds that character, not cramming, was the best test of fitness for government service.[10] In 1855, after Russell had tussled long and hard with Gladstone about the latter's sacking of a distant relative of his, Gladstone remarked, topically if insensitively, that Russell was 'like the soldiers in the Crimea, overrun with vermin'.[11]

Peelites and meritocratic Liberals played up Russell's perceived élitism because they wished to reorganise the party behind a policy of financial and administrative efficiency instead of his reformism. Supporters of Palmerston also smeared Russell with anti-populism in order to lower his reputation, exploiting his unwillingness to join Palmerston in bidding to the press and popular galleries on foreign policy issues. In dismissing Palmerston as Foreign Secretary in 1851, Russell had appeared to be doing the bidding of the Germanic court, just as he had been accused of un-English and illiberal prejudices when sympathising with the French during the Eastern crisis of 1840. Helped by his press contacts, Palmerston was adroit at presenting himself as an opponent of European despotism. Russell, by contrast, disdained flattery of the press as beneath the dignity, and unnecessary to the standing, of a *real* Liberal leader. Unfortunately this attitude and the abruptness with

---

8 D. McCarthy and A. Russell, *Lady John Russell: a memoir* (London, 1910), pp. 72–3, 87–8, 92–3.

9 *The diaries of John Bright*, ed. R. A. J. Walling (London, 1930), p. 185; E. Hodder, *The life and work of the seventh earl of Shaftesbury* (3 vols., London, 1886), II, 488; F. W. H. Cavendish, *Society, politics and diplomacy 1820–1864* (London, 1913), p. 283; M. C. M. Simpson, *Many memories of many people* (London, 1898), p. 165.

10 J. B. Conacher, *The Aberdeen coalition 1852–1855: a study in mid-nineteenth-century party politics* (Cambridge, 1968), p. 321.

11 '. . . and Mr Fortescue': a selection from the diaries for 1851 to 1862 of Chichester Fortescue, Lord Carlingford, ed. O. W. Hewett (London, 1958), p. 80. Gladstone, as Chancellor of the Exchequer, had removed the obstructive T. F. Kennedy, the brother-in-law of Russell's wife's brother-in-law, as a commissioner for woods and forests.

which it was conveyed, was bound to offend vain editors like Delane of the *Times*; Russell had no more permanent enemy than the *Times* during the last twenty years of his career, to his great disadvantage.[12]

In explaining the transition from whiggism to Liberalism, most twentieth-century historians have paid much more attention to Peelites, radicals and Palmerston than to Russell. It has also become an unquestioned (though not unquestionable) assumption that, from the 1860s, the existence of a commercial society and an increasingly democratic system required the party of movement to develop a new form of popular politics capable of joining up the parliamentary élite and the masses in a way that leaders of Russell's generation had not, and could not have, done. The most impressive and eloquent twentieth-century historians of Victorian Liberalism have tended to work within the Gladstonian, Fabian or Cobdenite traditions: Morley, Hirst and Hammond; Ensor, Briggs and Matthew; Taylor, Hanham and Vincent. In this context, Russell's reputation has not flourished; he is often marginalised as little more than a class-bound aristocrat, 'Finality Jack'. One distinguished historian describes him in the 1850s as 'an obsolescent Whig'; his modern biographer dismisses his opinions as 'partisan and antiquated views' based on Charles James Fox.[13]

These judgements will be challenged here. But they are not incomprehensible. Indeed Russell delighted in portraying himself as the defender of Fox's creed and the inheritor of a ready-made philosophical position. His nephew, the journalist G. W. E. Russell, had good reason to write that in sixty years of public life Russell never deviated from the creed which he professed on entering parliament in 1813.[14] One more blow to his reputation as a progressive in the 1850s was his determination to celebrate Fox's memory in four volumes of correspondence, published between 1853 and 1856, and three volumes of biography, which appeared from 1859. But did an admirer of Fox have to be an obsolescent whig? This essay argues otherwise. It first examines Russell's political creed, which has been largely lost to posterity, but was coherent, indebted to Fox, yet developed to suit new circumstances. It was very relevant to the needs of the Liberal party in the 1850s, as is shown in the second half of the essay, which analyses Russell's political situation in his years in opposition between 1855 and 1859. Despite his difficulties, he remained capable of building an attractive Liberal coalition, founded on a series of issues

---

12 *The history of 'The Times': the tradition established 1841–1884* (London, 1939), pp. 201, 592; A. I. Dasent, *John Thadeus Delane editor of 'The Times': his life and correspondence* (2 vols., London, 1908), I, 311, 313.

13 O. Chadwick, *The Victorian Church Part I* (London, 1966), p. 232; J. Prest, 'The decline of Lord John Russell', *History Today*, 22 (1972), 396.

14 G. W. E. Russell, *Prime ministers and some others: a book of reminiscences* (London, 1918), p. 21.

which foreshadowed the more policy-oriented Liberalism of the years after 1867. In so far as any one man deserves much credit for the scope of that new Liberalism, it was Lord John Russell.

I

Russell's position in the whig party of his youth has been distorted by historians' over-concentration on parliamentary reform, which he advocated. His major role was that of scholar and moralist, and it was a role which he never abandoned. The whigs liked to reserve cabinet places for licensed thinkers, learned men who could bring perspective and a historical dimension to knotty problems. Between 1830 and 1834, Russell was Paymaster-General, the same virtual sinecure which he gave Macaulay in 1846 in order to give him 'leisure and quiet' to continue his *History*.[15] By 1830, Russell had written not just about the British constitution but also about Europe in the eighteenth century, the Turks, the French revolution and his great-great-great-grandfather, as well as a book of essays on fashionable mores, two works of fiction, and a translation of Homer. He was 38, as yet unmarried, a shy, withdrawn bookworm. His reputation was as an earnest, emotional *littérateur*, a budding noble sage. Throughout his career, his political standing continued to be influenced by his intense religious belief and his developed political, historical and literary sensibility. Central to his political outlook was his stress on the importance of historical understanding and Christian charity.

Russell himself loved history intensely; he regularly read aloud to his family and 'could scarcely command his voice when the story was very touching'.[16] In his view, the purpose of history was *not* to supply precedents for current action.[17] Rather, it was a guide to human behaviour, national character, and the folly of overbearing government. It encouraged a statesmanlike breadth of understanding about the possibilities and foibles of the human condition.

The great lesson of history was the tendency of men in authority to lose their virtue, abuse their powers and repress human potential.[18] Bad government threatened the progress of civilisation. Spain had declined because of spiritual repression during the Counter-Reformation which, by undermining

---

[15] G. O. Trevelyan, *The life and letters of Lord Macaulay* (2 vols. in 1, Oxford, 1978 edn), II, III, 117. Russell joined the cabinet in June 1831, while retaining this post.

[16] B. Champneys, *The honourable Adelaide Drummond: retrospect and memoir* (London, 1915), p. 160.

[17] That was a Tory view, in his eyes, inappropriate for those who believed in progress: see e.g. his retort to historically based Tory criticisms of his 1839 education proposals in Parry, *Rise and fall*, p. 138, and his comments in *Recollections*, pp. 29, 177.

[18] Russell, *An essay on the history of the English government and constitution, from the reign of Henry VII to the present time* (London, 1865 edn), pp. xcvii, 236–7; and at Exeter Hall, *Times*, 14 November 1855, p. 10.

individual virtue, had made Spaniards only 'half men' and sapped national energy.[19] The most influential interpreters of Christianity had invented doctrines like the Athanasian creed, transubstantiation, or predestination, which justified amoral personal behaviour and preyed on the sinful, greedy, supercilious and aggressive aspects of the human character – so fomenting division, persecution, war, torture and slavery in the name of a God who had preached the duty of forgiveness, tolerance and eternal love.[20] Clumsy misuse of power was also possible in modern societies. Russell pointed to the rigid political economists of the 1820s; their ideals were benevolent but inflexible, taking insufficient account of the diverse customs, habits and manners of different communities and nations, and therefore repressing human energies – a mistake they would not have made had they, like the whigs, had a broad understanding of continental cultures.[21] The same fault could be found with radical constitutional reformers who sought to govern men by utopian theory, failing to understand that a constitution could no more be invented overnight than could a tree.[22]

In hundreds of speeches, Russell proclaimed his loyalty to the opposite ideal, Fox's great 'cause of civil and religious liberty all over the world'. Liberty was not to be confused with democracy, which threatened to unleash repressive passions and check progress.[23] A crucial benefit of real liberty was the spread of enlightened religious and moral principles. The English constitution was a good example: parliamentary government forced rulers to develop character in order to retain influence, while an enshrined freedom of conscience best facilitated the victory of Christian principles. The progress of western civilisation was intimately bound up with the values enjoined by Christianity: faith, hope and charity. The New Testament taught men that their sins would be redeemed by loving God with heart, soul and mind, and by loving their neighbours – the human race.[24] Studying the marvels of science, scenery and natural history instilled wonder at 'the perpetual efficaciousness of [God's] will and laws'; applying God-given human energy and industry to natural resources augmented wealth; developing one's mind and natural feeling through contact with literature and music deepened one's humanity; the duty of loving one's neighbour stimulated philanthropy,

---

[19] *Recollections*, p. 180; *Times*, 16 May 1856, p. 7. Similarly, the military failure of France in 1870 could be blamed on her inferior morality: Russell, *The foreign policy of England 1570–1870: an historical essay* (London, 1871), p. 92.

[20] Russell, *Essays on the rise and progress of the Christian religion in the west of Europe from the reign of Tiberius to the end of the Council of Trent* (London, 1873), passim.

[21] Russell, *Essays, and sketches of life and character* (London, 2nd edn, 1821), pp. 128–36.

[22] Ibid., p. 183; see *Recollections*, p. 179.

[23] See e.g., *English government*, pp. xcvi–xcvii, 252, 263–4.

[24] *Rise and progress*, passim, e.g. pp. 11–16, 23, 46.

nurturing the spark of divinity which God had planted 'in the breast of every man'.[25] The spread of 'sound, moral, and religious instruction' would lead men to redemption – and to 'the paths of duty', industry and 'advantage . . . to the country', thus diminishing popular vices and assuaging discontents.[26] So Christianity developed human virtues and energies, and hence civilisation. Conversely, the ultimate cause of the decay of empires was the loss of that virtue and energy, the triumph of the sinful rather than the moral qualities in human nature. If institutions were corrupt, a popular reform movement might save them; but if morals were rotten, there was no chance of regeneration.[27]

Underlying this argument was an appreciation of the immense power of public opinion, for good or bad. This was a natural response to the French revolution and the immense political and social turbulence of the early nineteenth century.[28] Russell held that opinion was 'queen of the world',[29] a force so potentially powerful that no individual could check it. This had great implications for the politician's role. In Fox's career, Russell admired most his courageous refusal to support Pitt's war against France in 1793, because he understood, as Pitt did not, that the popular uprising in France was too elemental to be stopped – especially by an alliance with autocratic powers.[30] Russell contrasted that situation with the one applying after Fox's death, when there were genuinely nationalist movements in Europe, which it was the duty of an imaginative statesman to harness against Napoleon.[31]

The politician's crucial task, then, was to assess the state of opinion. Usually, it was by no means impossible for 'sensible men' to guide it.[32] Some-times it was turbulent but immature and could be restrained; sometimes it was too sluggish and needed stimulating. The assessment and guidance of opinion made politics 'one of the noblest in the whole circle of human employment and arts'.[33] Very often, law had not caught up with opinion and needed adjusting. Sometimes constitutional structures needed altering in order to

---

[25] Ibid., pp. 57, 254; address at Leeds, 1852, reprinted in anon., *Literary addresses delivered at various popular institutions; second series* (London, 1855), pp. 139–42; Russell, 'The general aspect of the world: does it teach us to hope or to despair?' (1864), in *Rectorial addresses delivered in the universities of Aberdeen 1835–1900*, ed. P. J. Anderson (Aberdeen, 1902), p. 151.

[26] *Hansard*, XXXVIII, 914, 19 May 1837, and XCI, 966, 19 April 1847; Parry, *Rise and fall*, p. 134.

[27] *English constitution*, p. 341; 'General aspect', pp. 139–43 (on the fall of Rome).

[28] Russell blamed the French revolution on the conjunction of 'a monarchy apparently absolute, and [Enlightened] public opinion totally at variance with that monarchy': *Times*, 16 May 1856, p. 7.

[29] *Rise and progress*, p. 164.

[30] Russell, *The life and times of Charles James Fox*, vol. III (London, 1866), pp. 205–6, 357, 393–6.

[31] Ibid., pp. 400–4. Russell was better placed than most to appreciate this, because he had toured Spain in 1808–9, 1810 and 1812–13, and had been caught up in the romance of the patriots' struggle.

[32] *Rise and progress*, p. 165.

[33] Quoted in G. Waterfield, *Layard of Nineveh* (London, 1963), p. 298.

ensure a better representation of matured opinion and so allow law-makers
to do a better job. The politician must be alive to movements of opinion and
determine the most beneficial laws that they would allow. Keeping law
and opinion in some sort of accord was essential. On law and government
depended 'the prosperity and morality, the power and intelligence, of every
nation'.[34]

In Russell's eyes, his task as an honourable politician was to do what he
could to promote the Christian ideals which he equated with progress. This
imposed several responsibilities. It was important, for example, to be a patriot,
a judicious defender of Britain's place in the world as a bulwark of libertarian
values. Her 'eminence as the home of a vigorous and independent race of men'
ensured for her a great destiny abroad, and all patriotic politicians should
assert it, on Fox's principles – not by bullying, by populist gestures, or by
unjustified bloodshed, but equally not by succumbing to the cowardly and
selfish principles of peace without honour, or a feeble army and navy.[35] At
home, the crucial task was to use government to develop the moral rather than
the vicious qualities of humanity.[36] State power must not be used repressively,
or to weaken individual responsibility. The state's role was to reform
structures so as to check neglectful or corrupt administration, stimulate local
leaders to fulfil their responsibilities, and work with what appeared the virtues
rather than the vices of the population. These assumptions helped to under-
pin the 1832 Reform Act, the 1835 Municipal Corporations Act, and Russell's
Irish policy, subjects too vast to be discussed here.[37] But they also explain three
specific domestic initiatives which are relevant because Russell persisted with
them in the 1850s.

One was to ensure that neither politicians nor clerics infringed the culture
of religious toleration that promoted the spread of simple Christian morality.
Hence Russell's support for Dissenting, Jewish and Catholic emancipation. In
the 1840s and 1850s, he believed that the greatest threat to toleration was posed
by the High Church school which sought to constrain Anglican doctrinal
latitude – thus denying the Church of England's destiny as the nation's
church, the embodiment and protector of English freedom of thought.[38]
Hence his determination that the state's powers and patronage should be used

---

[34] *Hansard*, IV, 345, 24 June 1831.
[35] See e.g. *Foreign policy of England*. For Russell on Fox's principles in foreign policy, see
Memorials and correspondence of Charles James Fox, ed. Russell (4 vols., London, 1853–6), IV,
490–2. The quotation is from Russell's speech in *Transactions of the National Association for
the Promotion of Social Science 1858*, ed. G. W. Hastings (London, 1859), p. 24.
[36] *Times*, 14 November 1855, p. 10, and (on Ireland) *Recollections*, p. 313.
[37] See Parry, *Rise and fall*, chs. 3–6, 9; Brent, *Liberal anglican politics*, ch. 2.
[38] *Rise and progress*, pp. 307–8. For the background to this, and Russell's response, see
Chadwick, *Victorian Church*, I, ch. 4.

to assert that latitude, as over the Hampden appointment (1847) and the Gorham judgement of 1850. Hence also his shift of policy over church rates in 1859.[39]

A second, connected, duty was to promote access to education. Russell was a lifelong supporter of various voluntary educational societies, most importantly, the major undenominational association, the British and Foreign Schools Society, of which he was Vice-President and then President from 1824 until his death in 1878. From the late 1830s, he was also the politician most associated with the extension of state support for elementary education. He was drawn to this by a moral impulse to rescue children from vice and sensuality, which was intensified by the death of his first wife in 1838, his anxiety about Chartism, and his hostility to the attempt by the High Anglican National Society to increase its own influence over teaching.[40] For him, education must, first and foremost, be religious, in order to 'raise the character of the people'; ideally, it should also be historical, so as to assist 'sober and sound' judgements on current affairs.[41]

Finally, the legislative machine should encourage virtue not vice in other ways. The young Russell was particularly appalled by the savagery of the criminal law, especially when applied to the poor who had 'never been taught their duty to God and man'.[42] It was un-Christian; by lowering the state's character, it also discouraged loyalty to authority. In the 1830s, 'the humanity of the country' made possible the abolition of many capital statutes, on his initiative; this response demonstrated the state's benevolence, just as Fox had shown his 'love for the human race' in opposing the slave trade.[43] These principles help to explain Russell's involvement in education and public health reform, and his periodic attacks on the fortress erected by the legal profession to defend its profits at the expense of providing cheap justice to all. 'If you cannot afford to do justice speedily and well, you have no right to raise taxes – justice is the first and primary end of all government.'[44] But Russell was no sentimentalist about the rule of law. He had no illusions that an elementary

---

[39] He abandoned opposition to repeal when he became aware that the only alternative was undesirable: that nonconformists, in return for exemption from the obligation to pay the rate, should lose the right to participate in Church government. See J. P. Ellens, 'Lord John Russell and the church rate conflict: the struggle for a broad church, 1834–1868', *Journal of British Studies*, 26 (1987), 232–57.

[40] On Russell and education in 1838–9, see I. Newbould, 'The whigs, the Church, and education, 1839', *Journal of British Studies*, 26 (1987), 332–46. On the influence of his first wife's death, see S. Walpole, *The life of Lord John Russell* (2 vols., London, 1889), I, 329, and *Recollections of Lady Georgiana Peel*, ed. E. Peel (London, 1920), p. 25.

[41] *Hansard*, XCI, 1221, 22 April 1847; *Times*, 16 May 1856, p. 7.

[42] *Recollections*, p. 374.

[43] *Hansard*, XXXVIII, 914, 19 May 1837; Russell on Fox, in R. E. Prothero, *The life and correspondence of Arthur Penrhyn Stanley* (2 vols., London, 1893), II, 510.

[44] Quoted in G. W. E. Russell, *Prime ministers*, p. 23.

duty of the state was to keep down the 'evil . . . passions' in man.[45] As Home Secretary in the late 1830s, he was responsible for the move towards a more rigorous prison régime. He also remained a staunch defender of the discipline of the New Poor Law, which in his eyes was an attack on crime as well as pauperism.[46] In this and other ways, he, like many intellectual whigs of his generation, was confident that the state's power could be used to assist the process of reforming human depravity, aided by scientific inquiry into the causes of human behaviour (what was to become known as social science).

Where does parliamentary reform – the cause with which Russell will always be associated – fit into this model? It was a crucial part of the whigs' agenda in the specific circumstances of 1830 because they needed to abolish the rotten boroughs which underpinned Tory rule, and to diminish the power of some commercial vested interests which benefited from the peculiar seat distribution and franchise mechanisms. A rhetorical cry against 'old corruption' was also useful in holding together a large cross-class governing coalition, thus securing power and restraining some of the more utopian cries unleashed by the apocalyptic frenzy which accompanied the depression of 1829–30. Younger whigs like Russell hoped that these changes would provide the government with the broad and energetic backing needed to push forward a legislative agenda.[47] In other words, the concern was with the political tactics needed to bring about an activist programme, much more than with constitutional philosophy. Russell was hardly more wedded to Reform as an abstract principle than Fox. Indeed Russell, a young and ardent patriot during the final triumphant stages of the Napoleonic Wars, attributed Britain's astonishing commercial, cultural and military prowess since 1688 very largely to the openness of her 'pure and worthy' constitution.[48] After 1832, he never advocated wholesale redistribution of seats towards the principle of representation by numbers, and continued to defend the role of the small boroughs.[49] He had no interest in any change that might jeopardise the political influence of property. His main concern was always to use the virtuous opinion that would be infused into parliament by Reform to prod government into beneficial activity.[50]

Moreover, he continued to maintain that, however good the representative

[45] *Times*, 14 November 1855, p. 10.
[46] See Parry, *Rise and fall*, p. 125, and n. 86 below.
[47] For these views, see ibid., ch. 3.
[48] *English constitution*, pp. xxviii–xxix, 249 (the quotation comes from *Hansard*, second series, XLI, 1105, 14 December 1819).
[49] E.g. *Hansard*, CLVI, 2058–9, 1 March 1860.
[50] In calling for the extension of the suffrage to the upper working classes in 1860 he expressed his pleasure at the spread of 'true Christian feeling' in those classes: *Hansard*, CLVIII, 200, 26 April 1860.

system, politicians would and should retain considerable scope in preparing legislation. The art of government was to secure popular acquiescence, not to surrender to passion. 'It is the right of a people to represent its grievances; it is the business of a statesman to devise remedies.'[51] Those remedies would be successful according to the character and judgement of the statesman concerned. Similarly, it was the integrity and moral seriousness of political leaders which gained the respect of the House of Commons, 'the noblest assembly of freemen in the world', and permitted stable government – party government – to survive.[52]

So leadership style should be founded on fidelity to libertarian and moral principles. Russell's certainly was. He expected Liberal MPs to follow him as long as he articulated and upheld noble ideals. This was the way to avoid complacency in parliament, to discipline the party of government, and to rally the sympathy of reformers in and outside parliament. Acutely anxious of the weight of superstition, intolerance, apathy and narrow-mindedness in the world generally and in governing circles in particular,[53] Russell believed that consensual government usually meant bad government. As his confidant Dean Elliot (his wife's cousin) said in 1865, 'nothing had ever yet been done till what was called an "imprudent man" came'.[54] In the dog-days of Melbourne's government in 1839, Russell virtually appointed himself Colonial Secretary at a critical moment for the empire, and, arriving at the Colonial Office, announced that 'the thing we have to do here is to *decide*. We shall often decide wrong, but we must decide.'[55] The weedy history-lover Russell – a soldier *manqué* – believed that a parliamentary leader must be bold, courageous, virtuous and inspiring.[56] Opinion varied as to his success in actually *providing* such leadership, but he certainly tried to do so – sometimes too hard.[57] His assertive moralistic style contrasted with the more easygoing and consensual approach of the two Liberal prime ministers under whom he served, Melbourne and Palmerston. They were pragmatists, anxious not to offend 'average opinion' in the House of Commons, and therefore prone to inaction – arguably a wiser strategy.

---

[51] S. Reid, *Lord John Russell* (London, 1895), p. 85. See also *Hansard*, II, 1065–6, 1 March 1831.

[52] *Recollections*, p. 269.

[53] *Times*, 14 November 1855, p. 10.

[54] *The Amberley papers: the letters and diaries of Lord and Lady Amberley*, ed. B. and P. Russell (2 vols., London, 1937), I, 366.

[55] '. . . and Mr Foretescue', p. 67.

[56] In retrospect he saw himself as 'Commander-in-Chief' of the party of which he assumed the lead in 1835: *Recollections*, p. 133.

[57] It is surely significant that some of his worst mistakes – like the dismissal of Palmerston in December 1851 and the resignation of January 1855 – stemmed from hasty decisions intentionally made *alone* after much criticism of his vacillation and weakness, criticisms which obviously cut deep into his ego.

As far as possible, Russell chose his colleagues in his image. They should be disinterested, liberal, responsible and cultured: of good 'character'. Given the whig belief that liberty was rooted in British soil and that landlords had a duty to uphold the consolidated wisdom of their ancestors, many of these were bound to be landed, and some to come from particular liberal-evangelical families like the Elliots and Greys. Hence the 'family party' jibe. But Russell was also concerned with intelligence, breadth and culture. For example, he was criticised for appointing the brother of his wife's brother-in-law, Sir John Romilly, as Master of the Rolls in 1851. But Romilly used this post not only to accelerate the conduct of Chancery cases, but also to mastermind the publication of the state's historical papers – feeling ashamed, like Russell, of the philistinism of the English attitude to official historical records compared to that of the other 'governments of modern civilized nations'.[58] Russell did not uphold the idea of government by a landowning class. He went to the Lords in 1861 only when his health became too fragile for the Commons, and was never happy there, trying to speak of 'truth and justice to an assembly who did not care for such things at all'.[59] London society was 'always wrong';[60] that was why Lord and Lady John preferred the 'more popular and rational kind of society' to be met over 'pleasant little *teas*' at home, at which writers and scientists like Thackeray, Dickens, Panizzi, Joseph Hooker, Richard Owen, W. E. H. Lecky and J. L. Motley, or any visiting liberal foreign statesman or thinker, knew they would be welcome.[61] It was Russell who raised a storm in metropolitan drawing-rooms and newspapers by making the aggressively non-landed appointments of Goschen and Forster to senior positions in his 1865 government, in order to signal his determination to introduce parliamentary reform.[62] And it was Russell who invited John Bright to Woburn, around the time that the latter became the laughing-stock of the House of Commons for his inability to pronounce 'Pytchley Hunt' – leading a

[58] From 1853, he realised the government's long-standing theoretical commitment to publish the state's records: the Calendar of State Papers from 1547 onwards was produced from 1856, reaching 1603 by 1870. From 1857, he established the Rolls Series (*Chronicles and Memorials*), and in 1869 set up the Historical Manuscripts Commission in order to trace those records held in private hands. Until the end of Russell's last government in 1866, the annual grant for the editing of the Rolls series was £3,000, defended by the Treasury as an indirect contribution to 'the general information and education of the people'. See J. D. Cantwell, *The Public Record Office 1838–1958* (London, 1991), *passim* (quotation at p. 239). The quotation in the text is from M. D. Knowles, 'Great historical enterprises IV: the Rolls series', *Transactions of the Royal Historical Society*, 5th series, XI (1961), 141.

[59] *Amberley papers*, I, 482.

[60] McCarthy, *Lady John Russell*, p. 195.

[61] Lord Ribblesdale, *Impressions and memories* (London, 1927), p. 99. The quotation is at McCarthy, *Lady John Russell*, pp. 83–4.

[62] See e.g. Sir H. Maxwell, *The life and letters of George William Frederick fourth earl of Clarendon* (2 vols., London, 1913), II, 305–8.

candid friend to write to the Duke of Bedford: 'Hope you'll count your spoons.'[63]

This brief review of Russell's political philosophy has attempted to show that it was founded on but not circumscribed by Foxite ideals. It adopted the Foxite emphasis on the potential evil and folly of all government and the need to develop moral qualities in the governing class in order to minimise it. These qualities – of genuine feeling, broad historical and literary culture, cosmo-politan judgement and, therefore, judicious benevolence to humanity – would safeguard liberty and extend popular attachment to the rule of law. Russell inherited the notion that it was the peculiar duty of public-spirited whigs of proven character to provide this political leadership, not least because of their ability to build a firm party following that would give government a stable foundation.[64] But Russell's was a distinctively mid-nineteenth-century reading of Foxism, adapted to a world in which public opinion often seemed uncontrollably vital. Politics had to involve the leader-ship of a larger public than in Fox's day, and the inculcation of education and Christian morality. Revealed religion bulked larger in Russell's politics than in Fox's, largely because the future seemed so manifestly unknowable except to God. The alternative to the spread of Christian principles threatened to be social tension and perhaps divine retribution. Russell followed Fox in valuing the humane training of the traditional governing classes, and the same great teachers, Homer, Dante and Shakespeare, poets of the sublime and creators of true heroes.[65] But he was also concerned with raising the moral consciousness of a much broader public opinion, in ways as diverse as the promotion of elementary education and his presidency of the Royal Historical Society (made respectable because of his patronage in the early 1870s).[66] In his thinking about public opinion, Christianity and world progress, Russell was stimulated by the writings of historian contemporaries whom he admired, such as Milman, Lecky and A. P. Stanley ('my pope, but . . . not infallible').[67] But the essence of his religion was not very different from that which he was taught as a boy by his whig tutor, his father's domestic

---

[63] Recollections of Georgiana Peel, p. 122; Amberley papers, 1, 468.

[64] For whig thinking on these matters in the time of Fox, see A. D. Kriegel, 'Liberty and whiggery in early nineteenth-century England', Journal of Modern History, 52 (1980), 253–78, and idem, 'A convergence of ethics: saints and whigs in British anti-slavery', Journal of British Studies, 26 (1987), 423–50.

[65] E.g. Essays and sketches, pp. 67–9.

[66] The Royal Historical Society was established, on rickety foundations, in 1868. Russell became its second President in 1871 and remained in post until his death in 1878. He persuaded the queen to give it royal blessing in 1872, and was mainly responsible for the rapid expansion of membership. See R. A. Humphreys, The Royal Historical Society 1868–1968 (London, 1969), pp. 10–12.

[67] Prothero, Stanley, 11, 510; see Rise and progress, pp. v–vi.

chaplain, the poet, scientist, and inventor of the power-loom, Edmund Cartwright.[68]

What was Russell's appeal to Liberals? His name and inheritance counted for something. But surely what mattered more was his temperamental bias in favour of bold leadership, embracing educational, legal, social, Irish and church issues – with a view to using the power of the state to encourage private philanthropy and stimulate human virtue. These were the issues with which he became associated in the second half of the 1830s – adding further limited parliamentary reform to his list from the late 1840s, primarily in order to help them along their way. This was not an outdated programme in the context of the 1850s. Rather, his zealous and unworldly fidelity to principle alarmed many of his less emotional contemporaries. Had he been more relaxed and astute – more of a tactician – he would have been rather more successful; throughout his career, his problem was not a lack of radicalism but a surfeit of restlessness. It was Russell's policy – especially the religious and Irish reforms – which lost the Liberals their vast majority of 1832 in less than ten years. His tragedy was that thereafter he never enjoyed the parliamentary backing which he needed in order to make a success of its remaining aspects.

Yet it had to be like that, because his intensity and emotional commitment were fundamental to his politics and appeal. Russell learned from Fox that the political leader should stand or fall by his integrity. He also learned that domestic purity, admiration of virtuous figures from the past, and appreciation of the natural world, were crucial prerequisites in building that integrity. The Fox whom Russell venerated was not the young debauched rake, but the more mature cultured patriotic martyr. Reading Russell's account of him, we picture Fox thrilling to the deeds of Homer's patriotic heroes, savouring the poet's sublime descriptions, and corresponding with Parr and Wakefield about them.[69] We see him as the affectionate, benevolent gentleman at home at St Anne's Hill in Surrey, far from the corruption of the city and the tainted political arena, revelling in nature and domesticity, and drawing spiritual comfort from the song of the nightingale, to which he would go out of his way to listen.[70] The nightingale symbolised 'love, not fear'.[71] Its sound was graceful and sweet because it enjoyed 'the wildness of freedom' rather than the constraints of a cage.[72] Such domestic scenes encapsulated English libertarianism, threatened in the 1790s by Pitt's nationalist frenzy and

---

[68] Cartwright published sonnets to the adolescent Lord John which were written in order to impress on him the importance of conscientious labour and the development of (controlled) emotion, sympathy, benevolence and philanthropy: *Letters and sonnets, on moral and other interesting subjects, addressed to Lord John Russell* (1807).

[69] Russell, *Fox*, III, 242; *Memorials of Fox*, III, *passim*, and IV, 296ff.

[70] Ibid., esp. pp. 224, 247.   [71] Cartwright, *Letters*, pp. 98–9.

[72] Russell, *Hansard*, second series, VII, 74, 25 April 1822.

by continental carnage. The message of Russell's biography was that the tranquillity of St Anne's Hill gave Fox the opportunity to become a full man – and thus the great inspiration to all right-minded patriots. Pembroke Lodge had the same effect on Russell. Contemplating nature gave him serenity and allowed him to 'lift [his] heart to the Creator'; indeed he found it very painful to 'pick a flower [which] had been so many months perfecting'.[73] Difficult as it may be for the sceptical modern reader to accept, Russell's personality really seems to have been singularly straightforward and reverential. Chichester Fortescue was consistently struck by 'the great simplicity of his character and entire absence of affectation'; Dufferin thought his 'existence . . . flowed at a very high level of thought and feeling'.[74] Lady Charlotte Portal commented on 'the extraordinary beauty of that daily life – the most perfect man's life that I ever knew of'.[75] As with Fox, Russell's uncommon personal qualities underpinned his political attraction. Gladstone 'so long admired and loved [him] (and the political characters which attract love are not very numerous)'; Macaulay could 'not help loving him'; nor, apparently, could Palmerston, even after being dismissed by him in 1851; nor could Dickens.[76] Cobden and Bright, who had high standards in these matters, praised his moral power; the evangelical James Stephen, the civil servant under Russell at the Colonial Office, described his as the only 'dominant soul' among the politicians with whom he had worked.[77] Bagehot thought that he 'perhaps alone . . . has succeeded . . . in the oratory of conviction'; Baron Bunsen, on hearing him speak in the Commons, 'saw for the first time *man* . . . defending the highest interests of humanity with the wonderful power of speech'.[78] However flawed his tactics, however bad his behaviour to colleagues, however humiliating his reverses, he continued to command enough loyalty to rally a significant parliamentary and extra-parliamentary following because he projected something fundamental to Liberalism. One of the most recent historians to

---

73 Russell, 'Preface', to Mrs Cradock, *The calendar of nature or the seasons of England* (London, 1849–50), p. iii; *Recollections of Georgiana Peel*, p. 152.

74 ' . . . and Mr Fortescue', p. 68; Reid, *Russell*, p. 363. See also (Minto) McCarthy, *Lady John Russell*, p. 64.

75 Ibid., p. 274.

76 McCarthy, *Lady John Russell*, p. 273; Trevelyan, *Macaulay*, II, 242; G. Blakiston, *Woburn and the Russells* (London, 1980), p. 215; *The speeches of Charles Dickens*, ed. K. J. Fielding (Oxford, 1960), pp. 388–9.

77 J. Morley, *The life of Richard Cobden* (2 vols., London, 1908 edn), I, 393; G. M. Trevelyan, *The life of John Bright* (London, 1913), p. 358; *Sir James Stephen: letters*, ed. C. E. Stephen (pr. pr. 1906), p. 99.

78 W. Bagehot, 'The character of Sir Robert Peel', in *Biographical studies*, ed. R. H. Hutton (London, 1907 edn), p. 30; Baroness Bunsen, *A memoir of Baron Bunsen* (2 vols., London, 1868), I, 499–500 (applying also to Peel). For a similar comment to Bunsen's, see D. O. Maddyn, *Chiefs of parties, past and present, with original anecdotes* (2 vols., London, 2nd edn, 1859), II, 186.

understand his appeal – writing, it should be said, in the 1920s – observed that in the 1830s he created 'a moral atmosphere in which bad laws could not easily survive'.[79] Russell could not be ignored because he represented better than anyone else that vigorous (but intermittently flowering) plant, the Liberal conscience.

II

Russell in the 1850s can be seen as the elder statesman put out to grass or, more profitably, as the unfashionable critic of complacency. The political stagnation of these years had two causes: the disarray of the party system, and chauvinism. Russell sought to promote the agenda which he had tried to develop in the latter part of his own government of 1846–52. Frustrated then, he became even more so as the 1850s wore on, only to mount a recovery late in the decade.

The failure of the Liberals to win a majority on their own after 1841, and the distorting effect of the Peelites' presence after 1846, altered the options for the Liberal party and made it much more difficult for Russell to pursue his ideas. Most leading Peelites were willing to support Liberal governments, but they disliked Russell's restlessness and preferred the approach of centrist Liberals like Clarendon and Wood, who sought stability by associating government with the principles of economy and sound administration. After a lot of minor political turbulence, such a Liberal–Peelite coalition came into being in December 1852, headed not by Russell but by Lord Aberdeen. Given his position, Russell was an indispensable member of that government. Indeed he had to be Leader of the House of Commons – and was under the impression that Aberdeen would retire in his favour once the government had been established. But he found his position humiliating, because the Peelites had taken much more than their fair share of government posts, leaving his followers particularly ill-treated and weakening his influence over policy. Aberdeen showed no sign of resigning, and tension was soon inevitable, especially since Russell refused all departmental responsibilities after February 1853, leaving himself free to plan an agenda.

Over the next two years, Russell agitated emotionally on behalf of three issues with which, as a result of his previous initiatives, he felt his integrity was bound up. In each case he was defeated by his colleagues, adding progressively to his sense of humiliation. One cause was limited parliamentary reform, to which he had committed himself in 1851, and through which he hoped to diminish Conservative strength in parliament, revive the Liberal majority

---

[79] W. F. Reddaway, 'Lord John Russell', in *The political principles of some notable prime ministers of the nineteenth century*, ed. F. J. C. Hearnshaw (London, 1926), p. 158.

and purpose, and soothe the tempers of more moderate Chartists. But no
issue was more likely to unite the other weighty members of cabinet – Peelites,
centrist Liberals, and Palmerston – against him, and Russell finally had to
admit defeat in June 1854, withdrawing his bill. The second was national
education. In 1846, his government had subsidised the salaries of qualified
teachers; voluntaryist, Anglican and ratepayer pressure had prevented bigger
steps towards a rating system, but by 1852 he hoped that their opposition to
this enormously beneficial idea was waning.[80] In 1853 he brought in a bill
to introduce a permissive local rating system in boroughs, where gaps existed
in school provision – hoping to establish 'religion and morality on a still
firmer basis'.[81] Neither government nor average parliamentary opinion was
enthusiastic; this bill too was withdrawn. The third cause was patriotism. In
1850–1 Russell's intense Englishness had led him into trouble over the Durham
letter. Now, in 1853, he, with Palmerston, retorted by criticising the Peelites'
softness towards Russia. After the divided cabinet drifted into war in 1854,
Russell, who would have liked to be a bold, inspiring War Minister,[82]
consistently took the lead in demanding more decisive administration,
including an overhaul of the military departments. He lost most of the
arguments here too. By the end of 1854 he had been overruled on so many
issues that he felt that he was losing character by remaining in government.
When, in January 1855, the government had to face a motion calling for an
inquiry into wartime administrative failures, he decided that he could not
honourably resist it, and resigned – inevitably bringing down the government.

Russell considered that he had 'saved the army, what remains of it, and the
country'.[83] His former colleagues thought that he had betrayed them. When
asked to form a government, he agreed to try – what patriot would not? – only
to be rebuffed by almost all of them. Russell's reputation among the political
classes was thus gravely weakened even before his defensible but tactically
disastrous behaviour at the Vienna peace talks in the spring. He appeared to
be condoning peace with Tsardom, the great 'danger . . . to European
civilization'.[84] Abuse of him verged on the hysterical, and a cabal of junior
ministers, egged on by Delane, forced him out. The new prime minister,
Palmerston, had little choice but to accept their ultimatum, and may in any
case have thought that Russell's reputation was so tarnished that, for the first
time in twenty-five years, a Liberal government could afford his withdrawal.
Though he affected not to show it, Russell was utterly cast down.[85]

---

[80] *Hansard*, CXIX, 268, 9 February 1852.   [81] Ibid., CXXV, 548, 4 April 1853.
[82] ' . . . *and Mr Fortescue*', p. 68.
[83] W. M. Thackeray, *Letters and private papers*, ed. G. N. Ray (4 vols., London, 1945–6), III,
416.
[84] Campbell, in M. S. Hardcastle, *Life of John, Lord Campbell* (2 vols., London, 1881), II, 333–4.
[85] *Amberley papers*, II, 283.

The tone of the London press near and after the end of the Crimean War was not only very hostile to Russell; it was also narrowly chauvinist and complacent. So was parliament. One easy way for both bodies to obstruct reforms was to allege that they were 'un-English'. Fighting to rebuild his career in 1856, Russell more than anyone encountered this allegation. He was bound to lose the battles. But in the process he began a long-term recovery.

Russell's aim in 1856 was to use the issues with which he had previously been associated – decisive administration, legal and educational reform, and social inquiry – to exploit the dissatisfaction with the conduct of government that had welled up in 1854–5. He had disliked the excesses of the Administrative Reform Association, finding its anti-party and anti-establishment rhetoric utopian. But its bubble quickly burst; thereafter, its supporters' ardour and legitimate grievances remained to be tapped more constructively, and Layard, Samuel Morley, Goderich and Dickens were all to become firm allies of his in the next few years. Russell set himself up as an enemy of bureaucracy, arguing that the two things most necessary to frustrate what Dickens called 'the miserable red-tapist' were parliamentary reform and an infusion of energy and accountability into ministerial life – an infusion of the sort which he had supplied as Home Secretary in the 1830s, and from which he thought there had been a sad falling-off.[86] In 1856, he demanded a Minister of Justice, with the personal responsibility necessary to get parliament, which had become scandalously somnolent, to take its legislative duties seriously. The minister's main duty would be to make cheap justice a reality, for example by finding answers to vexed issues which had slumbered for decades – such as law amendment, and the reform of charitable trusts and county and ecclesiastical courts.[87]

Russell also wanted a responsible Minister of Education to be appointed, charged with promoting a national system on the lines set out in an ambitious series of resolutions which he introduced in March 1856 (schools, teaching religion, were to be managed from the rates in areas where existing provision was inadequate). He explained that a 'general and compulsory' system was necessary because the state education system in England was backward compared with 'the other enlightened nations of the world'.[88] This initiative

---

[86] For example, he criticised the decay in the administration of the New Poor Law since the 1830s: *Recollections of Georgiana Peel*, p. 287. Dickens had predicted that the withdrawal of Russell's Reform Bill of 1854 would mean an end to education, slum, sanitation and factory reform: E. Johnson, *Charles Dickens: his tragedy and triumph* (London, 1977 edn), p. 411.

[87] *Hansard*, CXL, 651, 12 February 1856, CXLIV, 558, 12 February 1857, and CXLVI, 774, 2 July 1857. In other words, Gladstone was not alone in bemoaning the 'declining efficiency of parliament' in 1856.

[88] *Hansard*, CXL, 1955, 6 March 1856, CXLIV, 797, 18 February 1857.

must have been designed to prick the bubble of fervent nationalism surrounding 'victory' in the Crimea. But it was politically unwise, since national pride inflamed the already vocal supporters of the status quo. Dissenters, Peelites and Tories all attacked Russell for betraying the values that had made England great. Edward Baines claimed that he was advocating the despotism of Berlin and Vienna. Gladstone alleged that he wished to endanger Britain's 'national character' by substituting mere 'technical instruction' and an 'alien and foreign' dependence on the state for 'real education' based on the 'sacred interests' of true religion. Disraeli was sure that Russell had 'mistaken ... the character of his countrymen'.[89] Russell retorted that those who prevented government from assisting education would maintain 'gaol and gibbet' but deny 'the duty of a Christian state to promote the cause of religion and morality'. And the charge of alien despotism was ridiculous: local ratepayers, not the state, would influence school syllabuses, and religious teaching would follow the liberal ideal of the Church of England, that 'nothing need be held as a matter of faith which is not either plainly contained in the Scriptures or which cannot be proved thereby'.[90] But his initiative stood no chance. Forced by government coolness to withdraw his substantive resolutions, he insisted on bringing the first, symbolic, one to the vote, only to have it roundly defeated by 260 : 158 – probably the lowest point in the history of parliamentary discussion of education.[91]

Anything touched by Russell was liable to the same complaint of 'unEnglishness':[92] even Panizzi's appointment that year as chief librarian of the British Museum, supported by Russell and Layard, was abused as an 'affront to British genius and character' by several newspapers and MPs.[93] In his view, Russell's cosmopolitan outlook was in the best whig tradition and not at all incompatible with patriotism; rather, it gave him a better insight into the peculiarities and needs of the English.[94] His view was that the *Times* was behaving unpatriotically in its hostility to the spread of liberty and morality. 'If England is ever to be England again, this vile tyranny of *The Times* must be cut off.'[95] There followed a comically incompetent episode, as Russell's

---

[89] Ibid., CXLI, 892–3, 952–8, 912, 11 April 1856.

[90] Ibid., CXLI, 912, 904, 11 April 1856.

[91] I calculate that Conservatives divided 166 : 23 against the resolution, and Liberal-Conservatives (i.e. the main Peelite body) 17 : 3. Liberals supported it by 134 : 79.

[92] For this view of his education plan, see e.g. *The Stanleys of Alderley: their letters between the years 1851–1865*, ed. N. Mitford (London, 1939), p. 136.

[93] E. Miller, *Prince of librarians: the life and times of Antonio Panizzi of the British Museum* (London, 1967), pp. 215–20; *Hansard*, CXLI, 1344, 21 April 1856.

[94] *Essays and sketches*, pp. 128–36. Russell was in fact educated in Europe much more than at Edinburgh, owing to his extensive travels as a teenager. He also lived in France a great deal in the 1820s.

[95] *History of 'The Times'*, p. 192.

interpreter to the world, Gilbert Elliot, dean of Bristol, tried to woo newspapers that would preach 'Liberal principles' – a hopeless plan, owing to the dean's lack of capital or contacts, and Russell's hesitation about appearing to oppose Palmerston or support his radical critics.[96] In autumn 1856, Russell was at the nadir of his whole career. He was consoled only by the fact that his hero had suffered similarly. In the 'deluge of folly and fury' of the 1790s, Fox had 'sought in a return to literary pursuits an occupation and an amusement'. So did Russell; in 1856 he finished editing Fox's correspondence and began writing the biography. In the closing passage of the former work Russell wrote Fox's epitaph for the 1790s, but perhaps another epitaph as well:

> The nation, inflamed by animosity, lifted up by arrogance, and deluded by the eloquence of men in power, assailed him as an enemy to his country, because he opposed measures injurious to her interests. [But he] preferred the welfare of his country, and of mankind, to the power and popularity, which were acquired by the wanton sacrifice of human life, and the disregard of justice, charity, and mercy.[97]

III

The parliamentary crisis of March 1857 seemed likely to intensify Russell's unpopularity. In fact, it was the signal for his revival. How did this happen?

The crisis was caused by the bombardment of Canton on the orders of Sir John Bowring, English plenipotentiary in China. Cobden and Russell condemned the action as neither legally nor morally defensible; Russell claimed that it lowered England's character, reputation and honour.[98] Each led a small band of supporters into the opposition lobby, and defeated the government.[99] But Palmerston, believing that they had ignored the national mood, called a general election to capitalise on the prevailing jingoism. Of all the rebels, Russell was the one most obviously at risk of losing his seat, since he was MP for the City of London. The great merchants of the City were enthusiasts for the development of the China trade and for Palmerston's aggressive commercial diplomacy in general. China was the source of big profits in the 1850s for merchants rich and well-established enough to exploit them. Such men were distinctly sobered by Palmerston's warning that unless the Chinese were disciplined the heads of 'respectable

---

[96] Koss, *Political press*, pp. 115–19.
[97] *Memorials of Fox*, IV, 491–2. For Russell's move towards planning Fox's biography, see Russell to G. C. Lewis, 3 September 1856, Russell papers, Public Record Office, 30/22/13B/188.
[98] McCarthy, *Lady John Russell*, p. 168.
[99] Dissident Liberals included Russellites F. T. Baring, J. L. Ricardo, and Lord Robert Grosvenor, and sympathisers from the administrative reform movement of 1855, such as Layard, W. S. Lindsay and A. J. Otway.

British merchants' might be on display on the walls of Canton.[100] A deputation of influential City men asked Palmerston himself to stand in the election (he declined).[101] Russell's three fellow-MPs for the City had supported Palmerston on the Canton vote. It was hardly surprising that the London Liberal Registration Association, the powerful caucus which dominated the constituency, was unsympathetic to Russell's re-election. It also believed that his recent and past mistakes had made his return virtually impossible; and his own agent, John Abel Smith, told him that the Pope would have as much chance of success.[102] The LLRA met on 10 March to select its candidates (assuming that they would be unopposed). Russell had not yet decided on his position, and indeed had sent out contradictory signals; but the meeting decided that he was irrelevant.[103] It decided to exclude him in the most pointed way by hoisting the trusty old radical anti-aristocratic flag: it declared that the City should be represented only by commercial men who could defend its economic interests. The meeting chose four candidates; Russell's replacement was Raikes Currie, an ageing radical, wealthy banker and East India proprietor.[104] There was another vacancy: this too was filled by an East India merchant, R. W. Crawford. The stage seemed set for the City to affirm its faith in Palmerston and its pride in British world power.

But the LLRA's action – 'a system . . . of intolerable dictation' – was the spur Russell needed to declare his candidature as an independent Liberal with a rival committee of volunteers.[105] As virtually 'all the merchant princes turned their princely backs' on him, he set out to appeal to 'the 20,000 electors of the City'.[106] The contest became one of the great events of the 1857 election. The LLRA required its four candidates to pledge that they formed a slate.[107] But this strategy succeeded only partially, because one of the four was Baron Lionel de Rothschild, head of the world's most famous banking house. Rothschild had been MP for the City since 1847, but, as a Jew, had been prevented from taking his seat by his inability to swear the explicitly Christian parliamentary oath. For the last decade, Russell had been the driving force behind the campaign for a new oaths bill emancipating the Jews, which the Lords had consistently defeated. The Jewish cause depended on Russell's high-profile support, and Rothschild infuriated the LLRA by refusing to

---

100 At the lord mayor's banquet at the Mansion-house: *Times*, 21 March 1857, p. 9.

101 *Stanleys of Alderley*, p. 146.

102 McCarthy, *Lady John Russell*, p. 169.

103 There is an extensive correspondence on the precise order of events in the Russell papers, 30/22/13C.

104 Currie had been a radical MP for twenty years. He praised Bowring (an old Benthamite) as 'a man of the people' rather than an aristocrat: *Times*, 14 March 1857, p. 10.

105 The quotation is from Russell's nomination speech: *Times*, 28 March 1857, p. 5.

106 McCarthy, *Lady John Russell*, p. 170; F. Bennoch, in *Times*, 28 March 1857, p. 5.

107 E.g. at the Cannon St meeting: *Times*, 25 March, p. 7.

advise electors to vote against him.[108] In private, he assured Abel Smith that he would 'make almost any sacrifice to prevent [Russell] being beat', and discreet financial arrangements may have been made to that end.[109] The distinguished banker and former Lord Mayor David Salomons, whom Russell, when Home Secretary in 1838, had appointed the first Jewish magistrate, led the formal Jewish movement for Lord John's return.

Meanwhile, Russell campaigned on the principle that 'peace' and 'economy' would give Britain 'leisure to pursue the work of legal, social, ecclesiastical, and political reform'.[110] As a first step, he came out firmly for a 'considerable extension of the suffrage' in line with the moral and educational progress of the upper working classes.[111] His emphasis on the connection between parliamentary and other reform capitalised on the irritation felt at Palmerston's and parliament's inaction since 1855, and was widely shared. The reforming Liberal judge W. P. Wood held that Palmerston was making the same terrible mistake as the Liberals had made in 1852, in not fighting the election on a principle.[112] Such views gradually began to make headway against the LLRA's organisation. At a series of noisy ward meetings in the last week of the campaign, motions supporting the LLRA slate were overturned by Russell's supporters, who advocated the reform cause and secured amendments calling for his return. At Cripplegate, for example, Samuel Morley asserted that Russell, 'with all his shortcomings', had 'more sterling principle in his little finger than Lord Palmerston had in his whole body'.[113] The tide of opinion was clearly flowing Russell's way; in the end, his triumph was plain. Sir James Duke, the sitting MP who shouldered nearly all of the constituency's commercial work, topped the poll (after some words of support for Russell), and Rothschild and Russell came next, almost together, well ahead of the two Palmerstonian East India men who had criticised Russell – with the usurper Currie the clear loser.[114] Russell had won against the *Times* and the 'servile

---

[108] In Cripplegate: ibid., 26 March 1857, p. 7. He had earlier said at the London Tavern that it would 'grieve' him if Russell were not elected: ibid., 18 March, p. 5.

[109] J. A. Smith to Russell, 4 April 1857, Russell papers, 30/33/13C/211.

[110] *Times*, 13 March 1857, p. 8.   [111] Ibid., 28 March 1857, p. 5.

[112] Wood to Russell, 12 March 1857, Russell papers, 30/22/13C/69. Wood, the son of a famous City radical MP, had been a law reformer and advanced Liberal MP, whom Russell had appointed Solicitor-General in 1851. He became a judge in Chancery in 1853.

[113] The LLRA slate was overturned by amendments during meetings in Cripplegate and at Threadneedle St on 25 March: *Times*, 26 March 1857, p. 7. In Bishopsgate on 26 March and Farringdon on 27 March, meetings passed resolutions urging 'strenuous support' for Russell and condemning the LLRA's attempt to fetter independent electors: ibid., 27, 28 March 1857, p. 5.

[114] The result was: Duke 6,664, Rothschild 6,398, Russell 6,308, Crawford 5,808, Currie 4,519. In his nomination speech, Duke declared that he would 'readily assist [Russell] in carrying out his contemplated reforms' and that he did not altogether approve of Bowring's conduct: *Times*, 28 March 1857, p. 5.

press'. He and his supporters toasted it as the people's victory.[115] It was also a reminder of Fox's triumph in Westminster 73 years before.

Russell's support came from a number of quarters (in addition to Jewish influence). His association with parliamentary reform seems to have brought him a lot of backing from shopkeepers and small masters. One leading Chartist told him that 'every Chartist entitled to vote' plumped for him, and that the unenfranchised strongly supported him too.[116] Despite his refusal to declare for the secret ballot, the City Ballot Society also appears to have worked for his return.[117] His advocacy of legal reform attracted many liberal barristers and solicitors.[118] It may also help to explain his following among small businessmen for whom 'cheap justice' and reform of the bankruptcy laws were urgent needs in their battle against 'vested interests'.[119] Most of Russell's commercial supporters seem to have been small traders in the domestic market, who would be helped by peace and economy, which would buoy domestic consumption, more than by an aggressive Palmerstonian foreign policy which would prop up the profits of the great merchant houses.[120] The

---

[115] Ibid., 30, 31 March 1857, p. 6, p. 7.

[116] C. W. Gregory to Russell, 28 March 1857, Russell papers, 30/22/13C/125 – quoting Milton to the effect that the nation was 'not dull and slow', but 'capable of reaching wherever the human faculty will soar', if led by men of 'energy and progress'. George Moore described Russell as the popular candidate, with crowds following him everywhere: S. Smiles, *George Moore: merchant and philanthropist* (London, 1878), p. 171.

[117] See F. Bennoch to Russell, 9 April 1857, Russell papers, 30/22/13C/235. The old philosophical radical T. P. Thompson, now a leader of the ballot campaign, backed Russell.

[118] I have not been able to trace a pollbook for the election. The following analysis of Russell's supporters relies on newspaper speeches and especially on my examination of his election committee, listed in *Times*, 27 March 1857, p. 3. I have used the *Post Office London Directory 1857*, and other reference works, to arrive at a rough-and-ready breakdown by occupation. There are 208 committee members listed with an address, whose occupations can be traced or guessed – with the caveat that the descriptions given in the Post Office Directory are often unhelpfully general. I estimate that 22 of these were barristers and 13 solicitors. These included Frederick Lawrence, later chairman of the City Garibaldi committee, and his friend J. H. Parry, the ex-Complete Suffrage Union activist, now a rising barrister; William Palmer, professor of civil law at Gresham College; Alexander Pulling, energetic law reformer; William Pritchard, high bailiff of Southwark and another active reformer; the learned Phillimore brothers, friends of Gladstone, who, as MPs, had joined the opposition to Palmerston on Canton; and a number of lawyers who were to become Liberal MPs.

[119] See the pro-Russell speech of Francis Line of the Tribunal of Commerce Association: *Times*, 26 March 1857, p. 5.

[120] One of Russell's supporters jeered at the big shipowners and merchants for whom the bombardment of Canton was 'a great pocket question': Dod, *Times*, 18 March 1857, p. 5. Only 109 of Russell's committee can be identified as commercial men (excluding booksellers *et al.*). They included 12 in the wine trade, 10 in silk, 9 in clothes, hats or shoes, and 9 in food and beverages. There were only 7 bankers, agents or stockbrokers and 2 shipowners. Without doing a very great deal of research, one can only guess how wealthy these men were, and where they traded, but the occupational breakdown suggests that Russell's support did come largely from those with domestic rather than far-flung interests. (Perhaps the large number of adherents from the wine trade is connected with Russell's support for free trade and

City's professional classes were also well represented on his side – men who wanted the City to return not just merchant MPs but also one with time and talents to 'devote himself to the higher questions of philosophical legislation'.[121] There were two great London headmasters, Mortimer of the City of London School and Kynaston of St Paul's, a strong contingent from the British Museum (headed by Panizzi),[122] some gentleman-scholars,[123] Edward Lloyd (the publisher of *Lloyd's Weekly London Newspaper*) and the radical publisher John Cassell. And there were surgeons, booksellers, printers and auctioneers.[124] Finally, there was a small minority of commercial men of great wealth and influence. They tended to be notable philanthropists, and were all anxious for the improvement and purification of institutions and the tone of public life (most had been active in the Administrative Reform Association).[125] Several were strong opponents of Palmerston's foreign policy. They included Samuel Morley (millionaire hosiery manufacturer and evangelical congregationalist), the Anglicans George Moore, William Leaf and Thomson Hankey, the unitarians Samuel Courtauld and A. J. Waterlow, and the Quakers G. W. Alexander, Charles Buxton and Henry Gurney.[126]

French and Spanish liberalism.) My speculations here follow those of V. A. C. Gatrell, that the Manchester election of 1857 saw a similar division of opinion between great and small merchants: 'The commercial middle class in Manchester, c. 1820–1857' (Cambridge PhD thesis, 1972).

121 The quotation is from Francis Bennoch's speech in *Times*, 28 March 1857, p. 5. Bennoch was deputy chairman of Lord John's campaign committee, a self-made silk merchant and twee Scottish poet: 'I love my books as drunkards love their wine / the more I drink, the more they seem divine': F. Bennoch, *Poems, lyrics, songs, and sonnets* (London, 1877), p. 64. He was a friend of radical German poets in exile like Ferdinand Freiligrath and Gottfried Kinkel.

122 Including Russell Martineau, philologist and lecturer in Hebrew language and literature at Manchester New College. He was son of the great unitarian preacher James Martineau. Lawrence and Parry (see n. 118) had had British Museum connections.

123 E.g. Henry Christy, the ethnologist, of a rich banking family, who devoted his life to travel, collection and research in prehistory and left his valuable collection to the British Museum; Samuel Sharpe, unitarian Egyptologist and benefactor of University College London; Felix Slade, antiquarian and promoter of education in the fine arts; and Sir Thomas Phillips, wealthy coalowner, Anglican educational reformer and an important cultural figure as Chairman of the Council of the Society of Arts 1859–62.

124 I estimate that there were 5 surgeons, 5 booksellers, 5 stationers/publishers, 2 auctioneers and 2 civil engineers on his committee.

125 Membership of the ARA itself is not significant, since it was equally possible for members to join the 'commercial men only' side in 1857. Indeed Crawford and Currie had both supported the ARA in 1855. There is an eleven-page list of its backers at the beginning of the multi-volume set of official papers of the ARA in the British Library.

126 Morley had been chairman of the ARA, hoping thereby to restore purity to public life and effect a revolution in the tone of opinion. He was appalled by the bombardment of Canton and by the tone and negativism of Palmerstonianism. Courtauld was a free-thinking unitarian crêpe magnate. Leaf was from a warehouse and banking family. Moore was a self-made lace merchant, an evangelical and a supporter of the Reformatory movement, the Bible Society, undenominational education and fallen women. All three gave generously to the ARA. Hankey was from a West India and banking family, the only 'princely' family to

The rallying of these groups in the same cause reflected broader trends of significance for the future direction of Liberalism. The post-Palmerstonian Liberal party was to rely on those, up and down the country, who in 1857 urged parliamentary reform – and there were many, despite Palmerston's superficial triumph.[127] It was also dependent on those who now believed that there was 'work to be done' at home – a group of which Russell was incontestably the leader after the 1857 election.[128] And it drew great strength from those who were repelled by the moral tone of Palmerstonianism at home and abroad. Hence the significance of the support for Russell in 1857 from Morley (leading Cobdenite, chairman of the electoral committee of the Liberation Society, and voluble voluntaryist) and Courtauld (one of the most high-profile campaigners against compulsory church rates); it marked an important stage in Dissent's rapprochement with the Liberal leadership. Equally signifi-cant was the increasing willingness of the main Peelites to move towards Russell and his stance on these three matters in 1857–8.[129] By September 1857, Althorp noted that Russell had 'taken the lead again on great National questions'.[130] He was very well received when he went to speak at Sheffield and Birmingham that autumn.[131]

Russell made many public appearances in these years, aimed at advertising his ideas and moulding opinion – a necessary task given the stagnation in parliament. At Exeter Hall he urged governors and citizens not to lend 'the helping hand of custom, folly, or intolerance to extinguish one spark of that divine flame which we call the soul'; he told the people of Liverpool that all classes had a duty to work together for reform; he warned that 'fearful . . . doom' and 'bloody and merciless retribution' might await those who preferred to 'eat, drink, and be merry'.[132] He spent a good deal of time urging voluntary philanthropy by the wealthy. He publicised the movements for national

support Russell, in his view: McCarthy, *Lady John Russell*, p. 170. Perhaps Hankey's loyalty was not unconnected with his extensive intellectual contacts with the continent; he corresponded with French political economists. He was Liberal MP for Peterborough. Alexander was one of the leaders of the anti-slavery movement.

127 As Russell recognised: to G. Elliot, 31 March 1857, Russell papers, 30/22/13c/163.
128 See e.g. *Spectator*, 24 October 1857, pp. 1110–11. Some journals had taken this line even before the election, e.g. *Leader*, VII, 1138–9, 29 November 1856.
129 Graham corresponded a great deal with Russell in 1858, principally on parliamentary reform, and declared his alliance with him in the Commons on 20 May 1858: *Hansard*, CL, 986. (See also ' . . . and Mr Fortescue', p. 130.) In the same year, Gladstone predicted that Russell would get the upper hand over Palmerston, because the latter had 'no legislative spirit or power': E. D. Steele, *Palmerston and Liberalism, 1855–1865* (Cambridge, 1991), p. 29.
130 *The red earl: the papers of the fifth Earl Spencer, 1835–1910: volume I*, ed. P. Gordon (Northampton, 1981), p. 44.
131 McCarthy, *Lady John Russell*, p. 171.
132 *Times*, 14 November 1855, p. 10, and 16 October 1858, p. 8; *Transactions of the NAPSS 1858*, p. 24.

reformatories, prison discipline and free drinking fountains; he drew attention to the Ragged School movement and the 'patient, daily work' needed to turn potentially criminal children into good members of society; and he lauded the crucial role of women in philanthropic movements, 'if in future sin is to have less dominion and religion more power'.[133] By 1859, his moralising speeches had made him one of the high priests of the Victorian middle-class philanthropic conscience, and it is appropriate that the most celebrated and message-laden liberal-religious melodrama of the year, Dickens's *A Tale of Two Cities*, was dedicated to him. One significant reformist lobby with which Russell liaised was the National Association for the Promotion of Social Science, established in 1857 in order to instil some continental-style rigour into discussion of Britain's legislative needs. Looking for high-profile political support, his old colleague (and fellow Francophile) Henry Brougham persuaded him to propose the inauguration of the Association at its first congress, and to preside over the section on jurisprudence and law amendment.[134] In this role, Russell advocated his Minister of Justice, the enlargement of the function of cheap, local courts, the reform of the bankruptcy law, and systematic law amendment carried not by executive diktat but 'by the action of opinion'.[135] (He then took charge of the NAPSS's bankruptcy reform bill until his return to government in 1859, when he gave it to the new Attorney-General; a diluted version passed in 1861.) Given the range of his interests, Russell was the obvious choice to succeed Brougham as the President of the whole of the second congress in 1858. In his address he duly urged the Association to follow 'Almighty Benevolence' by promoting legislation capable of raising the 'energy', 'tone' and 'moral character' of the population, which was threatened, among other things, by the inadequacy of religious education, the temptation of intoxication, inadequate sanitation, and over-rigid, energy-sapping prison discipline.[136]

Russell's interest in the Social Science Association was not sustained, probably because of his notorious dislike of detail, and perhaps also because he doubted its efficacy.[137] He continued to believe that the crucial stimulus to a legislative programme was parliamentary reform, which would galvanise the conscientiousness of parliament by forcing it to take more note of the virtuous elements of public opinion – fanned by the many moralistic novelists and voluntary bodies like the NAPSS. Prospects for Reform seemed to be

---

[133] On women, see ibid., p. 18; on Ragged Schools, see *Times*, 11 January 1856, p. 9, 26 September 1857, p. 10, and 25 October 1858, p. 10.

[134] Brougham to Russell, 21 August 1857, Russell papers, 30/22/13D/103.

[135] *Transactions of the National Association for the Promotion of Social Science 1857* (1858), pp. 29–35.

[136] *Transactions of the NAPSS 1858*, pp. 7–24.

[137] Though he presented its petition urging public health reform to the Commons in early 1859.

improving. The 1857 election made it clear that Palmerston was 'in great danger of being speedily upset' by his unwillingness to please reforming Liberal MPs.[138] This happened in February 1858, when Russell, with Bright and the Peelites, used the Orsini affair to defeat him, playing Fox against Pitt again by exploiting his apparent betrayal of patriotic libertarianism.[139] For the next sixteen months the Liberals were in opposition. Russell was able to put pressure on the minority Conservative government to settle the Jewish emancipation question, while it was forced to express an interest in parliamentary reform in order to stay in power. It was defeated on its Reform Bill of 1859, which did not please enough Liberals, and a speedy Liberal return to government could be predicted – probably on a reforming agenda, with Russell as prime minister.[140] But the latter prediction was not realised. When the Liberals formed the administration of June 1859, Palmerston took the highest post again, with Russell as Foreign Secretary.

Why, despite Russell's revival, was he unable to take the premiership in 1859? One reason was Palmerston's tactical superiority during the negotiations of June. But there were several more fundamental factors. The first was the eruption of the Italian crisis, pushing foreign affairs to the forefront. One of Palmerston's centrist henchmen, Charles Wood, wrote with evident relief in May 1859, 'War and Peace have . . . entirely superseded Reform.'[141] The great beauty of the Italian question was that it played to Palmerston's strengths, yet also appealed to Russell's (and Gladstone's) romanticism. Even Russell was prepared to subordinate Reform in the cause of Italian liberty. He was the more willing to do so because he thought that the subordination would be only temporary, since he had good bargaining counters, in the shape of a Cobdenite presence in the cabinet and Palmerston's agreement to bring in a Reform Bill in 1860.[142] That these turned out to be worth little was partly because Palmerston, eight years older than Russell, surprised most people by retaining more vigour over the next six years than his younger rival. But it was also because of the continuing complacency of parliament, which intensified

138 Hardcastle, *Campbell*, II, 349–50.
139 The Fox–Pitt comparison is especially apposite given the other controversies of early 1858 – about Indian government (after the Mutiny), jobbery (after the Clanricarde appointment) and jingoism (after the diversion of a naval force to Canton). On Orsini, see B. Porter, *The refugee question in mid-Victorian politics* (Cambridge, 1979).
140 This was predicted by Clarendon and Gladstone: ' . . . *and Mr Fortescue*', p. 139; Steele, *Palmerston and Liberalism*, p. 29. Robert Lowe, a consistent enemy of Russell, was not so charitable: *The Greville memoirs 1814–1860*, ed. L. Strachey and R. Fulford (8 vols., London, 1938 edn), VII, 331–2.
141 Steele, *Palmerston and Liberalism*, p. 124.
142 Cobden's man in cabinet was Milner Gibson. For Russell's reasoning on Italy and Reform, see Russell to Granville, 12 June 1859, Russell papers, 30/22/13G/266, and to Palmerston, 16 June 1859, 30/22/13G/282.

in reaction to John Bright's alarming campaign of 1858–9 for radical Reform, and was made yet worse because of the relative strength of the Conservative party after 1859 (the election took place under the short-lived Conservative government). Palmerston and Derby formed an unofficial bloc to resist a policy of 'movement'. This was a decisive 'tit-for-tat' against Russell, not only for 1851 but also for 'upsetting the coach' way back in 1834. Within a few months, a depressed Russell realised that the momentum for reform had ebbed away; this, combined with physical decline, persuaded him to go to the Lords in 1861.[143]

In the 1860s, Russell lost his vigour but not his principles.[144] He was the obvious prime minister when Palmerston eventually died in October 1865. It was equally obvious that his first legislative initiative would be a Reform Bill, intended as a rallying-call to the boroughs and a precursor of educational, social and Irish measures. The obstacle was, as ever, the tone of parliament and the upper reaches of the cabinet, reinforced by the *Times*. Russell was abused by his critics for his radical appointments, for depending too much on Bright and Gladstone, and for undue haste in promoting Reform. They urged that the question should be referred to a stately Royal commission – an astonishing call, in view of the frequency with which it had been discussed since 1848 and the moderation of Russell's bill of 1866.[145] But, unfortunately for Russell, Palmerstonian optimism and mid-Victorian prosperity had left the Liberal party no less conservative on Reform than it had been in the late 1840s. Lady Amberley's description of Russell as 'the head of the most advanced Liberals of the country; a proud position at 75' was a pardonable, rather than an absurd, exaggeration.[146] He hoped that the Reform Bill could be passed by 'pressing, pressing, pressing hard'.[147] But he often doubted if it could be passed at all. However, his disposition remained sunny; the cause would triumph in the end; his job was to promote it and await the result philosophically. Maintaining his spiritual well-being in face of the world's folly was equally important. The 1866 session was punctuated by parliamentary crises as dissident Palmerstonian Liberal MPs threatened to do what they finally did on 18 June, kill the bill and with it Russell's last government. On the first of these, the government was widely expected to fall. There was astonishment as it

---

[143] ' . . . *and Mr Fortescue*', pp. 165, 184.

[144] Russell is often assumed to have urged 'Rest and be thankful' in a speech at Blairgowrie in 1863. But he did not. He said that the country seemed to be of that opinion, and so there was no option but to consent; but he warned that there were 'other mountains to climb': *Times*, 28 September 1863, p. 7.

[145] For criticism of Russell, see e.g. Maxwell, *Clarendon*, II, 314, and Delane in P. H. Bagenal, *The life of Ralph Bernal Osborne* (pr. pr. 1884), pp. 222–3.

[146] *Amberley papers*, I, 485.

[147] M. Cowling, *1867: Disraeli, Gladstone and revolution; the passing of the second Reform Bill* (Cambridge, 1967), p. 104.

became clear that the prime minister was not on hand to deal with the potential crisis. That Oxford man-on-the-make Benjamin Jowett heard the explanation and recounted it scornfully. Russell 'had gone down to Richmond to hear the nightingales!' Jowett was the sort of man who considered that Russell had 'no sense and no knowledge of the world or of persons'. Much of London society would have agreed with him; but perhaps they did not know about Charles James Fox.[148]

IV

Russell's active political career ended at an unfortunate moment for his reputation. A new political era was beginning, and it was implausible that a man who had achieved nothing significant in domestic politics since 1850 would deserve any credit for influencing it. Yet Russell's legacy cannot be dismissed so simply. Though he had not anticipated the terms of the 1867 Reform Act, its galvanising effects on the Liberal party were more predictable. Knowing that his time was short, Russell used his last months as Liberal leader, in 1867, to publicise the two issues which he was most anxious for the party to rally around: Irish Church reform and elementary education.[149] The legislative activity of the Liberal government of 1868–74 was unprecedented, embracing not only both those questions, which dominated its first two sessions, but also other issues with which Russell had been concerned: the reform of public health, the poor law, the punishment system, licensing, the judicature and the bankruptcy laws, most of which were tackled in an appropriately moralistic spirit.[150] Of the seven cabinet ministers responsible for these policy areas, five had owed their primary political loyalty to Russell and the other two were adherents to the administrative reform crusade of the mid-1850s.[151] This is not to say that Russell was happy with all the details of

---

[148] *Dear Miss Nightingale: a selection of Benjamin Jowett's letters to Florence Nightingale 1860–1893*, ed. V. Quinn and J. Prest (Oxford, 1987), pp. 87, 204.

[149] See his motion on the Irish Church, in *Hansard*, CLXXXVIII, 354, 24 June 1867, and his *Letter to Chichester Fortescue, MP, on the state of Ireland* (1868) (followed by two other published epistles); and his motion on education, in *Hansard*, CXC, 493, 2 December 1867.

[150] See e.g. Parry, *Rise and fall*, ch. 10, and M. Wiener, *Reconstructing the criminal: culture, law and policy in England, 1830–1914* (Cambridge, 1990).

[151] Fortescue, the Irish Secretary, had first been appointed to that office by Russell in December 1865, and was a friend; Forster (Education) owed his first ministerial post to Russell (November 1865); Goschen (poor law/local government) was made a junior and then a cabinet minister by Russell in 1865–6, while his successor Stansfeld's career was rescued by Russell in February 1866 after he had resigned office in 1864 when associated with Mazzini and the conspiracy against Napoleon III. The Lord Chancellor, Hatherley, was the former W. P. Wood: see above, n. 112. The other two, Ripon (Forster's superior at the Privy Council) and Bruce (Home Secretary), were already well established in government before 1865.

the resulting legislation.[152] But he cared much less for the policy associated with the other members of the government, particularly the reforms in the civil service and army conducted by Gladstone's friends Lowe and Cardwell, and the foreign and later Irish policy of Gladstone himself, which he considered to be demeaning and irresponsible.[153] It is a moot point which of the Gladstonian or Russellite agendas (so to call them) did the more to destroy the 110-seat Liberal majority of 1868. At any rate, the upshot was the return of a majority Conservative government for the first time since Russell himself had achieved this feat in 1841. As ever, Russell's difficulty was not his class-bound outlook but his failure to humour the conservatism of English public opinion.

If one defines the dynamic of nineteenth-century Liberalism as the assault on the privileges of a ruling class and the move towards a more popular and ultimately a democratic government, then it could be argued that Russell deserves only a secondary place. If, however, one believes that Liberalism in the first two thirds of the nineteenth century was driven mostly by a moralistic anxiety to promote liberty, order, industry and patriotism through asserting Protestantism, parliamentary government and public responsibility for social ills, then he becomes crucial – and at least as important in the party's long-term evolution as Palmerston, the Peelites and the radicals.[154] Arguing for the second definition of Liberalism should not blind us to the existence of men who hoped for some form of the first; one cannot ignore the role of radicals and others who were suspicious of those politicians, like Russell, who were unembarrassed about their landed background and cool towards house-hold suffrage. Russell was also vain and capricious, and his pride in family and his quest for honourable fame could easily be mocked by these critics as the whims of a spoilt aristocratic brat.[155] However, in order to understand him this stereotype has to be subordinated, and more weight given to his self-image and his intense religious consciousness. It was these which defined the virtues which he aimed to promote, and the vices which he sought to attack, in his domestic, Irish and foreign policies. Russell's political identity was moulded by the opposition mentality of his Foxite forbears, and by his religious principles. These made it almost impossible for him to adopt the language of complacency and the political establishment with which his opponents associated him. He was not being hypocritical in urging, as he often did,

---

[152] He preferred concurrent endowment to disendowment in Ireland, while the 1870 Education Act was more lenient to the denominations than he had been – mainly under the influence of Lowe, who regarded all Russell's education schemes as impractically anti-clerical.

[153] There is entertaining abuse scattered throughout *Recollections*.

[154] This is the line taken by Parry, *Rise and fall*. It needs to be supplemented by further work.

[155] Among many examples, see Dasent, *Delane*, ii, 155, and C. S. Miall, *Henry Richard: a biography* (London, 1889), p. 96.

'friends of improvement [to] repeat the same thing . . . till some efficient inroad has been made upon the great mass of vice and misery'.[156] Yet this was the same man who believed that his tenure of high office was not only a duty but also a right. He was placeman yet preacher; he was both insider and outsider. Paradoxically, the man who served for over twenty-five years in British cabinets remained one of Fox's martyrs to the end.

156 *Times*, 25 October 1858, p. 10. For a similar sentiment in 1839, see Parry, *Rise and fall*, p. 127.

8

DOCUMENTARY FALSIFICATION
AND ITALIAN BIOGRAPHY
৩৩৩৩

DENIS MACK SMITH

E VERY country has been tempted on occasion to produce tendentious
accounts of its history and particularly in the biography of national
heroes. In extreme cases there can be actual manipulation of documentary
evidence, but much more common is casual misrepresentation to justify
someone's behaviour or perhaps to comfort national pride. Where a
presumption of deceit is obvious, the damage is no worse than marginal: for
example when a crucial but ambiguous letter from King Victor Emanuel to
Garibaldi in 1860 was reproduced in half a dozen different versions, or when
the execution of Mussolini in 1945 was described in many irreconcilable
accounts by presumed eyewitnesses who had private axes to grind. On other
occasions a reader is easily alerted to the chance that an author or editor might
be trying to ingratiate himself with a powerful patron. But in many cases
authenticity is hard to verify and there may be difficulty in deciding if a
memoir or diary, whether for political reasons or to make a more saleable
book, has been 'improved' or partially rewritten.

I

An easy method of falsifying written history is simple concealment of relevant
facts, and here a particular problem in Italy is that cabinet ministers illegally
used to retain important official documents after leaving office. Di Revel in
1867 was told by colleagues that this was a normal procedure and he should
follow suit for his own self-protection. Sometimes indeed it was done with a
deliberate intention to further someone's career by concealing information
from whoever replaced him in government. General Lamarmora, when he
became prime minister in 1864, was embarrassed to find that an important
treaty with France had mysteriously disappeared from the archives, and his
own highly confidential report of 1849 about an insurrection in Genoa
had mysteriously been purchased by a private citizen. Crispi, another prime

minister, discovered in 1888 that the archives of the Foreign Office had no trace of secret agreements for the past twenty-five years. One unfortunate result was that public opinion and politicians could be kept in ignorance about governmental commitments, for instance about the rash promise to send an Italian army to help Germany on the Rhine in any war against France. Nor was the important Triple Alliance with Germany and Austria published until 1915, more than thirty years after being signed, and not even the cabinet was consulted in 1915 when Salandra suddenly changed sides to fight against his ally of yesterday.

Raison d'état is of course properly invoked in every country to justify a degree of secretiveness. But it is worth remembering that Italian public opinion was persuaded into fighting two terrible world wars through this kind of secrecy, and on both occasions secretiveness was compounded with untruthful propaganda manufactured by a tiny group of politicians. Moreover in 1915, as in 1940, one may doubt if the national interest was well served.

Today Italians are confronted by a different aspect of conspiratorial secrecy ever since a few pertinacious magistrates in 1992 stumbled across a minor episode of embezzlement, because this fortuitous disclosure put them on the track of many much more substantial enigmas that for forty years had obscured the misconduct of a whole political class and perverted the working of parliamentary democracy. These unexpected revelations reinforce the suspicion that in no other western society are there so many potentially damaging mysteries of state. A murderous bombing outrage at Milan as long ago as 1969, first ascribed to left-wing terrorism and then to the neo-fascists, is still unexplained, and distortion of evidence by the police was a deliberate attempt to conceal the truth. Equally mysterious are later destructive bombings in half a dozen cities, which increased the suspicion that evidence was manipulated or invented for political reasons. Many years elapsed before journalists discovered that the official account of how in 1950 the famous bandit Salvatore Giuliano was brought to book had been an invention by the police to conceal their own complicity with the mafia. Further mystification still clouds the truth about the violent deaths in the early 1980s of the two Vatican bankers Calvi and Sindona, and of the oil baron Mattei in 1962, three people who were major players on the political scene and whose deaths left many major political problems unresolved. What we know is that all three were financing political parties across the board and obtained favours in return, favours that sometimes saved them from prosecution but also made powerful enemies.

Newspapers today continue to discuss other unexplained secrets from the past: many billions of *lire* missing from the public accounts; armed political coups involving General De Lorenzo in 1964 and Prince Borghese in 1970; the inexplicable disappearance of a passenger plane near the island of Ustica in June 1980; malversation of funds on an astronomical scale after several destructive earthquakes; clandestine political activity by an illegal masonic lodge that enrolled cabinet ministers, generals, judges and leading industrialists. And only since 1990 have magistrates at last begun to uncover many years of secret activity by an undercover military organisation code-named Gladio that was financed by the government but about which some prime ministers professed complete ignorance.

Most damaging of all, during fifty years of Christian-Democrat rule, governments have dragged their feet over investigating the camorra and mafia despite murders of many judges and police investigators brave enough to confront these dreadful scourges: one result of which is that three large regions of the country remain to a large extent outside the rule of law. Relevant evidence on this painful subject, according to parliamentary commissions of investigation, was suppressed as a matter of course, especially to avoid revealing many shabby connections between these illegal movements and prominent politicians – connections denounced a century ago by the prime minister Minghetti and others as a major problem for Italy. The judiciary since 1950 has asked parliament for permission to proceed against more than six hundred members of the legislature for suspected criminal activity, but permission was generally refused because many politicians were anxious to protect the murky world of politics from public scrutiny.

After the fall of Mussolini, unlike in some other defeated countries, an amnesty was quickly granted for the many atrocious crimes committed by fascists, so leaving another important gap in the archives. Governments have furthermore granted repeated amnesties for wholesale tax evasion and for hundreds of thousands of illegal buildings that everywhere caused havoc in towns and countryside. These amnesties, as well as letting many profiteers and *mafiosi* off the hook, have helped to conceal some facts of history. In other cases documents were clumsily forged for political purposes. De Gasperi, the most distinguished prime minister since the second world war, had to defend himself against the highly loaded allegation that in 1944 he wrote to Colonel Bonham Carter urging the British to bomb Rome, although Bonham Carter testified in court that this was untrue and he had never so much as heard of De Gasperi.

A better known example is a series of letters between Mussolini and Churchill that some Italians claim to have seen in authenticated copies and about which books are still written. Impossible though it may appear, Churchill in these letters is said to have begged Mussolini to fight on the German side in 1940 so that a defeated Britain would have one friend among the victors when the time came for peace negotiations. Equally incredible, other presumed letters from Churchill during the war continued to express admiration for the Duce and declared London's readiness for a compromise peace by surrendering part of the British empire to Italy.

Another victim of deliberate falsification was the influential communist thinker Gramsci whose writings were posthumously altered by his own party to omit criticism of Stalin and to delete unwelcome mention of similarities between communism and fascism. Such forgeries and perversions of the truth may have had a short-term political utility but in the long run produced a different result from what was intended.

II

The study of Italian fascism has presented particular difficulties in that an enormous amount of misinformation was printed during 1922–45 as journalistic propaganda, aided by the fact that most fascist leaders possessed newspapers of their own wherein they concocted legends about their own achievements and heroism. In November 1942, despite an acute war-time paper shortage, a periodical owned personally by Mussolini with an almost guaranteed circulation had one single issue that weighed over a kilogram when not the slightest criticism of fascism could be printed anywhere. By silencing open discussion the Duce made it hard for us to check some of his claims or estimate the degree of public support he enjoyed. The 'Protocols of the Elders of Zion', long after this book was proved a forgery, had two Italian editions in 1937–8 with tens of thousands of copies telling people about a Jewish plot to achieve world domination. Other inventions after 1945 were not so easily exposed. A fascinating book of memoirs by Quinto Navarra, who as Mussolini's personal servant lived in the Palazzo Venezia and saw more of him than anyone, seems in part to have been a compilation by two journalists in search of a good story. Even the documents published in 1985 by Mussolini's foreign minister Dino Grandi, though authenticated by the much respected historian Renzo de Felice, have been shown by the American professor Knox to be partly counterfeit.

Mussolini before he won power condemned censorship as a shameful scandal that should be abolished in the national interest but, once in office, it became the most important weapon in his armoury. Apart from rigorous controls over the press, he once admitted sending each month four tons of official documents to be burnt. Towards the end of his life he also ordered that his own private archives be destroyed to protect his reputation from criticism; though fortunately some survived and were photographed during the Anglo-American invasion with the result that Italian historians must sometimes refer to photocopies in Oxford and Washington. By his order the letters of D'Annunzio were 'corrected' before being published at state expense. More seriously, he mobilised Italian historians of the risorgimento under a central fascist directorate that sometimes issued orders about what results their research was expected to achieve. Not only is his own autobiography another diverting example of how propaganda can be used to colour the truth, but a 'definitive' and 'unexpurgated' edition of his abundant writings appeared under his personal imprimatur, and only critics outside Italy could draw attention to its extensive omissions and tamperings with the original text. Evidently he did not wish to remind Italians that he had once opposed censorship and dictatorship and militarism. Nor did he want them to recollect his earlier atheism and marxist sympathies. Nor were they allowed to know about his intention to 'chloroform' the Italian people and execute members of parliament who voiced public disagreement. On the other hand he positively needed to encourage Italians to welcome war against Britain, and for that purpose they were presented with a gallimaufry of improbable inventions about his invincible air force and army of eight million soldiers that without help from Hitler would guarantee victory after a few weeks of fighting.

The full extent of fascist falsehoods and disinformation will never be known because so much evidence has been destroyed. Nor can we measure its undoubted contribution towards Mussolini's defeat. There is nevertheless no doubt that his remarkable gullibility rendered him vulnerable to his own deceitful propaganda, and possibly he genuinely persuaded himself that his armed services were the best in the world. Public criticism was impossible and private criticism remained private. Information accepted by him as minister in charge of all three armed forces was often entirely false, as he had ample means of knowing. Another small but not untypical episode was his order to arrest a future pope, Cardinal Montini, until the police discovered that the only evidence was a letter forged by the anticlerical Farinacci. The brilliant journalist Malaparte admitted forging yet another letter to minimise Mussolini's involvement in the murder of Matteotti, and much of the other evidence produced after that assassination was for the same reason more or less fraudulent.

To prove the decadence and feeble pacifism of the British, Malaparte quoted abundant details from what he called an 'authoritative' English book entitled *1066 And All That*, in actual fact a famous and humorous work of fiction, but which he said reflected the views of the Oxford history school. The British were oddly censured by other official historians for having consistently opposed the unification of Italy in the nineteenth century. Even more oddly they were accused of ingratitude for refusing to admit that in the first world war they were saved from defeat by Italian victories. Ridicule was poured on the British CID, an acronym said to represent the 'Colonial Intelligence Department' for which young students were recruited from the 'University of Devon' near London. Many publications repeated word for word these ludicrous allegations, and a succession of books identified a dangerous enemy of Italy in a mysterious W. R. Juge who one may suspect to have been the inoffensive Dean Inge of St Paul's Cathedral. More consequentially, Grandi as ambassador in London, tried to ingratiate himself with the Duce by reporting in the middle 1930s that the British so admired Mussolini that they were on the brink of copying his fascist revolution; and Grandi added that in any case they could be fought with impunity since the finest regiments in the British army, which he carefully watched on parade, were no better than 'marionettes of wood' too cowardly to defend their country against the Italian blackshirt militia. We can only speculate on how far such reports helped to precipitate the declaration of war against Britain after 1939.

Another example of evidence being altered is the diary of Giuseppe Bottai, one of the less frivolous fascists and a minister who held office longer than anyone. Two editions of his diary have been published, one edited by Bottai himself in 1949 and a much longer version in 1982. Both are interesting and cover the same period, but almost every entry differs in each. The first and shorter edition cut out Mussolini's vulgar language and denunciation of the Jews, but contains revealing passages not in the second: for example it quotes Mussolini saying that already in 1936 he was planning a 'war of brigandage' against the western democracies, and in 1937 he intended to create an army of two million black mercenaries to dominate the whole of Africa. This earlier version refers to his envy of Hitler. It mentioned what Bottai called Mussolini's 'incredible' reluctance to be seen as needing expert military advice during the course of the second world war, and it quoted the Duce's astonishing boast a few days before the allied invasion in 1943 that an Italian victory was now assured. The second and much longer edition of Bottai's diary, while omitting some of these entries, contains many additional and fascinating comments, for instance about the barely literate general secretary of the fascist party who presumed to give public lectures on the subject of Ariosto's 'Divine Comedy'.

This is far from being the only instance of diaries and memoirs emended to impress posterity. Those of three important prime ministers, Menabrea for the 1860s, Crispi for the 1880s and 1890s, and Salandra after 1914, have evidence of alterations or deletions some of which were without doubt politically motivated. The diary of Cavour was first published in 1888 translated from the original French, but the manuscript then disappeared and only in 1991 were we given a corrected version ten times as long. Cavour's close collaborator Giuseppe Massari, who had himself produced a prudently doctored edition of Gioberti's correspondence, wrote a diary that is of the greatest importance for the years 1858–60, but which had to be republished in 1959 because an earlier edition of 1931 was disgracefully truncated and inaccurate.

For the period 1914–19 the substantial and important diary of the minister

Ferdinando Martini was published in 1966 in an excellent edition with only minor apparent omissions. It reveals that Martini was among the very few politicians to realise the damage done to Italian aspirations and self-knowledge through deliberate factual inaccuracies that by indulging patriotic pride made nonsense of many conventional histories of the risorgimento. It incidentally describes how Salandra as prime minister chose to prevent people knowing how he had dragged what he knew to be an unwilling country into the first world war: parliament was kept in recess on purpose and, for a crucial six months of 1914–15 when the whole world was in a state of convulsion, Martini records that not one word of foreign policy was mentioned in meetings of the Italian cabinet.

Another long diary of fundamental importance is that of Domenico Farini who as President of the Senate in the years 1887–98 was in daily contact with all prominent politicians. A fine two-volume edition of this diary in 1961, though slightly bowdlerised in deleting some strong language, corrects another published version of 1942 which, despite careful excision of critical references to the king, was halted by the monarchy before its second volume could appear. The earlier edition, as a product of the fascist period, had no difficulty quoting a prime minister confessing in 1894 that parliamentary government would never work in Italy, but omitted references to sexual peccadillos by the royal family and their unprintable involvement in bank scandals during the 1880s and 1890s. Farini was a devoted monarchist, but we can now see how his mention of 'abusi femminili' by the future King Victor Emanuel III was censured. Also deleted were references to how the Italian monarchy, which enjoyed the largest civil list of any sovereign in Europe, was presciently salting away much of its fortune in London – where, ironically, in the second world war it was invested in British war loan by the Custodian of Enemy Property and then preserved by the British courts from confiscation by the Italian republic after 1946.

Similar perplexity was created by two different published editions of a diary written by Marshal Cavallero who, as Chief of General Staff in 1940–3, had much first-hand knowledge about Mussolini as well as about relations with HItler and the second world war. A first edition of 1948 contains comments covering days left blank in the longer version of 1984, and the wording of other entries is so changed as to make them seem two different books. For unexplained reasons the second 'authentic' edition, though four times longer, omits passages which if true are not without interest: for example about how Mussolini, anxious for Germany to carry the main burden of war, ordered Italian naval units to stay close to the coast so as to avoid damage by enemy action; and about the way industrialists delayed conversion of their factories to arms manufacture in order to keep lines of peace-time production in existence; or about official encouragement of vicious blackshirt terrorism in the Balkans and how Mussolini ordered the property of Slovene 'rebels' to be confiscated for the benefit of hoped-for but non-existent Italian settlers.

III

The immense tragedy of fascism makes it easy to understand why contemporary politicians yielded to the temptation of fabricating history for political purposes. But liberal governments, both before 1922 and after 1946, sometimes acted similarly and with results that could also be unfortunate. The official publication of parliamentary debates in liberal Italy before 1922 was sometimes, perhaps often, doctored to conceal accusations of governmental malpractice, as we can tell from comparison with personal memoirs and newspaper reports of proceedings in the legislature. The liberal Giolitti, who dominated the years 1901–14, repeatedly refused requests to open the archives for the years after 1815 and candidly explained to parliament in June 1912 that it was inexpedient for 'beautiful legends' to be demolished by historical criticism. Some important episodes in Italian history could therefore be studied more easily in Vienna than in the archives of Turin and Rome.

One idea of what Giolitti meant by beautiful legends can be observed when he was premier during the war fought in 1911–12 for the conquest of Libya. We now know that vital facts were concealed and documents faked to justify the need for this war, and during the first five months of fighting the prime minister refused to let parliament meet to debate or question his momentous decision to invade Tripolitania. Subsequently he boasted that the outside world admired the fact that no colonial war had ever been fought with more brilliant success, whereas he knew that the effect abroad had been the very opposite. In private he confessed that the army commanders in Libya were absolutely incompetent ('sotto zero') and without a ten to one superiority in numbers were reluctant ever to engage the enemy. He even added that he had been obliged to falsify the news by inventing non-existent victories in order to sustain public morale. Subsequently every possible action was taken to keep secret that the war continued for many years after 1912 with many serious military reverses. Nor is it without interest that Mussolini, of all people, remarked that such gigantic examples of deception might have tragic results by concealing weaknesses in the army and its higher command. In 1915, after Giolitti had taken some of the relevant documentation away with him into retirement, his successor Salandra therefore led Italy into a world war expecting that a quick Italian victory was assured before the year's end. This erroneous expectation, like Mussolini's exactly similar mistake in June 1940, imposed a heavy burden on Italy's future development and damaged her claim to be considered one of the Great Powers.

Equally vital in an earlier period was the need to justify the Piedmontese victory in the risorgimento against criticism by other Italian patriots such as Mazzini, Cattaneo and Garibaldi. Plenty of historians dependent on government patronage for their jobs were available for this purpose. Dozens of volumes and thousands of documents were printed with minor or major inaccuracies, names of people left out, phrases inserted, and 'unpatriotic' remarks deleted. Dates were changed, for instance to defend King Charles Albert from the accusation that he signed a military convention with Austria the national enemy, and to prove that this same king in 1848 bravely declared war against Austria without waiting for Marshal Radetzky's defeat by a civic rising in Milan. The revolutions of 1848 were described as essentially patriotic by historians who in private confessed that this was a good deal less than the truth. In every school textbook the defeated King Ferdinand of Naples has ever since been disparaged as the wicked 'King Bomba' for his bombardment of the civilian population at Messina in 1847, whereas the subsequent Piedmontese bombardment of Genoa, Ancona and Gaeta was either applauded or ignored. This same desire for political correctness explains why the French success against Austria in the battle of Magenta was claimed as a great Italian victory (even by Salvemini in 1945), though the only Italian fatalities seem to have been among Italians fighting on the other side as part of the Austrian army, a fact that did not square with patriotic legend and had to be concealed. A *carbonaro* document was changed to prove that already in 1821 the Italian people were united in working towards national union and independence. An entire letter by Abraham Lincoln was forged to suggest that impartial outside observers were eager for Italy to annex Corsica, Dalmatia and Albania, a letter that was still being quoted by ministers in 1953 to support Italian territorial claims.

Other political reasons explain why Cavour's opponents among the patriots had to be traduced and depreciated. Garibaldi was defamed by the invention that in October 1860 he ordered his men to fire against the Piedmontese army, although his order had been to welcome them as brothers. Letters by Mazzini were similarly invented and other facts suppressed in order to counter an alternative interpretation of the risorgimento that was democratic, republican, and based not on nationalist *Machtpolitik* but on liberal patriotism and the desire to create a European federation of free peoples. Some historians concealed evidence in their possession with the aim of falsely depicting Mazzini as a cruel assassin and a communist in the pay of Austria, so that legends of his illiberal and anti-Italian activities became part of accepted opinion. When Felice Orsini attempted in 1858 to kill Emperor Napoleon III, Favour tried his hardest to persuade people that Mazzini was responsible; though, as Cavour knew, Mazzini was a bitter adversary of this would-be murderer. The unpalatable fact that Orsini was covertly paid from Cavour's secret service budget was carefully concealed. The prime minister even claimed to have positive proof that Mazzini intended to assassinate King Victor Emanuel, but this was a deliberate falsehood; nor has any evidence of any kind ever been produced.

Some of these fabrications, useful though they may have been at the time, are gradually being corrected in the present century now that the archives are more accessible. Great numbers of Mazzini's letters, hundreds of them buried after being arbitrarily intercepted by the papal and Piedmontese police, have now been exhumed and printed. An earlier and most defective edition of Ricasoli's letters is also in course of being replaced, though D'Azeglio and other leading characters of the risorgimento have not yet been so fortunate. Cavour, without doubt the most considerable politician in modern Italian history, posed a delicate problem for half a dozen editors who after his death published twenty volumes of letters covering his period in government. Cavour died with many state documents in his private possession: some of his papers were then dispersed or destroyed, some disappeared after being seized by the king, and most of the rest were inherited by a French citizen who did not share Cavour's liberal opinions. A commission was eventually appointed by the Italian government in 1913 to publish a corrected edition containing all that could be found, and today after eighty years and several false starts the result has at last passed a half-way stage. In the century after his death, researchers were nevertheless regularly refused access to the originals. But at least we are now able to see how earlier editors were instructed to alter the record.

Two of these editors, Michelangelo Castelli and Nicomede Bianchi, were the only scholars who, quite exceptionally, were given access to the State archives in order to support Cavour's political programme by writing a slanted version of events. This was a useful and perhaps excusable purpose during a critical period of nation-building. Less excusable is that later failures to correct the accepted story gave subsequent generations a dangerously inaccurate idea of the strengths and weaknesses of the new nation. Castelli wrote his own memoirs and a life of Cavour, both of them fascinating but both full of inaccuracies and inspired by the need to exalt every action of Cavour as laudable and successful. Two important volumes of Castelli's correspondence are equally unreliable.

Bianchi used his official position to write two books based on Cavour's letters and a third to demolish the reputation of Mazzini. In addition he produced eight substantial volumes of diplomatic documents covering the period before 1861, a publication that is still an indispensable basis for historical research. Bianchi in private explained that his allotted task was frankly that of political propaganda. He had to justify the Piedmontese monarchy which alone could make Italians 'glorious and feared by the outside world'. He had to praise the 'miraculous' achievements of Cavour and denigrate the 'wicked and crazy' democrats Garibaldi and Mazzini who were said to have destroyed Italy's reputation in Europe; though in fact these two great patriots were among the most admired Italians in the outside world. All the many facts that told in a different sense had to be omitted. Words and sentences were freely altered in what a later archivist, who had privileged access to the originals, has described as 'an enormous and persistent accumulation of systematic errors and suppression of the truth'. Many of these inaccuracies have still not been corrected because often the original documents have been lost or are unavailable for consultation. Bianchi furthermore used his position as chief civil servant in the Ministry of Education to make university professors swear an oath of loyalty to the régime, with results on public historical awareness that were no doubt intended and expected.

Subsequently in 1883–7 the diligent and meritorious Luigi Chiala produced six volumes of Cavour's letters and at other times edited half a dozen documentary collections that remain a primary source for any student of the risorgimento. Chiala had a delicate task of expurgation and told an American friend that he once suffered imprisonment for an indiscreet reference to King Victor Emanuel; but did an effective job as far as he was permitted. A quarter of his published documents were nevertheless incomplete or otherwise inaccurate. Cavour's scornful condemnation of Depretis and Crispi had to be discreetly removed because these two eminent politicians were in government at the time of Chiala's publication. Omitted, too, was Cavour's criticism of 'perfidious Albion' since this would have been equally ill-timed, and so were details of how this prime minister bribed journalists and foreign diplomats. Cavour's remark in 1856 had to be deleted where he condemned the unification of Italy as an absurd objective. Also cut out was his willingness to cede the island of Sardinia to the pope in return for annexing Rome, because this would have offended many patriots; and so was a reference to his own abortive plans for financing insurrections throughout Central Europe since it was expedient to blame these (and their failure) on Garibaldi.

Other politic deletions by Chiala were Cavour's gratuitous comments on the cowardice of Tuscans, and also his criticism of Naples as the most corrupt part of Italy that might have been kept in subjection by martial law. The prime minister's derision of Garibaldi as a 'savage' and a 'disgrace to Italy' was omitted as offensive to the memory of someone who after his death could safely be accepted as a national hero. Other expunged references included mention of Cavour's readiness in 1860 to fight a civil war against Garibaldi's followers. The official, but incorrect, story had to be that it was Garibaldi who wanted civil war; and no doubt the Italian public would have been appalled had they been allowed to know that Cavour ordered the Piedmontese army to prepare for the 'extermination' of thirty thousand of Garibaldi's volunteer soldiers who had just conquered half of Italy for their king. Yet another insufficiently patriotic fact was Cavour's remark that the Piedmontese annexation of Sicily was needed in order to thwart Garibaldi; so this too was left out.

Luigi Bollea, a schoolmaster with a passion for archival research, tried in 1916 to break this conspiracy of silence. But his book of documents was allowed publication only with further deletions and after years of difficulties with the government, including police harassment as well as legal action, and only after another more respected historian agreed to claim the work as his own.

Then in the 1920s a more substantial scholar, Alessandro Luzio, was put in charge of the official commission for re-editing Cavour's letters. Luzio was a devoted fascist who became vice-president of Mussolini's Royal Academy. He was also an embattled polemicist and vindictive to anyone he saw as a rival. Despite his fierce indignation when the Austrians gave him only limited access to the archives in Vienna, he himself jealously refused permission to scholars who wished to consult documents under his personal control, and he was outraged when Julia Ady 'pirated' documents of sixteenth-century Ferrara over which, in typical *stile fascista*, he claimed monopoly rights. Omodeo, the greatest contemporary expert on Cavour's career, was refused permission by Luzio to consult Cavour's papers. Omodeo, referring to this kind of petty and cantankerous scholarly rivalry, called it the greatest of all obstacles to historical studies in Italy and the chief reason why the best historians of the risorgimento were foreigners.

Before his death in 1946, Luzio's many published volumes nevertheless succeeded in correcting most of the errors introduced by his predecessors. Indeed he claimed to be producing a 'definitive' edition of Cavour's correspondence, though his own corrected volumes still contained a few examples of mutilation, or reproduced documents taken from Bollea without checking the originals, or else failed to recognise where Chiala had discovered a more authentic text. He also decided, somewhat arbitrarily, to print the letters not in chronological order but under separate subject headings. In 1946 Omodeo warned me, quite correctly, that my own request for permission to consult the Cavour archives would certainly be rejected, but I was then fortunate to enlist the support of important public figures including Croce, Chabod and the former prime minister Bonomi; and a few weeks later, Bonomi and Chabod were appointed to head a new commission to re-edit Luzio's work in a chronological sequence, and with proper public access.

Fifty years after the monarchy was abolished in 1946, a much greater mystery still surrounds the archives of the royal house, and my own repeated requests for information did not receive so much as an acknowledgement from ex-king Umberto. Many crates of documents were taken to Egypt by Umberto's father Victor Emanuel when he abdicated and later were sent to

Portugal and then Switzerland. Umberto bequeathed them at his death to the Italian State, but his heirs have continued to make difficulties and it is more than possible that in the interim much has disappeared or been destroyed. Whatever remains in existence could possibly illuminate many crucial events in national history, because the four Italian kings between 1849 and 1946 received copies of all important state documents, and the personal letters they wrote to ministers were generally returned to the royal archives when or before the recipients died. If need be, royal officials would arrive promptly to confiscate papers from the estate of important politicians, including Cavour, Rattazzi, D'Azeglio and Mussolini. Two or three scholars were allowed to see a few sections of this royal archive, and some documents selected by Umberto were sent in copy for publication in the official *Documenti Diplomatici Italiani*. For the rest we must rely on supposition.

This gap in our knowledge is the more significant in that the Italian constitution of 1848 made it a criminal offence for contemporaries to question the king's responsibility for political actions. Ministers alone could by law be held responsible, and the likelihood that a monarch worked against his elected government over vital issues of peace and war could at best only be hinted at. Until a new constitution was devised in 1947, historians had therefore to move carefully under a self-imposed censorship. Chiala planned an edition of the letters of Victor Emanuel II but for reasons that may be guessed it never reached the stage of publication. Although Comandini's book on Umberto I was printed, it was by order pulped before anyone could read it. The personal memoirs of Victor Emanuel III were shown by him to some loyal friends, but an official statement then declared that no such memoirs had ever existed. And although Umberto II said he meant to use his archives to write a personal history, we may doubt if he had any such intention.

Further speculation would be premature until we know how much of this material eventually reaches Italy, but it is undeniable that a good deal of written risorgimento history was slanted to protect the reputation of these heads of State. Victor Emanuel II for example was a very interesting person but not quite the *Re Galantuomo* of the textbooks, nor what the historian Zanichelli called the greatest Christian sovereign in all history. No one was allowed to know until long after his death that he told the Austrians of his regret at the introduction of constitutional government into Italy and of his conviction that Italians were completely unsuited to it. A strictly military education had taught him, as he confessed to a British ambassador, that there were only two ways of governing Italians, by bayonets or bribery. In contradiction to the public legend he privately informed Metternich and the pope that he was ready to help them by force of arms in crushing Mazzini's Roman republic and restoring absolutism throughout Italy. Later in 1867 he spoke of carrying out another massacre of Garibaldi's followers. At one point he sent a message to Berlin that he would join Prussia in fighting against France, but also promised the French that he would help them combat Prussia, and almost simultaneously informed the Austrians that he might assist them in defeating both France and Prussia. To the British he once suggested making war on the Sultan so that together they could divide and annex the Turkish empire. These astonishing facts were kept secret, even from his own ministers. Only with the greatest difficulty in 1870 did an unusually strong-minded prime minister save him from keeping an earlier promise to fight on the defeated side in the Franco-Prussian war. So untrustworthy was he that Cavour and other ministers, all of whom served him loyally and tried to cover up these aberrations, reached the point of saying that they would prefer to keep personal relations with him to a minimum; though no hint of their private feelings could ever be divulged in public.

IV

It must remain an open question how far secrecy and manipulation of documentary evidence has been damaging in its effects during the past two centuries of Italian history. Yet enough is known for us to be sure that Italy suffered from the irresponsible constitutional and military behaviour of its monarchs. Nor can there be any doubt that governments dangerously misled their successors through concealment or deliberate falsifications: for instance about the Austrian war of 1866, as well as about the Ethiopian war of 1894–6 and the Libyan war of 1911–12. Official reports on even earlier wars in 1848–9 and 1859 were also kept secret for many decades in order to preserve beautiful legends from scrutiny by parliament or historians, and this prevented important lessons from being learnt that would have been vital for the conduct of foreign policy. Again, after the military defeat of Caporetto in 1917, though a commission of experts was appointed to investigate what had gone wrong, its members were compelled to delete thirteen pages of their report concerning General Badoglio, the one man whose lack of competence was most suspect. The king was therefore enabled to promote this much criticised soldier to be Chief of General Staff, a post that he unfortunately held as late as November 1940 when the armed forces of fascism suffered another inexplicable defeat at the hands of the small Greek army.

In 1943 the inept Badoglio, after appointment by the monarchy to replace Mussolini as head of government, succeeded in fabricating another story to conceal his personal responsibility for the biggest military reverse in Italian history. His first mistake was to permit six further weeks of pointless fighting before reluctantly agreeing to General Eisenhower's terms for an armistice (albeit with mental reservations and no genuine intention of fulfilling its conditions). And then, just before the western allies attacked the German army near Naples, he persuaded them to weaken their carefully planned landing at Salerno in order to provide troops for a simultaneous attack on Rome. But a few days later, when American planes and paratroops were actually taking off from Sicilian airfields to land near Rome, he unexpectedly insisted on aborting an attack that he himself had requested. This disastrous behaviour not only imperilled the vital Salerno landing, but since the great bulk of the Italian army around Rome was left by him without any orders or information and without even a commander, the Germans captured over half a million men after a few hours of brave but completely disorganised resistance. An explanation was then hurriedly concocted to blame the American commander for letting this happen.

Italy suffered from the fact that military and civilian leaders in the previous two decades had been promoted less for their experience or competence than for reasons of political correctness and lack of strong personality. Mussolini not only distrusted subordinates who showed competence and initiative but himself had a very superficial feeling for history, and the contortions of his propaganda machine were an object lesson in how the achievements of a great country could be obscured and jeopardised through wilful ignorance of what could have been learnt from the past.

Fortunately the fifty post-fascist years have gradually and painfully produced a very different world. Evidence collected by the Italian anti-mafia commission and magistrates investigating *tangentopoli* has revealed in the 1990s how an otherwise healthy society had been perverted and endangered by the disingenuous fiction that things are as patriotic loyalty might wish them to be and not as they are in fact. Italian historiography, now unencumbered by political directives, has been able to confirm that Cavour, Giolitti and De Gasperi, despite or even because of circumstances that sometimes blighted their expectations, were statesmen of exceptional and admirable ability. Greater freedom of information is also permitting us to recognise how other lesser politicians such as Mussolini, Andreotti, and possibly Berlusconi, have had a major impact for good or ill on the fortunes of their country, and we can be moderately sure that their successes or failures will not in the long run be concealed by tendentious historical writing. 'Magna est veritas *et praevalebit.*'

9

KAISER WILHELM II
AND THE BRITISH MONARCHY

cxcxɔcx

DAVID CANNADINE

WE have recently and rightly been reminded that the Europe of the early modern period was a continent of multiple kingdoms and dynastic agglomerations: in the British Isles, the Iberian Peninsular, Austria-Hungary, and Brandenburg-Prussia, once-hostile and separate countries were held together, with varying degrees of permanency and success, by little more than shared allegiance to the same sovereign ruler.[1] By contrast, Europe on the eve of the First World War was a continent of unitary, integrated, nation-state monarchies, with their parliaments and bureaucracies, their railways and empires, their postal services and carefully guarded frontiers, extending from Portugal to Russia, the Netherlands to Italy, Spain to Germany.[2] But it is only in retrospect that this transition from royal to state authority seems both inevitable and irreversible. During the eighteenth century, and for much of the nineteenth, it was far from clear that sovereign nation states (and nation-state sovereigns) were going to be the culmination of the European story, as it had developed and unfolded down to 1914.

As historian and biographer, Derek Beales has devoted much of his life to the study of monarchs and monarchies in this confused, uncertain, intervening period, and he has ranged far and wide among continental royalty, from the Habsburgs to the Hanoverians, from Queen Victoria to King Victor Emanuel II. Thanks in no small part to his work, it is no longer 'peculiarly old-fashioned', as he himself once lamented it was, 'to find interest in monarchs, dynasties and marriage treaties'.[3] And throughout his writings, he has properly

---

[1] J. H. Elliott, 'A Europe of Composite Monarchies', *Past and Present*, 137 (1992), pp. 48–71; C. Russell, *The Causes of the English Civil War* (Oxford, 1990), p. 27.

[2] E. J. Hobsbawm, *The Age of Empire, 1875–1914* (London, 1987), esp. chs. 3, 4 and 6.

[3] D. E. D. Beales, *England and Italy, 1859–60* (London, 1961), pp. 4–7, 36, 43, 108–9; idem, *From Castlereagh to Gladstone, 1815–85* (London, 1969), pp. 21–7, 78–81, 80–3, 122–3, 226–8; idem, *The Risorgimento and the Unification of Italy* (London, 1971), pp. 64–84; idem, 'Gladstone and His First Ministry', *Historical Journal*, 26 (1983), pp. 987–99; idem, *Joseph II,*

stressed the many characteristics of early modern monarchies which survived throughout Europe beyond their time: multi-national realms, problems of succession, the education of princes, relations between monarchs and ministers, royal patronage of the arts, and dynastic connections, alliances and animosities.[4] Even during the late nineteenth century, as nation states consolidated around (and sometimes above) their sovereign heads, these traditional royal modes and preoccupations remained much in evidence. This essay will explore one instance of such a survival into the modern world, where, in the end, it failed to survive: the course and the consequences of the close family links between the British and German royal houses.

During the half-century before the First World War, the very period which witnessed the heyday of the modern nation state, the British monarchy became increasingly entangled with European royalty, largely because of the marriages contracted with the ruling families of the continent by Queen Victoria's many children. Of these alliances, none was more important – nor eventually more tragic – than that established between the British and the German royal families, thanks to the marriage of Princess Victoria (known as 'Vicky'), the eldest daughter of Queen Victoria and Prince Albert, to the Crown Prince Friedrich (known as 'Fritz') of Prussia, who eventually – if only very briefly – became Emperor of Germany. But it was during the reign of their son, Kaiser Wilhelm II, that connections between Germany and Britain became most important, most amicable, most controversial and – ultimately – most acrimonious. As such, they closely mirrored the relationship between the Kaiser and successive generations of the British royal family: with his grandmother, Queen Victoria; with his mother, the Empress Friedrich; with his uncle, King Edward VII; and with his cousin, King George V. What, then, were the Kaiser's attitudes to his British relatives? And how far did they influence, or were they themselves influenced by, his wish to make and to mould Germany's foreign policy?

I

By definition, the Kaiser's closest relationship with British royalty was with his mother, Princess Vicky. 'Between him and me', she once wrote, 'there is a

---

vol. I, *In the Shadow of Maria Theresa, 1741–80* (Cambridge, 1987), esp. chs. 1–3, 10 and 14; idem, *Mozart and the Habsburgs* (Reading, 1993), passim. The quotation is from Professor Beales's inaugural lecture, *History and Biography* (1981), reprinted below, p. 269.

[4] For another attempt to make this case with reference to the British monarchy, see D. Cannadine, 'The Last Hanoverian Sovereign? The Victorian Monarchy in Historical Perspective, 1688–1988', in A. L. Beier, D. Cannadine and J. Rosenheim (eds.), *The First Modern Society: Essays in English History in Honour of Lawrence Stone* (Cambridge, 1989), pp. 127–66.

bond of love and confidence which I feel sure nothing can destroy'.[5] But in practice, relations were rarely this serene. The princess was the most gifted child of Albert and Victoria, and the one who most conspicuously inherited her father's gifts of intellect and application. She was extremely well educated for her sex, an excellent linguist, and possessed of a life-long curiosity about politics, art, science, medicine, music and religion. In 1858, largely at her parents' behest, she had married Prince Friedrich. The couple were undeniably in love, but there were also broader considerations of dynastic interest and diplomatic ambition. For it was the dearest wish of Victoria and Albert that a united Germany should develop liberal institutions, and become Great Britain's foremost ally. And they saw in this marriage the one certain way of bringing this about. But this grand scheme never materialised, and in the tragic process of its non-realisation, the Princess's relationship with her son was profoundly affected, as was his attitude towards Britain.[6]

In part, this was because Vicky herself never settled happily or successfully in her new country. For her, England always remained 'home'. She disliked Wagner, thought the Prussians an 'odious people', and made her disapproval of all things Teutonic abundantly and tactlessly plain.[7] In supposing that she could recreate liberal England in her adopted country, she showed herself rigidly insensitive to political realities, and her evident lack of sympathy with the aspirations of German nationalism did not endear her to public opinion. As Crown Princess and later as Empress, she put the court, the aristocracy, the army and the bureaucracy against her, and thus lacked an appropriate power base from which to influence German politics.[8] More than was customary among German royal wives, she thrust herself forward, and the fact that she was widely (and rightly) believed to dominate her weak husband only did her reputation further damage.

But this was nothing compared with the greater tragedy which lay ahead. Early in 1888, her adored husband Fritz duly became Emperor, on the death of his long-lived father. But by then, he was already fatally stricken with cancer of the larynx, and he died after an ineffectual reign of only ninety-nine days. Even more unfortunately, the Empress was held responsible in some quarters for his death, since it was believed that she had insisted (despite the opposition of the German medical profession, Bismark, Wilhelm I, her own children, and public opinion) that an English physician attend the ailing

---

5 F. Ponsonby (ed.), *The Letters of the Empress Frederick* (London, 1929), pp. 119ff.

6 T. A. Kohut, 'Kaiser Wilhelm II and his parents: an inquiry into the psychological roots of German policy towards England before the First World War', in J. G. Rohl and A. Sombart (eds.), *Kaiser Wilhelm II: New Interpretations* (Cambridge, 1982), pp. 63–89.

7 M. Balfour, *The Kaiser and His Times* (New York, 1964), pp. 64–6, 68.

8 L. Cecil, 'History as family chronicle: Kaiser Wilhelm II and the dynastic roots of Anglo-German antagonism', in Rohl and Sombart, *Kaiser Wilhelm*, pp. 91–3.

Crown Prince – a physician who rejected the diagnosis of throat cancer, and refused to allow Friedrich to undergo the dangerous operation, recommended by the German doctors, which might have saved his life.[9] But this personal tragedy also had broader consequences. In England, when Albert died, Victoria remained queen regnant. But in Germany, when Fritz died, the Dowager Empress was left with no official role. The political influence that she had been brought up to wield was held by her for less than one hundred days.

To make matters worse, her relationship with her son, who had now succeeded as Kaiser Wilhelm II, had never been easy. Aside from the death of her husband, the greatest sorrow of her life was that Wilhelm did not turn out to be another Albert. His withered right arm (something for which the Empress was also blamed, since she had insisted on having an English doctor to deliver her first-born son) was an 'irrepressible source of sorrow for her', and the fact that he was 'not possessed of brilliant abilities, nor any strength of character or talents', only accentuated her feelings of disappointment.[10] She saw his own shortcomings as a blow to her own self-esteem, never gave him any encouragement, despite his heroic attempts to overcome his physical deformity, and insisted on a brutally regimented system of education for which he was quite unsuited. Even Queen Victoria thought she watched over her son with 'too great care'. But it was her husband's death which inevitably undermined their relationship still further. For his tragedy was his son's opportunity, and the Empress was obliged to endure the heartbreak of seeing her son wielding, from a very early age, the power which should have been her husband's – and her own.[11]

In his turn, the Kaiser fully reciprocated this dislike. Like his mother, he was strong willed, emotional and impulsive. Sooner or later, as he himself admitted, they were bound to quarrel. In his early twenties, he successfully broke away, first as a student in Bonn, and then as a subaltern in the Guards at Potsdam. He delighted in the company of his brother officers, became on very close terms with his grandfather and Bismark, and seemed, to the growing dismay of his mother, to have embraced wholeheartedly the Prussian values of 'blood and iron'. In 1881, he married Princess Auguste Victoria of Schleswig-Holstein-Sonderburg-Augustenburg, who was strongly anti-British, and who encouraged him in his hostility to his mother.[12] He disliked the control she exercised over his father, treated them both with great callousness during their brief and poignant spell of power, and when Friedrich

---

9   M. Reid, *Ask Sir James* (London, 1987), pp. 91–101, 261–6.
10   Ponsonby, *Letters of the Empress Frederick*, pp. 68, 119ff.
11   Balfour, *Kaiser and His Times*, pp. 76–7.
12   Cecil, 'History as family chronicle', pp. 96–8.

died, he surrounded the royal palace with troops, and forbade anyone, including his mother, to leave until it has been searched. This left the Dowager Empress with an abiding sense of grievance.[13] But to the Emperor, it mattered little: for the rest of her life, he virtually ignored her, and she rapidly ceased to be of any political importance.

As early as 1881, the Crown Princess wrote despairingly that 'this son has never really been mine', a view which Wilhelm echoed, but with rather different feelings. For he was determined to disassociate himself from the woman whom he once disparagingly described as the 'English princess'.[14] But inevitably, their relationship was more complex than that. It was not just that, in many ways, they were very similar people. It was also that Wilhelm craved her respect and approval, even as he knew he could never win it. And in the same way, he was captivated by his English relatives, and the English nation, even as he tried to reject them. He was brought up to speak English, to regard England as his second home, and to view the English country gentleman as the ultimate social ideal. And just as he rejected his English mother, yet sought her approbation, so his feelings about the English nation were equally contradictory. Nowhere was this shown more vividly than in his complex relationship with his grandmother, Queen Victoria.

II

During the last two decades of her reign, the Great White Queen was the undisputed doyenne of European royalty, and no member of her extended continental family occupied a more illustrious – or more uncertain – position than her eldest grandson, the Kaiser. Almost from the time of his birth, his grandmother saw him frequently, and after one of her earliest encounters with him, she happily pronounced him 'such a dear little boy, so intelligent and pretty, so good and affectionate'. But she soon came to share his mother's anxieties and disappointments and, by the time he was five, was already issuing warnings to Princess Vicky about his arrogance and pride. 'Why does Willy always sign himself "William, Prince of Prussia"?' she complained in January 1878 – 'his father never does'. But she did not need her daughter to give her the answer: Prussian presumption and bombast, malevolently fostered by Bismark and his grandfather.[15]

As Prince Wilhelm drew away from his mother, in the 1880s, it inevitably followed that his relationship with Queen Victoria became more uneasy. In November 1885, she cancelled a projected visit from her grandson, because she

---

13 Balfour, *Kaiser and His Times*, pp. 118–19.
14 Kohut, 'Kaiser Wilhelm II and his parents', p. 79.
15 E. Longford, *Queen Victoria: Born to Succeed* (New York, 1964), pp. 373, 423–4.

was so enraged by his hostile attitude towards the Battenberg family, whose matrimonial ambitions she was keen to promote. Wilhelm retaliated by dubbing her 'the old hag'.[16] She was distressed beyond measure at the way he treated his widowed mother in the aftermath of his accession: she was 'too furious, too too indignant', and sometimes she even wondered whether his head was 'quite right'. And she was no less enraged when, shortly after his accession, he refused to see the Prince of Wales in Vienna, on the grounds that his uncle was insufficiently deferential to his new rank. 'To pretend', the Queen exploded, 'that he is to be treated in private as well as in public as "His Imperial Majesty" is perfect madness! . . . If he has such notions, he had better never come here.'[17]

From 1889 to 1895, the Kaiser was a regular visitor to the annual Cowes Regatta, but his presence only made the Queen nervous and agitated. He invariably arrived with a massive suite, and turned Osborne into 'a German colony'. In 1893, he was firmly told that this time he must remain on board his yacht, and the British Ambassador in Berlin was instructed to 'hint that these regular annual visits are not quite desireable'. But the Emperor was not one to take hints. Not only did he arrive, but having won the Queen's Cup at Cowes Regatta, he kept the Queen waiting for dinner next day (as he did again in the following year). On neither occasion was Her Majesty amused. Nor was she in January 1896, when the Kaiser sent President Kruger a telegram, congratulating him on the defeat of the Jameson Raid. 'Sent off my letter to William', she noted with satisfaction, 'in which I gave him a piece of my mind as to this dreadful telegram'. Not until 1899 was he invited to Cowes again.[18]

Despite these political disagreements, personal relations between the Queen and the Emperor remained remarkably cordial. The Kaiser was genuinely eager to attend the celebrations for her Diamond Jubilee and her eightieth birthday, and instructed her physician, Sir James Reid, to keep him informed about his grandmother's health. His visit to England, in 1899, when anti-British feeling was very strong in Germany because of the Boer War, more than atoned for his failings at Cowes earlier in the decade.[19] Most importantly, the Queen knew how to deal with him. She might chide or scold him, but her criticisms were sympathetically and respectfully expressed in private. 'Though she had me as a child on her lap', Wilhelm later fondly recalled, 'and sometimes boxed my ears, the moment I became Emperor, she treated me with deference. She respected my position.' As a result, his feelings for her remained

[16] Cecil, 'History as family chronicle', p. 101; Longford, *Queen Victoria*, pp. 477–80.
[17] Longford, *Queen Victoria*, p. 507.
[18] Balfour, *Kaiser and His Times*, pp. 195–6.
[19] Reid, *Ask Sir James*, p. 124; Balfour, *Kaiser and His Times*, pp. 221–3.

loyal and loving, and he took great and genuine pride in being her eldest grandson.[20]

Appropriately enough, it was at the time of her death that he showed himself to his best advantage. Forewarned by Sir James Reid that the Queen was sinking, he at once rushed to her bedside, not as German Emperor, but as an anxious member of the British royal family.[21] Throughout her final days at Osborne, he impressed all who were present by his grave, dignified and uncharacteristically unostentatious demeanour, and in her last hours, he supported his grandmother on her pillow. After she had died in his arms, he helped to measure her for her coffin, and assisted the Prince of Wales and the Duke of Connaught in lifting her into it. Even the new king admitted that the Emperor had been 'kindness itself, and touching in his devotion, without a shade of brusquerie or selfishness'. In the eyes of the British royal family, and of British public opinion, it was his greatest moment.[22]

And the memory lingered on both sides. In 1911, the Kaiser was invited to London for the dedication of the Victoria Monument in front of Buckingham Palace. In accepting the invitation of King George V, he took the occasion to reiterate

> my devotion and reverence for my beloved grandmother, with whom I was on such excellent terms. I shall never forget how kindly this great lady always was to me and the relations she kept up with me, though I was so far her junior, she having carried me about in her arms! Never in my life shall I forget the solemn hours in Osborne at her deathbed when she breathed her last in my arms![23]

The fact that he was her eldest grandson was, he concluded, something he was 'always immensely proud of and never forgot'. There seems no cause to doubt his word. When war finally broke out in 1914, he was convinced that the King of England and the Emperor of Russia had played him false. 'If my grand- mother had been alive', he added, 'she would never have allowed it'.[24]

III

The admiration and respect which the Kaiser felt for his English grandmother were singularly lacking in his relations with his English uncle, King Edward VII. In part, this was the inevitable consequence of the King's

[20] Longford, *Queen Victoria*, p. 522; Cecil, 'History as family chronicle', pp. 221–3; Balfour, *Kaiser and His Times*, pp. 195–6.

[21] Balfour, *Kaiser and His Times*, pp. 230–2.

[22] Reid, *Ask Sir James*, pp. 191–221; Longford, *Queen Victoria*, pp. 560–5; P. Magnus, *King Edward VII* (Harmondsworth, 1967), pp. 336–7.

[23] H. Nicolson, *King George V: His Life and Reign* (London, 1967), p. 248.

[24] Balfour, *Kaiser and His Times*, p. 355.

fondness for his eldest sister and her husband, the Emperor's much-disapproved-of parents. Despite their very different temperaments, abilities and interests, the King was closer to Princess Vicky than to any of his brothers and sisters, and he mourned Fritz as 'the noblest and best man I had ever known', with the exception of Prince Albert himself.[25] Inevitably, his view of the Kaiser was clouded by his sense of the great personal and political tragedy by which his sister and brother-in-law had been visited, and the contrast between what was and what might have been seems to have tormented the King anew, every time he met Wilhelm.

In addition, the King's consort, Queen Alexandra, was vehemently anti-German. She never forgave Bismark for 'robbing' her father, the King of Denmark, of the Duchies of Schleswig-Holstein in 1864, and her detestation was subsequently transferred to the young Kaiser. In 1888, she described him as 'a mad and conceited ass . . . My hope is that pride will have a fall some day, and won't we rejoice then!' Two years later, when her son was made an Honorary Colonel of a Prussian regiment, she wrote to him scathingly: 'And so my Georgie boy has become a real live filthy blue-coated Piekelhaube German soldier!!! Well, I never thought I'd live to see that!' In 1902, she delivered another hostile diatribe: 'His country cannot disguise its true feelings against us – and all his future will show it with a vengeance.' And at her husband's funeral, the Kaiser tried to escort her into Westminster Hall, but she would not let him.[26]

Not surprisingly, then, the Emperor and the King never really saw eye to eye.[27] The Kaiser envied Edward his assured ease and grace, his unrivalled social prestige, as the cynosure of European high society. He seemed to epitomise the confidence and the condescension of the British, and this provoked Wilhelm to over-react, in a nervous, bombastic, tactless and self-assertive way. He disparagingly dismissed the King as 'the old peacock', as a morally corrupt monarch, with his debts, his gambling and his mistresses.[28] He constantly snubbed and ignored him, and during Queen Victoria's lifetime, tried unavailingly to use the superior status of his imperial rank to challenge Edward's social primacy when he was still Prince of Wales. Behind the King's back, the Kaiser freely criticised him; in his presence, he was constantly apprehensive of doing something incompatible with his dignity.

Wilhelm's insecurity, anger and resentment at his uncle were fully under-standable, because King Edward was never able quite to take the Kaiser

[25] Magnus, *King Edward VII*, p. 256.
[26] J. Pope-Hennessy, *Queen Mary* (London, 1959), p. 281; Nicolson, *King George V*, pp. 74–5; A. Edwards, *Matriarch: Queen Mary and the House of Windsor* (New York, 1984), p. 212.
[27] Cecil, 'History as family chronicle', pp. 102–5.
[28] Magnus, *King Edward VII*, pp. 286–7.

seriously.[29] As Prince of Wales, he envied his much younger nephew's power and prestige as head of state, and as King he found the Emperor's constant desire to interfere in English affairs intolerable. He constantly made indiscreetly disparaging remarks about the Kaiser, many of them in Germany itself, and thought him noisy, unstable, and certainly not a gentleman. Whenever they met, the King could never resist the temptation of pricking his nephew's bombastic and histrionic pretensions, and invariably gave the impression that he was dealing with an errant relative, rather than with a head of state. Not surprisingly, the Emperor much resented this. 'My uncle', he once complained, 'never seems to realise that I am a sovereign, but treats me as if I were a little boy'. 'Now Queen Victoria', he added, quite correctly, 'never made this mistake'.[30]

Their enmity began during the 1880s, initially because the Prince of Wales fully shared the views of his mother and elder sisters about the Battenberg family, and thereby incurred what one biographer describes as the 'bitter enmity' of the future Kaiser.[31] The rift was intensified by the tragedy of Fritz's brief reign, and the Prince of Wales was outraged at the way in which the new Emperor treated his mother during the early days of his own reign. Then, in September 1888, the Prince paid a private visit to Vienna. The Kaiser announced his intention of arriving on an *official* visit, and made it plain that no foreign royal personage should be in the Austrian capital at the same time. The Austrian Emperor, Francis Joseph, was much embarrassed, and in order to ease the position, the Prince of Wales tactfully withdrew. But he much resented what he regarded as a spiteful humiliation.[32]

By this time, the Emperor had convinced himself that the Prince possessed 'a false and intriguing character', while the Prince retaliated by describing Wilhelm to his elder sister as 'a bully, and most bullies, when tackled, are cowards'.[33] In the 1890s, their animosity was transferred to the sporting arena. The Prince of Wales enjoyed big yacht racing, and was proud of the fact that his own vessel, the Britannia, was the finest and fastest afloat. But the Kaiser aspired to become 'The Boss of Cowes', and injected an element of personal and national rivalry, by using what had previously been a cosmopolitan annual regatta as an opportunity to demonstrate the nascent might of the German navy. His giant purpose-built craft, Meteor II, outclassed all other yachts, when it first appeared in 1896. The Prince of Wales, much piqued, lacked the means to meet the challenge, and in the following year reluctantly abandoned the sport altogether.[34]

[29] Balfour, *Kaiser and His Times*, pp. 97–8.   [30] Cecil, 'History as family chronicle', p. 105.
[31] Magnus, *King Edward VII*, pp. 235–7.   [32] Magnus, *King Edward VII*, pp. 261–8.
[33] Cecil, 'History as family chronicle', p. 100; Magnus, *King Edward VII*, p. 268.
[34] Magnus, *King Edward VII*, pp. 300, 304–5.

Despite the Kaiser's impeccable behaviour at his grandmother's death bed, relations were not eased when Edward became King; nor would this have been possible in the context of growing Anglo-German antagonisms. The Emperor's visit to Sandringham in 1902 was not a success, and his provocative visit to Morocco three years later enraged the King, who dismissed his nephew as 'utterly false, and the bitterest foe that England possesses'.[35] Meanwhile, the Kaiser became increasingly convinced that the King's visits to the great capitals of Europe had only one purpose: the construction of an alliance which was to encircle Germany. In taking this view, he undoubtedly over-estimated the King's real influence and importance. But he came to believe that King Edward was 'the arch-intriguer and mischief-maker of Europe', and predictably, the German press took up this view with alacrity.[36]

Nevertheless, the public pageant of international royalty was amply kept up, and in the course of Edward's brief reign, each monarch paid very sumptuous state visits to the other's country. In November 1907, after threatening not to come at the last minute, the Emperor arrived in England.[37] The King absolutely declined to discuss any political matters, and his ministers were distinctly unimpressed by the Kaiser's weak grasp of affairs. But he scored one great public triumph. In London, on being given the Freedom of the City, he observed, to great applause, that 'Blood is thicker than water.' And on arriving at Windsor, he remarked that 'it seems like coming home again'. But all this goodwill was dissipated because he insisted upon remaining in England for another month, at Highcliffe Castle near Bournemouth, and accounts of his tactless, irresponsible and anti-British table talk subsequently leaked out. Not surprisingly, the King's return visit to Germany, in February 1909, was tense and unhappy, and the two sovereigns never saw each other again.[38]

According to Theodore Roosevelt, the Kaiser felt 'a real affection and respect for King Edward, and also a very active and jealous dislike for him, first one feeling and then the other coming uppermost in his mind and in his conversation'.[39] But on balance, it was the dislike which was much the stronger sentiment. In 1914, and again in 1918, he was convinced that it was his uncle who had brought about Germany's ruin: by thwarting the Reich's development, by his policy of diplomatic encirclement, and by propelling Europe into war. 'Even after his death', he exclaimed, 'Edward VII is stronger

[35] R. Hough, *Louis and Victoria: The First Mountbattens* (London, 1974), pp. 187–8; Magnus, *King Edward VII*, p. 380.

[36] Balfour, *Kaiser and His Times*, p. 265; Magnus, *King Edward VII*, pp. 417–18.

[37] J. Steinberg, 'The Kaiser and the British: the state visit to Windsor, November 1907', in Rohl and Sombart, *Kaiser Wilhelm II*, pp. 121–42.

[38] Magnus, *King Edward VII*, pp. 511–14; Balfour, *Kaiser and His Times*, pp. 296–7.

[39] Balfour, *Kaiser and His Times*, p. 264.

than I, though I am still alive'. And although he mellowed after his abdication and exile, his conviction that King Edward was the architect of Germany's ruin never left him. 'It is he who is the corpse and I who live on', the aged ex-Kaiser declared shortly before his death in 1941, 'but it is he who is the victor'.[40]

IV

Nevertheless, when King Edward VII died in 1910, the Emperor ordered all officers in the German Army and Navy to wear mourning for eight days, the German fleet in home waters flew its flags at half mast, and the Kaiser again travelled to England to be among the mourners. Although this time there was no death-bed tableau, the Emperor once more showed throughout an admirable and sympathetic self-effacement. He placed a wreath of purple and white flowers on King Edward's coffin, as it lay in state in Westminster Hall, and knelt with his cousin, now King George V, in silent prayer. As a gesture of respect, he Kaiser waited for his brother sovereign to rise first, and as a gesture of friendship, grasped his hand in a warm handshake. And once again, he was glad to be back at Windsor. 'I am proud to be able to call this place my second home', he recorded while staying there, 'and to be a member of this royal house, for everybody has treated me in the kindest way'.[41]

As this encounter implies, relations between the Kaiser and King George and his wife, Queen Mary, were much more cordial than they had been with King Edward and Queen Alexandra. Naturally enough, the new king had been brought up by his parents to see little merit in Germany, and even less in the young Emperor. But for him, the Schleswig-Holstein affair was past history, and although George V never really liked 'abroad', he always found the Emperor 'most kind and civil to me', and was himself quite ready to be friends with him'.[42] He greatly enjoyed his visit to Germany in 1892, and in the following year, his bride, Princess Mary, met the Kaiser for the first time at Osborne. She was dazzled by his glamour and charm, and retained a soft spot for him for the rest of her life. She greatly admired his courageous horsemanship, and her husband admitted that, for a man with only one useful arm, the Kaiser shot extremely well.[43]

Throughout the first decade of the twentieth century, they kept up a friendly if intermittent relationship with the Kaiser. In 1900, they asked him

[40] Cecil, 'History as family chronicle', p. III; E., Ludwig, *Kaiser Wilhelm II* (London, 1929), p. 394.
[41] Balfour, *Kaiser and His Times*, p. 308.
[42] K. Rose, *King George V* (1983), pp. 164–5; Nicolson, *King George V*, pp. 82, 93.
[43] Pope-Hennessy, *Queen Mary*, pp. 275–9; Balfour, *Kaiser and His Times*, p. 74.

to be godfather to their third son, Prince Henry, and two years later, the Prince of Wales (as he had by then become) travelled to Berlin to congratulate the Emperor on his forty-third birthday.[44] In March 1908, they met again in Cologne, where Prince George inspected the eighth Cuirassiers, of which regiment he had been Commander-in-Chief since 1902. When the Kaiser and his wife visited London, shortly after the new king's accession, for the unveiling of the monument to Queen Victoria, they thought their reception at Buckingham Palace was the most friendly they had ever enjoyed in England, and there were rumours that their daughter, Princess Victoria Louise, might be engaged to the King's eldest son, the future Edward VIII. And when King George and Queen Mary went on their family visit to Germany in 1913, they were treated with great kindness and hospitality, and were genuinely sad to leave.[45]

But although they liked the Kaiser personally, King George and Queen Mary distrusted his intentions in Europe, and his tactless outbursts at inappropriate moments only strengthened their suspicions. Even at King Edward's funeral, the Kaiser could not resist making unpleasant jibes about Britain and its position in the world. And his description of the new king to Theodore Roosevelt on that occasion was not exactly encouraging: 'He is a thorough Englishman, and hates all foreigners, but I do not mind that as long as he does not hate Germans more than other foreigners.'[46] Nor did he behave any better on his visit in 1911. There was a major misunderstanding between the two monarchs about Germany's intentions in Morocco, and on the eve of his departure from Portsmouth, the Emperor gave further offence by uttering renewed 'threats and curses against England'. By 1913, tension was so great that the Foreign Office advised the King that the visit to Germany in connection with the wedding of the Kaiser's daughter should be private, not official.[47]

As Europe rushed towards war during the summer of 1914, King George sent a telegram to the Emperor, making a 'personal appeal' to 'secure the peace of the world'.[48] But once battle was joined, the king had no doubt that his family's first duty lay to the British nation rather than to the international network of royalty. He changed the family name to Windsor, thereby provoking one of the Kaiser's rare jokes, when he remarked that he much looked forward to seeing the first performance of that well-known opera, 'The Merry Wives of Saxe-Coburg-Gotha'. In addition, the Emperor and his family were deprived of their honorary commands of British

[44] Nicolson, *King George V*, pp. 118–19, 144–5.
[45] P. Ziegler, *King Edward VIII: The Official Biography* (London, 1990), p. 43; Pope-Hennessy, *Queen Mary*, pp. 475–9.
[46] Edwards, *Matriarch*, p. 210; Balfour, *Kaiser and His Times*, p. 242.
[47] Nicolson, *King George V*, pp. 251–2; Pope-Hennessy, *Queen Mary*, p. 477.
[48] Sir G. Arthur, *King George V* (London, 1939), p. 295.

regiments, their Garter banners were removed from St George's Chapel, Windsor, and they were stripped of their honorary appointments to British orders of chivalry. At the same time, members of the British royal family renounced all 'German degrees, styles, dignities, titles, honours and appellations'.[49]

Neither the King nor the Queen ever forgave the Kaiser for what they regarded as his personal responsibility for the First World War. When she heard of his abdication on 9 November 1918, Queen Mary described it as 'retribution to the man who started this awful war'. And King George agreed. 'How are the mighty fallen', was his immediate reaction:

> He has been Emperor for just over thirty years, he did great things for his country, but his ambition was so great that he wished to dominate the world and created his military machine for that object . . . Now he has utterly ruined his country and himself. I look upon him as the greatest criminal known for having plunged the world into this ghastly war, which has lasted over four years and three months with all its misery.[50]

A few weeks after the armistice, his son Prince Albert, later Duke of York and King George VI, met the Kaiser's sister, Princess Victoria, in Germany. He wrote to his father: 'She asked after you and the family, and hoped that we should be friends again. I told her politely that I did not think it was possible for a great many years!!!' The King replied: 'Your answer to Cousin Vicky (who of course I have known all my life) was quite correct.'[51]

But despite these stern and sincere condemnations, even the First World War could not break entirely their family connections or their shared sense of royal identity. After the armistice, neither King George nor Queen Mary was every heard to say a harsh word against the Kaiser, and they considered he behaved with dignity and restraint in his Dutch retirement. When it was proposed by Lloyd George that the former Emperor should be extradited from Holland, and put on trial for war crimes, the King was incensed, and urged that this should not happen.[52] Interestingly enough, he had been encouraged to do so by the King of Saxony, the Duke of Wurtemburg and the Grand Duke of Baden, who addressed him on behalf of all the German princes, knowing that his 'family originated among us', not to allow others to lay hands on 'the Royal Dignity of a great and at one time friendly and related ruler'.[53]

King George V never again met or corresponded with his cousin, who was hurt at receiving no word of condolence from the British royal family on the death of his first wife in 1921. But in January 1936, the former Emperor

[49] Rose, *King George V*, pp. 173–5.
[50] Pope-Hennessy, *Queen Mary*, p. 507; Rose, *King George V*, p. 229.
[51] J. W. Wheeler-Bennett, *King George VI: His Life and Reign* (London, 1958), pp. 120–1.
[52] Rose, *King George V*, p. 231.   [53] Nicolson, *King George V*, pp. 438–40.

telegraphed his sympathy to the Queen, who responded with a grateful message, accompanied by a present.[54] And in October 1938, he wrote to Queen Mary for the first time since 1914, as her 'affectionate cousin William', saying how delighted he was about the Munich settlement, which he hoped had saved Britain and Germany from the 'fearful catastrophe' of another war. 'I kiss your hand', he concluded, 'in respectful devotion as ever'. 'Poor William', the Queen wrote, 'he must have been horrified at the thought of another war between our two countries'. She was so impressed by the letter that she passed it on to her son, King George VI, convinced that it would 'touch and interest you as it did me'. To this day, it remains in the royal archives.[55]

V

Even in Britain, which still possesses its royal house, it is not easy to imagine the time when most nations in Europe could proudly boast sovereigns as heads of state. In Germany, where the monarchy has been defunct for more than seventy years, such a state of affairs must seem literally unthinkable. And the idea that foreign policy might be regulated and controlled by a small number of hereditary monarchs, who were personally related, and who shared essentially the same outlook on the world, seems almost anachronistically quixotic. Nevertheless, during the thirty years before the outbreak of the First World War, the cousinhood of European royalty was a recognised element in the conduct of international relations, and in that cousinhood, no connection was more important than the love–hate relationship that existed between the British and German royal houses.

As the grandson and admirer of Queen Victoria, it is one of the great ironies of history that Kaiser Wilhelm II was uniquely placed to build good relations between Britain and Germany, in precisely the manner that Prince Albert and Queen Victoria had hoped might come about.[56] But he was temperamentally ill-equipped to carry out the task with which destiny and dynasty had entrusted him. Because he could never make up his mind whether he was German or English, his personal forays into foreign policy and Anglo-German diplomacy were invariably confused, unsettling and ill-sustained. The English did not understand why the German Emperor sought to meddle so readily in Britain's affairs, and the Germans did not understand why their Emperor was so fond of England.[57]

[54] Rose, *King George V*, p. 231.
[55] Pope-Hennessy, *Queen Mary*, pp. 281–2, 591–2; Balfour, *Kaiser and His Times*, pp. 419–20.
[56] Balfour, *Kaiser and His Times*, p. 166.
[57] Kohnt, 'Kaiser Wilhelm and his parents', pp. 84–5.

As far as the English royal family was concerned, this inevitably made the Kaiser very difficult to deal with. Neither Queen Victoria nor King Edward VII nor King George V possessed as much power in the making of Britain's foreign policy as the Emperor erroneously thought they did, and this inevitably made the relationship between the two royal houses confusingly asymmetrical. But in addition, the Kaiser seemed so inconsistent and so unpredictable, that it was often hard to know what to make of him, or of his utterances. He could behave impeccably, or abominably, on great public occasions. He could profess undying devotion one minute, and eternal enmity the next. He may desperately have craved the approval of three successive British monarchs, but he had little idea how to go about achieving this objective, and his bizarre vacillations in attitude and tone thwarted, rather than helped him realise, his objectives.

Of course, too much should not be made of these personal amities and animosities in the broader context of Anglo-German relations.[58] Even by the mid-Victorian period, the dynamics of international diplomacy were no longer determined, as Albert and Victoria still vainly believed, by family connection and dynastic calculation. By 1888, when Wilhelm became Kaiser, the future of European politics, in both its domestic and international guise, was no longer in the hands of Kings and Emperors. And by 1914, the fact that the King of England and the Emperor of Germany were cousins was of little real significance in accelerating or averting the coming catastrophe. Despite what they themselves may each have thought of the other, neither the King nor the Kaiser was personally responsible for the outbreak of war. The rise – and the resolution – of Anglo-German antagonisms was much more deeply rooted than that.[59] The Emperor may have been correct in observing that blood was thicker than water. But as historians and biographers have subsequently observed, and as he himself eventually discovered to his cost, it was iron that proved stronger – and more dangerous – than either of them.

[58] Cecil, 'History as family chronicle', pp. 109–11.
[59] For the fullest account, see P. M. Kennedy, *The Rise of Anglo-German Antagonisms, 1860–1914* (London, 1980).

10

THE HISTORICAL KEYNES AND
THE HISTORY OF KEYNESIANISM
୧୬୧୬୧୬

PETER CLARKE

JOHN Maynard Keynes lent his name to the most influential paradigm in the political economy of the mid-twentieth century. During the last thirty years a distinction – though not always the same distinction – has increasingly been drawn between Keynes and Keynesianism. To study Keynes himself points towards problems which are essentially biographical, just as the impact of Keynesianism indicates problems which are more broadly historical; one approach enters into disputes about intentions, while the other is more concerned with assessing outcomes; and the two projects need to be linked.[1] Major biographies by Donald Moggridge and Robert Skidelsky have now modified important features of Sir Roy Harrod's great monument to his friend, and thereby helped to retrieve the historical Keynes: a child born in the year that Marx died, a Victorian in his eighteenth year at the end of the old queen's reign, a man of only sixty-two at his death in 1946. Recently Keynes's early beliefs of which he gave a famous account, and his work on probability, have become the focus of lively debate among historians, philosophers and economists. All of this is relevant to understanding Keynes's own conception of political economy.

---

[1] This is essentially what I aim to do in this essay, integrating themes which I have explored in separate publications, notably: 'Hobson and Keynes as economic heretics', in Michael Freeden (ed.), *Reappraising J. A. Hobson* (London, 1990), pp. 100–15; 'The Treasury's analytical model of the British economy between the Wars', in Barry Supple and Mary Furner (eds.), *The State and Economic Knowledge* (Cambridge, 1990), pp. 171–207; 'The twentieth-century revolution in government: the case of the British Treasury', in F. B. Smith (ed.), *Ireland, England and Australia: essays in honour of Oliver MacDonagh* (Canberra; Australian National University, 1990), pp. 159–79; 'J. M. Keynes, 1883–1946: "The Best of Both Worlds"', in Peter Mandler and Susan Pedersen (eds.), *After the Victorians: essays in memory of John Clive* (London, 1994), pp. 170–87; 'Keynes in history', *History of Political Economy*, 26 (1994), pp. 117–35; 'The Keynesian consensus and its enemies', in David Marquand and Anthony Seldon (eds.), *The Ideas that shaped Post-war Britain* (London, 1996). These are cited below by short title. I am grateful to Bradley Bateman, Stefan Collini, Susan Howson, John Thompson and Maria Tippett for constructive criticism of earlier drafts.

The historical fate of Keynesianism is likewise now seen in a new perspective. In the period up to the 1960s, naive Keynesian triumphalism postulated a conversion to Keynes's ideas which was at once inevitable, beneficent, and permanent; since then, vulgar anti-Keynesianism has been premised on Keynes's alleged deficiencies in analysis, foresight and practical wisdom. A more subtle line of criticism has discriminated between the posthumous doctrine and its original begetter, who was necessarily silent throughout subsequent decades of debate around his appropriated name. Axel Leijonhufvud was influential in challenging the academic consensus about the nature of Keynes's own theoretical contribution to economics, back in 1968, while Terence Hutchison was notable in posing similarly awkward questions for latter-day Keynesians about the nature of Keynes's own policy advice.[2]

As Skidelsky rightly says: 'People who give mechanical replies to the question of what Keynes would have done in the 1980s or 1990s ignore the supreme importance he attached to getting the character of the age right as a first step to theorising and policymaking.'[3] Among historians it is now well recognised that a text – or at least a dead author – cannot properly be made to speak on issues, however portentous, which lay outside the author's cognisance at the time of writing, circumscribed by his or her own concerns. It is simply unhistorical to intuit undeclared doctrines from fragments and obiter dicta, and to father these constructs on unwitting historical figures, however eminent. It follows that the form in which influential ideas were conceived may well be different from that with which we have subsequently become familiar. The great eponymous 'isms' – Benthamism, Darwinism, Marxism, Freudianism, Keynesianism – have been particularly vulnerable. Indeed such distortions, which I would call ideological, may have been a condition of their influence, through the social purchase which they were thereby enabled to exert.[4] The present essay explores the tension between Keynes's own ideas and intentions, as formed in the course of his own lifetime (the biographical theme) and the ideological significance of Keynesianism, involving its selective reception and instrumental uses (the historical theme).

[2] Axel Leijonhufvud, *On Keynesian Economics and the Economics of Keynes* (New York, 1968); T. W. Hutchison, *Keynes versus the 'Keynesians'* . . . ? (Institute of Economic Affairs, 1977).

[3] Robert Skidelsky, *John Maynard Keynes*, vol. II: *The economist as saviour, 1920–1937* (London, 1992), p. 270.

[4] Peter Clarke, *Liberals and Social Democrats* (Cambridge, 1978), pp. 3–4, was my first effort at formulating this way of understanding ideology, and developed in 'Political history in the 1980s: ideas and interests', *Journal of Interdisciplinary History*, 12 (1981), pp. 45–7: reprinted in Theodore K. Rabb and Robert I. Rotberg (eds.), *The New History* (Princeton, 1982), pp. 45–7. Here I am recapitulating a point made in my historiographical survey, 'Keynes in history'.

I

When Robert Skidelsky produced the first volume of his long-awaited study of Keynes, *Hopes Betrayed* was an apt subtitle for a book which disappointed and disillusioned many of Keynes's admirers, for a mixture of reasons, private as well as public. *Hopes Betrayed* was a big Bloomsbury biography, of Holroydian proportions, in which Skidelsky rounded up the usual suspects and washed their dirty linen in public. To those who found this sort of thing unnecessary, there were really two answers. First, it could be said, here was a wholly necessary correction to the hypocrisy of the received version. For a long time after his death, Keynes's homosexuality had not been widely known. It was passed over by Sir Roy Harrod, in his official biography of the great man in 1951. Harrod seems to have been fearful that, if Keynes himself did not appear respectable, the probity of Keynesianism might be impugned at a critical stage in its reception as the conventional wisdom of Anglo-American political economy. When, in a more permissive era, the gaff was duly blown and the Keynesian boom simultaneously faltered, it looked like Harrod's worst-case scenario.

Skidelsky's other rationale was intellectual, more abstruse and arcane in its implications. Quite deliberately, *Hopes Betrayed* shaped an account of a young man cocooned in a world where the cult of personal relations precluded just the sort of public concerns and commitments which later made him famous. The book exploited the availability of the ton or so of Keynes's own papers to throw many sidelights not only on the official career of the rising civil servant and don but on the charmed path he had trodden from 6 Harvey Road, Cambridge, to Eton and back to Cambridge as a Kingsman; it showed how he had become both an Apostle and a disciple (of the philosophy of G. E. Moore); and surely satiated the most avid reader's curiosity about Maynard and Lytton and Duncan and Leonard and Virginia and Vanessa . . . Thus Skidelsky's first volume only took his hero to his thirty-seventh year – at which age Keynes had published nothing that would cause his name to be remembered as an academic economist. The point of Skidelsky's interpretation was to show a Keynes who had so little that was 'Keynesian' about him.

Here is a biographical problem with both intellectual and political implications. Much of the trouble stems from Keynes's brilliant memoir, 'My Early Beliefs', posthumously published in 1949, which has sometimes been perused in cold print without recognising its conventions of literary artifice. Keynes claimed that he, like other undergraduate Apostles who sat at the feet of G. E. Moore in Edwardian Cambridge, had 'a religion and no morals' and that 'we completely misunderstood human nature, including our own', through a misplaced attribution of 'rationality' to it.[5] The young Keynes was, on this reading, obsessed with questions of personal relations and private ethics but indifferent to public and civic responsibilities. This is the view persistently conveyed in volume one of Skidelsky's biography.[6]

Harrod's interpretation was governed by what he called 'the presuppositions of Harvey Road' – an over-arching assumption, which Keynes inherited from his parents, 'that the government of Britain was and would continue to be in the hands of an intellectual aristocracy using the method of persuasion'.[7] Thus in Harrod's treatment of 'My Early Beliefs', the supposed influence of Moore in temporarily distracting his impressionable disciple is not directly contested; but though Keynes may have walked the tightrope of high philosophical speculation, the presuppositions were invoked by Harrod as a kind of moral safety net which prevented Keynes from falling very far or with any real damage.[8] If Harrod was inclined to discount the iconoclasm of Keynes's account and to disclose instead an implicit recognition of public duty, to Skidelsky this stood out as another example of how the authorised biography had reflected a pious and unhistorical commitment to defend Keynes's reputation even from the self-inflicted barbs of autobiography.

Not that 'My Early Beliefs' is accepted uncritically by Skidelsky, for he admits that 'certain liberties with strict truth for the sake of effect and amusement would have been natural'.[9] Moreover, he also acknowledges that Leonard Woolf was one Apostle who directly repudiated its reading of Moore and his influence, maintaining that 'we were not "immoralists"'.[10] Yet despite saving phrases, the authority of 'My Early Beliefs' as a source remains integral to Skidelsky's interpretation. The point on which he fastens is that 'Moore provided no logical connection between ethical goodness and political, social or economic welfare'; hence a Moorite – and 'Keynes always remained a Moorite' – was consistent in evincing no interest in such matters.[11] Now the curious feature in what Skidelsky contends about the lack of connection between Moore's doctrine and Keynes's politics is that elsewhere in his volume

---

[5] Donald Moggridge and Austin Robinson (eds.), *The Collected Writings of John Maynard Keynes*, 30 vols. (Royal Economic Society, 1971–89) (hereafter *JMK*), vol. x, pp. 436, 448. This and the next three paragraphs summarise a case which I have more fully substantiated in 'J. M. Keynes, 1883–1946: "The Best of Both Worlds"'.

[6] Robert Skidelsky, *John Maynard Keynes*, vol. 1: *Hopes Betrayed* (London, 1983), pp. 119, 124, 229, 233, 262; cf. pp. 106, 117, 157, 209–10, 245–6, 400–1, cited by R. M. O'Donnell, *Keynes: Philosophy, Economics and Politics* (Basingstoke, 1989), p. 116, making the related point that Skidelsky's Keynes allegedly kept personal ethics in one compartment and relegated public duty to another.

[7] Roy Harrod, *The Life of John Maynard Keynes* (London, 1951), pp. 192–3.

[8] Harrod, *Keynes*, p. 80.   [9] Skidelsky, *Keynes*, vol. 1, p. 143.

[10] Leonard Woolf, *Sowing* (London, 1970), pp. 144–56, at p. 148.

[11] Skidelsky, *Keynes*, vol. 1, p. 146.

Skidelsky goes so far in supplying an account of the logical connection between them – through the theory which was ultimately published as the *Treatise on Probability* (1921). It has been left to Keynes's other recent biographer, Donald Moggridge, to integrate these concerns by making out a case for 'the important role of the period of the creation of *Probability* in bringing Keynes out from the inwardness and ultra-rationality of his "early beliefs" towards a view of the world that could link "science and art", his duty to his friends and an active role in the wider phenomenal world'.[12]

The fact is that Keynes's conception of probability offered a basis for actions to be judged on the basis of their *likely* consequences, rather than Moore's impossible requirement that consequences must be *certain* before any individual discretion could be justified. In general Keynes acknowledged that rules and conventions had a social utility, even though he made a persuasive case against Moore's insistence that they should *always* be obeyed. He was an immoralist in this narrow, tendentious, provocative, teasing definition rather than the broad, vernacular sense which Leonard Woolf correctly disputed. There was thus a firm common basis in Keynes's thinking about private and public claims; and, in licensing personal judgement, he implicitly assumed that it would have been formed and constrained by the same conventional morality which he refused to accept as a rigid and infallible commandment.

It is one of the strengths of Skidelsky's second volume, *The Economist as Saviour*, that it restores Keynes to his proper historical context without diminishing the significance of his intellectual achievement. Keynes branches out of Bloomsbury and transcends the Treasury; neither involuted aesthete nor disembodied expert, he emerges as a multi-faceted figure, subject to a complex play of personal, intellectual and political influences. Moreover, it is clear that the related issues of expectations, confidence and uncertainty assume a large part in the story – bulking larger than they did a decade ago in *Hopes Betrayed*. Part of the reason is technical: because Skidelsky has now integrated the research which philosophers have been doing on Keynes's conception of probability into his account of Keynesianism as a whole, in practice as well as theory. This has important implications for the status of the contributions to economic theory which Keynes made in his two major academic works, the *Treatise on Money* (1930) and the *General Theory* (1936).

Keynes's challenge to conventional political economy can be seen in both theory and policy – but not in that order. His quest for remedial policies did not wait for the fruition of his theoretical insights. While he was still essentially a neo-classical economist himself, accepting the theoretical assumption that disequilibrium created its own self-correcting forces – albeit

---

[12] See Donald Moggridge, *Maynard Keynes: an economist's biography* (London, 1992), chs. 5 and 6, at p. 165.

forces which might be thwarted in the real world – Keynes had already committed himself to a radical stance which invoked state intervention. His rationale was that government, representing the common interest, had a unique role to play. It could be described variously as that of supplying an initial impulse or a further acceleration, of priming the pump, or of offering a makeweight through public expenditure to a deficiency in effective demand. This is the vision of political economy which we immediately recognise as Keynesian.

'From 1924', Skidelsky suggests, 'Keynes knew what he wanted to do and, in very broad terms, why'.[13] This dating would not be accepted by all Keynesian scholars, most notably Moggridge; but it follows Harrod and it stands up well against the objections which have so far been raised against it. It sees the new departure in an article which Keynes wrote, under Lloyd George's prompting, in the Liberal weekly paper, the *Nation*, calling for a programme of public works. The reasoning was that the economy was 'stuck in a rut' and so needed 'an impulse, a jolt, an acceleration,' to break the cycle of low confidence and instead generate 'cumulative prosperity'.[14]

One irreducibly biographical and personal factor may well be relevant to the maturing of Keynes's vision. He got married. The significance of this step has been attested over the years not only by his mother but by so austere a scholar as Lord Kahn. Moggridge provides a telling epigraph to his chapter, 'Lydia and Maynard', from another Cambridge economist, Walter Layton: 'I have long felt that marriage was the one thing left that could give a fresh stimulus to your brilliant career & develop your full powers by harmonising the big reserves of your emotional nature with your intellectual life.'[15] Such contemporary testimony is now given further biographical reinforcement by Skidelsky, who provides the most convincing account of a relationship which successively swept Keynes off his feet and put him on his feet.

Perhaps it is not surprising that Lydia Lopikova made such a big impression on Keynes when she returned to London with Diaghilev's ballet at the end of 1921. His sexually ambivalent nature was no protection against infatuation with her, whatever astonishment this caused in Bloomsbury. Their relationship was sensual and loving, revealing a mutually supportive sympathy that was an education to both of them. That they remained childless was not through choice. If Bloomsbury frowned on the match, so much the worse for Bloomsbury. Vanessa Bell, with whose family Keynes had shared 46 Gordon

13 Skidelsky, *Keynes*, vol. II, p. 173; cf. pp. 178, 184.
14 *JMK*, vol. XIX, pp. 219–23. Moggridge, *Keynes*, pp. 420ff. disputes the interpretation in Harrod, *Keynes*, pp. 345ff., as supported in Clarke, *Keynesian Revolution in the Making*, pp. 24, 76–8.
15 Layton to Keynes, 19 August 1925, in Moggridge, *Keynes*, p. 395; cf. Richard Kahn, *The Making of Keynes's General Theory* (Cambridge, 1984), p. 169.

Square, began a vendetta which was maintained until the death of the two old ladies, ending separate lives in their Sussex farmhouses within a mile of each other. Lydia had a lot to put up with, but Maynard made his choice without equivocation or regret. The fractured friendships of Bloomsbury yielded, albeit with some nostalgic sadness, to the allure of the fractured syntax of 'Lydiaspeak' which provided so many fresh insights on the world. As Lydia said of one critic, 'he does not know that it is poor of him not to allow you to be more than economist, all your "walks of life" make a piquant personality . . . '[16]

It was, paradoxically, when Keynes became 'more than an economist' that his distinctive vision as an economist became apparent. This happened when he was dragged out of the Bloomsbury orbit, not only by Lydia but also by the gravitational pull of public affairs, and in particular the peculiar magnetism of Lloyd George. Keynes's overt political commitment in the 1920s was marked by his emergence as a leading publicist for the Liberal Party, now reinvigorated under the leadership of Lloyd George – the one political leader who sensed that the politics of the future lay in central issues of economic management, thus signalling the need for a more robust political economy than the axioms of 'laissez-faire'. 'I approve Keynes, because, whether he is right or wrong, he is always dealing with realities', was Lloyd George's compliment on Keynes's unemployment initiative in the *Nation* (a remark which Keynes recorded in a characteristic letter to Lydia).[17]

Keynes saw his opportunity for redefining the agenda of government in a way that spoke to new issues, which we immediately recognise as macro-economic. He began as a critic of the policy of deflation which was the necessary prelude for a return to the orthodox principles of sound finance, hallowed by Britain's pre-war prosperity. The rationale of deflation was to reduce costs to a competitive level, as a transitional adjustment to a new equilibrium, which would in turn permit Britain to return to the Gold Standard at the pre-war parity. Gradually it dawned on Keynes that, in the real world, the adverse consequences of deflation might be rather more than transitional. In that case it was frivolous to claim that 'in the long run' equilibrium would be restored. Keynes's point was that 'this *long run* is a misleading guide to current affairs. *In the long run* we are all dead.'[18] Hence the campaign which Keynes waged against the return to gold, if it entailed

---

[16] Skidelsky, *Keynes*, vol. II, p. 303.

[17] 'To you I can make boastings and not fear to be misunderstood – it is an internal boasting', he had to explain on finding that Lydia had treated his confidences as the sort of gossip too good to keep to herself. See Polly Hill and Richard Keynes (eds.), *Lydia and Maynard: the letters of Lydia Lopikova and John Maynard Keynes* (London, 1989), pp. 205, 207: an edition to which all scholars are now indebted.

[18] *JMK*, vol. IV, p. 65.

throttling trade through dear money. 'In a longer perspective', Skidelsky comments, 'it was the start of the Keynesian Revolution'.[19] In short, Keynes challenged laissez-faire as a *policy* well before he had developed a critique of the orthodox economic *theory* of the self-adjusting tendencies of the free market.

The theoretical message of the *Treatise* was that savings and investment, being different activities carried on by different people, could not simply be presumed to be identical. It required interest rate to bring saving and investment into equilibrium. As Moggridge has reminded us, it was the *natural* rate of interest which would do this, rather than the *market* rate which actually prevailed at any particular time; and 'the primary task of monetary policy was to prevent their divergence and to provide price stability at full employment'.[20] A reading of the *Treatise* which emphasises its 'orthodoxy' would point to the tendency towards equilibrium which Keynes's model assumes, so long as the natural rate prevails and is not thwarted in its assigned role. What Skidelsky chooses to emphasise, by contrast, is the *Treatise*'s preoccupation with the economics of disequilibrium, when the economy is in a position of sub-optimal output and hence unemployment. If the rate of interest – or 'bank rate' as Keynes normally said – is what restores equilibrium, it follows that banking policy plays a crucial role in stabilising the system. 'Order has to be created', Skidelsky asserts: 'it is not natural'.[21] Put in this way – and it is persuasively put – the *Treatise* carries us a long way into the world disclosed by the *General Theory*, in which the absence of self-righting forces in the economy is affirmed.

The inescapable point in the *Treatise* was that disequilibrium was a product of thwarted expectations. When enterpreneurs made their investments, they did so with an expectation of normal profit which failed to materialise. Only when expectations were fulfilled was equilibrium achieved; conversely, disequilibrium was only the problem so long as expectations were not fulfilled. Describing the *Treatise* in this way brings out the centrality of expectations to its model of the economy; but the epistemological frailty or subjectivity of those expectations, in generating the confidence necessary for investment, had still not become central to Keynes's theoretical analysis, still less to his policy advice. Indeed he often spoke at this time as though all that was needed was a magic tool-kit to sort out a mechanical problem. Confidence would be generated by recovery, not vice versa.[22]

---

[19] Skidelsky, *Keynes*, vol. II, p. 147.

[20] Moggridge, *Keynes*, p. 486, referring to the Wicksellian origin of this distinction.

[21] Skidelsky, *Keynes*, vol. II, p. 410.

[22] I have been led to appreciate the significance of this point by the insights in the work of Bradley Bateman, still unpublished, which has caused some modification of the interpretation set out in 'J. M. Keynes, 1883–1946: "The Best of Both Worlds"'.

Keynes's experience of actual historical developments – from the Wall Street crash of 1929 to the flight from sterling in 1931 – nudged him towards a partial recognition of the importance of business psychology in sustaining or undermining self-reinforcing cycles which took on a life of their own. Keynes had already given some hints, implying perhaps more than he fully intended, in the *Treatise*, where his analysis of 'bullishness' and 'bearishness' built directly upon the experience of boom and bust on Wall Street. His analysis concentrated on 'the fact that *differences* of opinion exist between different sections of the public'. The subjective nature of the estimates of the probabilities involved is the point to note; for it surely represents a shift from the strictly objective epistemology which had formerly underpinned Keynes's academic research on probability. Hitherto he had allowed for probabilistic judgements of the likely consequences of actions – but only for correct or incorrect judgements of those probabilities, given the same access to information, as in a market. Some passages of the *Treatise*, however, paint a picture with a different look to it. On the one side there was an untrammelled 'bullishness of sentiment'; on the other, stretching the established sense of a 'bear' as one who sold short on the stock exchange, he identified as bears those 'persons who prefer to keep their resources in the form of claims on money of a liquid character realisable at short notice.'[23] Who was in the right frame of mind, the bulls or the bears? It all depended, surely, on whether it was a bull market or a bear market. And what helped to determine that? Why, the relative numbers who were in a bullish or bearish frame of mind, of course! Keynes's arguments imply this, even if his intuitions may have run ahead of his strict formal intentions.

Keynes's concept of liquidity preference built on such foundations. What the *General Theory* did was to develop it as his theory of interest, once he had abandoned the conventional explanation of interest rate as the equilibrator of the economy. The *Treatise* too had attributed this role to interest rate, simply adding the twist that it was an inefficient equilibrator. But the *General Theory* attributed unemployment not to a disequilibrium but instead to an equilibrium – one which was not disturbed by any self-righting pressure from under-employed resources. Moreover, those bargaining over the price of their capital or their labour were impotent in the face of market failure of this kind. The strategies available to individuals (going liquid, cutting wages, reducing spending) were collectively self-defeating. Keynes thus broke the chain of rationality between individual decisions and an optimal outcome for the community which was implicit in the concept of 'the invisible hand' and which had long been regarded as a piece of common sense. 'It is natural to

[23] *JMK*, vol. v, pp. 223–5; cf. pp. 128–31. The notion of liquidity preference is clearly glimpsed here – though not yet its significance as the explanation of interest rates.

suppose that the act of an individual, by which he enriches himself without apparently taking anything from anyone else, must also enrich the community as a whole', the *General Theory* acknowledged. But its revolutionary message was that the theory applicable to the individual firm did not provide a theory of output *as a whole.*[24]

Though Keynes never used the term himself, plainly there is here a concept of macroeconomics, conceived as the study of the system as a whole, not simply of one sector, however great in magnitude, nor of any sub-set of economic agents, however numerous. Book Two of the *General Theory*, concerned with 'Definitions and Ideas', leads up to a clinching assertion in its concluding sentence of 'the vital difference between the theory of the economic behaviour of the aggregate and the theory of the behaviour of the individual unit'.[25] Indeed in the preface to the French edition Keynes tried to pretend that this was why he had termed it 'a *general* theory. I mean by this that I am chiefly concerned with the behaviour of the economic system as a whole, – with aggregate incomes, aggregate profits, aggregate output, aggregate employment, aggregate investment, aggregate saving rather than with the incomes, profits, output, employment, investment and saving of particular industries, firms or individuals.'[26] His criticism of neo-classical microeconomics – or what he called 'classical economics' – was precisely that it failed to grasp this macroeconomic dimension.

Keynes himself made two repeated claims about his own thinking during the early 1930s: first, that it underwent a revolution, and secondly, that this rested upon ideas which were 'extremely simple and should be obvious'.[27] There is surely strong reason to regard the fallacy of composition as the overarching concept which informed the creation of the theory of effective demand in the early 1930s. Though the concept was hardly new to the author of the *Treatise on Probability*, it took another decade before the author of the *General Theory* seized upon it as a key which could turn the lock of a door which he needed to open. When Keynes explained his new theory of effective demand for the first time, in his university lectures in the Michaelmas Term of 1932, he did so by outlining 'two fundamental propositions', both distinguishing between the choices open to individuals and the outcome necessarily true in the aggregate.[28] This distinction provided an analytical tool that could be applied to a variety of decisions: about holding money, about

[24] *JMK*, vol. VII, pp. 20, 293.
[25] *JMK*, vol. VII, p. 85.   [26] *JMK*, vol. VII, p. xxxii.
[27] *JMK*, vol. VII, p. xxiii (preface to the *General Theory*). I have substantiated the argument in this paragraph more fully in *The Keynesian Revolution in the Making, 1924–36* (Oxford, 1988), pp. 269–72 and 'Hobson and Keynes as economic heretics'.
[28] Lecture notes of R. B. Bryce, 24 Oct. 1932, transcript by Thomas K. Rymes (Marshall Library, Cambridge).

saving and spending, about cutting wages. In this sense, it is the general theory behind the *General Theory*.

'The precise use of language comes at a late stage in the development of one's thought', Keynes said in one of his lectures in 1933. 'You can think accurately and effectively long before you can so to speak photograph your thought.'[29] In the light of this remark, it is interesting to ponder an article which he had written a year previously, while he was struggling to express his new insights, about the essentially circular nature of economic behaviour. 'When we transmit the tension, which is beyond our own endurance, to our neighbour, it is only a question of a little time before it reaches ourselves again travelling round the circle.'[30] Here is an image which could equally well illustrate the centrality of the fallacy of composition in Keynes's current thinking – or the centrality of confidence, through the self-fulfilling nature of the expectations which it generated. The ambiguity may arise because Keynes was not yet in a position to photograph his thought, rather than because the sort of thinking which had now seized him was inaccurate or ineffective. In short, there may be more than one helpful way of describing the revolutionary shift in Keynes's ideas.

A further question arises about how Keynes's own agenda was to be implemented. This is really a political issue, about power and how to mobilise it. The conventional, constitutional mechanism under the parliamentary system is via public opinion, via the ballot box, via the election of sympathetic representatives, and via the formation of a ministry committed to the required policy. Keynes tried this road. He was instrumental in persuading the Liberal Party to stake its fate in the 1929 General Election on a pledge to reduce unemployment by means of a public investment programme. Keynes assumed a high public profile during the campaign with the pamphlet *Can Lloyd George Do It?*, written with Hubert Henderson. But the electoral verdict gave Lloyd George no chance to do it. Instead a minority Labour Government was returned, to which Keynes thereupon turned his attention. He sought to influence its policy through the various channels open to him in 1930, notably the new Economic Advisory Council and the Macmillan Committee on Finance and Industry, to both of which he had been appointed.

Keynes was certainly lucky to have another hat to wear, as an expert, now that his politician's hat had been knocked off. But does that justify Skidelsky in interpreting Keynes's politics as simply statist and élitist, or in identifying Keynes as a Liberal who ended up as a Whig? 'Keynes's anti-market, anti-democratic bias was driven by a belief in scientific expertise and personal disinterestedness which now seems alarmingly naive', Skidelsky states. 'This

---

[29] Lecture notes by Marvin Fallgatter, 6 Nov. 1933 (Rymes transcript).
[30] *JMK*, vol. XXI, p. 213 (*New Statesman and Nation*, 24 Dec. 1932).

runs like a leitmotiv through his work and is *the* important assumption of his political philosophy.'[31] There is something in this; but some qualification is also necessary. When Keynes explicitly called himself a 'leftish Liberal' in the 1920s, it seems perverse to insist that he did not know what he was talking about. Likewise, in the face of his reiterated appeals for a dialogue with Labour, and his uniformly dismissive comments on the lack of appeal of Conservatism, not to mention his apparent Labour vote in 1935, to conclude that 'it is easy to imagine Keynes at home, or as at home as he would ever be, in the Conservative Party of Macmillan and Butler' seems rather over-imaginative.[32] In this at least, it should be said, Lord Skidelsky is at one with Sir Roy Harrod, forty years earlier.

Exaggerating Keynes's technocratic bent, at the expense of his experiments in the method of democratic persuasion, creates not only a distorted impression but also a factitious problem. For it then becomes difficult to make sense of his explanation (in 1934) of why his policies had not yet been adopted: 'Because I have not yet succeeded in convincing either the expert or the ordinary man that I am right.' Only when *both* were convinced, he maintained, would economic policy, 'with the usual time-lag, follow suit'.[33]

The *General Theory* supplied a logical reason why there was no effective chain from understandable (and in that sense rational) microeconomic decisions to optimal (and in that sense rational) macroeconomic outcomes. This was a world necessarily bounded by uncertainty, and one therefore in which potent economic decisions had to be based on uncertain expectations. It follows that Keynes's politics of persuasion were part of a process whereby appropriate economic expectations were formed. Indeed Skidelsky shows clearly that such a climate of enlightened confidence constituted the context and premise for the successful implementation of Keynesian policies. Conversely, in the absence of either confidence or enlightenment, the best that could be hoped was to do good by stealth. As Keynes – willing, as usual, to settle for second-best – confided in June 1932, once Neville Chamberlain was firmly installed at the Treasury: 'There are enormous psychological advantages in the *appearance* of economy.'[34] A real iron Chancellor might be a disaster in a slump, but there was some compensation in having one who was lath painted to look like iron. Even so, Keynes's real thrust is better expressed in another comment on Chamberlain: 'Unfortunately, the more pessimistic the Chancellor's policy, the more likely it is that pessimistic anticipations will

[31] Skidelsky, *Keynes*, vol. II, p. 228.
[32] Skidelsky, *Keynes*, vol. II, p. 232; cf. p. 536 for Skidelsky's statement that Keynes, in the 1935 General Election, 'for the first and only time in his life, voted Labour'.
[33] *JMK*, vol. XXVII, p. 36 (*New Statesman*, 24 Nov. 1934).
[34] *JMK*, vol. XXI, p. 110 (Keynes to Macmillan, 6 June 1932).

be realised and *vice versa*. Whatever the Chancellor dreams, will come true!'[35]

II

What might be called the reception-literature of Keynesianism has hitherto focused mainly on its administrative impact. The actual behaviour of the policy-makers has been the focus – some would say the butt – of the public-choice school: essentially a model of decision-making which stresses the policy-makers' own microeconomic motives. Like other men, it is held, bureaucrats are to be seen as motivated by rational self-interest, in ways that subvert the purity of those naive presuppositions of Harvey Road.[36] The simplicities of the public-choice model may themselves be simplistic; but it is well worth asking what Treasury mandarins got out of their job, even if the answer turns on exploring a syndrome of psychic satisfactions rather than identifying crude material benefits accruing to them in pay or perks or even power. The social anthropology of Heclo and Wildavsky within the 'Whitehall village' suggests a more subtle and fruitful line of approach.[37]

The appeal of Keynesianism to the mandarin temperament should certainly not be overlooked. In the inter-war years the Treasury had been intellectually captive to the elegance of the self-acting model of the economy which legitimated 'sound finance'. The model of Keynesianism which they came to adopt in the post-war period also bore a mandarin stamp. Busy policy-makers, of course, did not spend their time poring over the *General Theory* to tease out its doctrine. It is interesting that Sir Richard Hopkins did not read the *General Theory* until he had formally retired as Permanent Secretary at the Treasury in 1945 (though he then read it twice in preparing for the National Debt Enquiry) while Hugh Dalton reread it both on becoming Chancellor of the Exchequer and after resigning from that post.[38] What politicians and civil servants wanted was a handbook readily applicable to specific policy issues – which was not, alas, what Keynes had purported to offer in the *General Theory*. 'It would need a volume of a different character from

---

[35] *JMK*, vol. XXI, p. 184 (*The Times*, 5 April 1933).

[36] See Gordon Tullock, 'Public choice', in John Eatwell, Murray Milgate and Peter Newman (eds.), *The New Palgrave*, 4 vols. (1987), vol. III, pp. 1040–4, at p. 1043. This sort of analysis is directly applied to Keynesianism in Britain in J. M. Buchanan, R. E. Wagner and J. Burton, *The Consequences of Mr Keynes* (Institute of Economic Affairs, 1978).

[37] Hugo Heclo and Aaron Wildavsky, *The Private Government of Public Money*, 2nd edn (London, 1981), esp. pp. lxxii, 2. I have developed these points in 'The twentieth-century revolution in government: the case of the British Treasury'.

[38] Susan Howson, *British Monetary Policy, 1945–51* (Oxford, 1993), pp. 18–19, 305–6. My treatment of many issues below is fundamentally indebted to this study.

this one', he stated, 'to indicate even in outline the practical measures in which they might gradually be clothed'.[39]

In the fullest study of wartime and immediately postwar macroeconomic policy-making, Alan Booth suggests that 'the "embedding" of Keynesian analysis in Whitehall' was the result of 'a complex interaction between economic theory, political power, administrative organisation and Britain's economic history in the period 1939–49'.[40] Even so Keynes's own role is difficult to discount; his influence was felt in virtually every corridor of Whitehall. But he was not the only economist who found and exploited new elbow room as a wartime policy adviser. Lionel Robbins, as Director of the Economic Section, emerged as 'a willing and effective public relations officer for the Keynesian cause' – and one whose credentials were the more impressive in view of his pre-war opposition to Keynes. Conversely, James Meade, already one of the architects of the *theory* of effective demand, now systematised a policy for its practical management. His work with Richard Stone in producing aggregate figures for national income can justly be described as 'a revolutionary departure in British official statistics'.[41] This led to the operationalisation of the concepts of the *General Theory* in a way which spoke to the macroeconomic issue raised by the war: how to control inflation.

Keynesian economic theory may have been devised at the bottom of the slump, but it was symmetrical in its policy implications, as its author explicitly affirmed. 'The best we can hope to achieve is to use those kinds of investment which it is relatively easy to plan as a make-weight, bringing them in so as to preserve as much stability of aggregate investment as we can manage at the right and appropriate level', he wrote in 1937, at the peak of pre-war British economic recovery. 'Just as it was advisable for the Government to incur debt during the slump', he argued, 'so for the same reasons it is now advisable that they should incline to the opposite policy'.[42]

Still, there is an obvious irony in the circumstances under which Keynesian ideas achieved their administrative breakthrough. Devised as a strategy to 'conquer unemployment' (as the claim had been made in 1929), a Keynesian macroeconomic analysis was in fact adopted by a hitherto sceptical Treasury in order 'to pay for the war' (in the language of 1939–40). Insofar as the Treasury became Keynesian it was not – in some belated act of intellectual atonement – to adopt a policy of expansion under conditions of deflation, but

[39] *JMK*, vol. VII, p. 383.
[40] Alan Booth, *British Economic Policy, 1931–49. Was There a Keynesian Revolution?* (London, 1989), p. 51.
[41] Ibid., p. 67.
[42] *JMK*, vol. XXI, pp. 387, 390 ('How to avoid a slump', Jan. 1937).

to impose a policy of restraint under conditions of incipient inflation. This explains the framework adopted in the 1941 Budget, defining the problem of war finance in Keynesian terms, as one of mobilising maximum resources. The Treasury could now seize upon the same intellectual arguments, which they had previously contested as the premise for expansionist policies, to support the sort of restrictionist measures which they characteristically favoured. Who had converted whom is a moot point.

Another great landmark was when the Coalition Government's White Paper on Employment in 1944 opened with its ringing commitment to 'the maintenance of a high and stable level of employment after the war'. True, many caveats followed, especially the remarkable comment in one paragraph that: 'None of the main proposals contained in this Paper involves deliberate planning for a deficit in the National Budget in years of sub-normal trade activity.'[43] Keynes's comment on the penultimate draft was that this section, with its feast of 'budget humbug', had 'the air of having been written some years before the rest of the report'.[44] It derived and survived, as he well knew, from drafts written by Sir Wilfrid Eady, Joint Second Secretary at the Treasury from 1942–52. Keynes had played some part in the debates within Whitehall and evidently found Eady's coy self-characterisation of his Treasury colleagues as 'obtuse, bat-eyed and obstinate' altogether too near the truth. Keynes brushed aside Eady's professions of incomprehension of the theoretical issues at stake, claiming that 'after all, it is very easily understood! There is scarcely an undergraduate of the modern generation from whom these truths are hidden.'[45] One difference that the *General Theory* made to policy-making was that its widespread acceptance by the rising generation of academic economists put the Treasury on the defensive, no longer confident of the sanction of orthodoxy.

With the danger of going down with the sinking ship staring it in the face, the Treasury took its cue from Sir Richard Hopkins, whose tussles with Keynes, stretching back to the sittings of the Macmillan Committee on Finance and Industry in 1930, had been an education for both of them. The bland drafting of paragraph 77 (which we now know to have been by Hopkins) shows the Treasury style at its best, effortlessly fudging a form of words which gave few hostages to fortune, claiming consistency with the past while simultaneously acknowledging a new departure:

> There is nothing to prevent the Chancellor of the Exchequer in future, as in the past, from taking into account the requirements of trade and employment in framing his annual Budget. At the same time, to the extent that the policies

---

[43] Employment Policy, Cmd 6527 (May 1944), foreword and par. 74.
[44] *JMK*, vol. xxvii, p. 367 (note by Keynes, 14 Feb. 1944).
[45] *JMK*, vol. xxvii, p. 325 (Eady to Keynes, 26 May 1943; Keynes to Eady, 27 May 1943).

proposed in this Paper affect the balancing of the Budget in a particular year, they certainly do not contemplate any departure from the principle that the Budget must be balanced over a longer period.[46]

The provenance of the White Paper is thus evident, as a Keynesian message, strained and filtered through the fine mesh of careful Treasury prose. The fact remains that everything else in it is by way of qualification to its initial and central claim.

> The government accept as one of their primary aims and responsibilities the maintenance of a high and stable level of employment after the war. This Paper outlines the policy which they propose to follow in pursuit of that aim. A country will not suffer from mass unemployment so long as the total demand for its goods and services is maintained at a high level.

That this claim was founded on a Keynesian multiplier analysis was subsequently made explicit.[47] 'My own feeling is that the first sentence is more valuable than the whole of the rest', Keynes said privately.[48]

The policy to be followed included not only strictly Keynesian measures for the counter-cyclical regulation of public investment but also parallel measures, chiefly due to Meade, for controlling swings in consumption expenditure by varying the rates of social insurance contributions. But if New Jerusalem was the ultimate goal, it was only to be reached by a hard and stony road. While the Government professed 'no intention of maintaining wartime restrictions for restriction's sake', they were nonetheless 'resolved that, so long as supplies are abnormally short, the most urgent needs shall be met first', and trusted that 'the public will continue to give, for as long as is necessary, the same whole-hearted support to the policy of "fair shares" that it has given in war-time'.[49]

The White Paper, in short, was not only a Keynesian document but one approved by Keynes himself, and attempts to suggest otherwise seem misguided. Keynes called the draft 'an outstanding State Paper which, if one casts one's mind back ten years or so, represents a revolution in official opinion'.[50] He had had to wait until nearly the end of his life to capture the ear of the opinion-forming élite; but that he had now done so was unmistakable. The White Paper went as far as was decent in making this plain:

46 Cmd 6527, par. 77.
47 Employment Policy, Cmd 6527, p. 3 (foreword); cf. par. 40.
48 Moggridge, Keynes, p. 709 (Keynes to A. Robinson, 5 June 1944); and see pp. 709–14 for a full and cogent account of Keynes's part in the drafting of the White Paper.
49 Cmd 6527, par. 17. Correlli Barnett has tendentiously presented this debate as a triumph for the 'glib confidence' of 'New Jerusalemism'; see The Audit of War (London, 1986), pp. 257–63.
50 JMK, vol. xxvii, p. 364 (note by Keynes, 14 Feb. 1944).

Not long ago, the ideas embodied in the present proposals were unfamiliar to the general public and the subject of controversy among economists. To-day, the conception of an expansionist economy and the broad principles governing its growth are widely accepted by men of affairs as well as by technical experts in all the great industrial countries.[51]

Though the canonical status of the *General Theory* was increasingly assured, however, it was more by vague invocation than by specific citation. What came to be justified under the rubric of Keynesianism might, in some respects at least, have surprised the historical Keynes.

The case for macroeconomic regulation of the economy was commonly meshed into a debate about planning, the buzz-word of the 1940s. It was in this guise that Keynesianism was assimilated to conventional arguments for socialism. True, Keynes had a longstanding record of wishing to regulate investment so as to make full use of resources, and in the *General Theory* he accordingly suggested 'a somewhat comprehensive socialisation of investment'. The Labour Party's nationalisation measures, however, hardly fulfilled his criteria of controlling the overall volume of investment, whether public or private – 'it is not the ownership of the instruments of production which it is important for the State to assume'.[52] Nonetheless, Labour appealed to a synergy between its nationalisation programme and a full-employment policy, under the elastic rubric of planning. In 1944 Dalton identified counter-cyclical control of investment as 'one of the strongest reasons for nationalisation' in the Labour Party's confidential discussions of postwar policy.[53]

In regulating the level of effective demand, Keynes's instincts were always to concentrate on investment. Practically all that the *General Theory* said about consumption was: 'The State will have to exercise a guiding influence on the propensity to consume partly through its scheme of taxation, partly by fixing the rate of interest, and partly, perhaps, in other ways.'[54] In practice, consumption proved easier to regulate than investment. Under the Labour Government, there was a commitment to macroeconomic management of the level of demand through fiscal policy, supplemented by the use of direct controls to keep inflationary pressure in check. 'Really, therefore', Dalton confided in his diary, 'though this is not the way anyone puts it – "always have a bit of inflationary pressure, but use physical controls to prevent it breaking

---

[51] Cmd 6527, par. 80.
[52] *JMK*, vol. VII, p. 378.
[53] Howson, *British Monetary Policy*, pp. 92–3. See Elizabeth Durbin, *New Jerusalems* (London, 1985), esp. pp. 216–18, for the earlier link between socialisation and full employment policies argued by the New Fabian economists; and Donald Winch, *Economics and Policy* (London, 1969), pp. 215–18 for a pioneering dissection of the muddled arguments for Keynesianism and 'planning'.
[54] *JMK*, vol. VII, p. 378.

through"'.[55] Publicly, this is how Sir Stafford Cripps explained the matter in his Budget speech of 1950: 'Excessive demand produces inflation and inadequate demand results in deflation. The fiscal policy of the Government is the most important single instrument for maintaining that balance.'[56]

By contrast, the use of monetary policy as an economic regulator smacked of the bad old deflationary days of the Gold Standard, and was abjured by Labour. In taking this line Dalton could initially claim both theoretical and practical endorsement from Keynes. Keynes repeatedly stressed the desirability of bringing down the rate to a low *and stable* level (in this sense 'fixing' the rate). True, there was a reference in the Employment White Paper to 'the possibility of influencing capital expenditure by the variation of interest rates', following a period of cheap money.[57] Keynes had simply commented: 'I have never myself been able to make much sense of that paragraph.'[58] In the last months of his life, furthermore, Keynes, had joined Joan Robinson in supporting Dalton's attempt at securing 'cheaper money' in the structure of long-term rates for government borrowing.[59]

Whatever the technical merits of this policy of fixed, minimal interest rates, both its provenance and its ideological dimension were clearly indicated in the *General Theory.* 'The outstanding faults of the economic society in which we live are its failure to provide for full employment and its arbitrary and inequitable distribution of wealth and incomes', Keynes claimed. Not only did he suggest that both flaws could be mitigated through a redistribution of income, which would raise the propensity to consume: he claimed that his theory held 'a second, much more fundamental inference' about inequalities of wealth, via the role now assigned to interest rates. If high interest rates became unnecessary to assure adequate saving, a régime of cheap money 'would mean the euthanasia of the rentier, and consequently, the euthanasia of the cumulative oppressive power of the capitalist to exploit the scarcity value of capital'.[60] It is little wonder that this apophthegm made a natural appeal to Labour supporters, not least Dalton himself. Indeed it led him to push cheaper money to a point where it became unsustainable, thereby disclosing a perverse effect of his monetary policy upon capital values. Though he was still bullish in November 1946 – '"The euthanasia of the rentier" is proceeding apace' – the moment of truth came that winter, with the issue of Government stock ('Daltons') at the unprecedentedly low level of 2.5 per cent. Its failure left the issue largely in the hands of the authorities. The perverse

---

55 Ben Pimlott (ed.), *The Political Diary of Hugh Dalton* (London, 1986), p. 465 (24 Jan. 1950).
56 Sir Stafford Cripps, quoted in Edward Bridges, *The Treasury* (London, 1966), p. 93.
57 Cmd 6527, par. 59. On this ambiguity see Howson, *British Monetary Policy*, pp. 44ff.
58 *JMK*, vol. XXVII, pp. 377–9 (Keynes to Sir Alan Barlow, 15 June 1944).
59 Howson, *British Monetary Policy*, pp. 149, 152.   60 *JMK*, vol. VII, pp. 372–6.

consequence came through an appreciation of the value of assets with a prospective annual return higher than these rock-bottom official interest rates. Here was the basis for the strategy, later urged by Crosland, Labour's pre-eminent revisionist, for raising interest rates as a means of depreciating capital values. When this point was put to Dalton in 1951, he noted ruefully: 'This is a new argument, not to be found in Keynes.'[61]

Though the Bank of England's discount rate remained fixed at the level of only 2 per cent until the Labour Government lost office at the end of 1951, there is evidence that Gaitskell, the new Chancellor, was ready to contemplate a rise in long-term rates to fight inflation.[62] It was left to the incoming Churchill Government to restore a flexible Bank rate. There was no talk of 'monetarism' in those days; but the scheme (ROBOT) that was broached for allowing sterling to float, under rather complex arrangements, went a long way down that road. The thrust of ROBOT was to charge the Bank of England with implementing a monetary policy that would make the defence of sterling its prime objective, necessarily at the expense of the full-employment objective. This would obviously have made life simpler for the Bank. In 1944 the Deputy Governor was reported to be 'uneasy at the prospect of our entering the post-war period without having any clear idea of what dials to watch in determining bank policy. Under the Gold Standard there were well understood indicators.'[63] The wistfulness of the authorities for the good old days of the 'knave-proof' fiscal constitution should not be underestimated. Though ROBOT was overruled on political grounds by the Churchill Government – since the Conservatives wanted to live down their reputation as the party of unemployment and the prime minister himself had had quite enough of the Gold Standard for one lifetime – the new government naturally imparted its own bias to the Keynesian consensus, just as the Labour Government had.

The Conservative version of demand management was to reinforce fiscal fine tuning with a monetary policy that now used interest-rate changes to the same ends. After twenty years at 2 per cent Bank rate was symbolically raised to 2.5 per cent in November 1951 and to 4 per cent a few months later. By 1957 the market was used to rates at around 5 per cent, and Peter Thorneycroft's

---

[61] See the authoritative treatment in Howson, *British Monetary Policy*, pp. 134–5, 191–5, 305–7; quotations from Dalton's diary at pp. 191, 305. Meade and Robbins had long advocated short-run variations in interest rates; see pp. 46, 49.

[62] Howson, *British Monetary Policy*, pp. 291–2.

[63] Note of a conversation with B. G. Catterns by Lucius Thompson-McCausland, 14 February 1944, quoted in Howson, *British Monetary Policy*, p. 59. On ROBOT see Alec Cairncross, *Years of Recovery: British economic policy, 1945–51* (London, 1985), ch. 9. The persistence of the 'knave-proof' appeal of the Gold Standard for the Treasury mind, as illustrated in this and the next paragraph, is one theme of my study, 'The Treasury's analytical model of the British economy between the Wars'.

'September measures' that year went to a 7 per cent rate, unprecedented since the disinflationary squeeze introduced in April 1920 by the Lloyd George Coalition. During 1957–8, however, it took only fourteen months for the rate to decline to 4 per cent – and a further thirty-two months before the Bank rate again reached its crisis level of 7 per cent in July 1961. 'Stop–go', of course, was one name for this kind of economic policy. In terms of intellectual consistency this was hardly Keynesian: instead, credit regulation to control the cycle of disinflation and reflation derived faithfully from the views which Ralph Hawtrey had long urged upon his colleagues (as some old Treasury hands recognised). It needs to be appreciated that the old dogs of the Treasury were not just learning new tricks but performing some of their old tricks too.[64]

Indeed, as the nature of the postwar economic problem revealed itself, the Treasury found itself in an all too familiar position. At the end of the war there had been a general expectation that the post-1945 experience would parallel that of post-1918: a couple of years of inflationary boom, with a slump around the corner. This fear was implicit in the 1944 White Paper. It was constantly in Dalton's mind, not only through his own memories but through reminders from Evan Durbin and the XYZ group of Labour economists. True, Dalton's Budget speech in April 1947 said that inflation rather than deflation was now the immediate danger. Yet Meade, writing in 1948, when inflation was already at the front of his own mind, prefaced his arguments with the comment: 'We are all agreed that measures must be taken to stimulate total monetary demand and to prevent it from falling below the level necessary to sustain a high output and high employment when the time next comes – as sooner or later it assuredly will come – when a deficient total demand threatens to engulf us in a major depression.'[65] Right through to 1949 fears of deflation continued, though by now intermittently, to grip the minds of the policy-makers, not least Sir Stafford Cripps; and in 1950 his successor, Gaitskell, was still keen to introduce a Full Employment Bill, despite the obvious lukewarmness of the old guard at the Treasury, led by Sir Bernard Gilbert and Sir Wilfrid Eady.[66]

It was only in 1951 that it really became clear that the scenario had changed. Here was the crucial turning-point, in perceptions of unemployment as much as in its incidence. It is hardly too much to say that in the next twenty years full employment came to be taken for granted. The attribution of this

[64] See G. C. Peden, 'Old dogs and new tricks: the British Treasury and Keynesian economics in the 1940s and 1950s', in Barry Supple and Mary Furner (eds.), *The State and Economic Knowledge* (Cambridge, 1990).

[65] J. E. Meade, *Planning and the Price Mechanism* (London, 1948), p. 12; cf. Howson, *British Monetary Policy*, pp. 146–7, 163.

[66] Cairncross, *Years of Recovery*, p. 426; Howson, *British Monetary Policy*, pp. 303–4.

Table 10.1. *Government income and expenditure as a proportion (%) of GDP*

	Income	Expenditure	Deficit/surplus	Defence
1951	32.9	27.0	+5.9	6.2
1952	33.6	30.6	+3.0	8.1
1953	31.8	31.0	+0.8	9.6

Calculated from Mitchell, *British Historical Statistics*, table 4, pp. 592–3 (public expenditure) and table 3, pp. 584–6 (revenue); table 4, p. 830 (GDP).

happy state of affairs to Keynesian influence may well rest on the unargued assumption, *post hoc ergo propter hoc*. Certainly the Keynesian triumphalist literature of the 1960s implies an economic-historical role for the *General Theory* which now looks implausible as a sufficient explanation for the long postwar boom. Yet it is not clear that the narrower question of why people stopped worrying about a slump in 1951 ought to be answered without reference to the historical Keynes, still less to Keynesianism.

After all, in the last slump Keynes had made his name by proposing a programme of public works, to be spread over two years, which would have raised government expenditure by about two per cent of gross domestic product (GDP). What he had actually wanted was roads or houses; but, in a famous passage in the *General Theory*, he ironically allowed for the conventional 'preference for wholly "wasteful" forms of loan expenditure rather than for partly wasteful forms', which still served to stimulate the economy so long as they provided the requisite 'pretext for digging holes in the ground'.[67] Suppose, then, that a rise in wasteful public expenditure – not by a mere two per cent of GDP but nearer double that – were to have been planned by government over two years beginning in 1951, would that not in itself have been enough to release loyal Keynesians from any fear of deflation? This is, of course, exactly what the Labour Government's rearmament programme amounted to in its macroeconomic impact. Though its implementation was trimmed back by the incoming Conservative Government, the impact of defence spending is clear. The flaw in this analogy is obviously that this was not deficit finance; but nor was the *increase* in spending covered by revenue; so in effect rearmament boosted demand through cutting the budget surplus by five per cent of GDP between 1951–3 (Table 10.1).

This stimulus to the economy may not have been beneficial, and it imperfectly fulfilled Keynes's dictum that 'wars have been the only form of large-scale loan expenditure which statesmen have thought justifiable'.[68]

[67] *JMK*, vol. VII, pp. 129–30.   [68] *JMK*, vol. VII, p. 130.

Nonetheless its part in changing perceptions about the British economy needs to be remembered.

It is, however, a further step – and a long one – to suggest an axiomatic identification of Keynesianism with a 'democratic deficit'. Notably through the influence of the Nobel laureate James Buchanan, such an axiom has become a staple of public-choice analysis. Here the 'specific hypothesis is that the Keynesian theory of economic policy produces inherent biases when applied within the framework of political democracy.'[69] Though this analysis was prudently limited by its authors to the political history of the United States, it may be thought curious that a hypothesis of such explanatory power, relying on a bias alleged to be inherent, should not yield equally demonstrable insights about the political legacy of Keynesianism in Britain.

Yet the fact is that during the period which is now regarded, for better or for worse, as the heyday of Keynesian influence, the Treasury maintained a generally tight fiscal stance. The two draconian budgets which Dalton introduced in 1947 finally removed the wartime deficit in government expenditure. Throughout the next quarter-century, a surplus was realised in every year except one. The exception was 1964–5, following Maudling's 'dash for growth', when an apparent deficit, itself amounting to less than one per cent of GDP, may well be a product of a change in accounting conventions. Only from 1973 did a series of deficits mount steadily, reaching a peak in 1976 at 6 per cent of GDP.[70]

After the Second World War, the total level of the public debt reached 275 per cent of GDP in 1947. Yet within five years it had fallen to 200 per cent, and in 1965 the national debt was less than current GDP for the first time since 1916. By 1980, after thirty years of alleged Keynesian profligacy, the debt amounted to less than six months' current production, whereas the national debt had been more than two years' production in 1931, supposedly the end of the era of sound money.[71] These figures may well conceal as much as they reveal; but they suggest the need for more sophisticated historical research on the empirical relationship between Keynesianism and government deficits.

The simplest interpretation is that the budget was balanced because low levels of unemployment provided no reason to unbalance it. It was a backhanded tribute to the success of full employment that other, and more

---

69 J. M. Buchanan and Richard E. Wagner, *Democracy in Deficit: the political legacy of Lord Keynes* (New York, 1977), p. x. It is congruent with their argument that they should see Keynes as an anti-democratic élitist (p. 7), imprisoned in the presuppositions of Harvey Road (p. 78).
70 Calculated from B. R. Mitchell, *British Historical Statistics* (Cambridge, 1988), table 4, pp. 592–4 (public expenditure) and table 3, p. 584 (revenue); table 4, p. 830 (GDP).
71 Ibid., table 7, pp. 602–3; table 4, pp. 829–30 (GDP).

traditional, priorities in budget-making found influential champions within the government apparatus. In this sense lip-service to Keynesianism served to license the Treasury's timeless mission – to act as a check upon human nature. Sir Bernard Gilbert, with his longstanding view of the Treasury's function as that of 'scraping the butter back out of the dog's mouth', perfectly exemplifies a cast of mind hardly ruffled by the advent of 'full-employment' rhetoric.[72] 'For some years it is likely that the policy will involve keeping the brake on with varying degrees of pressure, on both capital and consumer expenditure', Gilbert noted presciently in 1945. 'I see no difficulty about that, it is in harmony with all our past training and experience, and the constitution of the machinery of Government is well fitted for the exercise of negative controls.'[73] The result was a highly circumspect approach towards any possibility of an unbalanced budget. The prospect of a deficit, which suddenly (and misleadingly) appeared during the making of Butler's 1954 budget, thus 'produced a sudden reversion to pre-war principles', according to Sir Robert Hall, currently Economic Adviser to HM Government. Not only Butler and Gilbert but Sir Edward Bridges, as Permanent Secretary to the Treasury, apparently regarded the predicted deficit as worse than the predicted fall in employment with which it was associated, and Hall thus had 'quite a struggle to get them to realize that the principle of the Budgets since 1948 made the surplus or deficit accidental'.[74] Accidental? It sounds like *Animal-Farm* Keynesianism, with some budget outcomes (deficits) plainly more accidental than others (surpluses).

III

Keynes had, of course, addressed his *magnum opus* chiefly to his 'fellow economists', with a qualifying hope that it would be 'intelligible to others'.[75] How the *General Theory* was received, understood, and propagated by academic economists is an important topic which has not yet found its historian. There is a story to be told here in which names like Robertson, Hicks, Harrod, Hawtrey, Meade and Robbins will bulk large. But so will that of A. W. Phillips, and not only because of the eponymous 'Phillips curve' which came to express the supposed trade-off between unemployment and inflation. If the conception of Keynesianism which flourished by the 1950s can be called hydraulic, it was surely the ingenious Professor Phillips who set

[72] B. W. Gilbert in 1931, quoted in Eunan O'Halpin, *Head of the Civil Service: a study of Sir Warren Fisher* (London, 1989), p. 54.
[73] Gilbert to Bridges, 20 Mar. 1945, in Jim Tomlinson, *Employment Policy: the crucial years, 1939–1945* (Oxford, 1987), pp. 81–2.
[74] Alec Cairncross (ed.), *The Robert Hall Diaries, 1954–61* (London, 1991), p. 8 (8 April 1954).
[75] *JMK*, vol. VII, p. xxi (preface to the *General Theory*).

his stamp on this metaphor by causing an actual 'Phillips machine' to be constructed. It was developed at the London School of Economics in 1949–50, simulating the economy by pumping coloured liquids through transparent tubes, thus demonstrating to the sceptical how the flows could be manipulated by pulling the right levers.[76] Clearly Phillips himself was an engaging man and his machine achieved pedagogical triumphs which anticipated the advent of computer modelling. It is surely plain, however, that the inspiration for such mechanical exercises, so redolent of Heath Robinson, is hardly that of the historical Keynes.

The *General Theory's* insight about the fundamental role of expectations under conditions of uncertainty in influencing the behaviour of the economy was overlooked by the policymakers of the 1960s and 1970s at their peril. 'This is because they had inherited Keynes's machinery, but not the philosophy which sets limits to the scope and effectiveness of that machinery', is how Skidelsky puts it. 'Their hubris was inevitably succeeded by nemesis.'[77] In examining the ideological impact of Keynesianism in postwar Britain, it should not surprise historians to discover infidelity to Keynes's original intentions. Indeed such distortions may have been a price that had to be paid for the influence of the doctrine. It is not determinist or reductionist to recognise a natural selectivity in the reception of ideas by those to whom they appeal. Just as the Labour dialect of Keynesianism embraced planning and nationalisation as the means of economic management, so the Conservative patois spoke of regulation through monetary policy, while the mandarin idiom dwelt on the beauties of restraint and fine tuning by an omnicompetent Treasury.

The opaque historical consequences of Keynesianism were certainly not foreseen by the historical Keynes – only the fallibility of foresight itself. As Keynes told Shaw in 1935: 'When my new theory has been duly assimilated and mixed with politics and feelings and passions, I can't predict what the final upshot will be in its effects on action and affairs.'[78] He lived long enough, moreover, to glimpse his transformation from the begetter of ideas which he could recognise as his own to the status of father of an 'ism'. After he had dined with a group of Keynesian economists in Washington, DC, in 1944, he said at breakfast the next morning: 'I was the only non-Keynesian there.'[79]

---

[76] A. W. Phillips, 'The relation between unemployment and the rate of change of money wages in the United Kingdom, 1861–1957', *Economica*, vol. 25 (1958), 283–99; and see Nicholas Barr, 'The Phillips machine', *LSE Quarterly*, 2 (1988), pp. 305–37.

[77] Skidelsky, *Keynes*, vol. II, p. 410.

[78] *JMK*, vol. XXVIII, p. 42.

[79] Austin Robinson in Hutchison, *Keynes versus the 'Keynesians' . . . ?*, p. 58.

11

BASTIANINI AND THE WEAKENING
OF THE FASCIST WILL TO FIGHT
THE SECOND WORLD WAR

ల౩ల౩ల౩

OWEN CHADWICK

I T is well known that the Italian archives were maltreated, for the best of
reasons, in September 1943: partly by destruction, partly by export, partly
by concealment; in the effort to hide from the incoming Germans what some
of the Italian civil servants and generals had been doing.[1] It took a long time
after 1945 to recover what could be recovered and not everything could be
recovered and not everything that has been recovered is yet available in print.
But in 1990 *I Documenti diplomatici italiani* (series 9 vol. 10) printed Foreign
Office documents for those last months of Mussolini's power. They are edited
by Pietro Pastorelli, the professor of international politics at the Sapienza, who
has been president of the commission for the reordering and publication of the
diplomatic documents; and they are important. Some of these documents had
been published before in various collections but nothing before this has
enabled us to see the full force of the documentation; especially as it comes in
the letters of two leading Fascists, Alfieri the ambassador in Berlin and
Bastianini who from February 1943 was in effect running the Foreign Office.

The Fascist administration contained quite a number of sensible people.
For though it had promoted loyal party bosses to high posts – to be heads of
departments or even ambassadors for which some of them were not well suited
if ambassadors ought to be suave and groomed and courteous – it had also
used the civil service without many sackings and the civil servants did what

---

[1] For the treatment, destruction and first recovery of the archives see M. Toscano, 'Fonti
documentarie e memorialistiche per la storia diplomatica della seconda guerra mondiale' in
Rivista storica italiana 60 (1948) 83ff.; and F. Rave and G. Spini, 'Fonti documentarie e
memorialistiche par la storia della crisi dello Stato italiano (1940–1945)', *Rivista storica
italiana* 61 (1949) 400ff., 574ff. Best treatment in English is F. W. D. Deakin, *The brutal
friendship*, 2nd edn, London 1966. This article is based on the first A. B. Emden Memorial
Lecture at St Edmund Hall, Oxford.

civil services do, the best for whatever the government was in power without asking questions. But by December 1942 anyone with sanity must ask questions. The German Sixth Army was shut up inside Stalingrad after a Russian offensive ran right through its communications to the West; the Sixth Army did not surrender until 30 January 1943 but already in December, for the first time, every sane person must ask, can Hitler win this war? The Italians must ask it urgently because, to the pride of Mussolini and some of the people, and to the lament of more of the people, they had an army on the South Russian front.

I

Dino Alfieri was a Milan nationalist who was wounded in the First World War and at times the wound still hurt him. He joined the Fascist party early and held important posts in the civil service until he became the Minister of Culture, an office much weightier than it sounds because it was also responsible for controlling public opinion so far as Mussolini did not do that job himself. In 1939 he asked to be ambassador to the Vatican because he had an invalid son and needed to be in Rome, and won the assent of a disapproving Mussolini who thought him too big a man for a minor post. On 26 April 1940, as war loomed, Mussolini ordered him to be the ambassador in Berlin. The motive for this order was Mussolini's belief that in not less than six months and probably sooner Germany would have won the war. There would be a peace to settle and spoils to allot, and Italy must be represented by a capable man. Since Alfieri did not speak German and did not want to leave Rome he did not think himself a sensible choice. Nevertheless he and his wife arrived in Berlin on 17 May 1940. It was a good time for an Italian to arrive.

The choice turned out very sensible but not at all for the reason that it was so decided. He was chosen and sent to do a job totally unlike the job he was then called upon to do. Mussolini joined in the war, which he thought that Hitler had won, only to get a seat in making the treaty. The only instruction he ever gave to Alfieri, when he summoned him to the Palazzo Venezia to tell him what he was to do, was this: *work to get an atmosphere in Berlin that will be good for the coming peace conference.*[2] But then there was no peace conference; and two years later, by May 1942, Alfieri was beginning to be fed up with his job.[3] He told his boss Count Ciano that if you talk to the Nazis courteously they think you are weak and if you talk to them strongly they are offended, and they cannot be called comfortable friends.

[2] *Dictators Face to Face* 212 (henceforth *Dictators*). This was a 1954 English translation by D. Moore of the 1948 original Milan book, *Due dittatori di fronte.*
[3] DDI, 8, 595 (all references to series nine of DDI).

He thought it would help him if he were nominated a member of the Grand Fascist Council, and he received that honour a week later. It was a promotion which later risked his life and caused a death sentence to be pronounced upon him.[4] That future he could not know; and meanwhile the plea for the honour, and the acceptance of it, prove that in May 1942 he did not yet doubt Mussolini or the excellence of Fascism. And of course he threw into his reports the adulation of the Duce which is too characteristic of the reports of nearly all the Fascist ambassadors. When in September the news came to Berlin that Stalingrad had fallen to the German army and there was to be a victory parade in Berlin he went round to General Fromm to congratulate him and told him how proud the Italians were to be fighting with the Germans in the struggle against Bolshevism; and Fromm and Alfieri drank a toast in champagne to the success of the combined German–Italian armies.[5] But then nothing happened, no victory parade, no ceremony.

It has not been fully realised what a brilliant reporter was this ambassador. It has not been realised because the book which he himself wrote to describe his experiences is one of the bores of wartime memoirs and at times specious enough to be unpleasant. He was not the right man for post-war apologetic. This sounds like a complacent man, that form of autobiographer who likes to put in other people's reports on how good he was at his job, and so not indirectly sing his own praises. He quotes Morgagni, so loyal a Fascist that he shot himself at Mussolini's fall: 'Your intelligence and enthusiasm means so much to our country.' He quotes Mussolini: 'I realize that Alfieri is one of my best men. He has been successful in every sphere of his activities.'[6] Sometimes you like Alfieri, sometimes you think him a little ridiculous, sometimes you worry that he is so good a servant of a Fascist master, and in the end he wins your sympathy for the appalling predicament in which he found himself. Perhaps we may defend him even as an autobiographer and say that if you have been a Fascist cabinet minister and are writing after Fascism had become abhorrent your position is weak and you are more tempted than other men to quote persons who say complimentary things about you. But that was after the war. Yet soon after the war Alfieri's memoirs are frank on his getting on with some of the horrible men in Europe; he sounds as though he had no penitence, certainly not any touch of nausea, as he describes his part in the working of the Rome–Berlin Axis; and this complacency did not make the public think highly of his memoirs. Somehow he was out of date when he wrote of his past.

---

[4] He voted for the resolution of the Grand Council which caused the fall of Mussolini. The officers of the Salo republic came to arrest him but with the aid of friends he escaped into Switzerland. He was tried in absentia and sentenced to death. In 1946 he was tried as a war criminal and acquitted; then examined on whether he should be removed from the Foreign Affairs list as an 'undesirable' and again was acquitted.

[5] DDI, 9, 140.   [6] *Dictators* 200.

He still admired D'Annunzio as a great figure of Italian literature; at a time when to all the critics there was no more absurd posturer in literature. He is an admirer of Sir Nevile Henderson the British ambassador in Berlin in the Munich time; and after the war when appeasement was thought weak as water, that did not endear him to British readers. And sometimes, as is the way with autobiographies, the memory does not agree with the documents. Yet with ambassadors' reports, it is not always correct that the memory is more unreliable than the documents. For example, the documents show him as having no doubt that in the end Germany will win the war. The memory says that after Stalingrad he was sure that Germany could not win the war.[7] But the documents of an ambassador have a duty to express a faith in something which an inner conviction or doubt might not support.

But during the war, when he is reporting privately to his masters, he is eloquent, down to earth, amusing, unbuttoned. The dispatches to Rome from Berlin, that winter of 1942–3, make ever more enthralling reading as the situation went from bad to worse.[8]

Alfieri liked General Fromm who was only in command of the home army. He thought General Keitel pompous and too proud of himself.[9] For what he did have doubt about was the German conduct of this war in which the Italians were so inextricably mixed. He could say things to Ciano and Mussolini that no German could dare to say. He was totally against what was happening in Russia. He thought Hitler a poor general,[10] complained about the cruelty of some of his men in the East, and found the public speeches of the German leaders not at all to his taste. He thought some of the ritual absurd; he attended a Führer celebration that April, where the crowd was pressed together under stiflingly hot lights and the chorus (which consisted of ancient and ugly women) was too loud for the building and where (he says) the conductor Furtwängler waged a wrestling match with Beethoven.[11] He watched Hitler making his speech to the Reichstag in the Kroll Opera House at the end of April that year and was very unimpressed; he saw an orator who read all his speech and never took his eyes from the paper and went fast and as all the loudspeakers were raucous few people could get what he said and Alfieri looked round the audience and saw that as the speech went on and on they were bored, as he put it full of pesantezza[12] and the speaker had lost that rapport between orator and audience which Alfieri knew, from previous experience, he was able to evoke magically. And when at the end Hitler

7 *Dictators* 177.
8 By contrast the diary printed by 'L. Simoni', *Berlino, Ambasciata d'Italia 1939–1943* (1946), illuminates little.
9 DDI, 9, 146.   10 DDI, 9, 543.
11 DDI, 8, 508.   12 DDI, 8, 526.

received the usual ovation, he sat back bowed and looking despondent, as though he was bored by the applause. 'More than ever before', said Alfieri, 'he gave the impression of being shut up inside himself', being isolated because he wanted to be isolated, 'il grande solitario', the great hermit; so isolated that the ministers could not get decisions out of him unless they were to do with the military tactics.[13] Moreover Alfieri thought Goebbels guilty of the worst of taste. He disliked all the illegalities of the SS. There was a war to fight and it could not be fought only with soldiers and generals, there had to be a home front which would do its part; and this German government was both mishandling its military campaigns in the east and treating its home front as though it did not matter. Himmler he says never makes speeches. He knows he is unpopular. Perhaps he wants to be unpopular. What matters to him is that his power grows all the time.[14] At the end of September 1941 Alfieri reported lots of rumour, of plots, and palace revolutions, and offers of peace, and desperate deeds, and disgrace of Himmler;[15] and the official efforts to calm the public announcements do nothing but make them more nervous. For the Germans have lost their belief in the infallibility of their leaders. There is a spectre again – of lots of victories ending in defeat.

To Alfieri the worst form of the isolation of Hitler and the few colleagues who were the government of Germany was the consequent isolation of the German Foreign Secretary with whom perforce he must deal. He did not like Ribbentrop. He found him arrogant, vain, vague, continuously unsatisfactory whenever they met. But the problem was worse than Ribbentrop's human failings. The German Foreign Office was divided into two pieces – the civil service in Berlin, and their head with a few of his confidants in a forest near Hitler's forest headquarters – where Ribbentrop had to be if he was to get any decisions. While the Foreign Office gained more and more responsibility, every decision had to be referred to a very few people in a forest, never was there such a bottleneck; Alfieri compared it to a vase where the body is growing longer and longer to take more and more liquid while the neck remains just as small.

His predicament was that he was accredited to a government of which he did not now approve. What were his objections? This German government has no idea in its head except force – that is, winning the war by military means. But battles are won by military means, wars are also won by politics and there are no politics. The generalship is so inflexible, its idea is fight your way to somewhere and then resist to the last man, that is not generalship. But much worse for Alfieri was the treatment of the occupied territories. What is the point of this persecution of the Jews, which Alfieri knew a lot about in 1942 though later he said that he did not? What is the point of this maltreatment of

[13] DDI, 9, 221.   [14] DDI, 9, 198.   [15] DDI, 9, 157, 173, 198.

Roman Catholics, for it seems to have no advantages and some disadvantages, not least that it complicated the friendship with Italy? Above all, why should we alienate all Europe? – we must give the little countries hope, an assurance of a free and independent place in the new Europe, and then we shall swing them towards our side; and such assurances need politics.

Such were the reports which went to Count Ciano in the middle of 1942. Alfieri did not like Ciano. He rightly thought that this was nepotism, that Ciano had the job of Foreign Secretary only because he had married Mussolini's daughter. He accepted that Ciano was intelligent, lively, generous and educated. But Ciano rose up the Fascist ladder so fast and so easily that he really had no training for power and at times acted without thinking at all. He was 'volatile'. He was ambitious and could be harsh towards people who stood in the way of that ambition.[16] Such was Alfieri's opinion of his boss. Ciano also had a virtue which in our eyes is a virtue but which to Alfieri doing his job in Berlin was a defect. Where Alfieri only disliked Ribbentrop, Ciano loathed him. In private he talked about Ribbentrop in language that was not printable. He thought Ribbentrop not only stupid but consumed with arrogance. If like Alfieri you wish to influence the German government it certainly made it more difficult when your own boss loathed, and was loathed by, the member of that government to which you were accredited.

II

Such reporting as that of Alfieri must raise doubts in Rome, what are we doing in this war? Is it sensible to be where we are? It may still be sensible. It is certainly sensible if the alternative is a conquest of Europe by Stalin. But perhaps that is not the only possible alternative? At least that question began to be worth asking.

Ciano received other information which he did not like. An Italian industrialist in Germany reported the following joke as going about (this still in April 1942): 'The war in Russia will last two months, the war against England will last four months, the war against Italy will last four days.' It did not feel to Ciano funny, because he put the word JOKE into inverted commas.[17]

That 3–4 November came the disaster of El Alamein and then the news (end of November) of the cutting off of the German Sixth Army in Stalingrad. During these weeks Alfieri was rather silent except for the continual and mostly vain pressure on the Germans to give the Italians more materials with which to fight a war in Africa and aircraft to defend Italy from bombers.

Of one thing Alfieri was convinced and he soon persuaded Ciano of the

---

[16] *Dictators* 48, 101.   [17] DDI, 8, 458.

truth of this. Germany was treating all the little countries of Europe as though they were minor satellites. But they must be given a promise of a secure place in the future Europe – whether they were allies like Romania and Bulgaria, and he might have added Croatia and Serbia – or states of doubtful sympathy for Germany like Switzerland and Sweden. Goebbels in an article in *Das Reich* on 4 October said the opposite – the little countries must realise that they will be far better off if they surrender their statehood to be under a strong power.[18] In Alfieri's opinion nothing could do more to alienate the little peoples of Europe than such talk.

So there began to be an Italian quest to persuade the Germans – give Europe some hope for the future. Talk of the New Europe is too vague; you must try to start spelling out what it will mean politically. They knew that the Germans thought they, the Italians, were the only people who could influence the German government because Hitler so much admired Mussolini. But if they were to achieve this, it had to carry with it a far harder task. The system of government of the occupied territories – France, Serbia, Greece, Holland, Norway (Alfieri left out Poland and the Ukraine because they looked as though they might become part of the Reich, but he thought that Spain and Turkey really came into the same category) – was to exploit their economy for the benefit of Germany and especially the German war effort. To give Europe hope you had to give these states some prospect of stability. They are held only by fear. You cannot do that for long.

By the end of November 1942 it was evident to some German leaders, and to more Italian leaders, that the idea of total victory in Russia, which was Hitler's only idea, was likely to be an illusion. This mattered more to the Italians because they saw a threat from North Africa which the Germans did not even feel. Who will dare to tell Hitler that he ought to ask for a compromise peace with Russia or if that is not achievable to withdraw to some solid and easily defensible line? The Germans were all agreed that no German could dare to say it; and that there was only one person in all Europe who could say it with conviction and impunity and that was Mussolini, from whom Hitler would take what he would take from no one else.

On 6 December 1942 Mussolini met Goering at Görlitz and we have the minute of the conversation.

1. Russia. The Duce believes that the war in Russia is now pointless. Since at the moment we cannot get a Brest-Litovsk treaty (compensating Russia in Asia) we must get a defensive line which could be defended with minimum forces. Goering says that this could become Hitler's ideal.
2. Turn all the forces westward and to the Mediterranean because it is

[18] DDI, 9, 243.

clear that enemy no. 1 is Britain and that American air gives them the superiority.

Meeting between Ciano and Hitler at Görlitz 18/12/42:[19]

Hitler says that the odd defeats do not matter. We are in a struggle for civilization; if we are defeated we will never be able to stem the tide of Bolshevism. We have totally freed Europe from the enemy and ought not to risk that. Japan is unassailable in the east. The submarines blockade Britain. The Russian attacks have been contained with heavy Russian losses.

Our aims now are to beat the Bolshevist colossus to ensure safe living space for Europe.

We will help Italy in the south.

Ciano did not comment.

Second talk at Görlitz[20] (Goering, Ribbentrop, Keitel, Cavallero, also present):

Ciano suggests that the Duce would like a Brest-Litovsk treaty with Russia; aim, to release forces for the West; if a treaty is impossible, then find a line of defence easy to hold.

Hitler asks if the treaty is conceivable – the Russians would only use an armistice to prepare more attacks on us; there is no line conceivable which would ensure both Germany and Russia the necessities of life, raw materials, petrol etc. Italy also depends on these raw materials.

Suppose we had peace with Russia? Could Rommel do more in Africa? Very little, difficulty of transport.

We could not withdraw troops from Russia because we could not trust the Russian treaty.

We have enough in the West to defend against an Anglo-American landing. A treaty with Russia represents the squaring of a circle and is impossible.[21]

Ciano summarised all this for Mussolini, as he travelled back on the train on 19 December 1942. He said that it was a very cordial meeting but a separate treaty with Russia is impossible.[22]

There was beginning to be quarrelling among the soldiers – Germans blaming Italians for not holding the communication to Stalingrad, Italians saying that they gave warning that the defence of the communications was too thin.[23] Alfieri wrote again from Berlin 24 December 1942, much more

[19] DDI, 9, 408.   [20] DDI, 9, 413.

[21] Ciano Hitler etc. Görlitz, 18.12.42. Ciano spoke on the Italian need for reinforcements during 1943 and on bomb losses in Italian cities.

[22] DDI, 9, 418.

[23] Cavallero (CIGS) to Mussolini, 12 December 1942; DDI, 9, 421.

realistically, analysing the basis for all this German optimism, and saying that the Germans have an opinion quite out of reality – and they are getting further and further away from reality all the time.[24] The German method of propaganda is to announce only victory and to hide defeats, so when the defeats come, the disillusion of the people is all the greater. But the people still get good rations, and think that now they HAVE to win – and remember Versailles when there is talk of treaties.

> Germany is like a huge liner sailing in a mist and not sure of the course to sail. To avoid alarming the passengers the captain stands on a very high bridge and not even his officers can find out what he thinks. There is plenty of fuel in the tanks, the engines hum, the food on board is rationed to last a long time, everything is well – except no one knows whether it will find the harbour – nor whether it is capable of standing up to a storm.[25]

In this idea of Fortress Europe Germany is well protected. Italy is on the front line, on the walls. Germany now realises this and will help. This makes the bonds of the two countries tighter.

> I am told here that my suggestion of a peace with Russia is very important. It has been said to me that if the Führer cannot accept it for the moment, partly because of the reordering of the front, and partly because of the delicate situation in which he finds himself with his collaborators, the idea has been put into his mind and could later give useful results.[26]

On 21 January 1943 he told Ciano that the worse the news the more rigid grew Hitler and his companions; that in their minds was only a mirage, the will to victory; and this rigidity blinds their vision. 'A big dose of faith has become an absolute certainty' – they are simple.

> The formula started as 'fight to win'
>   then it became 'resist to win'
>   now it is 'win to survive'.

The leaders are almost all of the class which has never before held political power – they had no preparation for power – and hence they are dogmatists – their dogma that Germany is top nation, that it imposes its will on other

---

[24] DDI, 9, 458ff.

[25] Alfieri, 24.12.42, continued: the objects are still to get the line Volga Stalingrad Astrakhan to secure the flank to and over the Caucasus and the oil – and possibly from there southward – if it worked it would probably have won the war – but it didn't work at Stalingrad – why go on? essential strategically? prestige? – for whatever reason, a sanguine fight;
  fatal loss of a lot of men and Russia still dangerous;
  inability to free the Russian front for other purposes.

[26] Alfieri 475, 15.1.43, long and amicable conversation with Himmler. He gives good report of German morale and expresses lively devotion to Duce.

nations by force – and this excludes all possibility of peaceful compromise with other peoples on the basis of peace and common interests. The only policy is total victory or total defeat. Ought we not to tell the Germans what we think with absolute frankness? We are heavily involved – in a front line struggle – and they are having to reduce their help to us. 'The Duce said we march together to the end. It was a historic declaration – but to march together does not mean that one follows behind the other.' On the Soviet front we surely need a compromise peace – guaranteeing the eastern front and releasing forces for the West.[27]

III

On 6 February 1943 Mussolini suddenly did his famous Cabinet reshuffle, the like of which had never before been seen in Fascist Italy.

The important move was Ciano's dismissal from the Foreign Office. He was offered the choice between the governorship of Albania and the embassy at the Vatican and wisely chose the Vatican. The documents that were coming in from Albania show that it was hardly a job for a self-respecting person. Ciano much resented his dismissal. He had no desire to go to the Vatican.

The appointment of the Duce's son-in-law to the Vatican suggested to the world that this was Mussolini's first step in the search for a compromise peace as they thought it obvious that he would use the Vatican to this end and why else should so big a man be sent to so small a job? The American chargé inside the Vatican, Tittman, sent this very opinion to the Secretary of State in Washington, Cordell Hull. The Germans suspected the same for a moment.[28] Ribbentrop himself showed signs of worry and came to Rome to find out what was happening. Mussolini had no such idea in his head. He was one of the few people in Italy to whom it would not have occurred to try to use the Vatican in a quest for an armistice. He wanted to be rid of Ciano and did not mind where he went if it was consistent with a son-in-law's dignity; and he himself wanted the Foreign Office; for he rightly believed that he was the only person in the world who might persuade Hitler to a peace of compromise in Russia and so save Italy, and if he had the Foreign Office it could help him.

We notice that Alfieri's plan is not to get Italy out of the war. It is to get Italy out of the Russian war; so that German forces may be available to save Italy from the British and the Americans. There is no sign in the documents, yet, that he went on to ask himself the disturbing question, suppose that German armoured divisions enter Italy to help Italy, how easily will they get

---

[27] Alfieri 581, 3.2.42, on the history of the Jews under NS. He knows a lot esp. 582–3.
[28] 13 February 1943; Renzo De Felice, *Mussolini l'alleato*, Turin 1990, 1048.

out again? Evidently his distrust of the Nazis, though it was growing all the time, was not yet so vast as it was soon to become.

Three days after the removal of Ciano, a new character enters this business: Giuseppe Bastianini. Mussolini had taken Foreign Affairs but he was not at all well with his stomach ulcer and he had several other offices so this meant that most of the work was done by the under-secretary who was now Bastianini. Alfieri liked him; as courtly, and simple, and direct, though sometimes he found him taciturn. Bastianini became ex officio the person who had most chance of influencing what Mussolini should do. For someone like Alfieri life became a little easier; Ciano had not always done what Mussolini wanted and Bastianini always did; but also Mussolini often did what Bastianini advised.

As in effect the last of the Fascist Foreign Secretaries Bastianini also survived the war with a low reputation. The documents which he drafted and the policy which he followed will do little to raise that reputation. He had a lot of experience. At one time he was ambassador in London. He sounds in the documents a realist.[29] That was not how he appeared to some other Italian leaders who were already convinced that the only way to save Italy was to get out of the war and that as Mussolini would never get out of the war Mussolini must be ditched. Bastianini stood for the notion, which at that moment looked more realistic, that the only person who could get them out of the war without a German invasion of Italy was Mussolini and therefore Mussolini must be backed to the hilt. The difficulty of this realism was that Hitler had formed the same opinion. At all costs, according to Hitler, Mussolini must be backed to the hilt because he was now the only person capable of keeping Italy in the war; as Hitler said to Alfieri, he IS Italy. Bastianini thought the Duce was the only way out of the war; Hitler thought the Duce was the only way that Italy would stay in it.[30]

Bastianini started by sending a message to Ribbentrop that he intended to pursue the same policy of a close alliance with their ally Germany. That he should think he needed to send such a message in announcing his appointment is significant of the growing atmosphere of alienation between Germany and the directors of Italian policy.[31]

On 23 February 1943[32] Bastianini drew up an agenda for the Duce on his meeting with Ribbentrop. Number 1 is 'war aims' – all the rest is on the state of Italo-German relations in various countries – Alto Adige, Tunisia, Croatia,

---

[29] 6/11/43, Alfieri to Mussolini: Germany is very interested that Mussolini keeps Affari Esteri for himself – proof of his firmness in concentration for war and victory – shows Italy will be no easy target cf. 10/1–2.

[30] DDI, 10, 102, Alfieri to Bastianini, 3 March 1943.

[31] Alfieri to Mussolini, 12 February 1943; DDI, 10, 15ff. A good portrait of Bastianini is in Renzo De Felice's article on him in *Dizionario biografico italiano*.

[32] DDI, 10, 69.

Greece – all sore places – Croatia especially for it was an Italian sphere of interest and the German army and the Gestapo had taken over three quarters of the country. There was another delicate difficulty in Vichy where the Nazis were making the Vichy government arrest Jews and wanted an Italian cooperation which was not forthcoming. There was a dispute about Mihailovitch and the Chetniks in Yugoslavia – the Italians wanted to use them to help keep down the Communists, the Germans wanted to make no difference between Mihailovitch and the Communists.

And meanwhile Alfieri continued with his reports out of Berlin in which the German government appeared ever more bizarre and incapable. The Germans only know how to fight. They need the Italians, especially the Duce, it is the Italians who know how to civilise Europe. A New Order imposed by the Germans would only have a short life.[33] The Germans want us to help them to persuade their own government. The Nazi party is dividing – into the extremists, some of whom are near the Führer, deniers of tradition, wanting to exterminate Jews and persecute the Churches, and who see the future of Europe in racial terms with Germany in control; and the normalisers, who have a realistic view of the external life of the German people. It is from this second school that the critical voices are coming – critical of the treatment of occupied territories, of internal radicalisation, of undervaluing the Vatican and Catholicism – for a friendly attitude to the Catholic clergy could make an enormous difference in some other peoples. Alfieri happened to be at Hitler's headquarters on 31 January 1943 which was the day on which he made Paulus, the commander at Stalingrad, a field marshal; and Alfieri watched him with evident fascination; a man 'restless, excited, nervous, a prey to extreme agitation' pacing up and down the room, trying 'to make his words sound inspired', saying that he alone had taken the decision, and this supreme self-sacrifice of his soldiers, fighting to the last man in Stalingrad, would become a legend of heroism, which would add to the spiritual heritage of Nazism and be remembered with pride as we remember the glory of the warriors of Thermopylae. And then the very next morning the Russian radio announced that Paulus and his army had surrendered.

It was experiences like these which caused Alfieri to write to Italy: the Führer's spirit is now fanatical, pervaded with it, 'abbacinato' = blinded with brilliant light – fight the war with Russia to a finish at whatever cost in men and means – it is a state of absolute intransigence. He is shut up in his head-quarters, surrounded by very few collaborators, practically withdrawn from any contact with the life of his people. He does not notice what is happening to the German people, or how in the occupied countries resistance grows, and how this affects the foreign workers in Germany.

[33] DDI, 10, 114ff., 5 March 1943

The leadership is in euphoria the people are not. They hope that the Duce can help to bring Hitler out of his fanaticism.

The situation at the end of March 1943:

Bastianini agrees with Mussolini that the worst thing for Italy is if the Germans lose the war to the Russians and Bolshevism sweeps Europe and Italy itself is destroyed.

Since Hitler cannot now win the war in Russia, he must make a compromise peace on the Russian front and this is for Italy the best of all solutions because it will release force to defend Italy in the south and provide enough force to make the Western allies also go for a compromise peace.

But if Hitler is fanatical and will not make a compromise peace and the Duce cannot persuade him to it – then what? We cannot allow Italy to be destroyed because it is entangled in a German destruction. If Hitler is fanatical and Alfieri in Berlin is telling us that he is now fanatical – we have to go a different road – but what road is even conceivable? The question was raising its head even though it was a very difficult question for a responsible official like Bastianini to ask. Mussolini said in a speech in December that we march with Germany to the end. The speech much pleased Hitler. But Alfieri and Bastianini both interpreted it with a gloss. To march with someone does not mean that one party follows the other party unquestioningly and that it is always the same party which follows.

Meanwhile they must try to persuade Hitler and the letters from Mussolini to Hitler at this time, and in this sense, are well known – for example 8 March 1943 and 26 March 1943. Felice[34] has raised the disturbing psychological question whether Mussolini was not such a realist that he knew himself he could achieve nothing by these pleas and that it was necessary to present himself as the old Fascist master and so present himself to Europe as larger than he was. The documents do not make this a possible view. From Berlin Alfieri was feeding him with the doctrine that his pleas were achieving something – if not with Hitler himself at least with Hitler's small entourage.

Hitler agreed to meet Mussolini at the Castle of Klessheim outside Salzburg on 9–10 April 1943; and for the purpose the castle was lavishly redecorated with carpets and magnificent chandeliers and priceless tapestries and guards of honour and rolls of drums[35] and SS men who did nothing but salute at every door, so it was evident that the Germans wished to impress Mussolini and so thought that he needed impressing. But when it came to the crunch – whether Mussolini could tell Hitler that he ought to end the Russian war – Mussolini was a broken reed. Alfieri[36] described it thus: 'he no sooner found himself in the presence of Hitler than he was overcome by a feeling of embarrassment. His courage failed him . . . ' Alfieri found the atmosphere of the meeting

[34] Felice, *Mussolini l'alleato* 1015.   [35] *Dictators* 203.   [36] *Dictators* 225.

oppressive. He was charitable to Mussolini and attributed his weakness partly
to his stomach cramp and this is probably right, for Mussolini is now proved
to have had a stomach ulcer from the summer of 1942 and his close advisers
watched his decline with anxiety.

Bastianini's minute of the Klessheim meeting with Ribbentrop is in the
Documenti.[37] It was very simple. Ribbentrop said there was no policy but total
victory in Russia. Bastianini said that we are getting discontent in Italy.
Ribbentrop said, then suppress it, fiercely. You must use, he said, extreme
brutality. Bastianini said that would play into the hands of the Allies.

They met again next day. Bastianini was still more direct. You mean to get
total victory in Russia. How long will that take? Italy is in danger of being
eliminated while you are doing it. The day will certainly come when resistance
is impossible. Ribbentrop said simply, we will hold Tunisia and the Führer
will do all he can to help. But privately Bastianini thought already that for the
German military command Italy was expendable. The southern front did not
really matter to them. If Italy were lost to the Allies, it would always be
recaptured by the Germans once they had beaten Russia. Tripoli, Tunisia,
even Sicily were side-issues. They did not see that to Bastianini there was a
question whether if this happened the Italian people could any more stand on
the German side.

To us something important is evident from this minute; as yet Bastianini
has no idea of a secret getting out of the war and confronting the Germans
with a fait accompli. For if you mean to engage in what the Germans will
regard as a conspiracy, you do not start by telling them openly, soon we shall
be unable to carry on the war.

On 12 May 1943 the Pope offered Mussolini and Italy his help; and
Mussolini replied that we have no alternative but to fight on.[38]

The illusory policy of Bastianini was being encouraged by cryptic messages
from various of Germany's allies that the Duce must do something and that
everyone's hope was in him. Quisling sent a message from Norway that the
Nazis were maltreating his government and that only the Duce could help;
the Hungarian government and the Romanian government both sent
messages to the same effect – it was incongruous that at the moment when
Italy was at its weakest in modern history several countries in Europe should
be looking to Mussolini as their one hope of prising away the excessively heavy
hand of the Nazi régime in their territories.

---

[37] DDI, 10, 257.
[38] DDI, 10, 410, 412; but rumours of secret negotiations began to circulate already: 21 June 1943,
the Italian minister in Lisbon, Prunas, wrote to Mussolini about the rumours there which he
thought (rightly) to be part of the war of nerves; Italian agents were said to be in Algiers and
they included the Prince of Piedmont and Badoglio – soon denied as fantasy. Cf. Fransoni
to Mussolini, 26 June 1943, in DDI, 10, 591.

Inside the Italian Foreign Offices other voices warned Bastianini that he was not likely to persuade the Allies to accept Italian neutrality even if Hitler would allow it. They saw, intelligently, that Britain and America needed to invade Italy because they were afraid of Russia making a separate peace and to stop that they must be seen to open a second front and they could not yet open a second front in France and therefore they must invade Italy because they must be seen by Russia to stand on European soil.[39] So we have to fight on – none of us can persuade Hitler. Only the King and the Duce can decide if our attitude ought to be revised – for the rest of us the only thing is to fight on.

But if Germany loses the war in Russia, then we must get out before they lose because we must not also be swamped by the wave of Communist power which will sweep Europe. We may have to act in the autumn, to decide how to end our war.

IV

In July 1943 the Allies landed in Sicily and the new phase began. The first thing Alfieri did was to tell Mussolini that the Germans were already thinking of abandoning most of Italy to have a German fortress on the Appenines; in effect that while the Italians were forced to fight for Germany the Germans were thinking of leaving most of Italy to the enemy. 'If there are any disagreeable steps to be taken, any harsh words to be said, any difficult roles to be filled, you may make the fullest use of my services. The Foreign Minister can always – afterwards – discredit me, disown me and throw me into the sea.'

Hitler and Mussolini met at Feltre 19 July 1943. Alfieri and Bastianini drove together from the station to the airport to meet Mussolini. Bastianini said that now Mussolini was totally wrapped up in himself, was silent, you could not tell what he was thinking.[40] Alfieri said that Mussolini must be strong with Hitler and Bastianini said that he wholly agreed but he did not think that it would happen. It did not happen. Hitler launched into one of his monologues, growing ever more strident, and blaming Italy for all its weaknesses, and Mussolini just sat passively, for two hours, from time to time pressing his back where it was painful and occasionally 'giving a deep sigh like a man who is bored with listening to an interminable speech'.

In the lunch interval the three of them – Bastianini, Alfieri and General Ambrosio the chief of staff – took Mussolini aside and begged, pleaded, that he say something strong and demand that a way out be found – a separate peace, or if not, what? And suddenly Mussolini the broken man, who had said nothing all the morning, was pathetic.

---

[39] Cf. Babuscio Rizzo to Bastianini, 12 May 1943, in DDI, 10, 413; cf. *Actes et Documents du Saint-Siège relatifs à la Seconde Guerre Mondiale*, 7, (1973), 330–1.

[40] *Dictators* 236.

Can you suppose that I have not long been tormented with this problem? I may look indifferent but inside I am in an agony. What about this separate peace? We announce it on the radio. What will happen? The British and Americans instantly demand that we surrender. Are we ready to destroy the achievements of 20 years of Fascism? To acknowledge defeat, our first? To vanish from the international stage? It is easy to talk about a separate peace. But what would Hitler do? Do you think it conceivable he would allow us to keep our freedom of action?[41]

Alfieri said that neutral states might help a negotiation. Bastianini said he could consult them (he had already begun to do so). Mussolini would not hear of such talk. Then he had his private lunch with Hitler. They wanted afterwards to know whether he said anything of what they wanted. As he put on his flying jacket to fly back to Rome he said, 'I had no need to speak to Hitler in the way that you suggested.'[42]

The failure to speak at Feltre sealed the fate of Mussolini.

The plan could not work. Several responsible people and not only Bastianini – for example the two generals Caviglia and Ambrosio – argued that Mussolini should persuade Hitler that since Italy could not now fight a war it should be allowed by the Germans to get out of the war and in return should promise a strict neutrality in the conflict; and that simultaneously an approach should be made to the British and the Americans to get them to accept this neutrality – which, if they were sensible, they would do. And they all accepted that since Mussolini was the only person who could conceivably persuade Hitler to accept this plan, Mussolini must at all costs not be got rid of. But the one person who saw that this whole plan had no hope because whatever he said or did the Germans would never accept it was Mussolini himself. That complicated everyone's life but it imported reality into the situation.

Some older writers said that Claretta Petacci was part of the decline of Mussolini's national reputation and therefore a contributor to his fall. But historically she was a little thing; he needed her from 1936, it was only society gossip from 1938 and only really public in 1942. She was not an intriguer and made no attempt to influence him though intriguers sometimes tried to use her. Her existence did finally lower his image and prestige but it was lowered already for much bigger reasons. She probably helped to isolate Mussolini, that is to make it possible for him to shut himself away from other human company. But there were many bigger reasons – of which one was, in some ways, the biggest, that by early 1943 the Italian people hated the Germans and to many of them Mussolini seemed the chief link that tied them to Germany.

41 *Dictators* 246.   42 *Dictators* 248.

12

THE NEW DEAL WITHOUT FDR: WHAT
BIOGRAPHIES OF ROOSEVELT
CANNOT TELL US

രൗൌെ

TONY BADGER

FRANKLIN Roosevelt in the White House was much impressed by an
account of Abraham Lincoln's life in which Paul Angle chronicles
his 'Day-by-Day Activities' from birth to death. Roosevelt told his associates
one of the first tasks of historians should be to construct a similar day-by-day
chronology of his own life in the White House. On 26 January 1994 in the
Senate Majority Leader's Office the Roosevelt Library finally launched such a
project: *FDR: Day-by-Day*. The chronology will initially be based on the
White House Usher's Diaries, the Presidential Trip Logs, and the earlier
efforts of the documentary film maker Pare Lorentz to reconstruct every day
of Roosevelt's life. With additions from scholars, the Library aims to
create a constantly evolving database which will be available through the
Internet.[1]

The project testifies to a seemingly insatiable appetite for more and more
biographical detail about Roosevelt. There are no fewer than four multi-
volume biographies of Franklin D. Roosevelt, some still to be completed.
There is no let up in the production of single-volume biographies of the
President, both concise and substantial, popular and scholarly. In addition
there are at least two multi-volume studies of Roosevelt and his wife, Eleanor,
whose own life has been the subject of a plethora of biographies, including the
first of a projected two-volume definitive study. Most recently, the activities
of husband and wife in World War II have been massively chronicled.

As long ago as 1946 business historian Thomas C. Cochran lamented
the dominance in American historical writing of what he identified as 'the

---

[1] Geoffrey C. Ward, *A First Class Temperament: The Emergence of Franklin Roosevelt* (New
York, 1989) 609 n. 7; *The View From Hyde Park: The Newsletter of the Roosevelt Institute and
Library* 8 (Summer 1994) no. 2.

presidential synthesis' which privileged political history and distorted the analysis of long-term social and economic change. Yet clearly fifty years later, the 'presidential synthesis' still retains a powerful hold over writing on the New Deal. Why has this presidential synthesis continued to exercise such a powerful hold on the imagination of historians of the 1930s? Does the ever-increasing material on the life of FDR aid, or distort, our understanding of the domestic New Deal and the changes it wrought in American society?[2]

I

The continued fascination with Franklin Roosevelt is entirely understandable. Americans work out their lives in a political economy that still bears the imprint of the laws and agencies of Roosevelt's New Deal. The regulation of financial institutions, the welfare system, the framework of labour relations, and the subsidisation of agriculture reflect the parameters established in the 1930s. Political leaders, as William E. Leuchtenburg has shown, have laboured '[i]n the shadow of FDR' since his death. Liberal Democratic presidents in particular have repeatedly invoked his memory and been judged, usually unflatteringly, by the standards of the strong charismatic national leadership that he exemplified. One of Bill Clinton's first acts after his State of the Nation address in 1993 was to visit the Roosevelt birthplace at Hyde Park. Clinton appeared fascinated by the faithfully maintained details of the Roosevelt home. It appeared to one observer that the new President felt that by sitting at Roosevelt's desk, some of FDR's magic would somehow rub off on him. Clinton spoke at the local high school, constructed in the 1930s by the Works Progress Administration. At the presidential library he discovered that the University of Arkansas football stadium, where he had watched so many matches as a student in Fayetteville, had also been constructed by the WPA.[3]

Publishing concerns, institutional imperatives, the timing of particular revelations and historiographical trends interacted to translate that fascination into so many biographical studies. Memoirs of those cast loose by Roosevelt's death, FDR's establishment of a presidential library, revelations about both FDR's and his wife's sexual activities, and the burgeoning interest in women's history, all focused attention on the president and his wife.

No sooner than Roosevelt had died, than publishers moved to fill the gaping hole that had been left for many Americans when their commander-in-

---

[2] Thomas C. Cochran, 'The "Presidential Synthesis" in American History' *American Historical Review* 53 (1948) 748–59.

[3] William E. Leuchtenburg, *In the Shadow of FDR: From Harry Truman to Bill Clinton* (Ithaca, n.e. 1993); *The New Yorker* 8 March 1993 38–44.

chief, who had been in charge for thirteen years, died on the eve of victory in the European war. His longest serving Cabinet members – plucked from political obscurity by FDR in 1933 and now with no role to play in the Truman administration – worked to get out memoirs or diaries of their time with FDR. Mrs Roosevelt and her second son, Elliott, wrote their own accounts of life with the President. A host of associates capitalised on their work for Roosevelt to secure publishing contracts: two of his speech writers, his executive secretary, one of his personal secretaries, his physician, his secret service agent, and the chief of the White House press corps. Later, the White House maid and the President's portrait painter joined the ranks of the memoirists.[4]

An even more powerful stimulus to a biographical approach to the 1930s was given by Roosevelt's own sense of his place in history. Roosevelt had no desire to be commemorated by a great memorial: he asked for the simple small marble block which now stands, often unnoticed by visitors, in front of the National Archives. But he did have a very real belief in the importance of presidential records. He himself kept all his personal correspondence and ensured that his correspondence as governor and president was carefully retained. From 1938 the public papers of the Roosevelt presidency – largely speeches and messages to Congress – began to be published in year-by-year volumes with an interpretative introduction by the President. One of the early Public Works Administration projects was to complete the building of the National Archives started under Hoover. Until Roosevelt, presidential papers were the personal property of the outgoing president and might be taken away with them and sometimes even destroyed. Some parts of the papers of a number of Presidents did finally end up in the Library of Congress. In 1934 Roosevelt told his appointee as National Archivist, Robert Connor, that he thought all presidential papers should be held in the National Archives. The bulk of correspondence generated by the new responsibilities of the federal government under the New Deal and the sheer volume of letters sent by

---

[4] Frances Perkins, *The Roosevelt I Knew* (New York, 1946); John M. Blum, *From the Morgenthau Diaries* 3 vols. (Boston, 1959–67); Harold Ickes, *The Secret Diaries of Harold Ickes* 3 vols. (New York, 1953–4); Eleanor Roosevelt, *This I Remember* (New York, 1949); Elliott Roosevelt, *As He Saw It* (New York, 1946); Samuel Rosenman, *Working with Roosevelt* (New York, 1952); Charlie Michelson, *The Ghost Talks* (New York, 1944); William D. Hassett, *Off the Record with FDR, 1942–45* (New Brunswick, NJ, 1958); Grace Tully, *F.D.R.: My Boss* (New York, 1949); Ross T. McIntyre, *White House Physician* (New York, 1946); A. Merriman Smith, *Thank You, Mr President: A White House Notebook* (New York, 1946); Michael F. Reilly, *Reilly of the White House* (in collaboration with Frances Spatz Leighton), *The Roosevelts: A Family in Turmoil* (Englewood Cliffs, NJ, 1981); Elizabeth Shoumatoff, *FDR's Unfinished Portrait: A Memoir by Elizabeth Shoumatoff* (Pittsburgh, 1990). Anna Roosevelt's first husband contributed a vitriolic, far-right, assault on Roosevelt and the people round him, Curtis B. Dall, *F.D.R.: My Exploited Father-in-Law* (Torrance, CA., 1982).

ordinary Americans to FDR in the White House would have been impossible
for either the Library of Congress or the National Archives with their existing
resources to handle. In 1939, therefore, Roosevelt deeded to the federal
government 16 acres of land at Hyde Park and raised from his friends the
money to construct a library there. Congress authorised the National Archivist
to receive Roosevelt's papers and to administer them. By the end of World
War II the Library was functioning.[5]

As a result, historians could start archive-based work on the Roosevelt
presidency far more quickly than on any previous American president. Within
two years of Roosevelt's death his pre-presidential papers were open to
scholars. By 1950, 85 per cent of the Roosevelt papers had been cleared and
could be used – some five years before the Library of Congress was able to
release some of its Lincoln papers. According to William E. Leuchtenburg,

> Not enough has been said about what an extraordinary venture it was for those
> of us who went to Hyde park for the first time some forty years ago. There had
> never been anything like this before – the major part of all the records of the
> president of a large country opened to scholars only a few years after his tenure
> ended. We had absolutely no training in what to do with these papers. It is now
> commonplace for graduate students to be directed to the Truman Library or the
> LBJ Library or to Hyde Park, but our teachers had never seen the inside of a
> presidential library. How do you research not in a fragment of an illuminated
> manuscript but in thousands of boxes holding millions of pieces of paper?

Leuchtenburg recalls that frequently he would be there in the Research Room
alongside Arthur Schlesinger, Frank Freidel and John Blum. Because
Schlesinger worked so quickly, he would often slip pieces of paper to the other
scholars telling them about a particular file that he had seen that he thought
would be relevant to their particular work. The results of this mutually
supportive scholarship were an outstandingly rich decade of work in which
this first generation of New Deal historians established the defining historiographical frameworks for the study of the New Deal.[6]

It was inevitable and proper that their efforts to create the building blocks
for the edifice of New Deal studies should put Roosevelt at centre stage. Not
only their sources, but also their concern to establish a coherent narrative

---

5 Don Wilson, 'Prologue in Perspective: Presidential Libraries' *Prologue: Quarterly of the
National Archives* 21 (Summer 1994) 100–1; Frank Freidel, 'From Roosevelt to Reagan: The
Birth and Growth of Presidential Libraries' *Prologue: Quarterly of the National Archives* 21
(Summer 1994) 103–13.
6 Freidel, 'From Roosevelt to Reagan', 103–13. William E. Leuchtenburg, 'In the Shadow of
Leuchtenburg: A Response' (paper given at *The New Deal* conference, Sidney Sussex
College, Cambridge, 22 September 1993) Leuchtenburg to the author, 22 September 1993. By
contrast, serious archival-based reassessments of the Hoover presidency did not start until
1967.

of the 1930s, of the vast array of legislation and agencies that proliferated then, dictated their emphasis on the President and the dynamics of policy formulation. Frank Freidel started his multi-volume biography of FDR: by 1960 three volumes had been completed. Rexford Tugwell and James MacGregor Burns wrote substantial interpretative biographies, rich both in detail and analysis. The first three volumes of Arthur Schlesinger's masterly *Age of Roosevelt* confidently laid out a coherent and compelling picture of the ideological battles in Washington that produced the defining features of the New Deal: the emergency legislation of 1933 and the considered structural reforms of the Second Hundred Days of 1935. William E. Leuchtenburg produced what remains the best one-volume narrative of Roosevelt and the New Deal. It is not clear that all the subsequent biographical work on Roosevelt has substantially altered the pictures drawn by these pioneer historians. The broad sweep of Roosevelt's pre-presidential political career remains much as Freidel painted it. More than any later biographies, Tugwell and Burns raised analytical questions that got to the heart of interpretations of the New Deal and the options available to reformers in the 1930s: Tugwell lamented the lost opportunities for rational planning and allocation of the nation's resources. Burns regretted the president's preference for short-term solutions at the expense of long-term goals, particularly his failure to fashion a fully-fledged realignment of the political parties on clear ideological lines. No account has subsequently matched the richness of Schlesinger's dramatic narrative, nor identified with such a sure touch the critical policy issues at stake in the most diverse New Deal activities. No account has subsequently challenged the narrative framework that Leuchtenburg established, or so skilfully blended into that narrative analysis of the themes of the broker state, grass-roots democracy, administrative theory and party realignment.[7]

After this bold pioneering start, the historiographical emphasis moved away from Roosevelt. Historians worked on the implementation of New Deal policies, on the history of particular agencies and programmes and on the local impact of such programmes. It seemed to be increasingly difficult to retain the focus on Roosevelt *and* on the working out of the New Deal both in Washington and in the localities. It took Freidel fourteen years to take Roosevelt's story forward the eight months from his 1932 election to the end of the Hundred Days. He abandoned the multi-volume biography for a later

---

[7] Frank Freidel, *Franklin D. Roosevelt: The Apprenticeship; The Ordeal; The Triumph* (Boston, 1952–60); Rexford Tugwell, *The Democratic Roosevelt* (Baltimore, 1969 [1957]); James MacGregor Burns, *Roosevelt: The Lion and the Fox* (New York, 1956); Arthur M. Schlesinger, Jr, *The Age of Roosevelt: The Crisis of the Old Order; The Coming of the New Deal; The Politics of Upheaval* (Boston, 1957–60); William E. Leuchtenburg, *Franklin D. Roosevelt and the New Deal, 1933–1940* (New York, 1963).

single-volume overview. Schlesinger never returned to the projected further
four volumes that would have carried the story forward from 1936 both at
home and abroad.[8]

As academic historians moved away from the presidential focus to detailed
New Deal case studies, the focus on Roosevelt was sustained by revelations
about his private life. North Carolina newspaperman and former White
House press secretary, Jonathan Daniels, broke the story of Roosevelt's affair
with his secretary Lucy Mercer while he was assistant secretary of the Navy.
This affair was well known amongst the Roosevelt family and many
Washington insiders. What was new about Daniels's account was his
revelation that as a widow, Lucy Mercer Rutherford had stayed at the White
House while Eleanor had been away during the second world war and that she
had been at Warm Springs when Roosevelt died, only to be spirited away by
secret servicemen after the President's collapse. This revelation prompted a
reassessment of the important political relationship between FDR and his
wife. Joseph Lash, who as a young student had been befriended by Mrs
Roosevelt in the 1930s, explored this relationship fully and frankly in *Eleanor
and Franklin* emphasising just how close to break up the marriage had come,
how betrayed Mrs Roosevelt had felt, how emotionally distant relations had
inevitably become, and how determined Mrs Roosevelt had been to carve out
an independent career for herself. Writer Jim Bishop, who had made his
reputation dealing with the last days of presidents' lives, turned to the last year
of Roosevelt's life, focusing both on Mrs Rutherford and on the question of
Roosevelt's ill-health.[9]

Members of Roosevelt's family took up the case. In two volumes on his
parents and one on his mother's life after 1945, Elliott Roosevelt, the son who
had been closest to his mother, showed how Eleanor Roosevelt had been
unable to unbend sufficiently to satisfy the fun-loving side of FDR's
character. He suggested that Missy LeHand, FDR's long-time secretary, was
his lover and generally laid bare family tensions and resentments. James
Roosevelt angrily refuted this picture of family disaster and, in particular,
the contention that FDR had been sexually involved with Missy LeHand,
in his own book on his parents. Both sons turned their parents to
fictional advantage. Elliott wrote thirteen mysteries in which his mother
was the ace amateur detective; James, after completing an appointment as
Richard M. Nixon Professor of Political Science at Whittier College, wrote
a novel *A Family Matter*, in which Roosevelt shared the secret of the

---

[8] Frank Freidel, *Franklin D. Roosevelt: Launching the New Deal* (Boston, 1973); Freidel,
Franklin D. Roosevelt: A Rendezvous with Destiny (Boston, 1990).

[9] Jonathan Daniels, *Washington Quadrille* (New York, 1968); Joseph P. Lash, *Eleanor and
Franklin* (New York, 1971); Jim Bishop, *FDR's Last Year* (New York, 1974).

atomic bomb with Churchill and Stalin in an effort to secure post-war cooperation.[10]

It was not surprising that the Roosevelt children should have wondered whether it was their parents' relationship with each other and with them that made the children's lives so difficult and unhappy. The five surviving children had seventeen marriages between them; two of their spouses went on to commit suicide; a third attempted to murder James by stabbing him in the back with one of his own wartime souvenirs, a marine knife. It is difficult to estimate the effect, for example, on James and Anna Roosevelt of being placed in a chicken-wire cage and hung outside their upper-floor window high above the pavements of New York. This practice, favoured by Sara Delano Roosevelt to ensure that her grandchildren were exposed to enough fresh air, only stopped when a neighbour threatened to report Eleanor Roosevelt to the Society for the Prevention of Cruelty to Children. One of a succession of English nannies shut Elliott in a closet and turned the key in the lock so hard that it broke off. It was several hours before Elliott was rescued. This incident and many like them did not cost the nanny her job: she was only sacked when a drawerful of empty whiskey and gin bottles were discovered in her room.[11]

Nevertheless, it is difficult to disagree with the unflattering judgement of the radical Texas former congressman, Maury Maverick. On his death bed Maverick said to his son, 'Son, you and I have never been very close. But I want you to know that I'm proud of you son.' Then his last words to him were 'Yes, Son, I'm proud you didn't turn out to be a horse's ass like Elliott Roosevelt.'[12]

The interest in Mrs Roosevelt paralleled the rapid growth of women's history. But the role of the President's wife was also cast to centre stage by the opening in 1979 in the Roosevelt Library of 2,336 letters between Lorena Hickok and Eleanor Roosevelt, letters that express feelings of intense physical and emotional love between the two women. While Eleanor wished 'I could lie down beside you tonight and take you in my arms', Hickok remembered 'the feeling of that soft spot just north-east of the corner of your mouth against my lips'. These letters prompted discussion of Eleanor's sexuality and then extended accounts of her relationships with both Hickok and the other women in her wide network of female friends. Her most recent biographer, Blanche Wiesen Cook in the first of a projected two volumes, notes that much

---

[10] Elliott Roosevelt and James Brough, *An Untold Story: The Roosevelts of Hyde Park* (New York, 1973); *A Rendezvous With Destiny: The Roosevelts of the White House* (New York, 1975); *Mother R: Eleanor Roosevelt's Untold Story* (New York, 1977); typical of his mysteries, *Murder in the Oval Office* (New York, 1990); James Roosevelt (with Bill Libby), *My Parents: A Differing View* (Chicago, 1976); James Roosevelt (with Sam Toberoff), *A Family Matter* (New York, 1980).

[11] James Roosevelt, *My Parents* 36–8; Elliott Roosevelt, *An Untold Story* 78.

[12] Richard B. Henderson, *Maury Maverick* (Austin, 1970) xvii.

of the documentary record of her relationship with lesbian friends and with her younger male friend, Earl Miller, has disappeared or been destroyed. She considers this loss 'a calculated denial of ER's passionate friendships'. Rather she believes that Eleanor led a life 'dedicated to passion and experience' and that her relationships with Hickok and Earl Miller were 'erotic and romantic', 'daring and tumultuous'.[13]

But Franklin Roosevelt has not been left unattended. Most notably, professional biographer Kenneth Davis had completed a four-volume account of his life up to 1940 and Geoffrey Ward's surely definitive life has taken more than a thousand pages to leave Roosevelt still some years short of the White House, having just been elected Governor of New York in 1928.[14]

II

We now know what Roosevelt had for breakfast, what drinks he mixed for himself at cocktail hour, that he despaired of the food served at the White House. We know that from 1919 Eleanor and he slept in separate bedrooms. But does the biographical detail about Roosevelt that we now have in such abundance help us to understand the New Deal and to answer the questions we need to ask about the New Deal's legacy?

What the recent work has carefully clarified is the extent of the effect of polio on Roosevelt. A rehabilitation counsellor, a paraplegic polio victim and Geoffrey Ward have documented just how crippled Roosevelt was and 'the splendid deception' involving the collaboration of the media which ensured that neither photographic nor film evidence allowed the American people to see the true extent of his disability. Few Americans knew that the President was so wheelchair bound or had to be lifted like a baby to so many locations. As Geoffrey Ward has pointed out, Roosevelt was 'the most photographed and filmed American of his time'. Yet only three photographs of him in his wheelchair are known to have survived and less than a minute and a half of a 16-mm home movie documents the excruciatingly painful and ungainly way he walked on the arm of a bodyguard and with a cane. As Ward notes, Roosevelt's

13 Doris Faber, *The Life of Lorena Hickok: Eleanor Roosevelt's Friend* (New York, 1980); Blanche Wiesen Cook, *Eleanor Roosevelt* (New York, 1993) 10–15; Joseph Lash, *Love Eleanor: Eleanor Roosevelt and Her Friends* (New York, 1982). See also, Lash, *Eleanor: The Years Alone* (New York, 1975); *A World of Love: Eleanor Roosevelt and Her Friends, 1943–1962* (New York, 1984); and Lois Scharf, *Eleanor Roosevelt: First Lady of American Liberalism* (Knoxville, 1987).
14 Kenneth S. Davis, *FDR: The Beckoning of Destiny, 1882–1929; The New York Years, 1928–1933; The New Deal Years, 1933–37; The Time of Troubles, 1937–1940* (New York, 1971, 1985, 1986, 1993); Geoffrey C. Ward, *Before the Trumpet: Young Franklin Roosevelt, 1882–1905* (New York, 1985); *A First-Class Temperament.* See also, Nathan Miller, *FDR: An Intimate History* (New York, 1983); Ted Morgan, *FDR: A Biography* (New York, 1985).

'polished skill at duplicity, his positive delight in secrecy, in knowing things that others didn't . . . now superbly served his purposes'. But this refinement of our knowledge about Roosevelt's disability does not change our understanding of Roosevelt's political development. No one has revived Frances Perkins's argument that polio gave Roosevelt a sympathy for, and understanding of, the underprivileged which he had not had before. Roosevelt's progressive faith in the duty of government to aid the disadvantaged predated his polio. As for toughening his inner core, the trauma associated with the discovery of his affair with Lucy Mercer was arguably what 'toughened and matured' a Roosevelt used until then to having everything his own way.[15]

Is that affair with Lucy Mercer of interest to the historian? Does it matter who either Franklin or Eleanor Roosevelt slept with?

The partnership between FDR and his wife had always been regarded as unique and important in which Mrs Roosevelt acted both as the crippled politician's eyes and ears and as a formidable figure in her own right on the liberal wing of the Democratic Party in New York state and nationally. The evidence of physical and emotional distance revealed by the affair and by the testimony of the family helps explain Mrs Roosevelt's determination to get her message across to her husband, at times, particularly during World War II, when he did not want to listen. This distance makes the *political* partnership of two people the more, not less, remarkable. Mrs Roosevelt gave labour leaders, women and civil rights advocates access to the White House they would not have otherwise enjoyed.[16]

The evidence suggests it unlikely that Roosevelt had sexual relations with any women after the polio attack: it is equally clear that he relished the undemanding and relaxing attention of attractive women, especially Missy LeHand, when so many of his other friends and contacts needed something from him. We will never know whether Mrs Roosevelt slept with Lorena Hickok. The language she uses in the letters is physical and passionate – but so were many of the letters in 'the intense female friendships' that Carroll Smith-Rosenberg discovered in the nineteenth century in which women, very much restricted at home to a 'separate sphere' and assumed to be passionless, felt free to express their full emotional range in these letters to female friends. What is important, however, is that Eleanor Roosevelt's independent political and personal life was not the construct of Louis Howe and others, anxious to keep FDR's name alive politically when he was incapacitated by polio, but

[15] Ward, *A First Class Triumph* 704–35, 769–75, 781–3; Hugh Gregory Gallagher, *FDR's Splendid Deception* (New York, 1985); Richard Thayer Goldberg, *The Making of Franklin D. Roosevelt: Triumph over Disability* (Cambridge, Mass., 1981); Joseph Alsop, *FDR, 1882–1945: A Centenary Remembrance* (New York, 1982) 40–50.

[16] Doris Kearns Goodwin, *No Ordinary Time: Franklin and Eleanor Roosevelt: The Home Front in World War II* (New York, 1994) 27–30, 89–98.

rather a personal assertion by Eleanor herself of her rights to an independent life in the aftermath of the Mercer affair. This drive for independence was sustained primarily by a large number of female friends in New York involved in politics, social welfare and education, including some lesbian couples.[17]

Mrs Roosevelt's independent role has another importance. William E. Leuchtenburg looking back at his landmark book on the New Deal notes that 'in one respect I would write the book differently if I were to start out today ... I would say more than I did about the role of women in the Welfare State, and considerably more about ... the impact of the Great Depression and the New Deal on women.' Mrs Roosevelt was a central figure in a remarkable network of women bound together by ties of friendship, common experience, and, in Frances Perkins's words 'a cordial interlocking group of minds'. A generation born in the 1880s, the women were usually college-educated, social workers before the days of professional training, participants in the suffrage campaigns and in World War I relief work, and through their voluntary associations advocates of social reform even in the 1920s. The exigencies of the Depression gave them their opportunity in government. The emergency agencies of the New Deal needed their social work skills and the social welfare reforms of the 1930s drew on their expertise in consumer affairs, protective legislation, low-wage industries and social security. What Mrs Roosevelt gave this network was a dynamic role model, unrivalled visibility and prestige, access to the President, and jobs, as a result of the tireless barrage of patronage suggestions that she and Molly Dewson fired at Jim Farley. Franklin Roosevelt was not a passive participant in this process either. Roosevelt took women seriously. Not only did he respect his wife's political skills and determination but as Governor of New York he had grown accustomed to working with talented and forceful women.[18]

The recent biographies also, I believe, highlight three Roosevelt characteristics that do help explain some parts of the New Deal's successes and limitations: duplicity, optimism and luck.

Deviousness, the masking of true intentions, and a delight in secrecy appear

---

17 Goldberg, *Triumph over Disability* 166–7; Franklin Roosevelt's enjoyment of the relaxed company of younger women extended not only to Missy LeHand, but also especially to his cousin Margaret 'Daisy' Suckley. It was known that Margaret Suckley was with Roosevelt when he died, but the intensity of their relationship was unknown. When Margaret Suckley died, her diary and the many letters between her and FDR were discovered. Geoffrey Ward has edited these to reveal a touching and close relationship which lasted from the inauguration in 1933 to Roosevelt's death, Geoffrey C. Ward, ed., *Closest Companion: The Unknown Story of the Intimate Friendship between Franklin Roosevelt and Margaret Suckley* (New York, 1995); Cook, *Eleanor Roosevelt* 237–50; Carroll Smith-Rosenberg, *Disorderly Conduct* (New York, 1977) 53–76.

18 Leuchtenburg, 'In The Shadow of Leuchtenburg: A Response'; Susan Ware, *Beyond Suffrage: Women in the New Deal* (Cambridge, Mass., 1981).

to have been almost a reflex reaction on Roosevelt's part even in situations where political experience did not demand caution. It even extended to poker. It was his custom, while waiting for the message that Congress had adjourned, to play poker with Secretary of Treasury, Henry Morgenthau and others. Whoever was winning when the message came through collected the winnings for the evening. On one occasion, when Morgenthau was winning Roosevelt took the phone call from the Speaker of the House, but pretended it was from someone else. A good deal later, when he himself was in the lead, Roosevelt arranged for a call which he claimed announced the end of the congressional session. Only next day did Morgenthau discover that Congress had adjourned some hours earlier. Other examples were also perhaps harmless. It is not surprising that selective memory and a desire to embellish a good story invalidate, according to Geoffrey Ward, many of Roosevelt's accounts of his early life. It was clearly a more calculated presidential deception to attach a memo to a copy of the Inaugural Address implying that he alone had written it in four and a half hours on the evening of 27 February 1933, when in fact he was working from a complete draft from Ray Moley and the memorable phrase from Louis Howe about fear itself. In political terms, his delight in springing surprises exasperated congressional leaders and in some cases finally drove them into resolute opposition. His attempt to reform the Supreme Court in 1937 was almost fatally compromised from the start by his refusal to consult congressional leaders and the disingenuous explanation of the reform as a measure designed solely to promote efficiency in the federal courts.[19]

Roosevelt's serenity under the most intense pressure and in the most serious crises of Depression and War was in part accounted for by a resilient optimism that things would somehow turn out all right. Like a later president Ronald Reagan, this confidence that something would turn up rested on a faith in progress, in a benevolent divine presence and in the capacity of Americans to achieve what they set out to. At times, in tackling the banking crisis of 1933, in setting production targets for aircraft in World War II, and in his faith that the British would survive in 1940 without US intervention, this optimism was both justified and conveyed itself crucially to both political leaders and to public opinion. At other times, the reluctance to hear bad news or to think through overcoming all-too-real obstacles closed rather than opened up options for the President.

Finally, Patrick Maney has identified the importance of sheer good luck in Roosevelt's career. Some instances of what Maney describes as the Roosevelt luck will strike many as a mixed blessing. It is one thing to note that Roosevelt had the good fortune to come to public life in an era 'which came to accept as

---

[19] Ward, *Before the Trumpet* 186, 200; Goodwin, *No Ordinary Time* 159–60; James E. Sargent, *Roosevelt and the Hundred Days: The Struggle for the Early New Deal* (London, 1981) 37–41.

the norm change and reform and an expansive role for government, both at home and abroad' and that he was lucky first to run for office in a Republican district in 1910, a year when Democrats made an unusually strong showing. It is another to argue that he was lucky to have polio and thus sit out the ferocious ethno-cultural battles that split the Democratic Party in the 1920s, or that Pearl Harbor solved the President's dilemma of how to get into the war with Germany, or that he died at the right time: the irreconcilable nature of the wartime alliance he had created had not become apparent and the battle for ratification of US involvement in the United Nations would be in the hands of Harry Truman, who would not bring to that fight a legacy of incurable congressional suspicion.[20]

III

The biographical emphasis on Roosevelt nevertheless has only precisely circumscribed utility in assessing the achievements and limitations of the domestic New Deal. To understand the evolution of New Deal foreign policy it is essential to penetrate Roosevelt's mind, to understand his personal preoccupations and perceptions. But the president's thinking is not so important in attempting to understand the domestic New Deal.

I do not argue that there could have been a New Deal without Roosevelt. It is difficult to imagine the frantic excitement in Washington between 1933 and 1936 if John Nance Garner, Albert Ritchie or Newton Baker had been elected in 1932. Their narrow anti-statism and conventional thinking would have precluded a bold response to the Depression and it is salutary to remember that the Roosevelt nomination came within an ace of being thwarted after a campaign littered with political miscalculations.

Nor would I underestimate Roosevelt's personal political skills, which neither his predecessor, Herbert Hoover, nor his post-war successors possessed in like measure. The personal response of ordinary Americans to the patrician from Hyde Park is extraordinary. It is reflected in the crowds that lined the streets to see him, the thousands and thousands of letters painfully scrawled, often in pencil, on scraps of paper to the White House, the listening figures for the fireside chats, and the pictures of the President on the walls of share-cropper shacks. Industrial workers and African-Americans clearly identified with, and voted with great loyalty for, a man who could not have come from a more different background.

---

[20] Patrick Maney, *The Roosevelt Presence: A Biography of Franklin Delano Roosevelt* (New York, 1992) 11–13, 17, 27–8, 139, 192. While some of these points may appear to strain for effect, nevertheless, Maney's biography is easily the most thoughtful, politically astute, and historiographically up to date of the many single-volume biographies.

The emphasis on biography is also salutary in recreating the myriad of concerns that affected the President at any one time. As Doris Kearns Goodwin notes, historians too often impose a false sense of order and priority on their analysis of the past. 'But a president does not deal with issues topically. He deals with events and problems as they arise.' As someone who organised a book on the New Deal topically, I have to stand rebuked and also to acknowledge that Goodwin's most recent evocation of the White House during the war, 'a small intimate hotel' which hosted a 'series of house guests, some of whom stayed for years' goes a long way to elucidating the over-shadowing of domestic liberalism during World War II by focusing on the conflicting domestic and mobilisation priorities of the President and First Lady.[21]

Many New Deal emphases certainly reflect the long-standing personal predilections of the President. The pre-eminence given to agricultural policy, the desire for conservation, the hostility to the private utilities, the commitment to public power, the drive for rural electrification and the commitment to government responsibility for the long-term economic security of the citizen show in general the personal imprint of the President. Some policy initiatives can be directly and specifically attributed to Roosevelt, notably the establishment of the Civilian Conservation Corps in 1933 and the pushing through, against the scepticism of many professional foresters, of the plan to plant a 2,000-mile Shelterbelt of trees down the middle of the United States.

There are three areas where I think that Roosevelt's personal ideas go a long way to explain the limitations of the New Deal's ultimate legacy: public housing, social security and spending.

- Roosevelt never displayed much enthusiasm for government slum clearance and low-cost housing. His belated endorsement of Robert Wagner's 1937 Housing Act meant that low-cost housing in the United States never developed the legitimacy it enjoyed in Europe and met only a small part of the poor's housing need.
- In advocating the Social Security Act of 1935 Roosevelt never wavered in his insistence on the contributory insurance principle. The contributions of the workers themselves and payroll taxes funded old age insurance and unemployment compensation. 'With those taxes in', said Roosevelt, 'no politicians can ever scrap my social security program'. As politicians wrestled with the budget deficit in the 1980s and 1990s they could only be aware of the truth of Roosevelt's prediction: despite the spiralling cost of social security, no politician dared to eliminate those benefits to which those who paid social security contributions felt entitled.

[21] Goodwin, *No Ordinary Time* 11.

– His personal fiscal conservatism had a profound effect on the shape of the
New Deal. One of the main virtues of biographical studies of Roosevelt is
their demonstration of how committed he was to the economy in government programme in which he invested so much precious political capital
during the Hundred Days. He longed for the opportunity to balance the
budget and for fiscal 1937 he took the decisive, and often unpopular, steps
to bring the budget into balance. This commitment had far-reaching
consequences. The failure to spend enough may have delayed economic
recovery between 1933 and 1936. Roosevelt's caution certainly deprived
welfare programmes of vital funds that substantially inhibited their
effectiveness. But the decision of Roosevelt to balance the budget for fiscal
1937 had the most powerful effect. The recession that followed was the
single most important stimulus to the successful mobilisation of the
conservative bipartisan coalition that stymied hopes of progressive reform
for the next quarter of a century. Despite his renewed spending in 1938 and
the massive spending of the War, Roosevelt never came to accept the
notion of Keynesianism, even of the limited commercial variety that came
to characterise the political economy that the New Deal bequeathed at the
end of the war.[22]

IV

The emphasis on Roosevelt inherent in the biographical approach, however,
distorts more than it illustrates.

Even in the discussion of policy formation the Roosevelt focus tends to
downplay the contribution of other players, particularly in Congress. The
main thrust for industrial recovery policy and public works came from
Congress in 1933. The detail of tax policy was always powerfully shaped by
the Senate Finance Committee. Industrial relations policy owed virtually
everything to Robert Wagner.

But it is in examining the way New Deal programmes were implemented
that the biographical approach is inadequate and the implementation of New
Deal programmes frequently shifted the impact of those programmes and
determined the political and economic legacy of the New Deal in ways
Roosevelt had not intended.

New Deal programmes were, of course, not implemented by an army of
federal officials loyal only to their Washington masters. Some programmes
were run by state government agencies, but everywhere they were run by local
officials who might defer to local community sentiment rather than to direc-

---

[22] Anthony J. Badger, *The New Deal: The Depression Years, 1933–1940* (London, 1989) 108–16,
234, 241–2.

tives emanating from Washington. The forces of localism served to sanction racial discrimination, wide variations in size and fairness of government payouts, and pandered to the self-interest of local businessmen and farmers.

But the impact of New Deal programmes was often shaped by Washington bureaucrats following their own, rather than congressional or presidential, mandate. One of the leading exponents of policy history in the United States, Hugh Davis Graham, has noted that biography and traditional political history are good 'at reconstructing from archival records the origins of public controversy, the competition of political leaders seeking solutions, and the dynamics of executive leadership and legislative coalitions. This same tradition, however, has tended to limit historical attention to the open-ended process of implementation.' Attention to the role of the bureaucrats in that implementation is essential.[23]

The vast regulatory apparatus that governed the financial institutions, particularly the securities exchanges, and would for the next fifty years, was established by young lawyers working under both Jerome Frank and William Douglas with reference only to the broadest congressional authorisation. No agency was more important in revolutionising the distribution of credit and decentralising the distribution of financial power in the United States than the Reconstruction Finance Corporation, but Jesse Jones and his staff virtually ran an independent fiefdom. Policy was set in social security by bureaucrats for the Social Security Board who mapped out regulations and administrative procedures in the late 1930s. Arthur Altmeyer and his colleagues used the insurance ideology to fight off conservative challenges to social security, but they also used it to fight off liberal, social Keynesian challenges that would have aimed to fund adequate assistance programmes and provided for nationally guaranteed minimum incomes. The success of the social security administrators perpetuated the distinction between the deserving and the undeserving poor, which many New Dealers had striven to eradicate. The deserving received social security to which they contributed; the undeserving and helpless received assistance and welfare as a matter of grace not of right.[24]

In industrial relations, the end product of New Deal labour policy was a stable industrial relations system which revolved around conservative and 'responsible' unions that operated within an agreed consensus of capitalist

---

[23] Hugh Davis Graham, 'The Stunted Career of Policy History: A Critique and an Agenda' *The Public Historian* 15 (Spring, 1983) 14–33. I am indebted to Professor Graham for alerting me to this article.

[24] Jordan Schwartz, *The New Dealers: Power Politics in the Age of Roosevelt* (New York, 1993) 59–95, 157–94; Jerry Cates, *Insuring Inequality: Administrative Leadership in Social Security, 1935–1954* (Ann Arbor, 1982); Edward Berkowitz, 'The History of Policy: The Case of Social Welfare Policy' (Paper given at the annual meeting of the Organization of American Historians, 1995).

values. Union behaviour seemed very different from the supposedly explosive rank-and-file militancy of the 1930s. Unions were channelled into moderate and acceptable behaviour by the threat of congressional retribution, by the need to co-operate with the government in wartime mobilisation, and by a much more subtle and realistic management strategy in the 1940s. But the creation of stable and orderly labour relations was also the achievement of National Labor Relations Board and National War Labor Board professionals who, once they had restrained the worst excesses of employer anti-union practices, sought to curb union-worker autonomy as well. It was in these bureaucracies not in the White House that one had to look to understand many aspects of the political economy that emerged from the New Deal.[25]

The biographical approach also tends to overestimate the room for manoeuvre that any President enjoys. In the case of Roosevelt it ignores two fundamental and linked constraints – the circumstances of policy-making in the economic emergency of 1933 and the difficulty of avoiding the stifling impact of the dependence on conservative southern Democrats. Although the emergency conditions of 1933 theoretically gave Roosevelt the opportunity to exercise vast powers that had not been exercised since World War I, in reality the emergency severely restricted his options. The emergency dictated speed and the structure of the federal government in 1933 was simply inadequate for rapid, centrally directed radical reforms. The 'state capacity' simply did not exist to implement detailed government planning of the economy. If action had to be taken quickly, the government had to rely on existing local government bureaucracies and on the consent of those who were to be regulated, like farmers and businessmen. In turn, these often conservative forces were inevitably strengthened.

If speed in 1933 was the essence, Roosevelt had to work with the existing congressional Democratic leadership. The recognition that Roosevelt gave them and the patronage the New Deal distributed undoubtedly bolstered the position of conservative southern Democrats. In due course, southern Democrats worked to block the expansion of the New Deal into what they considered non-emergency areas and halted Roosevelt in his efforts to tackle the unfinished business of the New Deal attacking urban and rural poverty. What Roosevelt often saw as first steps, conservative congressmen were able to ensure were in fact last steps.[26]

[25] Howell Harris, 'The Snares of Liberalism? Politicians, Bureaucrats and the Shaping of Federal Labour Relations Policy in the United States, ca 1915–1947' in Steven Toliday and Jonathan Zeitlin, *Shop Floor Bargaining and the State: Historical and Comparative Perspectives* (Cambridge, 1985) 148–91.

[26] Badger, *The New Deal* 271–83, 307–9.

V

Constraints on policy implementation and formulation shaped the subsequent development of the New Deal political economy. The exact relationship between the changes wrought by the New Deal and the later political and economic development of the United States (and the relationship between the policies of the 1930s and the wider dramatic and longer-term social changes) has not been clarified by the 'presidential synthesis'.

Too often New Deal historiography has been trapped in a cycle of lamentation and celebration. Depending on their contemporary political stance, historians have sorrowed over radical opportunities missed by Roosevelt, deplored the shift to statism and bureaucracy in modern America which he instigated, or gloried in his democratic revitalisation of liberal capitalism. More time has been spent debating the President's intentions than in establishing the consequences, intended or unintended, of what he did. Biographies have exacerbated this myopic perspective.

It is not surprising that the earlier generation of Roosevelt's biographers should have worked within this framework: they started their work less than a decade after Roosevelt's death nor could they draw on the monographic case studies of agencies and programmes that proliferated later. When Leuchtenburg summed up their work in 1963, he was closer in time to the Hundred Days than we are to Watergate. (Even now Leuchtenburg can recall listening on the radio to Roosevelt's nomination at the 1932 Chicago convention. The immediate consequence of the Hundred Days for him was the presence at home of his father day after day – furloughed from his job in the Manhattan post office across from Pennsylvania Station under the 1933 Economy Act.) It was not surprising that these earlier biographical studies should have concentrated on the ways in which Roosevelt differed from his predecessor, Hoover, the ways in which the New Deal represented change from, rather than continuity with, what had gone before. Closely associated, for the most part, with the liberal wing of the Democratic party and the politics of Adlai Stevenson and John Kennedy, they tended to assume, and celebrate, a healthy continuity between the New Deal and post-war America. Leuchtenburg, Freidel and Schlesinger never abandoned these beliefs. Schlesinger, for example, vigorously resists any reincarnation of Hoover as 'progressive leader ... master modernizer or ... profound social analyst'. Leuchtenburg 'persists' in the view that the New Deal 'amounted to a watershed' which 'quite simply, changed the face of the land'.[27]

---

[27] Arthur M. Schlesinger Jr, *The Cycles of American History* (London, 1987) 37–87; Leuchtenburg, 'In the Shadow of Leuchtenburg: A Response'.

The subsequent failure to define more precisely the links between the New Deal and later social change is not only the result of the 'presidential synthesis'. Part of the blame must be laid at the breakdown of communications between New Deal historians and economic historians of the 1930s. Economic historians have been far more interested in attempting to isolate the cause of the Great Depression than in measuring exactly the impact of New Deal programmes and their contribution to recovery. More recently, Michael Bernstein's explanation of the persistence of the Depression in terms of the underdevelopment of crucial industrial sectors of the economy, Sally Clarke's careful assessment of the relationship between crop control programmes in the midwest, mechanisation and increased productivity, and Gavin Wright's longitudinal study of the South show the possibilities. Nevertheless, the work on the New Deal has little to match the integration of politics, economics and structures that characterises the work of the historians of the German and the European economy in the 1930s and 1940s such as Harold James, Richard Overy and Alan Millward.[28]

For a long time, the new social history equally ignored the role of politics and the state. American social historians have displayed much more interest in the impact of industrialization on the pre-industrial values of both immigrants and rural Americans than in the impact of the Depression and the New Deal. Much of the social history of the 1970s and 1980s ignored the 1930s or added a belated epilogue to studies of an earlier period. For all the work on women reformers in the 1930s, we still lack anything approaching a full history of the impact of the Depression on the family, on gender roles and on parent–children relationships. Despite the assertions that the Depression produced a security-conscious generation that dominated politics after 1945, no one has followed up Stephen Thernstrom's claim that the social mobility figures for Boston may have shown a break in the general upward pattern this century of social mobility, a blip which might well explain the post-war concerns. For all the studies of relief programmes for the unemployed, there are no studies of the effect of unemployment on infant mortality figures and on diet equivalent to the studies of Jay Winter for Britain. It is only the labour historians, examining the union breakthroughs of the 1930s, who have blended social and political history together to produce studies that integrate workplace experience, ethnicity, union activity, community

28 Michael Bernstein, *The Great Depression: Delayed Recovery and Economic Change in America, 1929–1939* (Cambridge, 1987); Sally H. Clarke, *Regulation and Revolution in United States Farm Productivity* (Cambridge, 1995); Gavin Wright, *Old South, New South: Revolutions in the Southern Economy Since the Civil War* (New York, 1986) 198–274; Richard J. Overy, *War, Economy and the Third Reich* (Oxford, 1994); Harold James, *The German Slump: Politics and Economics, 1924–1936* (Oxford, 1986); Alan Millward, *War, Economy, and Society, 1939–1945* (London, 1977).

organisation and political life, most successfully in Lizabeth Cohen's study of Chicago.[29]

Biographical studies cannot be expected to provide what the social and economic historians have failed to provide themselves. Their limited utility has, however, most recently been emphasised by major new studies which have shown just how much of the New Deal legacy to the post-war world was shaped in the years after 1937. Some biographical studies have never reached that far; those that have, have tended to focus on the political setbacks of 1937 and 1938 or on the foreign policy issues which grew in such importance as war approached. Recently, however, scholars such as John Jeffries have explored the ramifications of a Third New Deal after 1937. Alan Brinkley has demonstrated in masterly fashion how the rethinking by New Dealers of the fundamentals of social and economic policy and the political realities of war produced the particular mix of corporate and social policy, taxation and government spending, which characterised post-war liberalism.

What Brinkley describes is a 'commercial' Keynesianism in which government fiscal policy was the main engine of economic growth and the main economic tool of post-war administrations. Gone was the social agenda that New Deal planners had developed during the late 1930s and the war and which was encapsulated in Roosevelt's Economic Bill of Rights. In its place was a precisely circumscribed Keynesianism, very different from the 'social' Keynesianism found in Europe. 'Commercial' Keynesianism promised full employment without a massive increase in state bureaucratic power. This faith in a non-statist economic policy meant acceptance of the existing corporate structure, limited government regulation, and a restricted welfare state.[30]

VI

This shift simply highlighted the way that the biographical approach does not help understand just how many of the consequences of the New Deal were unintended, how the major trends in American social and economic development were not the ones desired by Roosevelt.

Roosevelt disliked welfare. His advocacy of the Works Progress Administration rested on the conviction that the government should get out of the business of relief. The federal government would provide jobs for the

[29] Stephen Thernstrom, *The Other Bostonians* (Cambridge, Mass., 1971) 233; Jay Winter, 'Unemployment, nutrition and infant mortality 1920–1950', in Jay Winter (ed.), *The Working-Class in Modern British History* (Cambridge, 1983); Lizabeth Cohen, *Making a New Deal: Industrial Workers in Chicago, 1919–1939* (Cambridge, 1990).

[30] John Jeffries, 'A "Third New Deal"? Liberal Policy and the American State, 1937–1945' (paper given at *The New Deal* conference, Sidney Sussex College, Cambridge, 20–2 September 1993); Alan Brinkley, *The End of Reform: New Deal Liberalism in Recession and War* (New York, 1995).

able-bodied unemployed: simple unemployment relief was returned to the states, even though relief administrators were only too aware that many states were either incapable of meeting or unwilling to meet relief obligations. Nevertheless, both FDR, and his work relief administrators and his Social Security Board, believed that welfare/relief would simply wither away, made unnecessary by social insurance and, if necessary, future emergency WPA-style works programmes. But the welfare state that Roosevelt bequeathed would foster an explosion of the very welfare he wished to see disappear. The key was in the small categorical assistance programme – Aid to Dependent Children in the 1935 Social Security Act. The federal government would match state government funds in programmes designed to assist the category of single mothers. The state programmes that were to be assisted were tiny, the recipients were mainly widows, the programme was instituted without much debate. The relatively ungenerous matching provision of federal funds for this programme, compared to aid to the blind and the old, reflected the almost unthinking inclusion of a programme which had very little political visibility. Incremental increases in both benefits and eligibility and the changing structure of rural and inner-city poverty transformed this marginal programme designed to help widows, into the greatest single provider of assistance in the American welfare system. It became the programme that underpinned the whole system. By 1960 3.5 million families were in receipt of benefits from the Aid to Families with Dependent Children; by 1970 10 million families were helped.[31]

Once the banks were saved in 1933, rescuing American agriculture had been the first priority of Roosevelt's Hundred Days. Roosevelt wanted to keep people on the land – not from any romantic 'back-to-the-land' notions, but as a matter of public policy at a time when there were no urban jobs for a surplus rural population to flee to. Price-supports were designed to raise farm income to acceptable levels, federal underwriting of rural credit aimed to save farms from foreclosure, rural electrification promised not only to modernise farming but to eliminate the drudgery of rural life and to make staying on the land physically and culturally attractive. At best, by 1940 the New Deal had acted as a 'holding operation' for American farmers: it did enable most of them to stay on the land in a decade when economic opportunity elsewhere was non-existent. But the New Deal was only temporarily slowing the transformation of American agriculture. In 1933 Roosevelt's farm advisers believed that solving the farm problem was the key to restoring the economy as a whole. By 1940 they believed that urban prosperity was the key to solving the farm problem. During the war, the 17 million new non-farm jobs enabled the

31 Linda Gordon, *Pitied But Not Entitled: Single Mothers and the History of Welfare* (New York, 1994) 209–306.

surplus rural population to flee the land. Farm price-supports and wartime prosperity drove unprecedented mechanisation and technological advance. The massive flight from the land, the virtual disappearance of the family farm, the decline in the number of farms, and the vast increase in their size were developments that Roosevelt neither desired nor foresaw.[32]

For city dwellers, Roosevelt promised in 1938 'an attack on the slums of this country which must go forward until every American family has a decent home'. But, as we have seen, his commitment to low-cost government housing was minimal. His vision for a decentralised urban America was better captured by the Greenbelt programme in which the crowded inner-city population would be dispersed into planned 'new town' environments just outside big cities. But only three communities were ever built and the rent levels designed to make the projects financially self-liquidating put them out of reach of low-income slum dwellers. What the New Deal did instead was unwittingly to foster suburban sprawl. By 1935 its Home Owners' Loan Corporation had already rescued one in ten of the nation's owner-occupiers by refinancing their mortgages over a much longer period than the usual five-year repayment. Aiming to revive the construction industry by reviving the housing market, the Federal Housing Administration insured private lenders and encouraged them to cheapen the cost of housing by reducing the down-payments they required, lengthening the repayment periods, and lowering their interest rates. The American housing industry, noted economist Isador Lubin, was a high-cost, low-volume industry. It was as if, he argued, the car industry built 85 per cent Cadillacs and 15 per cent Fords. What the FHA did was help create a low-cost, high-volume industry. Only in the suburbs was the cheap land available that would make possible mass-production housing. By the early 1940s the San Francisco area was already developing suburbs on the lines of post-war Levittown. The FHA fostered this development: its loans were for newly purchased single-family homes, rather than for the renovation of existing property or the building of housing for rent; the agency insured loans for predominantly white borrowers and red-lined or steered clear of blighted inner-city areas. This suburbanisation of America was not the decentralisation of urban America that Roosevelt had dreamt of.[33]

In 1940 the South, as in 1930, was a poor, rural, one-crop, segregated society in which too many people chased too little farm income and blacks were economically and politically powerless and racially segregated. Government spending on defence industries and military facilities in World War II

---

[32] Badger, *The New Deal* 147–89.

[33] Kenneth T. Jackson, *Crabgrass Frontier: The Suburbanization of the United States* (Oxford, 1985) chs. 10–12; Robert Fishman, 'Housing in the 1930s: The Origins of an American Industrial Policy' (paper given at the annual meeting of the Organization of American Historians, 1995).

and after kick-started the region into self-sustaining economic growth. Urban jobs absorbed the surplus rural population, provided the market for a diversified agriculture, created the purchasing power to sustain a regional consumer-durable manufacturing base, and ultimately created the living space and bargaining power for an indigenous black civil rights movement. Wartime prosperity gave farmers both the capital and the incentive to mechanise and diversify. The New Deal did play a role in transforming the region, as it did also in the West. As Jordan Schwarz has shown, New Deal programmes created the infrastructure that made the Sunbelt possible. Cheap public power and the regional availability of credit facilitated industrialisation. Government capital through public works programmes revitalised southern cities, providing the investment in infrastructure that private capital had supplied a generation earlier in northern cities. As Gavin Wright has shown, the Fair Labor Standards Act of 1938 integrated the South into a national labour market. As Pat Sullivan will show, southern black leaders in the 1930s saw the New Deal's economic rescue of the region as a precedent for future federal intervention in the region's race relations.

Roosevelt was optimistic about the South; he eagerly anticipated a 'new generation of leaders' in the region. But the South was modernised by a very different strategy and under very different leadership than Roosevelt had hoped for. A younger generation of southerners, both in Washington and back in the states, had been inspired by the New Deal to advocate a liberal modernisation strategy for the region. Prosperity would come through the creation of mass purchasing power – enabling tenants to purchase their own land, raising minimum wages and extending social security. A precondition of change had to be the protection of the civil rights of both labour union organisers and blacks, most notably extending the right to vote. But it was conservatives, not liberals, who masterminded the economic modernisation of the South, putting their faith in seeking industrial development through tax incentives and the attractions of a low-wage, non-unionised work force, a modernisation which they believed would not disrupt traditional patterns of race relations in the region. Eventually, they would also recognise the need to attract high-tech industry and business leaders would be compelled by economic necessity and by federal, and local black, pressure to accept racial change. But neither the leaders who mediated the racial changes of the region in the 1960s and 1970s, nor the white voters who shifted to the Republican party in the 1970s and 1980s, shared the economic liberalism that informed Roosevelt's endorsement of the description of the South in 1938 as the region's number one economic problem.[34]

---

[34] Bruce Schulman, *From Cotton Belt to Sunbelt: Federal Policy, Economic Development, and the Transformation of the South, 1938–1980* (New York, 1991) 63–112; Wright, *Old South, New*

VII

Scholars will soon be able to surf the Internet and to find out more and more about Roosevelt's daily life. To question the utility of that enterprise is not to denigrate biography nor to privilege large impersonal forces at the expense of great men. It is to argue that historians know as much as they need to know about the life of Franklin D. Roosevelt. It is to argue that New Deal historiography has been better at assessing Roosevelt's intentions than the consequences of his actions. It is to argue that the historiography has more convincingly described policy formulation and policy alternatives than policy implementation and that historians have assessed with greater conviction the changes in the 1930s compared to what had gone before than those changes in comparison with what came after. What biographies of FDR have not told us, and cannot tell us, is what we need now to know about the New Deal: its exact relationship to the immense transformation of American society in the second half of the twentieth century.

South 198–234; Patricia Sullivan, *Days of Hope: Race and Democracy in the New Deal* (Chapel Hill, forthcoming) chs. 1–3; Anthony J. Badger, 'How Did the New Deal Change the South?' in Steven Ickringill ed., *Looking Inward, Looking Outward* (Amsterdam, 1990) 166–83.

HISTORY AND BIOGRAPHY:
AN INAUGURAL LECTURE

෭ഽഌഽഌഽ

DEREK BEALES

M R Vice-Chancellor,
Mr Gladstone, who will play a large role in this lecture, wrote in his diary, while he was an undergraduate at Christ Church: 'I wish I were duly convinced of the extreme importance of residence at Oxford.' This University's dispiriting notice to a new professor explains that he need not give an inaugural lecture 'in his first term or in his first year', or at all. On such a time-scale it cannot be too late to applaud the readiness of another Christ Church man to leave Oxford, even at the cost of coming to Cambridge, albeit under an assumed name, Lord Dacre of Glanton. Historians ought not to quote out of context, and so I continue Gladstone's diary entry: 'I wish', he said, 'I were duly convinced of the extreme importance of residence at Oxford, both as regards individual progress in religion, and influence exercised directly or indirectly on others' – and then, as so often, he spoils it all by a qualification – 'especially in a case where the individual has the reputation of possessing more [influence] than he actually has'.[1] In my opinion all the

---

This is so much a *pièce d'occasion* that to rewrite it would totally change its flavour. I will not attempt to explain all the allusions, but it will help the reader to know that the presiding Vice-Chancellor was Sir Peter Swinnerton-Dyer, Bart., of a Shropshire family. I wish it were possible to reconstruct the brilliant impromptu speech he made at the end of the lecture.

[1] *The Gladstone Diaries*, ed., M. R. D. Foot, 1 (Oxford, 1968), 301: 25 April 1830.

Many of my colleagues in Faculty and College have helped me in writing this lecture, usually without realising it. Dr D. N. Cannadine criticised an early version. Prof. R. Hatton kindly provided me with copies of two articles: her own 'The Joys and Sorrows of Writing Historical Biography' (The Roy M. Wiles Memorial Lecture 1979 (McMaster University)), and R. Pillorget, 'Die Biographie als historiographische Gattung. Ihre heutige Lage in Frankreich', forthcoming in *Historisches Jahrbuch*.

I derived stimulus from the Anglo-American Historical Conference on this theme, held at the Institute of Historical Research in July 1980.

See the symposium on 'Biographie und Geschichtswissenschaft', vol. VI of *Wiener Beiträge zur Geschichte der Neuzeit* (1979).

electors to the Chair of Modern History wield an influence as powerful as it is beneficent; and no member of this formidable audience contributes more to my sense of inadequacy as I speak than Lord Dacre, who has furnished in his own inaugural and valedictory lectures[2] incomparable models of the blend of wit, style and wisdom appropriate to such occasions.

Perilous though it is for me to mention it, we must all wish that Professor Gallagher were still with us to prophesy, and perhaps witness, the discomfiture of another inaugural lecturer.[3]

Under my umbrella title, 'History and Biography', I shall consider from several angles the place of biography and the biographical approach in the study and writing of history. Since I am in the middle of a book on Joseph II of Austria and much of my lecturing concerns Gladstone, I felt almost obliged to choose this theme.

It has been put to me that an inaugural lecture offers an opportunity for an ego-trip. I shall not stop to enquire what degree of licence I could claim if I embarked on such a journey. The only indulgence I ask for is to be permitted a little personal reminiscence or intellectual autobiography. I am anxious to tell my tale before the genre attains a new and alarming scale and sophistication with the publication of Mr Cowling's forthcoming volumes.[4]

Ever since Gibbon gained 'a clearer notion of the Phalanx and the Legion' from service in the Hampshire militia,[5] historians have automatically asked themselves whether their scholarship too has benefited from a similar experience. Between school and University I was briefly conscripted into the Royal Artillery. I cannot report that I learned anything about techniques of warfare. My battery moved only once to its desolate Welsh firing-range, and we took the wrong fuses. I discovered not only how grotesquely inefficient armies can be, but also that, while soldiers can easily steal for themselves enormous rations of free time, it is hard indeed for them to use their leisure – shall I say seriously? In so far as I did so, it was in listening to music on the Third Programme and reading talks published in *The Listener*. I believe that their strikingly high quality at that period was an early instance of creative direction on the part of Dr Laslett. For me the most important article was a review by Max Beloff, commending to English readers a French book which he claimed inaugurated an epoch in historical writing. It was Braudel's

---

Cf. also L. Stone, 'The Revival of Narrative: Reflections on a New Old History', *Past and Present*, 85 (1979), 3–24.

[2] H. R. Trevor-Roper, *History Professional and Lay* (Oxford, 1957); 'History and Imagination', *Times Literary Supplement*, 25 July 1980, pp. 833–5.

[3] See R. Cobb, 'Jack Gallagher in Oxford', *Cambridge Review*, 102 (7 Nov. 1980), 21–4.

[4] M. Cowling, *Religion and Public Doctrine in Modern England* (Cambridge, 1980), the preliminary volume to a larger work.

[5] E. Gibbon, *Memoirs of My Life* (ed. G. A. Bonnard) (London, 1966), p. 117.

Mediterranean . . . in the Age of Philip II.[6] I resolved to obtain it. The local librarians gulped, but they obliged. Several months later, when my zeal had a good deal cooled, it was further chilled by the vast volume's arrival. But 'I read, I applauded, I believed.'[7] I was exalted by its image of the Mediterranean as a glowing, ageless world of its own – and, beyond that, an El Dorado of bottomless archives. Almost the only history book I had by then bought was Burckhardt's *Renaissance*. Braudel's vision merged in my mind with Burckhardt's, particularly with the photographs in the Phaidon edition, summoning me to the wonders of Italy.

In the 1950s and 1960s, Tripos examiners ritually observed in their reports that no candidate appeared to have read Braudel. On that evidence I was unusual. However, few primary sources are so unreliable as examiners' reports, unless as a record of exasperation recollected during convalescence.

One sentence only of Braudel's stuck complete in my head. It concerns Charles V, the emperor who in the early sixteenth century united under his rule Spain, Germany, the Netherlands, most of Italy and much of America. 'Charles V', Braudel announced, 'was an accident calculated, prepared, desired by Spain'. The epigram is crucial to the argument of the book. Charles V and his unwieldy empire are not to be treated, in the manner of previous historians, as the chance product of dynastic marriages. They were planned. 'Europe', he continued, 'was moving of its own accord towards the construction of a vast state'. He discerned during this period profound tendencies operating in favour of political concentration.[8]

These assertions fall within a general critique of *histoire biographique*. Certainly Braudel rejects total determinism. But, he says, 'the zones between determinisms, in which one can take to the woods of freedom, are not numerous, and few men are to be found there'. Some 'strong personalities', like Don John of Austria and Pope Pius V 'undoubtedly succeeded in disrupting, disturbing the normal direction of the century's destinies'. That explains why their work was never followed up. 'All efforts against the prevailing tide of history, which is not always obvious, are doomed to failure.'

His final passage on Philip II points out that the king never used the word 'Mediterranean' in Braudel's sense. Philip had not been taught the right kind

---

6 M. Beloff, 'A Challenge to Historians', *The Listener*, 42 (10 Nov. 1949), 816–17. F. Braudel, *La Méditerranée et le monde méditerranéen à l'époque de Philippe II* (Paris, 1949).

7 Gibbon, *Memoirs*, p. 59 (referring to his conversion to Roman Catholicism through reading Bossuet).

8 'Charles de Gand est un hasard calculé, préparé, voulu d'Espagne' (Braudel, *Méditerranée*, p. 519). In the 2nd edn (Paris, 1966) the sentence survives (II, 21), but changed into the perfect tense. The English edn (F. Braudel, *The Mediterranean and the Mediterranean World in the Age of Philip II* (London, 1973)) does not convey the full force of the statement (II, 672). The second quotation is the published translation of the version in the 2nd French edn (same pp.).

of geography. Here, writes Braudel, is further proof of the distance between mere 'biographical history' on the one hand and 'the history of structures and . . . expanses' on the other.[9]

His presentation of the case against biography, and more generally against historians' former preoccupation with individuals, may be taken as the case of the whole school he represents and adorns, associated with the journal *Annales*. It constitutes the most powerful argument that the proponent of biography now has to meet, because historians writing in this spirit have published so much that is impressive and influential, first and foremost Braudel's *Mediterranean* itself.[10]

I shall now dare to ask whether Braudel's view of the empire of Charles V can be sustained. It once seemed to me not just intoxicating but persuasive. Historians here as well as in France have long been taught to study 'problems in preference to periods',[11] trends and processes rather than events and individuals. It is peculiarly old-fashioned to find interest in monarchs, dynasties and marriage treaties. How satisfying that one of the classic accidents of traditional historiography should turn out to be nothing of the kind, but instead an outcome willed by Spain, towards which Europe was moving of its own accord, the upshot of profound tendencies! But I fear it's pure moonshine.

The very phraseology of the epigram deceives. 'Charles V', he begins – but he must mean the empire, not the person – 'was an accident calculated' and so forth 'by Spain' – yet there was no such thing in the late fifteenth century as a Spanish collective will. A handful of rulers and their councillors were the match-makers, chief among them King Ferdinand of Aragon and Queen Isabella of Castile. We may safely rely on the dictum of Professor Elliott: 'The union of Spain and the Habsburg lands was the last thing that Ferdinand and Isabella would have wished.'[12] It needed a stillbirth and at least three unexpected deaths in the prime of life to bring about the empire of Charles V.

In the sentence 'Europe was moving of its own accord towards the construction of a vast state', there is no conceivable meaning we can attach to the word 'Europe'. I see no evidence for such a movement in western Europe other than the simple existence of the empire of Charles V. This phenomenon

---

[9] The splendid passage about 'strong personalities' and 'le maquis de la liberté' comes from the 1st edn, pp. 1098–9. For 'the prevailing tide of history' see the English edn, II, 1244.
    The last word on Philip II appears in the English edn, II, 1236–7; I have modified it slightly on the basis of the French (2nd edn, II, 514).

[10] See P. Burke's introduction to a collection of articles from *Annales: Economy and Society in Early Modern Europe* (London, 1972).

[11] Lord Acton, 'The Study of History' [his Inaugural] in *Lectures on Modern History* (ed. J. N. Figgis and R. V. Laurence) (London, 1906), p. 24.

[12] J. H. Elliott, *Imperial Spain, 1469–1716* (London, 1963), p. 125.

cannot be attributed to profound historical tendencies. The emperor is the trend. As such, he must deserve study for himself.[13]

Here is another case. The concept 'enlightened despotism', commonly applied to the second half of the eighteenth century, used to be employed in its natural sense, connoting that the despots themselves mattered. Professor Soboul has now declared that enlightened despotism should be regarded as a social movement, deriving from the intensification of serfdom in eastern Europe in the early modern period, *deuxième servage*. Though the régimes concerned appeared liberal and egalitarian, in reality they were serving the interests of the all-powerful territorial aristocracy.[14]

This approach takes no account of the fact that, whereas two of the most famous rulers involved, Catherine II of Russia and Frederick II of Prussia, unquestionably worked with and for the aristocracy, the third, Joseph II, sought to undermine it. A century afterwards, the long-term plans of both Frederick and Joseph seemed to their successors too embarrassing to be revealed to historians. In Prussia Bismarck refused to allow the disclosure of Frederick's deep-laid schemes of military aggrandisement. In Austria-Hungary what had to be concealed was Joseph's secret intention 'to humble and impoverish the great'. He had told his horrified mother, Maria Theresa: 'It is the lords I am attacking.'[15] In the last years of his life he legislated against them despite the opposition of many of his advisers and nearly the whole nobility. It was against the trend as well – or at least it was against the dominant trend. He largely failed. But we can hardly suppose the attempt to have had no repercussions. And if we wish to understand the attempt, we must study its author.

I turn now from great rulers to local professors. It was fifty years ago yesterday that the first holder of the Chair of Modern History, Professor

---

[13] It seems to me in fact that the converse of Braudel's argument would be more plausible: namely, that Charles V's empire defied the trends of history, because it was impossible to govern and hold together so many territories at once, as witness the very early devolution of power in Germany to his brother Ferdinand (1522). This interpretation leaves Charles V less important than I suggest in the text, but still requiring study as someone trying to cope with historical tendencies that made his inherited position untenable.

My purpose in taking this illustration was to show that what seems to me an accident of dynastic policy could appear so vastly important to Braudel that he simply had to treat it as the outcome of a profound trend.

[14] A. Soboul, 'Sur le système du despotisme éclairé', *Les lumières en Hongrie, en Europe centrale et en Europe orientale* (Budapest, 1977), pp. 19–29.

[15] A convenient account of Frederick's *Rêveries politiques* can be found in E. Bosbach, *Die 'Rêveries Politiques' in Friedrichs des Grossen Politischem Testament von 1752* (Cologne, 1960). On Joseph's long-term plans as expressed in his *Rêveries*, see my article in *Mitteilungen des österreichischen Staatsarchivs*, 33 (1980), 142–60.

For further discussion of Joseph II and enlightened despotism see my article, 'Writing a Life of Joseph II: The Problem of his Education', *Wiener Beiträge zur Geschichte der Neuzeit*, 6 (1979), 183–207.

Temperley, delivered his Inaugural.[16] We have therefore reached an appropriate moment for a first survey of its history. But what does the history of a Chair amount to? Since this one involves no administrative duty, its history must be an account of the work and influence, and to some extent the personality, of the successive incumbents during their tenure. In other words it must be a sort of collective biography.

But historians ought, where possible, to generalise. Unfortunately, only four persons have held the Chair. Analysis of just four cases cannot, I presume, yield statistically significant results. Yet historians and others habitually generalise on the basis of such small samples. In many of the weightiest matters larger samples simply cannot be found. Lengthy and influential works base their conclusions about the leaders of the British Labour Party on the seven known instances.[17] Pregnant lessons are drawn from comparisons between Lutheranism and Calvinism, the French and Russian Revolutions, the unifications of Italy and Germany, the British and American Constitutions, the premierships of Gladstone and Disraeli, and the two World Wars. Let us see what we can get from analysis of the four Professors of Modern History.

First, as to subject of study, the Chair has always been filled by a student of both English and European history, whose period of interest has included the eighteenth and nineteenth centuries. This custom accounts for the widespread feeling that ideally the University should possess a Chair of pure English history as well.

Secondly, as I think of the group of all Cambridge Professors of History over the last half-century, what seems to me especially remarkable is the

---

[16] H. Temperley, *Research and Modern History* (London, 1930). The lecture was delivered on 19 November 1930.

I should like to have found time to echo Temperley's remarks on the need for historians to travel, though I should have had to point out that cost and restrictions are greater now than in his day.

It is tempting to interpret his warning against the declamatory style of the French (p. 7) as a prescient shot directed against *Annales*, but it looks as though he was thinking of older writers.

I offer these pages as a contribution to the work of the newly founded Society for the Study of the History of the University of Cambridge, noting that G. S. R. Kitson Clark, 'A Hundred Years of the Teaching of History at Cambridge, 1873–1973', *Historical Journal*, vol. 16 (1973), does not mention the Chair of Modern History and scarcely alludes to its holders (see p. 550).

[17] The figure seven includes Mr Foot, who was elected Leader a few days before I gave the lecture. It does not include the five mere Chairmen who led the Parliamentary Party before 1922. See H. Pelling, *A Short History of the Labour Party* (London, 1962), p. 52.

R. T. McKenzie, *British Political Parties* (London, 1955) attempted to analyse the position of the Labour Party leader while acknowledging that there had been only two clear examples down to that time, MacDonald and Attlee (see p. 335). In later editions he has been able to use a larger sample.

diversity of their backgrounds. Scarcely a majority read History as undergraduates; only a minority were undergraduates at Cambridge; a sizeable
group began their careers outside Britain. It is impossible to imagine the
Faculty and the subject without the writings, teaching and inspiration of a
classically educated monk, an Austrian doctor of both laws, an American who
came to history by way of psychology and law, a Württemberger who went to
school in Prague, and a Bessarabian magician. In France the law ensures that
almost all academic posts are held by Frenchmen.[18] In this country it is
already officially laid down that schoolteachers must have passed a
Certification of Education course, at least when their subjects are not
considered of special national importance. Many lawyers seek to require that
those intending to practise must have studied Law as undergraduates. A
misguided professionalism might well have insisted that History Professors
must have read History, as it is sometimes urged that History undergraduates
must have taken the subject at 'A' Level. It is surely manifest how much we
should have lost if such prejudices had operated in the choice of History
Professors in general.

But the Professors of Modern History display no such interesting diversity.
All have been English, not even Welsh or Scottish. The first was actually born
in Cambridge itself. Doubtless it is significant that all were born within the
area of the Danelaw. It is notorious that King Alfred founded this University
precisely in order to reindoctrinate the recovered districts in Anglo-Saxon
attitudes.[19] At least the last three holders of the Chair have been 'scholarship
boys'. All read both parts of the Historical Tripos. Once arrived as undergraduates at Cambridge, none left it, except for war service, until after he had
been elected to the Chair. All but one stayed throughout his working life a
Fellow of one of the smaller Colleges. The most outlandish characteristic I can
think of about them, or at least about the last three, is that all have been
musicians, my predecessor easily the best.

I wrote this passage before I came upon Braudel's account of his own
intellectual formation and of the history of *Annales*, which was founded just

---

[18] I am grateful to Dr P. J. Collier for sharing with me his knowledge of the French educational
system.

The fact that history and geography are studied together in French Universities must have
greatly influenced the style and content of French historiography. Similarly, the approach of
English historians has obviously been much affected by our separation between English and
European (i.e. Continental) history in school and University courses.

[19] I derive this fantasy from blurred recollections of a brilliant speech given by the late
John Saltmarsh to a dinner of the Confraternitas Historica, the History Society of my
College.

The place of these societies in the story of Cambridge History should not be forgotten. I
owe a good deal to the opportunity – or the necessity – to give regular papers at meetings of
the Confraternitas.

one year before the Chair of Modern History. I thought I had written a spoof. It turns out to be a parody. His article consists entirely of appreciations of individuals, until suddenly he recollects himself.

> Who will not smile [he says] to see me write a history *historisante* . . . I have spoken of men, of occurrences. But it is very evident that this little stream, narrow and lively . . . ran through a vast countryside, during a particular epoch of history . . . and in a particular country, France . . . Is it by chance that Henri Berr, Lucien Febvre, Marc Bloch and myself all four came from eastern France? That the *Annales* began at Strasbourg, next door to Germany and to German historical thought?

He had already pointed out that Strasbourg University had been lavishly funded by the French government to educate away the effects of the German occupation of Alsace-Lorraine.[20]

Can I do better than that in explaining or palliating this uniformity of background of the Professors of Modern History? First, it has not in every case and in every respect been willed by the Electors. That might be taken to suggest that powerful trends are at work, against which mere human wishes are pitted in vain. Secondly, if there is one lesson that analysis of groups, such as MPs, has taught us, it is that correlations between background and outlook are few and weak.[21] When we are dealing with a handful of individuals, the discussion becomes almost absurd. I doubt whether Bessarabia pullulates with Postans. I am certain Yorkshire doesn't bristle with Butterfields. If you had only Sir Herbert's writings and knew nothing of his origins and personality, I wonder whether you could tell that he was a Yorkshireman. I do not find his works direct and plain-speaking, pragmatic and down-to-earth, stolid and consistent. Confinement to Peterhouse did not prevent his mind ranging adventurously and provocatively over the whole field of modern European, including English, history. He moulded Peterhouse rather than Peterhouse him. Intellectual formation is far more powerful than social or geographical origin or physical location.

This might be added. The study of English history, which tends to become parochial, has benefited greatly from the work of others than those brought up in England. It is a pity that so few continental scholars have written on the history of Victorian Britain. Earlier centuries have been more fortunate.

---

20 F. Braudel, 'Personal Testimony', *Journal of Modern History*, 44 (1972), 448–67 – the quotation from p. 467. The series of essays on 'History with a French Accent', of which this is one, constitutes a valuable assessment of Braudel's work (pp. 447–539).

21 I am thinking particularly of the work of W. O. Aydelotte on the Parliament of 1841–7. His first article, 'The House of Commons in the 1840's', *History*, 39 (1954), 249–62, which stressed correlations between MPs' economic interests and their votes, was disavowed in his 'Voting Patterns in the British House of Commons in the 1840s', *Comparative Studies in Society and History*, 5 (1962–3), 134–63.

Conversely, what marks out the great names of the Cambridge school of modern European history is the place they have earned in the historiography of the countries they have studied: Temperley in eastern Europe, Butterfield in Germany, Charles Wilson in the Netherlands, John Elliott in Spain, David Thomson, Betty Behrens and Patrick Bury in France, Trevelyan and Denis Mack Smith, my research supervisor, in Italy. While there are subtleties and perhaps depths that one can never fully grasp about the history of a country other than one's own, one may also perceive things about it that natives largely neglect or take too much for granted.

What might prevent the maintenance of this tradition would be the further decline of the teaching and study of foreign languages in British schools. You can be among the world's best historians of Britain, the United States and many Third World countries without knowing a word of any language other than English. But you cannot be a European historian worthy of the name on English alone. It is not a case of learning just one language at school. The more, the better. In addition, if European history is to prosper here, the Faculty will have to go on arranging languages tuition for undergraduates; and it is indispensable that we should continue to offer options in the Tripos, particularly Special Subjects, requiring knowledge and use of foreign languages, even though they are likely to attract fewer students than those whose materials are all in English.

I cannot salute my predecessor, Charles Wilson, to his face, because he has been recalled to Florence. His work has ranged astonishingly widely and his approach has been exceptionally broad, but his central contribution has been to economic history. This is a field where, if anywhere, scientifically ascertained laws might be expected to govern the work and fate of individuals, laws which ought to be applicable throughout history even if men in past ages were unaware of their existence. In some writings on economic history, individual men and women, whether rulers, owners, inventors, investors, designers, peasants or labourers, pass unmentioned. Pilgrim advances steadfastly towards the sublime condition of self-sustained growth, fighting Giant Capital and the Labour Lion, undaunted by Hobgoblin *crise* and the Foul Fiend *conjoncture*. Charles Wilson rejects these dismal stories. He helped to found the now flourishing study of entrepreneurs and their businesses; he has been determined to relate economic to political development; and he has refused to be imprisoned in the 'mythology of trends'.[22] His work has shown

---

[22] I will cite just three short works of Professor Wilson's to illustrate these points: 'The Entrepreneur in the Industrial Revolution in Britain', *Explorations in Entrepreneurial History*, vol. III (1955); C. H. Wilson, *History in Special and in General* (Cambridge, 1964) [his Inaugural, delivered on 12 March 1964]; and 'The Relevance of History', *Mededelingen van de koninklijke Academie voor Wetenschappen, Letteren en schone Kunsten van Belgie*, Klasse der Letteren, Jaargang XXXVII (1975), pp. 1–13.

that even in economic history you cannot satisfactorily explain what happened in the past without recourse to the biographical approach.

Sir Herbert Butterfield was Professor of Modern History when I was an undergraduate. I heard his lectures in this room. He therefore seems to me the ideal incumbent. It would have vastly amused him that I should be speaking on what the Faculty calls a 'general historical question'. I once brashly told him that the history of historiography, on which he had just published a book, was considered in my College a waste of time, serving only to prevent historians getting on with their proper task of writing straight history. My old supervisor, David Thomson, was certainly a splendid advertisement for this view – though I have to acknowledge that he eventually brought out a book on *The Aims of History*, but it was too reasonable to provoke much controversy.[23] When I had uttered this heresy, Sir Herbert shook with laughter. I presumed at the time that what delighted him was the thought that here in front of him he had a perfectly unreconstructed specimen of a breed he had thought extinct.

But it was characteristic of him, having stressed one side of an argument in one place, to put the other point of view elsewhere. He is best known as the hammer of the Whig historians. That, as the Regius Professor has shown, meant first and foremost Acton.[24] Butterfield maintained that it was the duty of the historian to shed the prejudices of his day and to look at the past for its own sake, not restricting his attention to the glamorous periods and the successful men and countries, rather seeking to understand every age and group.[25] But his mind was too creative to remain content with so passive a role.

> [The books of early historians, he wrote] are to be handled rather in the way that the economic historian might handle the stale records of a defunct business house: so that we may learn whether there is not a history to be wrung out of them totally unlike anything that the writers of them had ever had in mind.[26]

There was a deep paradoxicality, an inspired perversity, about Butterfield, as he was sure there is about history.[27] He once told with glee how at a general

---

[23] D. Thomson, *The Aims of History* (London, 1969).

[24] O. Chadwick, *Freedom and the Historian* (Cambridge, 1969), pp. 37–8.

[25] H. Butterfield, *The Whig Interpretation of History* (London, 1931).

[26] H. Butterfield, *Man on his Past* (Cambridge, 1969), p. xiii. Cf., from his Inaugural as Professor of Modern History (*The Study of Modern History* (London, 1944) [delivered on 14 Nov. 1944]): 'the climax of the historian's endeavour, when, instead of learning things with servility, we reign over the field with a presiding mind' (p. 27).

[27] E.g. Butterfield, 'Some Trends in Scholarship, 1868–1968, in the Field of Modern History', *Transactions of the Royal Historical Society*, 5th series, 11 (1969), 159.

On pp. 179–82 and 184 Butterfield tells us something about Temperley, as he does at greater length in his introduction to the reissue of H. Temperley, *Frederic the Great and Kaiser Joseph* (London, 1968).

election, being lucky enough to possess the vote in more than one
constituency, he had been able to support candidates of all three major parties.
What is more, all three won. It was 'the shock of my life [he said] – I felt it
too terribly on my conscience'.[28] No sooner had he turned the profession
against Whig historiography than he moved to assail the arch-Tory,
Namier.[29] This is why I wonder whether his delight at my unreconstructed
pragmatism might after all have represented his latest view. The moment
he identified a bandwagon, even when he had started it off himself, he
decamped.

Anyone working on Victorian Britain in Cambridge during the 1950s and
1960s was bound to be influenced by Dr Kitson Clark. Now Kitson was a
plainer man than Butterfield, and a more recognisable Yorkshireman. Dr
Robson has recently presented to the Faculty some of Kitson's papers, which
contain an exchange between him and Butterfield on Tripos reform. Kitson
had composed a wise and judicious paper advocating some very reasonable
changes. Butterfield replied that he agreed with what Kitson had written, but
this was not to be taken to mean that when it came to it he would support
him.[30] Their outlooks were very different. Kitson wrote some puzzled
and reverent passages about the mysterious process of population growth and
industrialisation.[31] But I doubt whether he would have accepted that you were
entitled to write intellectual, political or religious history 'totally unlike
anything [contemporaries] had in mind'. What interested him was Maitland's
'common thought of common things'. He wanted, like G. M. Young, to 'go
on reading until you can hear people talking'.[32]

We here encounter a crucial division of opinion, and plainly it is Kitson's
attitude that is the more friendly to biography. In a moment I shall consider

---

[28] H. Butterfield, *Raison d'Etat. The Relations between Morality and Government* (Martin
Wright Memorial Lecture, Brighton, 1975), p. 15.

[29] H. Butterfield, *George III and the Historians* (London, 1957).

[30] I have left this passage as it stood in the lecture. However, looking at the documents again, I
find that it was with reference to a particular proposal of Kitson's that Butterfield used
roughly these words (Butterfield to Kitson Clark, 10 Feb. 1950).

   An earlier exchange in 1943–4 was more overtly hostile: Butterfield asked for his letter to
be returned, and Kitson wrote to R. E. Balfour (14 Dec. 1944) saying that Butterfield
evidently thought him (Kitson), 'in anything which concerns the teaching of history', 'a very
wicked man indeed'. He went on: 'However, I am very anxious not to hamper Butterfield in
the development of his own ideas, and look forward to the publication of his Inaugural
Lecture, which I think may possibly make them clear. I gather it was delivered with great fire
and force of attack.'

[31] G. Kitson Clark, *The Making of Victorian England* (London, 1962), chs. III and IV.

[32] Perhaps it is sufficient, as it certainly is fitting, to refer to Kitson Clark's edition of G. M.
Young's *Portrait of an Age* (London, 1977), here the Maitland question appears in the above
form on p. 18 of the introduction Young wrote for the second edition, and the original
version is given on p. 194.

   The Young quotation can be found on p. 9 of his *Last Essays* (London, 1950).

these two approaches by reference to the study of Gladstone. But before I do so, another general issue must be broached.

Writers on the nature of history commonly suggest that on one side there are plain facts, and on the other side biased historians.[33] But in reality most historical facts are known to us only because they have been recorded by individuals, often with comments and always selectively. The recorders themselves have to be studied if the facts are to be properly used. For example, the statistics compiled by Gregory King formed the basis of much English social and economic history of the seventeenth and eighteenth centuries. A look at King's career, methods and attitudes has shown that he prepared his tables on dubious principles to further a polemical purpose.[34] Similarly, in order to make discriminating use of the inviting figures in the religious census for England and Wales taken in 1851, you need to know how the organiser, Horace Mann, collected his information and what he thought about religion and society.[35] There is nearly always a conflict of evidence, and all the testimony is slanted in some way or other. So, at least on many subjects, the historian cannot inject much in the way of new prejudices because contemporaries harboured so many themselves.

Now in studying Gladstone and developments connected with him, historians are faced with this problem in its most acute form. He not only filled 15,000 columns of *Hansard*, he published at least 200 books or articles, he composed thousands of memoranda, his diary runs to 41 volumes, and several hundred thousand of his letters survive.[36] Throughout his working life of nearly seventy years he self-consciously related his actions to what he discerned as the tendencies of history.

He had a Braudelian gift for trends. He claimed that, if he had 'a striking gift', 'it [was] an insight into the facts of particular eras, and their relations one to another, which generates in the mind a conviction that the materials exist

---

[33] This seems to me at the root of E. H. Carr's argument in *What is History?* (London, 1961). It is true that he acknowledges in his first chapter, 'The Historian and the Facts', that the facts come to historians already processed. But I think the dichotomy of the chapter-heading takes possession.

Cf. E. H. Dance, *History the Betrayer* (London, 1960).

[34] G. S. Holmes, 'Gregory King and the Social Structure of pre-industrial England', *Transactions of the Royal Historical Society*, 5th series, 27 (1977), 41–68. E. Le Roy Ladurie, 'The Chief Defects of Gregory King', in *The Territory of the Historian* (Hassocks, 1979), pp. 173–91.

[35] The problems are well explained in D. M. Thompson, 'The 1851 Religious Census: Problems and Possibilities', *Victorian Studies*, 11 (1967–8), 87–97.

[36] On the magnitude of the Gladstone material, see A. T. Bassett, *Gladstone's Speeches: Descriptive Index and Bibliography* (London, 1919); the volume of the British Library's MSS catalogue which Bassett edited, *The Gladstone Papers* (London, 1953); C. F. G. Masterman, preface to abridged edn of Morley's *Life of Gladstone* (London, 1929), p. xxii, *The Gladstone Diaries*, ed. M. R. D. Foot, vol. I, introduction.

for forming a public opinion, and for directing it to a particular end.[37] He spoke of having to connect himself 'with silent changes, which are advancing in the very bed and basis of modern society'.[38]

> Logical continuity [he asserted] and moral causation are stronger than the conscious thought of man; they mock it, and play with it, and constrain it, even without his knowledge, to suit their purposes.[39]

Sometimes he compared the trends of history to the process 'which incessantly removes and replaces the constituent parts of the human body', at other times to the movements of the earth's crust.[40] Again,

> great discoveries are commonly to be found in germ either unobserved or imperfectly developed, long before their publication, which marks the stage of maturity in their idea, and makes them part of the general property of mankind.[41]

Instances can certainly be found when he allowed his judgement of social tendencies to be influenced by political convenience. It didn't take him long after the American Civil War to transform what he had previously treated as the simple stoicism of the Lancashire operatives during the cotton famine into a glorious example of political intelligence.[42] It was not radicals so much as Gladstone who popularised the notion that the Hyde Park riots of 1866–7 extracted from the government the Reform Act of 1867.[43]

He thought so incorrigibly in terms of trends that there are moments when he sounds like a social commentator of the present day. He told the Mechanics Institutes of Lancashire and Cheshire that this was

---

[37] *The Prime Ministers' Papers: W. E. Gladstone*, I: *Autobiographica*, ed. J. Brooke and M. Sorensen (London, 1971), 136.
   I was tempted to dilate on this theme, under the title wished on to Professor Chadwick by *Who's Who: Action and Gladstone*.

[38] Gladstone, *Chapter of Autobiography* (London, 1868), p. 7 [the second para. of the tract].

[39] Gladstone, 'The Evangelical Movement' [*British Quarterly Review*, 1879], in *Gleanings of Past Years* (London, 1879), VII, 225.

[40] *Chapter of Autobiography*, p. 60; speech on the Reform Bill, 27 April 1866 (Bassett, *Gladstone's Speeches*, p. 376).

[41] Gladstone reviewing Martin's *Life of the Prince Consort*, vol. II [*Church of England Quarterly Review*, 1877], in *Gleanings*, I, 67.

[42] See the speech quoted above on Reform (Bassett, *Gladstone's Speeches*, pp. 375–6), for the myth complete. For the stage of mere stoicism, see *Proceedings at the opening of Farnworth Park* . . . [12 Oct. 1864] (Bolton, 1865), esp. p. 29.

[43] For the myth complete, see Gladstone, *Speeches . . . in South-West Lancashire, October, 1868* (Liverpool, n.d.), p. 73.
   Cf. M Cowling, *1867: Disraeli, Gladstone and Revolution* (Cambridge, 1967), esp. pp. 42–4, 272–5.

the age of humane and liberal laws, the age of extended franchises, the age of warmer loyalty and more firmly established order, the age of free trade, the age of steam and railways; so it is likewise . . . the age of examinations.[44]

But his history was generally both serious and professional. Modern scholars have adopted, perhaps unconsciously, many of his interpretations of his own age. His accounts of the Oxford Movement, and especially of its relationship with the Evangelical Movement, are the basis of the received view.[45] His numerous articles on the politics of the 1850s, mostly written within a few months of the events discussed, supply the framework of modern analyses.[46] His descriptions of Victorian Cabinet government are far superior to those of all his contemporaries except Bagehot, and I suspect that Bagehot learned a good deal about it from Gladstone during their frequent meetings in the early 1860s, before *The English Constitution* appeared.[47] Gladstone's lecture on Wedgwood and his article on Macaulay still figure as essential reading on the men concerned.[48]

---

[44] Speech on the death of the Prince Consort, 23 April 1862, in *Gleanings*, I, 20.

[45] I am thinking particularly of *A Chapter of Autobiography* and the article on the Evangelical Movement (*Gleanings*, vol. VII). But there are many writings both from the 1840s and later which contribute to the story. Among the most interesting is 'The Present Aspect of the Church' [*Foreign and Colonial Quarterly Review*, 1843], which, as Gladstone himself wrote when reprinting it (*Gleanings*, vol. V), 'may . . . serve as part of the materials, from which the religious history of a critical period will have finally to be written' (p. I n.).

[46] Probably the most notable is 'The Declining Efficiency of Parliament', *Quarterly Review*, 1856. For modern historians' use of this and other articles of Gladstone, see J. B. Conacher, 'Party Politics in the Age of Palmerston', in P. Appleman, W. A. Madden and M. Wolff (eds.), *1859: Entering an Age of Crisis* (Bloomington, 1959), pp. 163–80; Beales, *England and Italy, 1859–60* (London, 1961), esp. ch. II.

[47] See esp. Gladstone's reviews of successive volumes of Martin's *Life of the Prince Consort* and his article 'Kin beyond Sea' [*North American Review*, 1878], all collected in *Gleanings*, vol. I. On p. 248 he acknowledges Bagehot's work. But he had already done so in 'The Session and its Sequel', *Edinburgh Review*, 126 (1867), 561–2.

The piece of evidence that comes nearest to proving Gladstone's influence on *The English Constitution* is this. On 15 Oct. 1863 Gladstone complained to Bagehot that the latter had used in an article some views and information about Sir George Lewis derived from a confidential talk with Gladstone, and got one point wrong. Bagehot replied on 19 Oct., admitting the faults, and particularly his mistake in assuming that Lewis must have informed the Cabinet of his differences with Gladstone over the Budget of 1860. Bagehot went on: 'One's ignorance of Cabinets is so total that I could not have imagined his not doing so' (B[ritish] L[ibrary], Add. MS 44401, fos. 135–6, 144–7).

Gladstone recorded in his diary his reading of *The English Constitution* on 18, 21, 28 Feb., 2, 5, 6 and 7 March 1867 (ed. H. C. G. Matthew, *The Gladstone Diaries*, VI (1861–1868) (Oxford, 1978), 501–5). Many meetings between the two men are mentioned in this volume.

[48] 'Wedgwood', address at Burslem, 26 Oct. 1863, in *Gleanings*, II, 181–211, set in recent years for a Special Subject in Part II of the Historical Tripos; 'Macaulay' [*Quarterly Review*, 1876], *ibid.* pp. 265–341, of which D. Knowles wrote (*Lord Macaulay, 1800–1859* (Cambridge, 1960), p. 5): 'it is noteworthy that [Gladstone's] judgments on Macaulay's personality and qualities as a historian are in all essentials those that a critic of today might reprint as his own'.

For nearly forty years he was a friend of the historian Acton. Late in life, Gladstone came to depend on Acton for historical assistance. 'I want', he wrote to him in 1887, 'to get at all the learning in the world on the history of pork-eating . . . It is connected with serious questions of ethnography.'[49] Acton saved Gladstone from some embarrassing gaffes in his Romanes Lecture of 1892.[50] But it looks to me as though the boot was on the other foot in the early 1860s, at least so far as modern English history was concerned. Acton was still under thirty and had yet to undertake his tour of continental archives. When in 1863 the young man needed an article for his journal on the origins of the Crimean War, and wanted to get at the truth of Palmerston's resignation in 1853, he applied to Gladstone. Gladstone at first enquired rather testily whether Acton had checked the dates in *The Times*. On being told yes, he sent into the country for his diaries and arranged for Acton to discuss the matter with several surviving members of the Aberdeen Cabinet.[51] This is a rather more scholarly approach than Acton displayed in the next year, when he published an edition of a spurious work ascribed to Frederick the Great, hotly maintaining its authenticity on wholly insufficient grounds.[52] Gladstone's splendid article on Macaulay was written unaided, and it is revealing how Acton received it. The historian complained that Macaulay had

---

[49] Gladstone to Acton, 16 May 1887 (Cambridge University Library, Acton MSS, Box 9).

[50] The main issue seemed to be Occam's association with Oxford (e.g. Gladstone to Acton, 10 Oct. 1892, *eodem loco*).

On the relationship between the two men in the years after 1879 see O. Chadwick, *Acton and Gladstone* (London, 1976). The Romanes lecture is mentioned on p. 30.

[51] Gladstone to Acton, 27 Feb., 2, 4, 12 and 14 Mar. 1863, Cambridge University Library, Acton MSS, Box 9; Acton to Gladstone, dated only by the day of the week but docketed 26 and 28 Feb., 11 and 13 Mar. 1863 (BL Add. MS 44093). The Acton MSS also contain a page of notes by Acton on his conversation(s). The article was in fact written by Lathbury, and appeared in *Home and Foreign Review*, 2 (1863), 398–432. See also *ibid.* 4 (1864), 308–10. There is further information on this and the *Matinées royales* article in J. L. Altholz, D. McElrath and J. C. Holland (eds.), *The Correspondence of Lord Acton and Richard Simpson*, III (Cambridge, 1975), 72–97.

The Kinglake article has not been taken into account by writers on the origins of the Crimean War.

It is interesting that Gladstone was so ready to give information about Cabinet discussions and to offer his diary as a historical source.

In all the writing on the relationship between the two men, including a chapter called 'The Influence of Mr. Gladstone' in D. Mathew, *Acton* (London, 1946), I do not think it has been suggested that Gladstone should be considered a historian and might have influenced Acton in that capacity.

[52] 'Confessions of Frederick the Great' [*Home and Foreign Review*, 1863], reprinted in D. Woodruff (ed.), *Essays on Church and State* (London, 1952), pp. 353–73 [see nn. on pp. 473–4]; *Les Matinées Royales, ou l'Art de Régner* (London, 1863). Both these pieces were the work of Acton, but published anonymously. The article amounts to an introduction to the edited documents.

Nothing in the spurious 'Confessions' was nearly so shocking as the authentic political testaments proved to be.

never described the English public mind in 1680. The statesman had been more interested in disputing, with the aid of a scholarly work by a Fellow of St John's, Macaulay's picture of the Restoration clergy.[53]

Gladstone considered himself an expert on Homer, but Professor Lloyd Jones doesn't believe he would have made a good classical scholar.[54] Though the prime minister never, I think, claimed to be a historian, this was his true academic bent.

Gladstone is a unique case. I doubt whether anyone left behind a larger quantity of evidence essential to students of his time. I cannot think of any other great man who was quite so assiduous and skilful in relating his actions to what he discerned as historical trends. But a large number of prominent figures come near him. I will mention only Clarendon, Frederick II, Napoleon, Bismarck, Salisbury and Churchill. If few historians rank as great men, most great men rate as historians. No doubt it is right to apply the laws of modern economics to the Middle Ages and the approaches of modern geography to the reign of Philip II. But most of the generalisations were made by some contemporary, and if they were not, historians must at least be wary of them. One of the principal uses of a biography is to help us appraise the evidence left by the subject. Where a biography is not available, the historian should still enquire into the character, experiences and attitudes of those on whose testimony he relied.

What one remembers in general about the excellence of one's supervisions is seldom backed by detailed recollections. I cannot match Butterfield's memory of Temperley teaching him, standing on a chair, brandishing a poker and declaiming Swinburne.[55] But I recall just one remark from a supervision with Dr Smail. I had been reading an essay of a type I now recognise as peculiarly irritating. It was heavily dependent on a book which for excellent reasons the supervisor had not recommended. 'That essay', said Dr Smail as I

---

[53] The MS of the article on Macaulay survives in Add. MS 44695. There is no sign of Gladstone's having received any help with it, and Acton's extremely interesting comments on it (to Gladstone, 21 June [1876], in J. N. Figgis and R. G. Laurence (eds.), *Selections from the Correspondence of the first Lord Acton*, I [no more published] (London, 1917), 260–1 – from BL Add. MS 44093) clearly refer to the final text as published in the *Quarterly*. The work by a Fellow of St John's is C. Babington, *Mr Macaulay's Character of the Clergy in the latter part of the Seventeenth Century Considered* (Cambridge, 1849).

Acton plainly did not believe in deep, silent, unconscious historical tendencies. His history was intellectual, of the conscious mind of Man.

I have not been able to consult the PhD thesis of Ward W. White (Catholic University of America, 1972), but I have used his essay in D. McElrath, *Lord Acton. The Decisive Decade, 1864–1874* (Louvain, 1970).

I hope to pursue this discussion further elsewhere.

[54] H. Lloyd-Jones, 'Gladstone on Homer', *Times Literary Supplement*, 3 Jan. 1975, pp. 15–17.

[55] Butterfield, *The Study of Modern History*, p. 1.

concluded, 'reminds me of the Marmaduke Smith Memorial Lecture, in which many historians are learnedly cited but the listener is left uncertain what the speaker himself thinks'.

I shall now try to ensure that this lecture is not open to that criticism. I am not maintaining that all history is biography. Of course it isn't. There are branches of history in which men have played a negligible part – to take an extreme example, most of the history of climate. Even in intellectual and political history, where it is usually conceded that individuals matter, other influences count as well. Biography is not dominant even here. Despite the claims of the History of Parliament Trust, the history of parliament is much more than a collection of biographies of MPs. This would still be so even if the Trust included MPs' opinions as well as their backgrounds, and brought in the peers. A true history of parliament involves study of elections, debates, procedure, groupings, relations between the Houses, the work of the legislature and its connection with public feeling.

Few individuals can be known to the historian in detail. Many biographies are of limited use to him. The most valuable are those, like Professor Hatton's *George I* or Professor Plumb's *Walpole*,[56] which place their subject in his historical context, which illuminate times as well as life. On the other hand, it is not only pure biographies which vindicate the biographical approach. No mere biography could have done so much for the reputation of one man as Professor Elton's work has done for Thomas Cromwell, though equally this revolution in Tudor studies is partly dependent on the biographical approach.[57]

What I have tried to show is that biography has been too much disparaged. When a great historian can mistake a person for a trend, when it is thought more important to analyse social background than opinions, then the time has come for a reaction. The case of Gladstone illustrates how much more remains to be said even about a man who has already attracted a score of biographies, and how necessary it is for historians to take a biographer's look at those who have supplied their evidence.

To talk of trends is not in itself objectionable, but it is shorthand. Certainly, millions of individuals have found no defence against the juggernauts of history: the Cathars of Montaillou, the American Indians, or in the twentieth century those who fought in the trenches, the kulaks and the Jews of continental Europe. But it must be remembered on the other side, first, that the juggernauts are powered and directed by men; secondly, that history is concerned with trends as they affect people; and thirdly, that individuals'

---

56 R. Hatton, *George I* (London, 1978); J. H. Plumb, *Sir Robert Walpole* (2 vols. so far: London, 1956, 1961).
57 Professor Elton's latest synthesis is *Reform and Reformation* (London, 1977).

reactions to trends, even the reactions of those who never gain the woods of freedom, constitute the historian's prime material.

Mr Vice-Chancellor, Lord Acton's peerage, his polyglot learning and his Catholic statesmanship rested on the wasting foundation of a Shropshire baronetcy. When he went among those whom he called his 'bucolic neighbours',[58] he would give instructive lectures on topical subjects to the Bridgnorth Literary and Scientific Institution.[59] I calculate that the shortest of these weighty discourses lasted an hour and three quarters. Cambridge is brisker and more humane. All that remains for me to do is to thank you for your attention and responsiveness during these 47 minutes.

This Inaugural Lecture was given in the University of Cambridge on 20 November 1980.

[58] Acton to Gladstone, 1 Nov. 1868 (BL Add. MS 44093).
[59] Some at least of these have been reprinted, e.g. 'The Civil War in America' [18 Jan. 1866], 'The Rise and Fall of the Mexican Empire' [10 Mar. 1868], 'The War of 1870' [25 Apr. 1871], in Figgis and Laurence (eds.), *Historical Essays and Studies by . . . Acton* (London, 1908). In *The History of Freedom and Other Essays* (same editors, London, 1922), the essays on 'The History of Antiquity' and 'The History of Freedom in Christianity' had the same origin.

DEREK BEALES: A CHRONOLOGICAL
LIST OF PUBLICATIONS
ఴఴఴ

Abbreviations

Cambridge Review	CR
English Historical Review	EHR
German History	GH
Historical Journal	HJ
History Today	HT
Mitteilungen des österreichischen Staatsarchivs	MÖSA
New York Review of Books	NYRB
Rassegna storica del Risorgimento	RSR
Times Literary Supplement	TLS
*	Review

1954

'Gladstone on the Italian Question 1860', *RSR* 41 (1954), 96–104

1955

'Historians in Sicily', *The Bull and the Porcupine* [Sidney Sussex College, Cambridge] 1 (1955), no. 3, 16–17

1956

'Il Risorgimento protestante', *RSR* 43 (1956), 231–3

*E. E. Y. Hales, *Mazzini and the Secret Societies* (London, 1956), *HT*, November 1956, 783–4

1957

'Britain and Sicily, May–August 1860', *Archivio storico messinese*, 3rd series, vol. VIII (1956–7), 3–5

'Removing Bias from History Books: Report to Council of Europe' ['from a special correspondent'], *The Times*, 3 October 1957

*Conor Cruise O'Brien, *Parnell and his Party, 1880–90* (Oxford, 1957), *CR*, 12 October 1957, 25–7

1958

'Sir Lewis Namier and the Party System', *CR*, 31 May 1958, 599–603

1959

'An International Crisis: the Italian Question' in P. Appleman, W. A. Madden and M. Wolff (eds.), *1859: Entering an Age of Crisis* (Bloomington, Indiana), 181–96

'Simpatie e incomprensioni dell'Inghilterra vittoriana' in *Il '59* (Milan, 1959) [*L'osservatore politico letterario* 5, numero 6], 69–78

*Rosario Romeo, *Risorgimento e capitalismo* (Bari, 1959), *Economic History Review*, 2nd series 12 (1959–60), 337–8

1960

*R. B. McDowell, *British Conservatism, 1832–1914* (London, 1959), *CR*, 27 February 1960, 413

*H. J. Hanham, *Elections and Party Management: Politics in the Time of Disraeli and Gladstone* (London, 1959), *CR*, 5 March 1960, 439–40

1961

England and Italy, 1859–60 (Nelson, London, 1961), pp. xii + 196

*E. E. Y. Hales, *Revolution and Papacy, 1769–1848* (London, 1960), *HJ* 4 (1961), 234–6

1962

'Party Politics', review article on Sir Ivor Jennings, *Party Politics* (3 vols., Cambridge, 1960–2), *HJ* 5, 191–8

*Harold Acton, *The Last Bourbons of Naples* (London, 1961), *CR*, 19 May 1962, 459–61

*Valdo Vinay, *Evangelici italiani esuli a Londra durante il Risorgimento* (Turin, 1961), *Journal of Ecclesiastical History* 13 (1962), 270

1963

'L'opinione pubblica inglese di fronte all'unità italiana' in *Atti del XL Congresso per la Storia del Risorgimento* [1961] (Rome, 1963), 77–86

Translation of reviews of Italian books in *Economic History Review*, 2nd series, 15 (1962–3), 596–9, 600–3; 16 (1963–4), 189–95, 405–6

*G. Giarrizzo (ed.), *Le relazioni diplomatiche fra la Gran Bretagna e il Regno di Sardegna*, III Serie: 1848–60, vol. VI–VIII, *RSR* 50 (1963), 570–1

1964

Articles in *Encyclopaedia Britannica* (revised edn, 24 vols., London, 1964): 'Joseph Cowen', VI 681; 'Edward George Geoffrey Smith Stanley, 14th Earl of Derby', VII 274–6; 'Giuseppe Garibaldi', IX 1144–6; 'Sir William George Granville Venables Vernon Harcourt', XI 90.

*Edward Crankshaw, *The Fall of the House of Habsburg* (London, 1963), *Stortfordian* [Bishop's Stortford College], no. 234 (Spring Term 1964), 17–18

*N. Blakiston (ed.), *The Roman Question* (London, 1962), *EHR* 79 (1964), 876

*Federico Chabod, *A History of Italian Fascism* (transl. by Muriel Grindrod, London, 1963), *History* 49 (1964), 106

1965

*W. L. Burn, *The Age of Equipoise. A Study of the Mid-Victorian Generation* (London, 1964) *HJ* 8, 417–20

*Carla Ronchi, *I democratici fiorentini nella rivoluzione del '48–'49* (Florence, 1963), *EHR* 80 (1965), 618–19

*N. Coppola (ed.), *Vittorio Imbriani intimo* (Rome, 1963), *EHR* 80 (1965), 625–6

*Stuart J. Woolf, *Studi sulla nobiltà piemontese nell'epoca dell'assolutismo* (Turin, 1963), *History* 50 (1965), 88

*Raymond Grew, *A Sterner Plan for Italian Unity: the Italian National Society in the Risorgimento* (Princeton, 1963), *History* 50 (1965), 96–7

1966

'Mazzini and Revolutionary Nationalism' in David Thomson (ed.), *Political Ideas* (London, 1966), 148–60 [pp. 143–53 in the Pelican edition (Harmondsworth, 1969)]

1967

'Parliamentary Parties and the "Independent" Member, 1810–1860' in Robert
Robson (ed.), *Ideas and Institutions of Victorian Britain: Essays in Honour of
George Kitson Clark* (London, 1967), 1–19
*Donald Southgate, *'The Most English Minister . . . ':The Policies and Politics of
Palmerston* (London, 1966), *Canadian Historical Review* (1967), 385–6
*Norman Gash, *Reaction and Reconstruction in English Politics, 1832–1852*
(Oxford, 1965), *HJ* 10 (1967), 313–16
*Massimo d'Azeglio, *Things I Remember* (ed. and transl. by E. R. Vincent,
London, 1966) and Ronald Marshall, *Massimo d'Azeglio: An Artist in
Politics, 1798–1866* (London, 1966), *EHR* 82 (1967), 628–9

1968

*G. Santoro, *L'economia della provincia di Salerno nell'opera della Camera di
Commercio, 1862–1962* (Salerno, 1966), *EHR* 83 (1968), 419
*Ronald Butt, *The Power of Parliament* (London, 1968), *CR*, 31 May 1968,
523
*Donald Southgate, *'The Most English Minister . . . ': The Policies and Politics
of Palmerston* (London, 1966), *History* 53 (1968), 150–1

1969

From Castlereagh to Gladstone, 1815–85 (A History of England, vol. VII, Nelson,
London, 1969; also published in the Norton Library History of England,
New York, 1969), pp. 328
'Il governo inglese e la visita di Garibaldi in Inghilterra nel 1864' in V. Frosini
(ed.), *Il Risorgimento e l'Europa: Studi in onore di Alberto Maria Ghisalberti*
(Catania, 1969), 27–40
*John P. Mackintosh, *The British Cabinet* (2nd edn, London, 1968),
Cambridge Law Journal 27 (1969), 309–11
*John Vincent, *The Formation of the Liberal Party, 1857–1868* (London, 1966),
HJ 12 (1969), 181–5

1970

Articles in *Encyclopaedia Britannica* (revised edn, 24 vols., London, 1970, 'Sir
James Lacaita', XIII 568; 'David Pacifico', XVII 14; 'Henry John Temple, 3rd
Viscount Palmerston', XVII 187–90; 'John Russell, 1st Earl Russell', XIX
771–2; 'Christian Friedrich, Baron von Stockmar', XXI 263–4
'David Thomson, 1912–70', *Journal of Contemporary History* 5 (1970), 195

1971

The Risorgimento and the Unification of Italy (Allen & Unwin, London, 1971), pp. 176

The Political Parties of Nineteenth-Century Britain (Historical Association Appreciations in History No. 2, London, 1971), pp. 23

From Castlereagh to Gladstone, 1815–85 (paperback edition with corrections, Sphere, London, 1971), pp. 317

1972

*F. Curato (ed.), *Le relazioni diplomatiche fra la Gran Bretagna e il Regno di Sardegna*, III. Serie: 1848–60, vols. IV–V (Rome, 1968–9), *EHR* 87 (1972), 438–9

1974

'Peel, Russell and Reform', review article, *HJ* 17 (1974), 873–82

[with N. Blakiston] 'La Gran Bretagna' in *Bibliografia dell'età del Risorgimento: in onore di A. M. Ghisalberti* (4 vols., Florence, 1971–7), III (1974), 323–8

*Jasper Ridley, *Garibaldi* (London, 1974), *New Statesman*, 25 October 1974, 588–9

1975

The Cambridge Historical Journal, 1923–1957. The Historical Journal, 1958–1974. Index (Cambridge, 1975), pp. 82

'The False Joseph II', *HJ* 18 (1975), 467–95

*Denis Mack Smith, *Cavour* (London, 1985) and *Cavour and Garibaldi* (2nd edn, Cambridge, 1985), *TLS*, 10 May 1985, 514

1976

*Toni Cerutti, *Antonio Gallenga: An Italian Writer in Victorian England* (London, 1974), *American Historical Review*, 81 (1976), 179–80

*Denis Mack Smith, *Mussolini's Roman Empire* (London, 1976), *New Statesman*, 24 September 1976, 411–12

1977

Contributions to discussion at 3rd Mátrafüred colloquium [1975] in *Les Lumières en Hongrie, en Europe centrale et en Europe orientale* (Budapest, 1977), 60–2, 136–8

*Joseph Hamburger, *Macaulay and the Whig Tradition* (London, 1976), *Times Higher Education Supplement*, 13 May 1977, 20

1978

'Victorian Politics Observed', review article, *HJ* 21 (1978), 697–707

Revision of David Thomson, *England in the Nineteenth Century* (new edition, Harmondsworth, 1978)

1979

'Writing a Life of Joseph II: the Problem of his Education', *Wiener Beiträge zur Geschichte der Neuzeit* 6 (1979), 183–207

1980

'Joseph II's "Rêveries"', *MÖSA* 33 (1980), 142–60

[with T. C. W. Blanning] 'Prince Kaunitz and "The Primacy of Domestic Policy"', *International History Review* 2 (1980), 619–24

*Paul P. Bernard, *The Limits of Enlightenment: Joseph II and the Law* (London, 1979), *Cambridge Law Journal* 39 (1980), 222–4

*Ernst Wangermann, *Aufklärung und staatsbürgerliche Erziehung: Gottfried van Swieten als Reformator des österreichischen Unterrichtswesens 1781–1791* (Vienna, 1978), *History* 65 (1980), 128–9

*William J. Callahan and David Higgs (ed.), *Church and Society in Catholic Europe of the Eighteenth Century* (Cambridge, 1979), *History* 65 (1980), 491–2

1981

History and Biography (Cambridge, 1981) [inaugural lecture as Professor of Modern History], pp. 36

The Risorgimento and the Unification of Italy (Longman, London, 1981) [revised version of the Allen & Unwin edition of 1961, with a new preface], pp. 176

From Castlereagh to Gladstone, 1815–1885 (Norton History of England, revised edition, New York, 1981), pp. 328

*Owen Chadwick, *The Popes and European Revolution* (Oxford, 1981), *TLS*, 28 August 1981, 979

*Thomas Pinney (ed.), *The Letters of Thomas Babington Macaulay*, vols. v and vi (Cambridge, 1981), *Times Higher Education Supplement*, 25 September 1981, 17

1982

'Italy and her Church', review article, *HJ* 25 (1982), 229–38

'Gladstone and His Diary: "Myself, the Worst of All Interlocutors"', review article on M. R. D. Foot and H. C. G. Matthew (ed.), *The Gladstone Diaries*, vols. I–VI, 1825–1868 (Oxford, 1968–78), *HJ* 25 (1982), 463–9

*Max Egremont, *Balfour: A Life of Arthur James Balfour* (London, 1980), *Victorian Studies* 25 (1981–2), 511–12

1983

'Gladstone and his First Ministry', review article on H. C. G. Matthew (ed.), *The Gladstone Diaries*, vols. VII–VIII, 1869–74 (Oxford, 1982), *HJ* 26 (1983), 987–98

1984

*Matthias Buschkühl, *Great Britain and the Holy See, 1746–1870* (Dublin, 1982) and *Ignaz von Döllinger: Briefwechsel 1820–1890*, vol. IV, Briefwechsel mit Lady Blennerhassett, 1865–1886 (ed. Victor Conzemius, Munch, 1981), *TLS*, 23 March 1984, 297

*Karl A. Roider, jr, *Austria's Eastern Question, 1700–1790* (Princeton, 1982), *Journal of Modern History* 56 (1984), 547–9

*Geoffrey Symcox, *Victor Amadeus II* (London, 1983), *HT*, November 1984, 56

*Jay Winter (ed.), *The Working Class in Modern British History. Essays in Honour of Henry Pelling* (Cambridge, 1983), *CR*, 20 November 1984, 191–3

1985

[Edited, with Geoffrey Best], *History, Society and the Churches: Essays in Honour of Owen Chadwick* (Cambridge, 1985), pp. ix + 335

'Christians and *philosophes*: the case of the Austrian Enlightenment' in Beales and Best, *History, Society and the Churches*, 169–94

'Die auswärtige Politik der Monarchie vor und nach 1780: Kontinuität und Zäsur' in *Österreich im Europa der Aufklärung* (ed. R. G. Plaschka and G. Klingenstein, Vienna, 1985), I, 567–73

1986

Obituary of R. C. Smail, *The Times*, 21 July 1986

*Elisabeth Kovács, *Der Pabst in Deutschland. Die Reise Pius VI. im Jahre 1782* (Munich, 1983), *History* 71 (1986), 541–2

*Wolfgang Altgeld, *Das politische Italienbild der Deutschen zwischen Aufklärung und europäischer Revolution von 1848* (Tübingen, 1984), *American Historical Review* 91 (1986), 684
*Alvise Zorzi, *Venezia Austriaca 1798–1866* (Rome, 1985), *TLS*, 22 August 1986, 922

1987

Joseph II, 1: In the Shadow of Maria Theresa, 1741–80 (Cambridge, 1987), pp. xviii + 520
'Social forces and Enlightened policies' in *Seventh International Congress on the Enlightenment: introductory papers* [Budapest, 1967] (Oxford, 1987), 33–43 [reprinted in *Transactions of the Seventh International Congress on the Enlightenment* (3 vols., Oxford, 1987), 1, 151–61]
'Sur les débuts des Lumières autrichiennes' in *Début et fin des Lumières en Hongrie, en Europe centrale et en Europe orientale* [6th Mátrafüred colloquium, 1984] (Budapest, 1987), 95–7
*Norman Gash, *Lord Liverpool* (London, 1984), *Journal of Modern History* 59 (1987), 831–3
*Franco Venturi, *Settecento riformatore*, vol. 4: *La caduta dell'Antico Regime, 1776–1789*, tome II: *Il patriotismo republicano e gli imperi dell'Est* (Turin, 1984), *TLS*, 6 March 1987, 237

1988

'Claims to continuity: Europalia 87', *TLS*, 29 January 1988, 113
Articles in John Cannon, R. H. C. Davis, William Doyle and Jack P. Greene (ed.), *The Blackwell Directory of Historians* (London, 1988): 'Biography', 40–1; 'Pietro Giannone', 156–7; 'Franco Venturi', 429–30
*Béla Köpeczi (ed.), *L'absolutisme éclairé* (Budapest, 1985), *EHR* 103 (1988), 744–5
*Hervé Hasquin (ed.), *La Belgique autrichienne, 1713–1794. Les Pays-Bas méridionaux sous les Habsbourg d'Autriche* (Brussels, 1987) and Janet L. Polasky, *Revolution in Brussels, 1787–1793* (London, 1987), *HJ* 31 (1988), 503–6
*Dino Carpanetto and Giuseppe Ricuperati, *Italy in the Age of Reason, 1685–1789* (London, 1987), *HT*, March 1988, 56
*John Martin Robinson, *Cardinal Consalvi, 1757–1824* (London, 1987), *TLS*, 22 January 1988, 76

1989

'Printing Satires', review article on *The English Satirical Print* (7 vols., London, 1986), *HJ* 32 (1989), 449–51

*Franco Venturi, *Settecento riformatore*, vol. v: *L'età dei lumi, 1764–1790*, tome I (Turin, 1987), *EHR* 104 (1989), 989–90

1990

'Social forces and Enlightened policies' in H. M. Scott (ed.), *Enlightened Absolutism* (London, 1990), 37–53

'Dialogue with Documents. Modern History', *History Sixth* 6 (March 1990), 30–1

'Reform, Revolution and Religion in the Risorgimento', *History Sixth* 6 (March 1990), 46–9

*Gerda Lettner, *Das Rückzugsgefecht der Aufklärung in Wien 1790–1792* (Frankfurt, 1988), *GH* 8 (1990), 90–2

1991

'Garibaldi in England: the politics of Italian enthusiasm' in John A. Davis and Paul Ginsborg, *Society and Politics in the Age of the Risorgimento: Essays in Honour of Denis Mack Smith* (Cambridge, 1991), 184–216

'Was Joseph II an Enlightened Despot?' in Ritchie Robertson and Edward Timms (ed.), *The Austrian Enlightenment and its Aftermath* (Edinburgh, 1991) [*Austrian Studies* 2], 1–21

*Roy Porter, *The Enlightenment* (London, 1990), *Journal of Ecclesiastical History* 42 (1991), 522

1992

'Historians and the Aims of Joseph II', *Early Modern History*, January 1992, 16–19

'The electorate before and after 1832: the right to vote, and the opportunity', review article on Frank O'Gorman, *Voters, Parties and Politics: The Unreformed Electorate of Hanoverian England, 1734–1832* (Oxford, 1989), *Parliamentary History* II (1992), 139–50

*Michael Hughes, *Law and Politics in Eighteenth-Century Germany* (London, 1988), *European History Quarterly* 22 (1992), 127–8

*C. Mozzarelli and G. Olmi (ed.), *Il Trentino nel Settecento fra Sacro Romano Impero e antichi stati italiani* (Bologna, 1985), *EHR* 107 (1992), 487–8

*Alvise Zorzi, *Canal Grande* (Milan, 1991), *TLS*, 24 July 1992, 12

1993

[With T. J. Hochstrasser,] 'Un intellettuale piemontese a Vienna e una inedita storia del pensiero politico (1766)', *Bollettino storico-bibliografico subalpino* 91 (1993), 247–309

Mozart and the Habsburgs [the Stenton Lecture, 1992] (Reading, 1993), pp. 23

'Mozart's Vienna' in *Die Zauberflöte* (Covent Garden programme, London, 1993), 36–41

*Paul P. Bernard, *From the Enlightenment to the Police State. The Public Life of Johann Anton Pergen* (Urbana, Illinois, 1991), *GH* 11 (1993), 103–4

*W. R. Ward, *The Protestant Evangelical Awakening* (Cambridge, 1992), *Archives* (1993), 235

1994

'Walter John Strachan', *St Catharine's College Society Magazine*, September 1994, 40

*John Stoye, *Marsigli's Europe, 1680–1730: The Life and Times of Luigi Ferdinando Marsigli, Soldier and Virtuoso* (London, 1994), *TLS*, 22 April 1994

*Oswald Hauser (ed.), *Friedrich der Große in seiner Zeit* (Cologne, 1987), and Heinz Duchhardt, *Friedrich der Große, Franken und das Reich* (Cologne, 1986), *GH* 12 (1994), 413–14

1995

'The impact of Joseph II on Vienna' in Moritz Czáky and Walter Pass (eds.), *Europa im Zeitalter Mozarts* (Vienna, 1995), 301–10

*'Saint of Nationalism', review of Denis Mack Smith, *Mazzini* (London, 1994), *NYRB*, 2 March 1995, 6–9

*Jean Bérenger, *A History of the Habsburg Empire, 1273–1700* (transl. C. A. Simpson, London, 1994), and Franz A. J. Szabo, *Kaunitz and Enlightened Absolutism, 1753–1780* (Cambridge, 1994), *HT*, March 1995, 53

*Rebecca Gates-Coon, *The Landed Estates of the Esterházy Princes: Hungary during the Reforms of Maria Theresia and Joseph II* (London, 1994), *TLS*, 16 June 1995

*'Benevolent Dinosaur', review of Alan Palmer, *Twilight of the Habsburgs: the Life and Times of Francis Joseph* (London, 1995), *NYRB*, 2 November 1995, 40–3

1996

'Court, Government and Society in Mozart's Vienna' in Stanley Sadie (ed.), *Wolfgang Amadè Mozart* (Oxford, 1995), 1–16

INDEX

cɔeɔeɔ